Sarah Lubjuhn

The Bait must be Attractive to the Fish and not to the Fisherman
Entertainment-Education Collaborations between Professionals
in the Sustainability and the Television Field

To Daniel, Carmen & Werner, who have taught me the greatest lessons about life

Sarah Lubjuhn

The Bait must be Attractive to the Fish and not to the Fisherman

Entertainment-Education Collaborations between Professionals
in the Sustainability and the Television Field

Bibliografische Information der Deutschen Nationalbibliothek
Die Deutsche Nationalbibliothek verzeichnet diese Publikation in der Deutschen Nationalbibliografie; detaillierte bibliografische Daten sind im Internet über http://dnb.ddb.de abrufbar.

© 2013 Oldib Verlag
Waldeck 14, 45133 Essen
Umschlagbild: Daniel Kehrer
Herstellung: Presseldruck, Remshalden
ISBN 978-3-939556-35-0

Dieses Werk ist urheberrechtlich geschützt. Jede Verwendung, die über den Rahmen des Zitatrechtes bei vollständiger Quellenangabe hinausgeht, ist honorarpflichtig und bedarf der schriftlichen Genehmigung des Verlages.

Table of Content

Abbreviations...8
Acknowledgements..9

PART I...12

1. Introduction..13
    1.1 Definitions and Basic Principles.. 16
    1.2 Research Interest and Research Question................................... 18
    1.3 Multidisciplinarity of the Thesis.. 22
    1.4 Overview of the Chapters.. 23
    1.5 Summary... 25

2. Learning from Entertainment-Education Theory for
Collaborations in Germany... 26
    2.1 Definition.. 27
    2.2 Developments and Diffusion..30
    2.3 The E-E Strategy.. 34
    2.4 Theoretical Aspects of E-E Collaborations................................ 49
    2.5 Results and Critical Reflections of Entertainment-Education in
        Non-Western Countries.. 63
    2.6 Results and Critical Reflections of Entertainment-Education in Western
        Countries... 67
    2.7 Who watches E-E Television Formats? A localization of Target Groups....74
    2.8 Summary... 80

3. Entertainment Television, Entertainment-Education and Prosocial Themes 82
    3.1 Approaches at the Interface of Television and Society 83
    3.2 Entertainment Television Research... 88
    3.3 Theories in the Field of Entertainment Television Genres..........94
    3.4 Ethical Aspects and E-E Television... 104
    3.5 Summary... 116

4. Good Practice Examples of Two Media Centers in
the USA and the Netherlands... 118
    4.1 Theoretical Notions from the Dialectical Tension Concept for Prosocial
        Change.. 119
    4.2 Hollywood, Health & Society Program, USC Norman Lear Center, Los
        Angeles, USA... 123
    4.3 Center for Media & Health, Gouda, the Netherlands................148
    4.4 Summary... 168

PART II...175

5. Research Methodology...176
5.1 Research Question..177
5.2 Introduction to the Data Collection and Analysis
    with the Grounded-Theory Methodology..178
5.3 Data Collection...180
5.4 Data Analysis...187
5.5 Summary...195

6. Conditions and Characteristics of Entertainment-Education Collaborations....197
6.1 Media Legislation Rules..198
6.2 Developments in the Television and the Sustainability
    Field Contributing to the E-E Collaboration Situation in Germany..........204
6.3 Field Logics and Motives..212
6.4 Forms of E-E Collaborations in Germany..215
6.5 Applying Theory and Research in E-E Collaborations..........................216
6.6 Follow up activities...219
6.7 Summary...221

7. Place of Gift Exchange and Correlations to Common Sense and
Zeitgeist (According to the Third Reich Experience and the Media)...............223
7.1 Theoretical Foundation of the Research Theme...................................224
7.2 Place of Gift Exchange...224
7.3 Common Sense According to the Third Reich Experience
    and the Media..232
7.4 Zeitgeist According to the Third Reich Experience and the Media..........246
7.5 Recent Circumstances...248
7.6 E-E Implementers Carefully Observing Common Sense,
    Zeitgeist, and Recent Circumstances..249
7.7 Integrative Model of the Place of Gift Exchange, Common Sense,
    Zeitgeist and Recent Circumstances...251
7.8 Putting Germany and International E-E Collaborations into a Context.....253
7.9 Summary...255

8. Entertainment-Education Collaboration Forms and Stages
on the Place of Gift Exchange...257
8.1 First (and Follow up) Face-to-Face Meeting(s)....................................258
8.2 E-E Co-production and Inscript Participation......................................267
8.3 E-E Service...285
8.4 E-E License..300
8.5 Integrative Model: Condition and Forms of
    E-E Collaborations in Germany..308

 8.6 Critical Reflection on the E-E Collaboration Forms in Germany..............309
 8.7 Summary..310
 Epilogue II...314

9. Theoretical Concept on Entertainment-Education Collaborations
 in Germany, Discussion and Recommendations..318
 9.1 The Research Subject Paradigm and Theoretical Concept.......................318
 9.2 Consequences for E-E Definition..319
 9.3 Discussion and Recommendations for Future E-E Developments............321

References..330
Weblinks... 358
Appendix..359

Abbreviations

CDC	Centers for Disease Control and Prevention
CMH	Center for Media & Health
GGD Amsterdam	Public Health Service of Amsterdam (Geneeskundige en Gezondheidsdienst (GGD) Amsterdam)
E-E	Entertainment-Education
esp.	especially
FCHE	Federal Centre for Health Education (Germany)
HH&S	Hollywood, Health & Society
e.g.	for example
et al.	et alii (m.), et aliae (fem.), et alia (neu.)
etc.	et cetera
i.e.	that is
ibid.	ibidem
NCI	National Cancer Institute (USA)
OTEC	Education Technology Expertise Centre (The Netherlands)
UCLA	University of California, Los Angeles
USC	University of Southern California
WGAW	Writers Guild of America West

Acknowledgements

This research study has been a journey full of 'reciprocity', a journey of giving, receiving and reciprocating. For me it was the chance to learn and to grow with a heart's theme and to really try to understand the processes behind. After some years of work as a communication researcher in the field of applied sustainability, the question started to trigger me, how entertainment media can be used to reach German audience coming from lower socio-economic backgrounds with sustainable lifestyle issues in their everyday life. This question was at that time quite unusual and my work was specifically focused on cognitive, factual, rather than affective communication approaches. I discovered the scientific works on Entertainment-Education (E-E) and one of the first items I read was Martine Bouman's book "the Turtle and the Peacock". I was triggered by the question in how far effective collaboration processes between sustainability and entertainment TV professionals can contribute to change processes among audience members to live a more sustainable lifestyle. I felt privileged to have the possibility to do in-depth work on E-E collaboration practice in Germany.

From many people I received wonderful gifts. They supported me in so many different ways and speaking with the words of Marcel Mauss, I am not sure if I ever can reciprocate all of those, but I hope so and the following lines can be understood as a small contribution of reciprocating, of honoring their beautiful gifts.

I am thankful to the German National Academic Foundation, who financially and ideationally supported me and invested in this new area of research from 2008 to 2010.

I want to thank my PhD supervisors Prof. Dr. Jo Reichertz, Dr. Martine Bouman and Prof. Dr. Christoph Fasel for their guidance and support during my research. Prof. Dr. Jo Reichertz advised me during the whole PhD process, especially during the German E-E study and I thank him for the many lessons he taught me. I owe very much to Dr. Martine Bouman, who advised me through her E-E expertise in many stages of my work. She taught me much about Entertainment-Education and she introduced me to many pioneers of the E-E field, always willing to share her networks and experience. Her support was invaluable and I am very thankful for that. Prof. Dr. Christoph Fasel supported me with his advice and expertise and I am thrilled by his activities of establishing interfaces between consumer research and Entertainment-Education. I thank him for his helpful advices and for letting E-E ideas develop in the many talks we had.

I am also thankful to my colleagues from the Department for Communication Studies, University of Duisburg-Essen for the encouragement and willingness to share their thoughts and opinions with me. I would like to specially thank Julia-Lena Reinermann for her support in many stages of my work, Dr. Oliver Bidlo and Nadine Marth for their reflections and assistance in the analysis process of the data, and Kathrin Bosnjak, who discussed with me and commented on my media chapter. From the Wuppertal Institute I thank Dr. Christa Liedtke for her strategic advices, Dr. Oliver Stengel and Kristin Parlow for giving their comments on my chapters. For the coding support during the analysis process I want to thank my coding partner Nicole Schmidt.

Furthermore, I would like to attribute special thanks to all my colleagues in the sustainability communication field; several of them also have become increasingly interested in Entertainment-Education and it was always enriching to share ideas with them. Especially, I want to thank my dear friend and colleague Dr. Nadine Pratt as well as Dr. Thomas Hanke and Sandra Kolberg. All of them I thank for the reflections we shared on the E-E collaboration topic.

My credits also go to the study participants from sustainability organizations, the entertainment television and media legislation field. I thank them for openly talking about their E-E collaboration experiences. The dokFORUM and the ARUS PhD programme at the University of Duisburg-Essen furthermore made it possible that I could travel to several national and international conferences to present my research theme, which I appreciated much.

There are several colleagues from the international E-E field, which I want to especially thank here: Dr. Martine Bouman and her team (especially Hester Hollemans and Peter Fokkens) from the Center for Media & Health as well as Sandra de Castro Buffington and her team (especially Kathy Le Backes) from Hollywood, Health & Society, Norman Lear Center, University of Southern California. They supported me during my research visits in 2008 and beyond through their networks and their expertise. They opened up doors to television professionals, health experts and other scientists and they commented on my chapters. I experienced this as a great support and I cannot describe how important their cooperation has been to me. Furthermore, I would like to thank Vicki Beck, former director of the Hollywood, Health & Society, who took her time to explain me the first developments of the program and who made comments on my media center chapter.

During my visits at the Center for Media & Health Peter Fokkens was so kind to offer me accommodation. This has been a wonderful support to me and I want to thank him as well as Dr. Martine Bouman for their kind hospitality.

I had the pleasure and honor to meet and discuss my work with Prof. Arvind Singhal from the University of Texas at El Paso. He supplied me with valuable insights, sent me articles and research reports. For me he is a very outstanding person, a real bridge builder, and each time I could meet him, there were several very inspiring lessons I took back home with me. I thank him for each of this moments shared. I met Prof. William Brown from the Regent University for the first time in May 2008 in the Netherlands, when he was doing a sabbatical break at the Center for Media & Health. I really appreciate the talks with him, his advices and comments specifically on ethical considerations as well as celebrity endorsement in E-E projects. I am thankful for his kind cooperation. Another E-E friend has been Maaike de Jong. I am pleased about her comments on my E-E chapter and I cherished each time, when I had the possibility to discuss with her. My special thanks also go to my E-E colleague Florian Wirth from the University of Munich. He commented on and corrected several of my PhD chapters, and it has been a precious gift and support to me.

Esther Asiama and Joshua Simpkins edited my English and gave me useful hints. I thank both for the great dedication in this process and especially I thank Esther Asiama for being the wonderful person and best friend she is. Most of the data analysis and writings I did in Namibia, Windhoek, where I found a place of peace and calmness, a situation, which I cherished much. I want to thank my Namibian colleagues and friends for their patience in listening to my PhD stories during lunch hours and evenings we shared. And I would like to say thank you very much to the family clan in Bielefeld, especially to Inge, Daria and Jörg, who didn't got tired of asking how my PhD research comes along.

I want to *especially* thank my beloved partner Daniel Kehrer, who assisted me in so many different ways, which makes it impossible to fully mention them here. By the end of many working days he listened to my stories, he gave critical reflection and inspiration and he also turned my 'ugly duckling' draft figures into 'beautiful swans'. All has been of great value to me. I owe him so much. He is the shining star, the love, the heart and the freedom. There are no words.

I am also deeply thankful to my beloved parents. They have given me a lifetime of encouragement and love. Whithout them I would not stand where I am today. They supported me wherever they could and I thank them for their assistance, for each conversation on my work, and for every moment we share.

Through the thesis I grew in many ways and it brought me to the point where I stand today. My family and friends – and here I want to additionally mention my dearest friend Chirin, Christiane, Uwe, Carolee, Klaus and Kristin – were the biggest gift I could have in this life phase. They intuitively understood how to support me best. Nothing means more to me.

Sarah Lubjuhn,
Windhoek, June 2013

PART I

1. Introduction

> "To reflect the principle of LOHAS [Lifestyle of Health and Sustainability] in a [daily soap] character would be a very interesting undertaking, and could be pursued. However, there is the danger that the LOHAS would apply only to his/her lifestyle and that the character would be seen as too one-dimensional. Awareness of sustainable consumption should be more anchored within the general life attitudes of the character for it to be truly convincing. For me it is important that credibility is maintained in everything I do. Many people take up the cause of doing something for the environment because it is something that is at the moment chic. The creation of sustainable and long-term awareness raising is something much more important. We are all responsible for the future of our planet, and we want to make our contribution."
>
> - Rainer Wemcken,
> Managing director of Grundy
> UFA and Producer of Geman
> daily soaps.
> In: BNE Journal, November 2008

Germany and other countries are currently facing a turning point concerning their reactions to global scenarios such as the North-South divide, global environmental challenges, unbalanced population growth or global health problems, such as epidemics. The progress of industrial production and consumption caused non-sustainable prosperity, which can primarily be characterized by unequal distribution of wealth and negative ecological consequences (Schmidt-Bleek, 2007).

The concept of sustainable development, which was defined for the first time in 1987 in political debates, recognizes the relation of ecological, social, health and economic questions and the human needs for development for present as well as future generations. Thus it pays strong attention to the global challenges and how to approach them. A sustainable development of a society strongly depends on each societal member and how they deal with ecological, health and other social issues in their everyday life (UN, 1987; chapter 2). Educational processes, which are orientated on the ideal of a sustainable development, always need *communication*. "Only by and in the form of communication, an event or object has a societal relevance and significance" (Ziemann, 2007: 123). Cultural background and the everyday life are the basis for communication processes, which allow concepts of a jointly experienced sustainable life. Through symbols, pictures and metaphors, sense structures can develop and through them problems can be solved (Bittencourt et al., 2003). Sustainability communication[1] has a central role in the education and development of sustainable knowledge, attitude and behavior. Through sustainability communication individuals can actively participate in the evaluation of sustainable development processes and receive orientation and ideas for everyday life (Michelsen & Godemann, 2007). In other words, the important objective for a change to more sustainable lifestyles is created through communication and implicates a mental and cultural change (Reichertz, 2007b) and sharpens awareness of individuals.

Mass media can be a crucial driver for these mental and cultural change processes. It helps to create interpretational offers that may support changes in attitude and behavior, especially because it creates frames for the perception of problems and the construction of social reality (Berger & Luckmann, 2000). One reason for this development is the decrease of traditional socialization agents such as the church, school, family, as well as fading societal classes and gender roles (Reichertz, 2007b). Thus, the mass media has an important status for socialization and identity development in individualistic societies (ibid.). Mass media helps to make interpretational offers regarding a sustainable development available to the public (de Witt, 2007). In this context, *television* (chapter 3) is a "specific technical and social organized form of symbolical communication" (Plake, 2004) and a key medium of German society (see below). It is not only carrier and facilitator of messages, but furthermore identifies stakeholders with role model character, because television can offer new world views to his recipients and at the same time creates new social knowledge.

Television in Germany is also used to transport sustainability issues, such as ecological, health or social themes. However, this does not apply to all broadcasted program genres: on the one hand a variety of programs are offered on the German television market, which convey sustainability related data, facts and sophisticated elaborations in information-orientated genres (such as in *plant e. (ZDF-Umwelt) (ZDF)* or *Quarks & Co. (WDR)*). On the other hand, **sustainability themes in fictional and entertainment genres** (e.g. in daily soaps or reality shows) are only **sparsely covered** (Glathe, 2010; Lubjuhn & Reinermann, 2010; Schwender et al., 2008). Especially the television entertainment field bears potentials in which strategies need to be developed and implemented in order to portray sustainability themes with high quality standard (e.g. in terms of accuracy and authenticity).[2]

---

[1] Sustainability communication should be defined here according to Ziemann (2007: 126) as a "global societal process promoted by mass media which consists of the recursive structure of contributions and arguments in context with better life in terms of ecological, economic and social issues".

[2] Another aspect in the sustainability media debate is not only centered on what the television stations convey to their audience members, but on what their corporate sustainability performance is. For German media organizations it can be testified, that in comparison to other countries (Ries, 2004) and, in comparison to other corporate business sectors, they seems to adapt processes of a sustainable organization culture less fast. For example sustainability reports or other sustainable measurements are still rare. However this is another field,

When now focusing those organizations that on a daily basis deal with sustainability themes such as German ministries, research institutions or other (non-)governmental organizations, we can find parallels to the 'sustainability gap' in the television field: people from environmental, health and social organizations, whose task is to promote sustainable lifestyle patterns, preliminary try to reach the public *through cognitive-orientated communication approaches* (giving facts, figures, handing out brochures, etc.). They frequently use these approaches for nearly all societal members, not comprehensively differentiating between various target groups (compare Bonfadelli & Friemel, 2006). *Affective communication strategies*, such as the E-E strategy (chapter 2), which are used in entertainment media, are yet rarely applied in Germany (Lubjuhn & Pratt, 2009; Schwender et al., 2008). One central reason is that their initiators from sustainability organizations often lack of the comprehension that *the message needs to fit to the target group members rather than the sender* (the bait must be attractive to the fish and not to the fisherman, chapter 6.2.2.1). Hence, also in the sustainability field, potentials to reach people who are perceptive for an affective communication approach via entertainment media (e.g. those who are coming from lower socio-economic milieus, chapter 2.7) are not comprehensively exhausted yet and developments are standing at some kind of starting point.

Both potentials, i.e. (1) to increasingly, accurately and authentically depict sustainability themes in entertainment formats (potential in the entertainment TV field) as well as (2) to increasingly and effectively make use of affective-orientated strategies for communicating sustainability themes (potential in the sustainability field) seem to make a good match when combining them. These potentials can be used (to a certain degree) when both fields *utilize synergies* and *learn from each other*.

But, how can this happen? How can the number of entertainment professionals who are interested or personally engaged in specific sustainability themes increase? How can the number of sustainability professionals experimenting with an affective, entertainment orientated approach increase? How can we get away from 'single case actors' and come to majorities? To answer these questions investing in strategic and directed collaboration processes between both fields is significant.

This thesis will exactly focus on these collaboration processes of the *entertainment television field* and the *sustainability field*. It asks how both fields can utilize synergy potentials for *strategic and directed collaboration processes to enhance an accurate and authentic depiction of sustainability content* (e.g. also by applying scientific theories), so that the audience members can learn from it, change their attitude or even behavior towards more sustainable lifestyles.

Therefore the thesis uses the scientific field of Entertainment-Education, where collaboration processes between prosocial and entertainment media professionals have been examined for several decades. Although in recent years German professionals from the sustainability and the entertainment TV field also have increas-

---

which might be discussed and researched, but should not be the main focus of interest here.

ingly become interested in the Entertainment-Education approach, collaboration processes between environmental, health and social organizations on the one hand and entertainment TV makers on the other hand have not been the focus of research interest so far, and there are many unanswered questions. Hence, research in this field is necessary to give deeper insights into the collaboration practice and to show where exactly the above-mentioned potentials are.

In the next four sections some matters that need to be explicated will be touched upon. Section 1.1 defines some of the concepts used in this thesis. Section 1.2 touches on the research interest and the question of the thesis. Section 1.3 deals with the interdisciplinary background of the thesis. In section 1.4 an overview of the thesis chapters is provided and section 1.5 finally summarizes this chapter.

1.1 Definitions and Basic Principles

The thesis exclusively focuses on various conditions and forms of collaborations between governmental (related) authorities specialized on environmental, health and social related issues and entertainment TV professionals who facilitate messages to a mass audience in Germany. It examines specific features of teaming-up strategies. The basic terms and issues are defined and can be characterized as follows:

1. ***Clarifying the terms Entertainment-Education collaborations and formats***: In national and international scholarly literature, a collaboration between prosocial experts from governmental (related) authorities and entertainment TV makers are betokened as *Entertainment-Education (E-E) collaborations*. In the thesis this expression is used to characterize the collaboration activities. Moreover, media formats depicting prosocial/sustainability issues (see below) are labeled with the term *Entertainment-Education programs (or formats)*. Thus, when prosocial experts and TV makers team up in a collaboration, they may create E-E television programs.

2. ***Focusing exclusively on mass entertainment TV programs***: The approach of combining educational contents with entertainment via intentional prosocial messages within radio, film, theater, music, lyrics or television programs is described as *Entertainment-Education strategy* (see chapter 2). This thesis exclusively focuses on E-E collaborations in entertainment television formats in which governmental authorities and TV makers implement partner activities on (episodes of) a daily soap, telenovela, reality show, etc. (see chapter 2.4) to reach a broader mass audience. There are several reasons why this thesis analyzes E-E collaborations in the field of entertainment TV and not, for example, in print or radio. Firstly, entertainment TV can be considered as a media genre which bears high **potential to change attitude and behavior** towards a more sustainable lifestyle (see chapter 3). Secondly, mass entertainment TV is able to reach many **mainstream German media users** who are primarily people from middle or lower educational backgrounds (see chapter 2.7). For more highly educated people, or the so-called information-elite, a variety of

TV formats for sustainability exist in Germany, as mentioned above. However, studies on how TV formats reach the German users of mainstream media have not yet been carried out systematically. A third argument for choosing TV for an E-E collaboration focus is that *television is the most used medium in Germany*. 87.1% of media users watch television more than once a week (ARD, 2009). Television viewership has continued to increase, and between 2000 and 2009 it went up from 187 to 193 minutes per day (ARD, 2008). Television is furthermore increasingly consumed in Germany by nearly every age group, and it will not loose its orientation function in a foreseeable time (Volpers et al., 2008).

3. *Defining prosocial change/sustainability themes*: In this thesis the term 'prosocial change' will be used in part I of the thesis to describe 'socially desirable'[3] issues or developments to which a society should aspire. In part II of the thesis, the term 'sustainability' will be used to describe the same socially desirable developments. The author has decided for this separation because part I of the thesis will give a theoretical background on E-E (collaborations) and in this scholarly field the term 'prosocial change (communication)' is usually applied and has a long history of usage (e.g. Singhal et al., 2004, Singhal & Rogers, 1999). In part II, E-E collaborations are portrayed for Germany. In Germany 'sustainability (communication)' is a rather new term without a long history of usage mainly applied by German communication scholars who want to describe the process of how the society achieves a socially desirable or 'sustainable' development'[4] (Michelsen & Godemann, 2007). A more detailed reflection on the term of sustainability is given in chapter 5, where the German analysis starts.

When this thesis talks about prosocial change themes (part I) and sustainability themes (part II), a clear focus is meant. Here, especially the dimension of the *applicability in everyday life of audience members* plays a striking role. Prosocial change/sustainability topics include: (a) How to *consume in a sustainable manner and deal with social topics*: e.g. topics like green consumerism and social issues like fair trade but also topics like gender empowerment or racial tolerance. (b) How to *live environmentally friendly*: e.g. topics dealing with climate change issues, energy/resource efficiency. (c) How *to live a healthier life*: e.g. topics dealing with healthy lifestyles, obesity or diabetes. So when this thesis deals with so-called prosocial change/sustainability ex-

---

[3] In contrast to prosocial behavior, antisocial behavior can be described as behavior that is "undesirable or detrimental to others individuals and/or society" (Nariman, 1993: 7). Further debates on ethical aspects of the terms are presented in chapter 3.4.

[4] According to the Brundtland Commission (Hauff, 1987: 46), "sustainable development is a development that meets the needs of the present without compromising the ability of future generations to meet their own needs. It contains within it two key concepts: the concept of 'needs', in particular the essential needs of the world's poor, to which overriding priority should be given; and the idea of limitations imposed by the state of technology and social organization on the environment's ability to meet present and future needs".

perts, these people have an expertise in the social, environmental or health field. When an expert who has an expertise in one of these three fields is cited, then this person will be named as 'health expert' or 'environmental expert'.

4. ***Defining collaboration partners***: In this thesis, the focus of collaborations lies on ***governmental*** (related and on their behalf working) ***institutions*** teaming up with ***entertainment TV makers***. So, when in the following chapters prosocial change (part I)/sustainability (part II) organizations are mentioned, this comprises ***governmental (related) authorities*** on
   - federal,
   - federal state and
   - regional levels, but also
   - research institutions, which implement projects on behalf of these governmental authorities and who have expertise in the environmental, health or social field.

   Another focus of collaboration institutions also could have been possible, for example examining the collaborations between NGOs (like the *Red Cross* or *Green Peace*) or private businesses partnering with entertainment TV makers. The focus on governmental (related) organizations had been chosen because a greater potential has been conferred to them to serve as an 'enabler of prospects' when it comes to mainstreaming accurate and authentic sustainability themes in Germany's entertainment television (Lubjuhn & Hoffhaus, 2009).

5. ***Partnership of agents with different aims and prospects***: This thesis conceives prosocial/sustainability experts and entertainment TV makers and their respective organizational environments as agents with *two completely different objectives*. The primary aim of prosocial experts is to foster generally-accepted, educational messages (such as 'save energy, resources and money') that may spur a positive change in knowledge, attitude and behavior. In comparison to that, entertainment TV makers reinforce conditions of the free media market and competition,[5] short-term thinking, and pressure rule their everyday life. Therefore, television professionals primarily pursue an economic motive (Bouman, 1999; Bourdieu, 1998). Their first and foremost aim is going for high quotas and both different perspectives need to be importantly accounted for when dealing with the collaborative environment.

1.2 Research Interest and Research Question

The interest in entertainment television formats as a vehicle to promote prosocial messages[6] has grown tremendously during the past several decades. A variety of studies published in the international literature point out that E-E collaborations set incentives for the learning processes of audience members and show them proso-

---

[5] This circumstance indeed applies more to commercial broadcasters rather than to public ones.

[6] In the chapters 1-4 the term 'prosocial' will be used (see explanations in section 1.1).

cial alternatives for their action in everyday life (Arendt, 2008; Beck, 2004; Kaiser Family Foundation, 2008; Hether et al., 2008, Hether & Murphy, 2009; Lampert, 2007; Lacayo & Singhal, 2008; Lopez-Pumarejo, 2006; Lubjuhn & Bouman, 2009; Morgan et al., 2009; Movius et al., 2007; Murphy, Hether & Rideout 2008, Murphy et al., 2008 ; Papa & Singhal, 2008; Singhal & Rogers, 2004; Singhal & Dura, 2008, Whittier et al., 2005; Wilkin et al., 2007).

There is a substantial body of international literature (Beck, 2004; Beck, 2009; Bouman, 1999; Dutta-Bergman, 2004; Figueroa et al., 2002; Kaiser Family Foundation, 2004; Greenberg et al., 2004; Li, 2008; Nariman, 1993; Poindexter, 2004; Ryerson, 2008; Sabido, 2004; Singhal & Rogers, 1999; Sood, 2002; Sherry, 2002; Tufte, 2004; Usdin et al., 2004; Van Leeuwen et al., 2012) dealing with the communication of prosocial messages through entertainment television and the collaboration issue.

In contrast, the German literature provides a relatively small but growing number of discussions in the field of Entertainment-Education and collaborative processes in media formats (Arendt, 2008; Lampert, 2007; Lubjuhn & Bouman, 2009; Lubjuhn & Hoffhaus, 2009; Lubjuhn & Reinermann, 2010; Reinermann & Lubjuhn, 2011; Reinermann et al. (2012); Schulz et al., 2008; Schwarz, 2004). 'What are specific communication strategies and strategic measurements for teamwork?' 'What is the status quo of the collaborating stakeholders?' 'Who teams up with whom?' 'How do the partners work together?' 'What are potentials and pitfalls while collaborating and how can they be solved?' 'How should E-E collaboration be designed for an "effective and efficient teaming up" so that both sides are satisfied?' On the international level, scholars have been doing research regarding these and other questions (Beck, 2004; Beck, 2009; Bouman, 1999; Brown & Singhal, 1997; Bouman & Brown, 2008a; Papa & Singhal, 2008) while the German scholars have not yet been discussing conditions, forms, processes, activities and strategies in this context. This leads to the main research question of this thesis:

What are the conditions and forms for Entertainment-Education collaborationsbetween entertainment television professionals and sustainability experts from governmental (related) authorities?

Altogether, five central sub-questions resulting from the main research question may help to provide an answer. The following sub-questions A1 and A2 will be answered in part I of the thesis:

A1 Analyzing theoretical debates: What is the status quo in scientific debates in the field of Entertainment-Education and prosocial entertainment television and how might this provide hints for answering the main research question?

A2 Analyzing significant E-E media center approaches: Which insights can be composed from two significant international E-E media centers in order to get closer to the conditions and forms of E-E collaborations in Germany and effective future collaboration practice?

The outcomes of the scientific debates (A1) and the international approaches (A2) will serve as a basis for a concept for an in-depth analysis of German E-E collaboration practice in part II of the thesis.

Part I consequently contains:
- theoretical debates in Entertainment-Education (chapter 2) and prosocial entertainment TV (in chapter 3) as well as
- the analysis of international good practice approaches (chapter 4), providing insights for the German collaboration practice.

In part I important prerequisites are provided to answer the main research question. The results of part I will be integrated in the in-depth analysis of Germany's E-E collaboration practice in part II of the thesis (chapter 5-9). Part II then touches the new contribution in terms of a qualitative study, which leads to answering the main research question. The following sub-questions B1, B2 and B3 will be posed in order to answer the main research question:

B1 Researching conditional collaboration factors: What are significant conditions (i.e. external and internal conditions as well as crucial characteristics) of present E-E collaborations in Germany which influence the collaboration process?

B2 Investigating collaboration practices and their forms in depth: Based on the conditions and characteristics, how can the present collaboration process between sustainability experts and television professionals in Germany be described in different forms and stages with regard to the development and implementation of collaborations?

B3 Developing a theoretical concept and making recommendations for the future: Based on the conditions, characteristics and forms, how can the theoretical concept of E-E collaborations in Germany be summarized and what are the best recommendations for the German collaboration context when managing E-E collaborations in the future?

Part II accordingly consists of:
- a methodology chapter in which the data collection and analysis procedures according to the study are illustrated (chapter 5),
- the depiction of the crucial conditions and characteristics of E-E collaborations in Germany (chapter 6),
- an in-depth presentation of the main E-E collaboration field in practice, the place of gift exchange, as well as co-relations of the place of gift exchange to the fields of common sense and zeitgeist (chapter 7),
- the portrayal of the different E-E collaboration forms and stages regarding on the 'place of gift exchange', the main category resulting from the analysis (chapter 8) and
- a summary of the E-E theoretical concept for Germany as well as final discussions and recommendations for future E-E activities (chapter 9).

Given this background, the thesis is divided into four striking steps while on its way to answering the main research question and it is separated into two different parts as the following figure illustrates:

Figure 1.1: Procedure of answering the main research question within the thesis

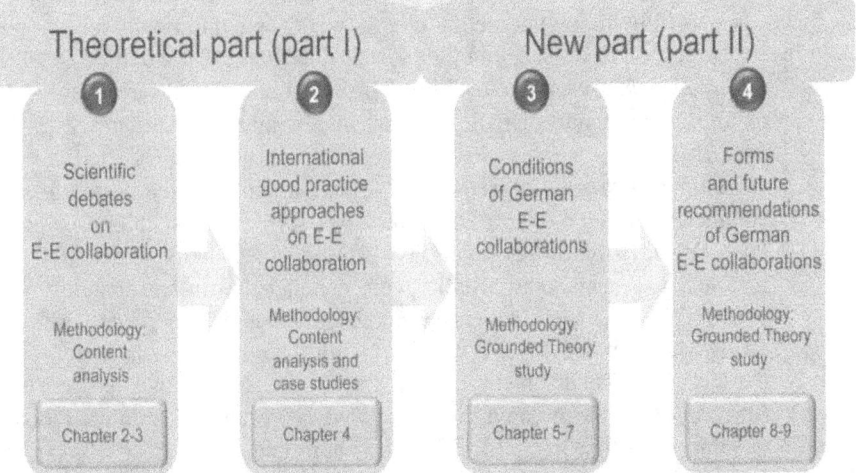

In part I and part II different methodologies are provided. The methodology used in part I applies content analysis and case study research to E-E collaborations. It focuses on theoretical notions of Entertainment-Education (sub-questions A1) and international good practice approaches in E-E collaboration processes (sub-questions A2). The following methodologies are used:

- **Content analysis (step 1)** analyzing literature on the theory and practice of E-E strategy, prosocial media and the television field.
- **Content analysis (step 2)** examining policy papers, strategies and legislations, which affect E-E collaborations in the international field.
- **Case studies (step 2)** analyzing two of the most significant E-E collaboration research institutes in the United States and the Netherlands.[7] In this context the aim has been to identify structures which contribute to the suc-

---

[7] These institutes are the Hollywood, Health & Society program, Norman Lear Center, University of Southern California, Los Angeles, USA and the Center for Media & Health, Gouda, the Netherlands (chapter 4).

cess factors of these E-E collaboration approaches in science, practice and policy through:
- Review of collaboration methodologies based on the results of both research institutes: training methodologies for E-E collaborations, E-E modules, published and unpublished project reports, scripts and grants.
- Participatory observation of E-E consultations, E-E workshops, E-E awards and E-E Master Classes.
- Qualitative interviews with health experts (N=7), television professionals (N=7), staff members of the research institutes (N=8) and around 40 further informal talks with E-E researchers, practitioners and pioneers.

These methodologies were used to answer the sub-questions A1 and A2 in part I of the thesis. In part II the following methodologies were applied to finally answer the main research question through responding to sub-questions B1, B2 and B3:
- *Grounded Theory study (step 3 and 4)*: Selection criteria were established to form a status quo of E-E collaborations within the German television industry.
- *Grounded Theory study (step 3 and 4)*: An in-depth qualitative study was conducted through narrative interviews with sustainability experts (N=10), television professionals (N=13), media legislation experts (N=2). Informal E-E collaboration talks were conducted with sustainability experts (N=7), television makers (N=2) and media legislation experts (N=2), all of which totaled 17 E-E collaborations. The data was analyzed using the Grounded Theory methodology. In this context the insights from the first part of the thesis came in and the analysis results led to future recommendation for the German E-E collaboration field.

1.3 Multidisciplinarity of the Thesis

This dissertation project is based on several disciplines, including communication science, educational science, health science and applied sustainability research. The perspective of communication science is most relevant regarding the structure of the collaborative process between prosocial experts and entertainment television makers. This process needs to be explored and analyzed within the context of concrete interactions in practice. Communication science also plays a decisive role while examining principles in the theoretical debates (chapter 2 and 3). Studies and results based on educational science, health science and applied sustainability research are of high relevance as they refer to the content of E-E collaborations: prosocial messages. These messages are implemented in the TV program content, they are as well integrated in follow up activities (workshops, events etc.) or even in an integrated campaign approach on the prosocial theme.

The perspective of communication science primarily elucidates the *structural level* of the research topic: the concrete collaborative relation between prosocial experts and television makers. In contrast, the focus of educational science, health science and applied sustainability research primarily refers to the *content level* of the collaborations. On the content level, the prosocial theme depicted in the television program plays the crucial role in the collaborative process. The relation of these disciplines is located in an intersection area as follows:

Figure 1.2: Location of the research theme from an interdisciplinary perspective

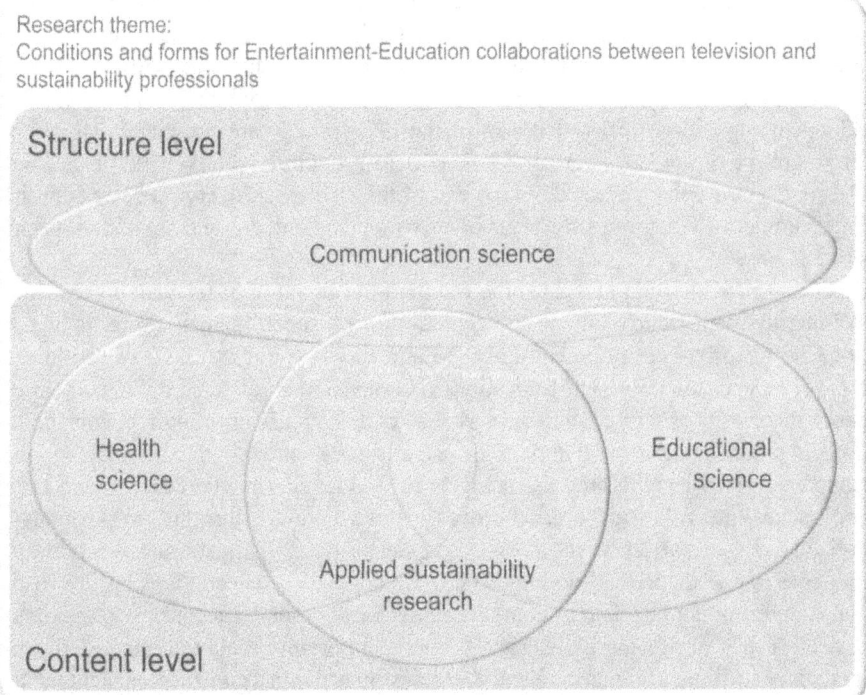

The four disciplines incorporate their perspectives into the thesis. The central perspective of the thesis comes from communication science, as communication science provides answers for concrete conditions and forms of E-E collaborations in Germany.

1.4 Overview of the Chapters

This thesis is divided into two parts. The part I (chapters 2-4) refers to sub-questions A1 and A2. There the theoretical and practical notions of the E-E strategy as well as the international practice approaches in E-E collaboration are analyzed. Part II (chapters 5-9) alludes to the sub-questions B1, B2 and B3. This part concentrates on the conditions, characteristics, forms, stages and recommendations for E-E collaboration processes in Germany. In part II, the main research question – the question regarding conditions and forms for E-E collaborations – is answered.

Chapter 1 provides the background of the thesis. The central definitions, which the thesis is based on, are presented. The research interest, the central research question and the interdisciplinary background are explained.

Chapter 2 probes the E-E strategy, development, diffusion and the most important theoretical incentives, most of which originate with communication science, social science and social psychology. Topics introduced and discussed will be the social marketing perspective, Bandura's theory of social cognitive learning, Sabido's prosocial entertainment theory, the parasocial interaction and identification theory, the closely related concepts of celebrity identification, audience-centered theories and further theories used in the field of Entertainment-Education will also be examined. Furthermore, theoretical aspects on E-E collaborations are provided and achievements and critical reflections of the E-E strategy are presented. The main target groups of the E-E strategy – lower socio-economic groups, children and adolescents – are also elaborated. At the end of the chapter an overview regarding the Entertainment-Education effects shows which potentials and boundaries the strategy has.

Chapter 3 provides and evaluates the role and the function of television according to Entertainment-Education and the depiction of prosocial themes. From its inception, the historical development and the main research traditions of television are presented, and Entertainment-Education and television is reflected in the context of genre theories. Another crucial emphasis is on the discussion of ethical considerations in television in general and on the use of the E-E strategy in particular.

Chapter 4 gives insights into the analysis of two leading media centers[8] and their approaches into E-E collaboration processes for conveying insights for Germany's E-E analysis in part II of the thesis. For the purpose of illustrating the two approaches, some theoretical notions from the concept of dialectic tension in prosocial change are applied, and both media centers are presented according to the main dialectics they are facing. After each section, important points that made the centers successful are summarized and Germany may learn from these insights. The first part of this thesis, in which the first two sub-questions A1 and A2 are answered, is then summarized and concluded in Epilogue I.

Chapter 5 focuses on the illustration of the Grounded Theory methodology, which is used for the analysis of E-E collaboration processes in Germany. After the introduction of the Grounded Theory for the on-hand study, detailed insights are given about how the data collection and analysis with collaborating sustainability experts and entertainment makers proceeded in the study.

In chapter 6, 7 and 8 the results of the qualitative research study on E-E collaborations in Germany are provided. Furthermore, the theory of gift exchange according to Marcel Mauss is presented as a crucial guidance for the explanation and inter-

---

[8] For the first cases study, the program "Hollywood, Health & Society" at the Norman Lear Center of the University of Southern California, Los Angeles, USA is analyzed. The Center for Media & Health, Gouda, the Netherlands is the basis for the second case study.

pretation of the analysis results. Chapter 6 accentuates and discusses the striking conditions and characteristics of E-E collaboration processes as experienced by the study participants. Chapter 7 pays attention to the main category, the place of gift exchange, which was stipulated through the analysis. On the place of gift exchange E-E collaborations take place in practice. Furthermore, the reciprocal effect of the place of gift exchange with two other significant fields is outlined: common sense and zeitgeist according to the Third Reich Experience and the Media. Chapter 8 is an in-depth portrayal of E-E collaboration forms and stages as they relate to the place of gift exchange in practice where at least four different collaboration forms are presented and discussed. Part II, which refers to the sub-questions B1, B2 and B3, is subsequently summarized and evaluated in Epilogue II.

Chapter 9 summarizes the theoretical concept of the research subject and a discussion and recommendations for Germany's future collaboration activities in Entertainment-Education are given.

1.5 Summary

The first chapter outlines that this thesis focuses exclusively on E-E collaborations between sustainability experts from governmental (related) authorities and TV entertainment makers in Germany. The main interest of the thesis is centered on *conditions and forms* of collaboration processes.

While on the international field there are several approaches and strategies for fostering prosocial topics though collaboration approaches exist, Germany has only made half-hearted steps in this direction so far. Thus, to discover conditions and forms of E-E collaborations the thesis first presents *theoretical debates* in the field of Entertainment-Education and prosocial media and TV to find useful hints for further collaboration developments in Germany. Secondly, the two most *significant international approaches* of E-E collaboration practice are examined in order to learn from them for applications in Germany. The results of these two different parts (theoretical debates and international E-E practice) are used as a base for part II of the thesis, where a qualitative study will examine communication practice of German E-E partners and the main research question will be answered.

2. Learning from Entertainment-Education Theory for Collaborations in Germany

> "The entertainment-education strategy is as wholesome a communication strategy as can be: It is theory-driven and applied, speaks to one's heart and head, is commercially viable and socially ameliorative, covers media production and reception processes, and is research-anchored and creatively stoked. Further, its purpose is to show the possibilities, not to prescribe, allowing the audience members, who choose to tune in, to make their own meanings or co-create new ones in conversation with others. What more could one ask for?"
>
> - Arvind Singhal, 2010

The first step to answering the main research question is to deal with the E-E strategy (i.e. the definition, the development and diffusion, the theories, effects and target groups) as it is discussed and reflected in scholarly literature. The aim of this chapter is to learn what the implications of the E-E strategy are (sub-question A1, chapter 1.2) and to provide answers regarding conditions and forms for teaming up processes between educational (governmental authorities) and entertaining (TV makers) agents in Germany (see part II of the thesis).

In literature, applying the E-E strategy is described as purposively designing and implementing prosocial media messages. These messages entertain and educate simultaneously in order to boost knowledge about certain issues, create a positive attitude about it or even change behavior. In western as well as in non-western countries[9] many (research) programs and collaborations have been established which use promotional health, social and environmental messages in television entertainment plots in order to reach huge segments of the public (Nariman, 1993).

Singhal & Rogers (1999: 13) state that "the idea of combining entertainment with education is not new: It goes as far back in human history as the timeless art of storytelling". Singhal, Pant & Rogers (2000: 173) add that "for thousands of years, music, drama, dance and various folk media have been used in many countries for recreation, devotion, reformation and instructional purposes". The idea of *consciously and strategically combining entertainment appeals with educational*

---

[9] The author prefers to write western and non-western countries and not developed and developing countries. There are two reasons for this: Firstly other E-E literature also prefers the differentiation between western and non-western countries (Bouman, 1999; Singhal & Rogers 1999) and, secondly, the terms developed and developing countries seem to be more 'discriminating' than the expressions western and non-western.

messages in television, radio, comic books or rock music has been well-documented over the past 25 years, specifically in communication science as well as in the field of social psychology (Singhal & Rogers, 1999: 14).

To better understand the E-E approach, an overview of the theoretical notions behind the E-E strategy is worth examining.

2.1 Definition

Health promotion (HIV/AIDS, drugs, obesity, etc.) and social themes (gender empowerment, domestic violence, etc.) have played an integral part in the development of E-E scholars, governmental authorities and other experts working with prosocial topics. They have used the idea to interweave educational messages within entertainment programs since the late 1950s. Entertainment-Education also plays a role in the environmental field and several studies were provided about environmental topics (IPC, 2010; Singhal et al., 2000).

There are many variations of entertainment and education possible. Following Singhal & Rogers (1999: 11-13) some media formats emphasize pure entertainment (many of them with 'antisocial' values like crime, unhealthy lifestyles, disregard for the environment, etc.) while others focus on boredom-pedagogy. Entertainment Education is in the middle and combines the better of the two (see illustration 2.1).

Figure 2.1: Localization of E-E programs

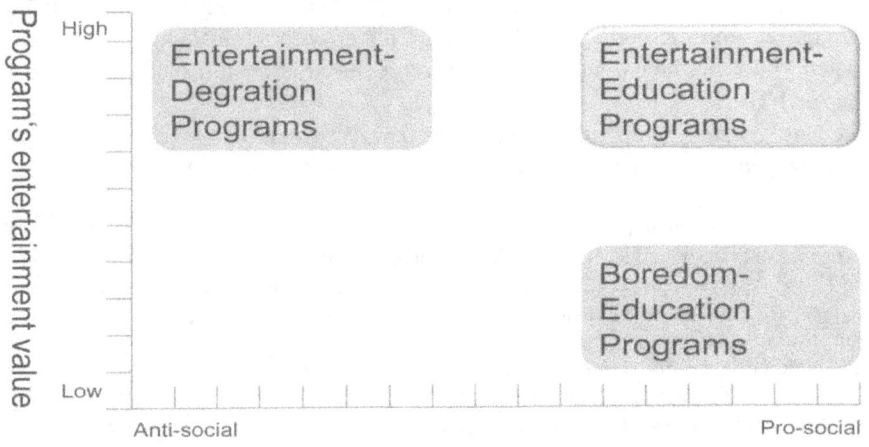

Source: Singhal & Rogers (1999: 12)

E-E media formats provide a high entertainment value and prosocial values at the same time (Singhal & Rogers, 1999). According to Lacayo & Singhal (2008), the terms Entertainment-Education and Edutainment are synonymously used in international literature. The abbreviation for both terms is enter-educate.[10] In contrast to Lacayo & Singhal, Lampert (2007: 70) suggests differences between the two. She argues that Edutainment aims just at providing knowledge (similar to infotainment) whereas the Entertainment-Education strategy has the additional purpose of changing attitude and behavior.[11]

Nowadays several definitions exist which emphasizes different aspects of the E-E strategy. One definition, which includes the recent developments and discussions in the E-E field, is the following:

"Entertainment-education is a theory-based communication strategy for purposefully embedding educational and social issues in the creation, production, processing, and dissemination process of an entertainment program, in order to achieve desired individual, community, institutional, and societal changes among the intended media user populations" (Wang & Singhal, 2009: 272-273).

Wang & Singhal (2009) choose the term *"theory-based communication strategy"* in their definition. It emphasizes the theoretical framework of Entertainment-Education and it hints at the theoretical foundations involved in the E-E format that will be discussed in this chapter and which also need to be reflected in the German collaboration context in part II of the thesis.

Another aspect of the definition is *"purposefully embedding educational and social issues in the creation, production, processing, and dissemination process of an entertainment program"*. In particular, the passage *"purposefully embedding educational and social issues"* suggests that this thesis should put the collaboration process of the educational and the entertainment professionals (e.g. how they initiate the contact with each other, which steps are undertaken to create a joint program content) into the foreground as this is the core research interest of the thesis (see chapter 1.2).

The part *"creation, production, processing, and dissemination process of an entertainment program"* refers to the process-based character of Entertainment-Educa-

---

[10] The terms of infotainment and emotainment also exist. They were designed by the media industry itself. Infotainment describes formats which combine informational and entertaining elements (see chapter 3.3.2). Emotainment is entertainment with a lot of emotions: one example comes from the German TV show *Super Nanny* (RTL), in which families coming from lower socio-economic milieus receive help through a pedagogue on how to educate their children. A second example is the German TV show *Das Medium* (RTL), in which the audience is guided through emotional and difficult times in their life. In addition, there are two other terms, advertainment and ecotainment, which are frequently used in the marketing and advertising field. Advertainment describes an entertaining form of advertising that typically uses the stylistic device of humor. Advertainment also includes advertising games such as the *Moorhuhn*. The term of ecotainment has been established by Lichtl (1999) and describes a marketing strategy based on an emotional communication concept for effectively spreading ecology relevant content, products and services.

[11] According to Aufenanger (2004) since the 1990s the term Edutainment has been increasingly used in Germany in the field of learning software programs whereas Entertainment-Education is known (even though not broadly) as a strategy which has its origin mainly in the health communication field.

tion in which the E-E format is to be designed and implemented. As a strategy it requires much more than just the 'end product'. This pays respect to the fact that the E-E strategy applied in practice needs time, energy, and endurance. Additionally, it concedes that also resistance, tensions and dialectics are possible while establishing and implementing the strategy (Papa et al., 2006).

Reflecting on these factors critically, the author suggests a formulation "in which educational and entertainment professionals purposefully embed prosocial issues in the creation, production, processing, and dissemination process of an entertainment program".

In the definition of Wang & Singhal, the E-E strategy aims to *"achieve desired individual, community, institutional, and societal changes among the intended media user populations"*.

Importantly, this part of the definition refers to a change on the (1) individual, (2) community, (3) institutional and (4) the societal level. Because of the "and" the definition indicates that the change should take place simultaneously on all levels. Indeed, also Singhal, Rao & Pant (2006) describe synergetic effects, when changes on one level stimulate changes on another. As the change can, but must not happen simultaneously on all levels, the author thinks that this perspective is too broad and she would suggest writing "or" instead of "and".

In context with these four levels used for the E-E definition for the purposes of this thesis, there are various theories emphasizing different stages of prosocial (knowledge, attitude and behavior) change (Abraham et al., 1998; Bartholomew et al., 2006; McGuire, 1989; Prochaska et al., 1992; Singhal & Rogers, 1999). For instance, Prochaska et al. (1992) distinguishes between five different stages of change starting with 'precontemplation' and ending with the stage of 'maintenance'. An E-E soap opera for example reaches the audience members by changing their short-term behavior, but a change of the long-term behavior (maintenance) cannot be realized. Bouman (1999: 25) thus suggests including all different stages of prosocial behavior change in an E-E definition. According to Wang & Singhal and the mentioned reflections above and according to the research subject, the following definition of the E-E strategy is a reformulation that fits better within the context of the thesis:

"Entertainment-Education is a theory-based communication strategy in which educational and entertainment professionals purposefully embed prosocial issues in the creation, production, processing, and dissemination process of an entertainment program in order to achieve different stages of change either on individual, community, institutional or societal level among the intended media user populations".

Through this reformulation, the E-E definition is focused on the research objective of this thesis and has its origin in international scholarly literature. As will be outlined in chapter 2.4, this definition refers to E-E co-productions and inscript participation partnership arrangements.[12] How far this reformulated definition can be

---

[12] As will become clear in part II of the thesis, co-productions and inscript participations are

applied in the German collaboration field will be discussed in part II of the thesis. Thus it must be regarded as a sensitizing concept (see chapter 5 and 6).

2.2 Developments and Diffusion

The growth of using Entertainment-Education as a prosocial communication strategy began with the growth of the electronic media all over the world. Different origins of the E-E strategy go back into the 1940s. In 1944 the Australian radio series *The Lawsons* was produced. This series aimed at fostering health behavior within the public. *The Archers*, a radio drama broadcast by the BBC starting in 1951, was one of the first E-E series to promote agricultural innovations for farmers in Britain after the Second World War. Today it is still broadcasted in Britain being the longest-running radio series in history.

The E-E strategy for television began with the widely popular Peruvian soap opera called *Simplemente María*. Between 1969-1971 it became the most popular TV program throughout Latin America. The main character María, a very poor girl, moved to the big Peruvian capital Lima to find a better life. There she became a maid and a seamstress in the household where she worked. Her "cinderella" (Lampert, 2007: 73) story inspired thousands of people to buy Singer sewing machines, which were used in the program (Singhal & Rogers, 1999: 41). María also visited literacy classes and many people enrolled in those classes and subsequently created literacy clubs, thus emulating María's behavior (Singhal & Rogers, 1999: 42). All these effects were unintended. The Mexican producer Miguel Sabido was the first person to recognize the immense power of using entertainment media in a systematic way to enhance changes in the public. Hence, *Simplemente María* can be considered as a landmark in understanding the power of Entertainment-Education. Sabido produced twelve E-E soap operas from 1967-1997 addressing prosocial issues such as adult literacy and family planning (Singhal & Rogers, 1999: 52). Sabido's work inspired the production of *Hum Log (We People)*[13], an Indian soap which was broadcasted in the early eighties and focusing on issues such as the status of women in society, education, the dowry system and family planning.

Simplemente María and *Hum Log* fostered prosocial messages with a high impact. The audience changed their beliefs and actions[14] as they identified with the protagonists in these programs (Singhal & Rogers: 36-44 and 96-102). The E-E strategy succeeded in both programs beyond anyone's expectations, and it has been used ever since in television communication programs all over the world to promote

---

also used in Germany's collaboration practice, but they do not come to the fore as much as e.g. in the Netherlands (chapter 4.3) or in non-western countries.

[13] *Hum Log* celebrated 25 years of existence in 2009.

[14] According to an effect study the respondents claimed to have realized through *Simplemente María* that the treatment of maids was very bad. Furthermore, they stated that there had been reports about families who started to get increasingly interested in their maids' lives and treat them better, e.g. allowing them to go out for night classes (Singhal & Rogers 1999: 42).

prosocial issues. Sabido's formula is applied mainly in non-western countries to enhance aspects of a prosocial development.

Next to Sabido's activities, other stakeholders from western organizations started to design and implement entertainment programs aimed at using television for promoting health and environmental messages for both western and non-western country settings. In the 1970s, the 'Hollywood lobbyists' pleaded for more prosocial messages within the media. "A "Hollywood lobbyist" is a group, usually with an office in Los Angeles, that seeks to persuade scriptwriters and producers of prime-time television shows to include issues like abortion, designated driving, or the environment in television episodes (Montgomery, 1998)" (quoted after Singhal & Rogers, 1999: 18). A good example for Hollywood lobbyism is the *Harvard Alcohol Project* (Montgomery, 1993; Singhal & Rogers, 1999). The Center of Health and Communication of the Harvard School of Public Health succeeded in implementing the idea of the 'designated driver', a person who purposely abstains from alcohol, within more than 160 series like *Cheers, Bill Cosby* or *L.A. Law.*

Within the 1980s, E-E radio, television, music and theatre projects were primarily promoted in non-western settings by US institutions like the John Hopkins University (Popular Communication Services) in Baltimore (JHU/PCS) as well as the Popular Communication International (PCI) in New York. All of these activities focused on pedagogical concepts to boost health-promoting behavior and social change regarding issues such as HIV/AIDS and birth control in non-western countries[15] and were mostly part of and funded by USAID (Piotrow & de Fossard, 2004; Poindexter, 2004).

Various articles, papers, workshops and conference reports have contributed to a sound theoretical E-E framework used in entertainment formats and positive effects on audience members were documented (Poindexter, 2004; Sherry, 2002). These results are limited to a non-western country perspective.

Nonetheless, the developments of the E-E strategy in western countries have increasingly moved forward during the last two decades, as scholars and practitioners have become more and more interested in E-E projects and investigate results on the effects of the program (see section 2.6). There are fewer results compared to the results for non-western countries. However, there are interesting examples and issues, both in the USA and Europe.[16]

Since the 1980s, different initiatives have arisen to integrate health issues like contraception and HIV/AIDS in US television programs. One of these projects is *The Media Project*, an initiative of the *Advocates for Youth*. The prosocial messages of this project were embedded in series like *Emergency Room* or *Dawson's Creek*

---

[15] In Germany there were also single efforts regarding the implementation of the E-E strategy in western countries. Many of these activities were provided by the Konrad-Adenauer foundation in Bonn (Konrad-Adenauer-Stiftung, 2001).

[16] Although the next section intends to give a brief overview of the E-E diffusion in the USA and Europe, chapter 4 will depict the striking examples, which the thesis aims to learn from for Germany.

(Kaiser Family Foundation, 2004) – TV shows that are also broadcasted in Germany.

Numerous US children's programs like *Sesame Street, Electric Company* and *Mister Roger's Neighborhood* (Singhal & Rogers, 1999) have used Entertainment-Education to prepare children for classroom learning and further educational processes. Furthermore, there were efforts by the *UCLA School of Public Health* and the *Department of Film and Television* in which they collaborated with the *Immunization Branch of the California Department of Health Services* to launch E-E campaigns (Glik et al., 1998). Other players in this field of Entertainment-Education are the *Robert Wood Johnson Foundation* and the *Kaiser Family Foundation*, both of which have collaborated with *Viacom* on the project *Know HIV/AIDS*. With the *Science & Entertainment Exchange* program of the National Academy of Science, there is another player "that provides entertainment industry professionals with access to top scientists and engineers to help bring the reality of cutting-edge science to creative and engaging storylines".[17]

A comprehensive approach has been established through the *Norman Lear Center* and its program *Hollywood, Health & Society* at the University of Southern California using the E-E strategy in US television prime time shows. The *Hollywood, Health & Society* program has established a network with many collaborating Hollywood scriptwriters, producers and health experts (such as doctors or university professors). The program is funded by the US government and other (non-)governmental institutions (see chapter 4.2). It has implemented scientifically validated health lifestyle stories in prime time shows such as *Maude, All in Family, The Jeffersons*, and more recently *Emergency Room, Scrubs, Private Practice, Law & Order* and *Grey's Anatomy* (NLC, 2008), to mention only a few.

By comparison Europe provides fewer studies and evidence highlighting how the E-E strategy was or is disseminated (with the exception of the Netherlands). As mentioned before, *The Arches*, broadcasted by the BBC, can be considered as one of the first examples of an E-E production. In the 1980s, BBC launched the series *EastEnders*, which consistently involved health and environmental issues. At the end of the 1990s, the BBC World Service Trust was founded. This independent charity uses media and communication campaigns trying to reduce poverty and promote human rights (BBC World Service Trust, 2008), primarily doing projects in non-western countries.

In the Netherlands, the E-E strategy was used in the late 1980s and the early 1990s for the first time in series like *Familie Oudenrijn* (1987), the *Way of Life Show* (1988), *Villa Borghese* (1990) and later on in the series *Costa!* (2005). For ongoing research and examples of program implementations, the findings of Bouman (1999, 2005, 2011a), Bouman & Draaisma (2006) and Bouman et al. (2009) are highly significant. Since 1999, the Center for Media & Health (previously called Bouman E&E Development) – directed by Bouman – has been analyzing and im-

---

[17] Retrieved from Science & Entertainment Exchange 2011: www.scienceandentertainmentexchange.org (3rd March 2011).

plementing collaborations between health communication and television professionals (chapter 4.3). They utilize strategic and theory-based E-E activities that may help stakeholders in their partnership (i.e. facilitating the collaboration process for both sides).

Comparing the Dutch, US and the UK activities to those in Germany, the E-E strategy is not as widely disseminated. However, as chapter 1 makes clear, several collaborative activities are taking place trying to promote health and environmental messages via entertainment television in a comparable way (part II of this thesis).

Following Tufte (2004, 2005), the development and the diffusion of social change practice can be separated into three different 'generations' [18]:

1. The first generation approach used to spread information, raise awareness and change behavior. This approach was largely based on the social learning theory, positing that individuals learn by observing and imitating others who serve as role models and thereby gaining a sense of self-efficacy (see section 2.3.2). Tufte (2005) criticizes this approach because it ignores the know-ledge and needs of the target community (also known as 'banking education approach' [19]).
2. The second approach emerged in the mid to late 1990s. It identified structural barriers to both behavior change and individual behavior; it started to address society as a unit of change. Another cornerstone of the second generation was the introduction of participatory approaches.
3. The third generation emerged recently and identifies the root of problems not in the lack of know-ledge but in structural inequalities and power imbalances. The aim of this approach is to empower ***individuals and their communities to seek and create social change by changing their individual lives as well***. This also means that cultural change must not come from external agents but from the community itself via promoting dialectic processes of the debate and collective actions.

In recent publications, Singhal, Wang & Rogers (2011: 19) point at five emerging trends in which E-E scholars and practitioners should attend: integration of Entertainment-Education with (1) social movements, (2) invitational approaches, (3) the positive deviance approach to change, (4) new digital technologies, and (5) trans-

---

[18] Tufte (2005: 173) provides a detailed overview regarding different notions of the three generations. It is important to note that these different generations also include elements from one another.

[19] Several authors have described the banking education approach. One of the first to point at this approach was Paulo Freire. With banking education he referred to educational pedagogy, which is linked to the process of banking. "In the banking concept of education, knowledge is a gift bestowed by those who consider themselves knowledgeable upon those whom they consider to know nothing" (Freire 2006: 72). Examples for this kind of concept are "the teacher teaches and the students are taught; the teacher knows everything and the students know nothing; the teacher thinks and the students are thought about; the teacher talks and the students listen – meekly; the teacher disciplines and the students are disciplined" (Freire 2006: 73).

media storytelling and they conclude: "These converging and powerful trends suggest that E-E is a highly flexible and versatile strategy for social change: As part of a communication campaign, E-E can be global and local, a stand-alone intervention and a component of a larger project. The field of E-E continues to keep an open and proactive perspective in its theoretically grounded and research-informed practices" (ibid.).

2.3 The E-E Strategy

E-E collaborations all use a multidisciplinary background to reach the audience with prosocial messages. Therefore, the focus is largely on various social and psychological processes that take place while and after media consumers (have) encounter(ed) an E-E narrative. According to Tufte (2005), changes took place in this context. Scholars have recently discussed the danger of this individualistic, cognitive-proceeding centered and 'mechanistic' approach for social change (Dutta-Bergmann, 2005; Dutta, 2006; Singhal & Rogers, 1999). They have made suggestions to use a more holistic approach (e.g. taking the cultural background of the media users and the platforms and features on which the messages are sent into consideration) (Wang, 2008).

The following sections provide an overview on important theoretical notions that have influenced Entertainment-Education. These are the social marketing perspective, Bandura's social cognitive theory, Sabido's prosocial entertainment theory,[20] the parasocial interaction theory, the identification theory, the celebrity influence concepts, audience-centered theories and further theories in use in Entertainment-Education.

2.3.1 Social Marketing

Governmental (related) authorities often struggle with the problem of how to get the audience interested in prosocial topics. In order to solve this problem they have applied the strategy of social marketing for their own principles, especially in using mass media to spread their messages. This is particularly true for the systematic application of marketing[21] concepts and techniques to achieve specific prosocial behavior goals with regard to the public (see also NSMC, 2006). Kotler and colleagues were one of the first who conveyed marketing principles into the social field (Kotler, 2006). Kotler & Zaltman (1971: 5) (also see Cheng et al., 2011) define social marketing as "the design, implementation, and control of programs calculated to influence the acceptability of social ideas and involving considerations of product planning, pricing, communication, distribution, and marketing research".

---

[20] Sabido's theory is already a connection between the social marketing and the social cognitive theory.
[21] Kotler et al. (2011: 39) define marketing as „a process in the economic and social context, through which individuals or groups satisfy their needs and wishes by generating, offering and exchanging products and other valuable things".

Cheng, Kotler & Lee (2011: 21) introduce the traditional marketing toolbox of the four P's, that can be adapted to prosocial campaign development to "create, communicate, and deliver values for their targeted behaviors", whereas "the synergy of the 4Ps (...) makes a truly successful social marketing campaign possible" (ibid.). The four P's are specified as follows: (1) *Product*: the characteristics of the product/behavior, (2) *Price*: costs and values of a behavior including social, economical and psychological costs, (3) *P*lace: where the product or the behavior is available (4) *Promotion*: where the pro-duct is sold/where the behavior is sent via prosocial messages.

The literature also refers to a fifth variable, the *P*ositioning, which means framing issues so that the target group remembers them (Corcoran, 2007: 90). In value and experience marketing (Doyle, 2008; Joseph, 2010; O'Sullivan & Spangler, 1998), the framework moves beyond these P's. In the context of E-E television interventions, it also might be important for researchers to address the insights coming from these upcoming marketing fields.

In recent years, governmental (related) authorities dealing with health, social or environmental issues have increasingly integrated social marketing into their communication campaigns as practitioners realize how the use of models developed in other sectors could be translated into their practice. The social marketing frameworks have proved to be particularly adaptable. Over the last couple of years, there has been growing evidence to suggest that social marketing can improve the impact and effectiveness of communication campaigns ((NSMC), 2006). The strengths of social marketing are that its features can be adapted to each stage of the prosocial communication campaign design. These include the audience segmentation, consumer research, competition and monitoring, all of which are depicted below.

Audience segmentation: Hill (2004) points out that social marketing borrows strategies of business marketing, which includes identifying target groups (see section 2.7) and so-called consumer orientation. Consumer orientation asks for the specific needs and wishes of the consumer. Thus, when one wants to reach certain people (e.g. mothers), one has to find out what they need and want. The audience segmentation concept does research on target groups and it pre-tests the campaign messages. In addition, it splits the public into different subgroups that have different psychological and social characteristics. These components can be applied to the practice of promoting prosocial themes.

Consumer research sees in the consumers' wishes and needs (preferences, beliefs, opinions, etc.)[22] the basis for a social marketing strategy. Consumer research can be useful during the conceptualization stage of projects that seek to mainstream prosocial topics through media.[23]

---

[22] Pine & Gilmore (1999) add that especially in non-western countries, audience members cannot be easily investigated in this context. They argue that other strategies are needed.
[23] For example in the collaboration of the German Federal Ministry of Education and Research, the University of Hohenheim and RTLII in the format *Welt der Wunder,* consumer research had been applied to find out more about the audience members, who received proso-

Competition: Social marketing can also research the commercial viability as well as the products and services offered. A focus on promoting prosocial topics to the public could include (1) examining unsustainable (i.e. unhealthy or environmentally damaging) behavior that competes with sustainable behavior or (2) doing research on other prosocial messages that are being promoted.
Monitoring: Social marketing uses evaluation from the start of the planning process to its end. For advocating prosocial topics, evaluation is a vital part to find out whether TV or other media formats are achieving their objectives (also see chapter 3.2). Thus, it is important to measure the impact a TV format has on the audience members.

Although there are many advantages to using the social marketing strategy in communicating prosocial issues (through the media), social marketing is not without its criticism. Most of the common criticism is that social marketing 'manipulates' people who are thus 'persuaded' to live a more sustainable life in the same way that marketing 'persuades' consumers to buy products (Bruhn & Tilmes, 1993; Hill, 2004). And, the social marketing perspective focuses on the individuals, meaning that social or economic conditions are often ignored (Bruhn, 2006; McDaniel et al., 2005).

Apart from these two arguments, Hübner (2005) refers to the problematic of diffusion of social marketing. He maintains that the social marketing perspective in Germany is still considered as something 'strange' to governmental organizations working with health, social and environmental topics. They have little or no experience in the field of marketing activities. Therefore, many misunderstandings and problems arise; for instance they put marketing on the same level with advertising activities (Hübner, 2005). Nonetheless, social marketing has increasingly become an integral part of their strategies guided by discussions about ethical correctness (Andreasen, 2001; Guttman, 2000).

On the international level, various social marketing instruments are used by health and environmental governmental organizations and television makers to design and implement entertainment messages. Following Bouman (1999: 27) "Various techniques of social marketing are used in the design of entertainment-messages (e.g. formative evaluation, audience segmentation, needs assessment, product development, pre-testing). Research-based knowledge about characteristics, needs and preferences of the target audiences can substantively inform and support the design of entertainment-education programmes. This may include inviting audience representatives to participate in the design process or to organize focus groups to obtain actual information and feedback from the specific target group".

In recent years, researchers have developed E-E approaches including both qualitative and quantitative methods[24] that go with the principles of social marketing de-

---

cial messages in the storylines (Schwender et al., 2008).

[24] An extensive overview regarding the methods in use in E-E projects can be found by Sood et al. (2004). Sood and colleagues (2004: 133) stress that "the current standard for evaluating entertainment-education programs consists of baseline and follow-up surveys, compar-

scribed above.

2.3.2 Bandura's Social Cognitive Theory

Besides the social marketing approach, the E-E strategy is based on the social learning theory or social cognitive theory, as it is nowadays called. According to Bandura (2004: 76) "social cognitive theory provides an agentic conceptual framework within which to analyze the determinants and psychosocial mechanisms through which symbolic communication promotes personal and social changes. To be an agent is to influence intentionally one's own functioning, and life circumstances. In this transactional view of self and society, people are producers as well as products of their social environment. By selecting and altering their social environment, they have a hand in shaping the course that their lives take". For the E-E approach, "shaping the course", and the intersection of being "producers as well as products of their social environment" is important. Bandura deals with the issue of ***how people learn from situations by observing the behavior of others (vicarious learning)***. This is a vital point that needs to be taken into consideration while creating and implementing prosocial messages with the potential to positively influence audience members. Bandura (1977) claims that the audience can learn new behaviors by observing role models in the mass media and then model the same behavior. If there is a high degree of identification,[25] this modeling effect occurs between the viewer and the media personality.

Bandura (1977 and 1979) suggests that an individual (among other ways) learns by observing and imitating the overt behavior of other individuals who serve as models. He identifies three different narrative possibilities rising from theoretical and empirical types of social modeling:

1. *Prestige model*: Characters who exhibit socially and culturally admired behaviors. This model should represent a high potential of identification for the audience.
2. *Similarity modeling*: Different media characters who appeal to various population segments portray advantages of adopting prosocial behavior.
3. *Transitional modeling*: Characters who exhibit a negative role model adopt a positive, prosocial behavior. These characters are mainly constructed by offering plenty of parallels to the audience, showing them different options of actions and consequences.

Another pillar of the Bandura's social modeling theory are four different psychological processes: (1) *attention*, (2) *retention*, (3) *production* and (4) *motivation*. Obviously, attention is needed when having people watch and then accurately perceive the role model and her or his behavior. With the help of these models, the audience can identify, experience and eventually learn new behaviors, without ne-

---

ing those individuals exposed versus those not exposed to the entertainment-education programs, ideally with a treatment and control group".

[25] Bandura (1986) defines identification as the process by which an individual adopts a model's behavior and/or personality patterns.

cessarily applying these behaviors. Retention is related to seeing the modeled behavior repeated in the program so that the audience will remember it. Recall is important in this kind of process. Retention should lead to production, which is putting into action the behavior patterns the audience has seen in the prosocial programs. Motivation refers to the process of cognitively sharing the character's experiences via her/his imagination (i.e. the learner must want to demonstrate what she/he has learned) (also see Dunlap, 2005).

By witnessing the positive and negative role models who go through changes in behavior, the viewers may be motivated to adopt the positive behavior or modify the negative behavior patterns.

Bandura (1997) distinguishes two motivational influences of social modeling in E-E programs: presenting the behavior change as a beneficial decision for individuals (vicarious motivation) and as an attentional involvement using emotional appeals to foster prosocial interaction between the viewer and the role model. Following Bandura (1997, 2004) a desired behavior change depends on five factors: (1) *self-efficacy*, (2) *collective efficacy*, (3) *outcome expectations*, (4) *aspirations* and (5) *perceived impediments*. Other features of the social modeling process are (1) the symbolic coding, which summarize the main messages in an epilogue at the end of the program and (2) social support, in which influences coming from the social groups are used to sustain the prosocial behavior shown in the program. For example in the collaboration in the German series *Lindenstraße* (episode *Suche Klima, biete Schutz*), TV messages have been used as the main component to promote prosocial issues to a mass audience. This was additionally supported by other public follow up communication activities, such as a festival, discussion rounds and a bicycle rally for saving the environment (Lubjuhn & Reinermann, 2010).

Miguel Sabido (section 2.3.3) integrated many of these theoretical E-E aspects of Bandura's theory in the design of his soap operas (Singhal & Rogers, 1999). In recent years, Bandura has become increasingly interested in E-E applications of his theory (Bandura, 2004). He has made a great contribution towards refining the strategy.

An additional key to the E-E strategy and its effects on the audience lies within Bandura's **concepts of self-efficacy** (Bandura, 2004; Gecas, 1989; Schwarzer, 1992) and **collective efficacy** (Bandura, 2004). The concept of self-efficacy is linked to the behavior change that a person *considers* or *enacts* (ibid.). It can be described as an individual's perception of her or his capability "to deal effectively with a situation and to control this situation. Efficacy beliefs influence how people think, feel, motivate themselves, and act" (Bandura, 1995: 3, also compare Strong 2008: 57).

This means that the person recognizes her or his own behavioral responsibility and has the awareness that she or he can individually influence decisions and achieve the desired goals. As described above, the feeling of efficacy can be applied to one's individual behavior (self-efficacy) as well as to societal or cultural behavior (collective efficacy). According to Bandura (2004: 80), "social cognitive theory extends the conception of human agency to collective agency. The strength of families, communities, school systems, business organizations, social institutions, and even nations lies partly in people's sense of collective efficacy and they can solve the problems they face and improve their lives through unified effort. People's shared belief in their collective power to realize the futures they seek is a key ingredient of collective agency".[26] That means that Bandura's theory offers models not only for enhancing the self-efficacy but also for learning to influence the social and cultural environment for a change (e.g. founding self-help groups, etc.) (Bandura, 2004: 81).

Research in recent years is largely based on Bandura's previously established theory, focusing on (1) the various social and psychological processes that happen while and after media users encounter an E-E narrative and (2) how to take the socio-cultural environment of individuals into consideration (Chatterjee et al., 2009; Morgan et al., 2009; Moyer-Gusé, 2008; Schuh, 2008; Wang, 2008). Sabido also used Bandura's results as a grounding for his theory, but he dealt with other levels and components, as the following section will outline.

2.3.3 Sabido's Prosocial Entertainment Theory

Miguel Sabido is a pioneer in the field of the E-E strategy. As a writer and producer of television and theater in Mexico, he successfully implemented the E-E strategy in a dozen of the soap opera programs he developed. His work has had a fundamental impact on the diffusion of the E-E strategy. The process of theorizing Entertainment-Education started with Sabido's analysis of the previously mentioned soap opera *Simplemente María*, which captured the hearts of Peruvians and others. Sabido developed a theoretical concept for Entertainment-Education, which is based on, among others, Bandura's social learning theory (1979 and 2004), the drama theory of Bentley (1967), the theory of stereotypes and archetypes by Jung (1958 and 1970), and MacLean's theory of triune brain (1973).

Sabido was primarily influenced by *Bandura's social cognitive theory*, which was described in the previous paragraphs. He used it to describe the concept of E-E programs and the effect on the audience. He incorporated principles of Bandura's theory into the design of positive, negative and transitional role models.[27] The *theory of drama* provided Sabido with hints regarding the design of the plot as well as

---

[26] One example of collective efficacy is an episode of the South African E-E program *Soul City*. According to Usdin et al. (2004: 154) "neighbors collectively decide to break the ongoing cycle of spousal abuse in a neighboring home. When the next wife-beating episode occurred, they gathered around the abuser's residence and collectively banged pots and pans, censuring the abuser's actions".

[27] Positive role models support prosocial behavior, negative ones reject it and transitional role models develop from antisocial to prosocial characters (Nariman, 1993). The positive and the negative role models defend resp. attack prosocial behaviors. In fact, the positive ones are rewarded and the negative ones are punished. The doubting, transitional role models begin to change their awareness, attitudes and behavior towards prosocial issues, and for that they are rewarded.

the characters and their relationships to each other. On the basis of *Jung's theory of archetypes*, Sabido developed archetypical characters for his E-E programs, which can be clearly identified by the audience. The *theory of the triune brain* distinguishes between three different regions of the brain (cognition, emotion and instinctive behavior). Sabido used this approach to explain that the media should activate all three regions for stimulating prosocial reflection or behavior patterns. Compared to regular dramas and soap operas, the E-E strategy (1) does not only stimulate emotions (the feeling of losing a loved one), but (2) it also portrays instinctive behavior by a special manner of production (showing a fight) and (3) it also shows cognitive components by summarizing information and central messages in the epilogue of some of the E-E programs.

Beside the theoretical foundation, Sabido was one of the first to use formative (pre-production), process (production) and summative (post-production)[28] research (see section 2.4.3) to design and implement programming that would not only have entertainment value but also contain messages of social value and would give people an understanding of acceptable social behavior (Sabido, 2004).

To sum up, several theoretical notions inspired Sabido, and he formed his own theoretical contribution based on them. Following Singhal & Rogers (1999: 58), further contributions to the E-E strategy of Sabido have been (1) providing a moral framework[29] for the specific educational issue, (2) using formative and process research (section 2.4.3.1 and 2.4.3.2), (3) providing multiple transitional role models as well as positive and negative characters for the educational issues depicted, (4) providing epilogues delivered by a credible individual at the end of each episode[30] and (5) conducting summative research (section 2.4.3.3) to measure the effects of Entertainment-Education on behavior change.

2.3.4 Parasocial Interaction and Identification Theory

Like social cognitive theory and prosocial entertainment theory, parasocial interaction theory (Horton & Wohl, 1956) and the identification theory (Kelman, 1958; Kelman, 1961) focus on the audience of E-E media programs and how they may be convinced to change their knowledge, attitude and behavior towards a prosocial

---

[28] Sabido's production techniques are described in detail in Nariman (1993).

[29] Singhal & Rogers (1999: 58) state that „the moral framework is usually derived from a nation's constitution, its legal statutes, or from documents, such as the UN Declaration of Human Rights, to which the country [in which the E-E intervention takes place] is a signatory". More details on the moral framework can be found in Singhal & Rogers (1999).

[30] As chapter 4 and part II will also clarify, the use of Sabido's methodology is much related to the television system (media legislations, role of the state, role of commercial and public broadcasters, etc.) of the country, in which an E-E program is introduced. Sabido's methodology works perfectly for non-western countries where the governmental authorities can – to an ultimate extent – influence the media system. Given this background, chapter 4 will illustrate how governmental authorities handle E-E collaborations in the US and the Netherlands. Based on these insights, it will be the task of the thesis to illuminate conditions and forms of E-E collaborations in Germany and to give future recommendations.

way of being. Both theories are described separately and in greater detail because they have obtained immense recognition in the field of Entertainment-Education in recent years (see above).

E-E programs are designed to stimulate and enhance the parasocial interaction (PSI) and identification between television viewers and television characters. Both theories describe different levels on which viewers can be influenced regarding a prosocial change by (positive) media characters.

2.3.4.1 Parasocial Interaction Theory

Merton pioneered the parasocial interaction theory in 1943 while doing research on the Kate Smith 18-hour singing marathon on television. Merton's research influenced scholars like Horton and Wohl (1956) and others (Rubin et al., 1985; Rubin & McHugh, 1987). Much of the research on PSI focuses on the perceived relationship that people have with media characters and how this influences E-E effects (Horton & Wohl, 1956).

Entertainment-Education uses the PSI concept for audience analysis watching audiences identify with positive characters when overcoming the difficulties they are confronted with or with transitional characters when dealing with struggles. These problems are often similar to reality as experienced by the audience. For example, one result of such PSI is the thousands of letters that are sent by audience members to radio or television personalities in E-E programs (Strong, 2008; Sood & Rogers, 2000). Strong (2008) strengthens that during the last two decades, the parasocial relationship between television consumers and different types of television people, defined as either fictional or real mediated personalities, has been described in various research studies (Babrow, 1987; Grant et al., 1991; Houlberg, 1984; Klimmt & Vorderer, 2003; Levy, 1979; Rubin & McHugh, 1987; Rubin et al., 1985; Singhal & Rogers, 2002; Sood, 2002; Tuner, 1993; Vorderer et al., 2004; Zillmann, 1994). In this context, the theory of PSI has been conceptualized as a measure to analyze ***cognitive***, ***behavioral*** and ***affective*** audience involvement before, during and after media exposure.

The cognitively orientated PSI can be defined as the degree to which the audience carefully pay attention to the television characters in the media messages and reflect on their educational or prosocial content after their exposure (Sood & Rogers, 2000).[31] For example, a media user considers Philip, a character in the German soap opera *Gute Zeiten, Schlechte Zeiten (Good Times, Bad Times)* a great personality and also a good singer after reflecting on his activities in the show. The behavioral orientated PSI is the degree to which audience members talk to mediated television people (also see Strong, 2008). In real life, this means talking to other

---

[31] Bandura (1995) describes cognitive PSI as being important to understand self-efficacy, which influences behavior change. The effects of E-E programs are connected to the ability (through the television character portrayals) to enhance the understanding of self-efficacy among the audience members. Bandura's theory of social learning and self-efficacy is described in chapter 3.3.1.

people (neighbors, family and friends) about the television personality in their everyday life (Sood & Rogers, 2000). An example would be that a media user tells his close friend that he will buy the new CD of the soap star Philip from *Gute Zeiten, Schlechte Zeiten* or that he will found an environmental activism group, as Philip did in the soap storyline. So the media user changes something due to the dialogue with others on what she or he saw on TV.

Beside TV, the parasocial component in new media (online parasocial interaction) might be a significant issue to put in the focus of interest, also when establishing a research agenda for Germany.

2.3.4.2 Identification Theory

Identification theory is based on the *affectively* orientated parasocial interaction. Affection means in this context the feeling that a media character is liked, much as a friend in real life. For example, a media user may like the attitude of the soap star Philip (e.g. his activities like founding an environmental activism group) or his appearance and would love to have him as a real friend.

In classical identification theory, a person takes on the identity of another person (Kelman, 1961), and this is the first type of role identification. The second type of role identification is 'reciprocal role identification', in which "the roles of two parties are defined with reference to one another" (Kelman, 1961: 64), such as in the case of a soap character and her or his fans. Both soap opera stars and audience members exchange and share reciprocal relationships that are played out in soap opera magazines and on soap opera web sites. Identification can be differentiated from compliance because, referring to the identification process, the audience member believes in the attitudes, values and behaviors she or he adopts from other people. In compliance processes the person just displays the attitudes, values and behaviors to evoke a favorable reaction from another person or a group she or he wishes to please (Kelman, 1958).

Identification is very close to parasocial interaction. Sood (2002) considers both to be closely related types in her model of audience involvement. She defines PSI as cognitive, behavioral and affective forms of interaction with media people. Identification is a form of 'referential affective audience involvement', in which television viewers relate to quiz show hosts, reality show participants (similarity identification) or relate to fictional characters in soap operas or serial dramas (wishful identification). Sood's (2002) and more recent studies from other communication scholars have not been adequately distinguished where the process of PSI ends and where audience identification begins (also see Strong, 2008). Or maybe there is actually no difference between the two of them, describing the same thing with different terms. In either case, as Strong (2008) also stresses, both processes seem to overlap and both have cognitive, behavioral and affective dimensions.

2.3.5 Celebrity Influence

Brown and colleagues (Brown, 2008a; Brown & Brasil, 1995; Brown & Basil, 2010; Brown & Fraser, 2004; Brown & Fraser, 2007) extended the parasocial interaction and identification theory to celebrities and their involvement in E-E communication campaigns. Their research explains that television consumers form bonds with sports stars (Magic Johnson, Mark McGuire, and Diego Maradona), recording artists (Elvis Presley), religious leaders (Pope John Paul II. and Cardinal Stephen Kim), racecar drivers (NASCAR legend Dale Earnhardt), politicians (Governor Arnold Schwarzenegger) and other celebrities (Princess Diana and Steve Irwin) through various mediated and interpersonal communication measures (Brown, 2008b; Brown, 2009; Brown, 2010; Brown & deMatviuk, 2010; Brown et al., 2008).

By listening to the celebrities' music, watching their series, seeing their films, attending their sport activities and festivals or collecting their memorabilia, fans establish a strong PSI and identify themselves with the media stars. According to Brown & Fraser (2007: 52), "the growing influence of celebrities can be seen in the worlds of economics, politics, media, and culture. Their international influence is extensive owing to the pervasive reach of entertainment media". Brown & Fraser explain (2007: 57-58) that developing a relationship with another person (parasocial interaction) and identifying with her or him are different matters.

In academic literature, PSI has often been applied to measuring audience involvement, whereas celebrity identification has garnered only a small amount of research attention (Brown & Fraser, 2004). For understanding the persuasive influence celebrities can have on audience members, the parasocial interaction theory and the identification theory can be combined according to Strong (2008: 50-51):
1. "Parasocial interaction theory provides insight into how audience members establish seemingly interpersonal relationships with celebrities, and
2. identification [theory] explains how these relationships can change values, beliefs and behavior of audience individuals".

Strong (2008: 51) goes on stating: "The processes of identification, when extended into the realm of the mass media, provides an appropriate theoretical basis for assessing the role of celebrities in E-E campaigns". Within the concept of identification lies a behavior change (Kelman, 1958), whereby a person 'adopts' or 'takes over' the behavior of another person. Focusing on celebrity identification, media scholars point out that media users normally lack aspects in their lives (work, income, popularity, etc.) that can be considered as similar to the unique status of celebrities (Brown & Fraser, 2004; Dyer, 1991), but they nonetheless want to become a certain celebrity, imitating their perceived image and behavior patterns (Adams-Price & Greene, 1990; Stack, 2000). Schuh (2008) refers to this context by differentiating between similarity identification and wishful identification. She also identifies interpersonal communication of the media users via a 'human to human' mediation of narrative engagement (such as via face-to-face interactions, landline telephone, mobile phone or computer-mediated means such as email or discussion forums) as a striking component in the field of celebrity effects.

In recent years, celebrities have become increasingly involved in E-E campaigns, as evidenced by the collaboration in the German daily soap *Gute Zeiten, Schlechte Zeiten (Good Times, Bad Times)*, in the weekly soap *Lindenstraße* (Lubjuhn & Reinermann, 2010) as well as in the interactive E-E internet film Experience Snd-Bites (www.SndBites.nl) by the Center for Media & Health (Bouman & Hollemans, 2012).[32] As the aim of the E-E strategy is to enhance the knowledge of personal and social need, influence attitudes or change overt behavior through entertainment (Singhal & Rogers, 1999; Singhal, 2004), it makes good sense to invite celebrities to play a role in this task, when also reflecting the different modeling types that Bandura has established (section 2.3.2). For example, a celebrity can take over a prestige model in a storyline.

Research suggests that Entertainment-Education may be more effective when celebrities are strategically used within the overall E-E campaign (see Singhal & Rogers, 1999 for many examples). Celebrities have been used in many non-western and western country settings for communicating health, social and environmental related issues to a broader public.[33] Brown & Fraser (2004) argue that celebrities can have a vital role in social or health related campaigns (for instance Michael J. Fox for Parkinson's disease, Lance Armstrong for testicular cancer or in Germany the soccer player Philipp Lahm for HIV/AIDS). They receive instant recognition and the media intensively covers their activities. Even though celebrities have been used as a vital component of E-E campaigns, the theoretical groundwork of their role has not been firmly established in communication theory (Brown & Fraser, 2004; Brown & Fraser, 2007).

To clarify and to summarize, the effects of using celebrities to promote prosocial issues with and without an E-E approach can be examined more closely in the following figure.

---

[32] This is one reason why the research on celebrity influence is depicted in detail here.

[33] For instance in India, the first E-E television serial *Hum Log* (see above), used Ashok Kumar, a famous Indian film star, to increase the status of women and to promote family planning. Viewers of the program wrote letters referring to epilogues they had seen and communicating that they have changed their values, beliefs and behavior (Singhal & Rogers 1999: 84-89). Many other examples can be found in Kincaid et al. (1991), Rimon (1989) and Silayan-Go (1990). In the USA, celebrities have been also instrumental in a number of communication campaigns and TV series. The designated drivers campaign, incepted by the Harvard School of Public Health in 1988, is one of those famous examples (see above). Within a national wide campaign and the support of many Hollywood celebrities the social norm was successfully promoted that drivers should abstain from alcohol (DeJong & Winsten, 1990; Winsten & DeJong, 2001).

Figure 2.2: Effects on celebrity involvement in E-E campaigns for prosocial issues

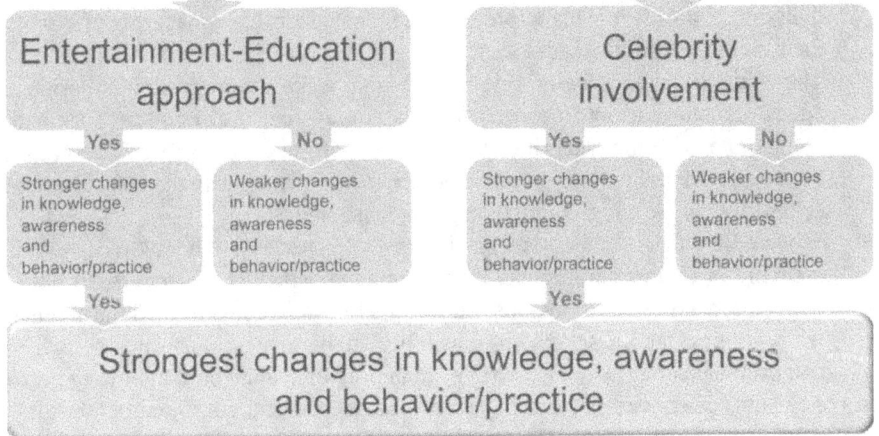

Source: Own illustration based on the results of celebrity effects of Fraser & Brown (2004: 106-108)

The illustration shows that a prosocial issue can be promoted through an individual/educational approach aimed at changes in personal lifestyles. By using an individual/educational approach, policy departments, health and environmental organizations or development planners often design communication campaigns to address their prosocial issue to the public. In the next step, the educational organization gets in touch with television people from the entertainment field or, more generally, speaks with media professionals and discusses collaboration options. In this stage, the decision needs to be taken about whether to apply an E-E approach to the media format or not (e.g. using research on the format or let the collaboration be guided by communication experts in order to ensure an effective collaboration for both parties as is done in the USA or the Netherlands).

If educational organizations decide to so implement such an E-E approach, the TV format and the communication campaign will produce stronger changes in knowledge, awareness and behavior/practice associated with both the format and campaign than without using the E-E approach (Brown & Fraser, 2004). The same thing goes with celebrities as spokespeople: the prosocial media format and the communication campaign, which involve positive celebrity role models as spokespeople to a specific issue, will provide stronger changes in knowledge, awareness, and behavior/practice associated with the format and the campaign than those which use non-celebrity spokespeople (Brown & Fraser, 2004).

Besides the obvious benefits of featuring celebrities in E-E media formats and campaigns, media scholars also point out some disadvantages (Bouman, 1999; Brown & Cody, 1991; Singhal & Rogers, 1999):

1. Celebrities receive large amounts of money for the advertising work. Celebrities are often doing the work on spreading prosocial issues more for money than out of altruism. This is problematic, because it has a negative effect on their credibility for the audience.
2. The challenge of employing celebrities is that some governmental authorities, educators and other prosocial professionals may find it difficult to work and collaborate with the celebrities because they are not familiar with the entertainment business culture. For instance, a host of demands in the contract with celebrities can be a nightmare to negotiate and satisfy.
3. When celebrities become associated with E-E messages, a dramatic change in their life or a moral failure can be damaging. Singhal & Rogers (1999) mentioned, for instance, a famous Latin America singer named Johnny Who, while singing about sexual responsibility in his songs, was later seriously compromised after he got a young woman pregnant and would not marry her.

In conclusion, celebrities need to be carefully screened and consulted before they are involved in an E-E media format and an E-E communication campaign. Nonetheless, Brown & Fraser (2004) maintain that the advantages of using celebrities for Entertainment-Education outweigh the potential disadvantages.

2.3.6 Other Audience-Centered Theories

Attracting and interacting with target groups is a well-known problem for prosocial change organizations. When applying a media approach, most of them have made the experience that the audience often does not notice the health, social or environmental messages. For these organizations it is difficult to motivate people to change their awareness, attitude and behavior. On the international level, governmental organizations have started using audience-centered theories when applying Entertainment-Education in practice. They examine how television viewers interact and react to E-E formats.[34] The following concepts belong to the audience-centered theories: PSI and identification theory (see section 2.3.4), the celebrity influence (see section 2.3.5) as well as the uses & gratifications theory and the two-step-flow concept. While the first three were described before, the last two of them will be discussed shortly in the following.[35]

---

[34] The motivation behind this lies also in the shift in thinking about mass media theory to the question, what it is that people do with mass media as well as the insight that the 'banking education approach' (Tufte 2005, see section 2.2) does not work.
[35] These theories have been chosen for a short discussion, because they have often been ap-

The uses & gratifications theory asks from the viewpoint of the audience 'what they do with television' and not 'what television does with them'. The theory sees the audience as active users who satisfy and gratify their needs with the help of television (also compare Strong 2008: 54). E-E programs meet these needs, which are triggered by motivations like entertainment (fun, joy, excitement), escapism (to forget their sorrows and problems), information (to learn something), social interaction (to talk about the topics with others) and identification (to have others to identify with) (ibid.). The more the needs of the audience are satisfied, the greater and more enduring the post-exposure effects (McQuail et al., 1972).

Lazarsfeld, Berelson & Gaudet (1944) first introduced the two-step-flow model. It describes how individuals (opinion leaders) pass on their own interpretation of the media content and thus influence the audience. The term 'personal influence' was coined to refer to the process occurring between the media's direct message and the audience's ultimate reaction to that message. Opinion leaders are quite influential in making people change their attitude and behavior and are quite similar to those they affect. The two-step-flow theory has improved the understanding of how the mass media influences decision-making; however, in today's media environment it is less qualified for sense making. The multi-step flow theory of mass communication or the diffusion of innovation theory seems to be more appropriate here (Rogers, 1976; Rogers, 1995).

In all, the audience-centered theories allow scholars to examine how the viewers use Entertainment-Education in an intermediate process. In E-E program evaluation studies, audience feedback mechanisms and measures of involvement, parasocial interaction and identification are used to analyze the endorsement and likeability that E-E characters have. Subsequently, it is examined how these qualities are linked to the behavior changes of viewers. These kinds of studies have not been implemented in Germany's E-E environment so far, and future activities may deal with the question of to what extent this application contributes to effective E-E collaboration practice.

2.3.7 Further Theories in Use in E-E

This section presents basic supporting theories in use, when governmental (related) organizations and television professionals design and implement E-E projects on the international level. Additionally, some of the extended and updated versions of these theories are briefly depicted.

Most of the early upcoming social change behavior theories used in the field of Entertainment-Education are cognitive processing theories (this is especially true for the original versions of the theories but not for the extended ones, which have been developed in recent years). They address individuals' psychological beliefs and perceptions about their social environment as driving forces for behavior change.

---

plied in the E-E context. Other theoretical notions with frameworks based on new media interactivity might also be significant to address (McMillan, 2002; Stacks & Salwen, 2009: 389-405), but cannot be dealt with here.

The most striking theories to have influenced the E-E strategy are Becker's health belief model (1974)[36], Fishbein & Ajzen's theory of reasoned action (1975) and its extensions, Ajzen's theory of planned behavior (1980)[37], Petty & Cacioppo's elaboration likelihood model of persuasion (1986b)[38] and its applications by Bouman (1999), Slater (1997) and Slater & Rouner (2002). Slater (1999) suggests that narrative engagement through absorption and identification with characters is the most critical for attitudinal (and maybe behavioral) change. Recent research from Bae (2008) based on the elaboration likelihood model and the theory of planned behavior stresses the role of emotion (sympathy and empathy) and issue involvement, and suggests incorporating these constructs in a new model for prosocial behavior change.

Other theories in use, which deal with the process of motivating people to change their attitude and behavior, are the persuasion theory by Hovland and his associates (Hovland et al., 1949; Hovland et al., 1953), the social comparison theory (Festinger, 1954), the attribution theory (Heider, 1958; Kelley, 1973), principles of social proof (Cialdini, 1985), the social adaptation perspective (Kahle & Homer, 1985; Kamins et al., 1989) and the dual-process models like the heuristic systematic model (Chaiken et al., 1989).

The main focus of these theories is on the *cognitive components*, which include evaluation, recall, critical judgment, and inferential judgment (Brown, 2008a; Johnson & Eagly, 1989). At the heart of these theories lies the assumption, that people will change their behavior when they know the objective risks and when they recognize them as real threats. Recent research has extended these models and proposes the *affective components* of narrative engagement of audience members as important and possibly leading to changes in knowledge, attitude or even behavior (Bae, 2008; Bilandzic & Busselle, 2008; Chatterjee et al., 2009; Morgan et al., 2009; Movius et al., 2009; Murphy et al., 2011; Schuh, 2008; Van Leeuwen et al. 2012).

This change from cognitive (what people think) to affective (what people feel) orientated research regarding behavior change also influenced the thinking of prosocial change organizations to some extent. In former years, they tended to work with

---

[36] The health belief model identifies six predictors for individual intention of behavior change, namely susceptibility, perceived severity, perceived benefits, perceived barriers, cues of action, and self-efficacy (Janz et al., 2002; Janz & Becker, 1984).

[37] The theory of reasoned action and the theory of planned behavior make the point that attitudes, norms and perceived personal control concerning a target behavior determine the individual behavioral intention for change.

[38] The elaboration likelihood model suggests two key paths of information processing: A central and a peripheral path. The central route means that the audience carefully thinks about the argumentation in the messages, which leads to stable attitude and behavioral changes. When the audience is either not able to motivate and/or unable to process a message, they process it peripherally, which means that they rely on cues when assessing the message. Typical peripheral cues include the use of heuristics like 'If professionals say it is good, then it is good' or 'If my best friend uses condoms, then so should I'.

cognitive approaches to deliver messages to the public, while in recent years, they have started to involve models that refer to both cognitive and affective processes. These developments have led them to become more open-minded about collaborating with entertainment TV makers in formats communicating prosocial themes and trying to reach mass audience (Bouman, 1999; Lubjuhn & Pratt, 2009).

Further theoretical notions applied in E-E programs are *step and stage theories*. Step and stage theories are predominately found in the field of advertising. One of the early formal advertising models introduced by St. Elmo Lewis (1898) theorized four different levels of response to a media message: attention, interest, desire, and action (Strong, 1925). This corresponds with a progress from low to high involvement. Step and stage theories are very heterogeneous in explaining different steps to audience behavior change.

In the field of Entertainment-Education, there are many models and theories in use in creating a successful framework for media formats as well as campaigns for changing audience members' knowledge, attitude and behavior. It is simply not the case that 'one model fits all' for a TV format or a communication campaign that uses different settings, methods and messages for different audiences. For the collaborations established in Germany so far – and likewise for future collaborations – it is recommended that the above-mentioned theories and theoretical notions be increasingly applied. The analysis in part II of the thesis critically reflects on the use of theoretical concepts; it poses the question of how theoretical notions and research are to be incorporated in German collaboration practice and what future developments in this field can look like.

2.4 Theoretical Aspects of E-E Collaborations

The latter section described the theories involved in E-E interventions for reaching the target group members with prosocial themes. This section will now depict the theoretical aspects, which come in when prosocial and entertainment partners collaborate to create an E-E format. These theoretical aspects are the foundation for part II of the thesis.

Bouman describes theoretical aspects of E-E collaborations in several scholarly publications (1999, 2004, 2005). She differentiates between four main types of partnership arrangements in E-E collaborations. These are E-E production, E-E co-production, E-E inscript participation and E-E lobbying. Later she replaces the word E-E lobbying with E-E service[39] (Bouman, 2010; Bouman & Brown 2011). In this chapter the focus will be on E-E co-production, E-E inscript-participation and E-E service as the main types of partnership arrangements and not on E-E production.[40] This distinction serves as an orientation for later theoretical analysis. The

---

[39] This term came up through the analysis processes in part II and was solidified in several discussions with Bouman (e.g. Bouman, 2010).

[40] E-E production is defined by Bouman (1999: 123) as "an initiative of a prosocial organization to act as an independent producer and design and produce one's own entertainment program for prosocial purposes and 'sell' it to a broadcasting organization. (...) Being now the

different forms can be considered as *ideal typical partnership arrangements, distinguished here for analytical reasons*. The borders between them may be fluent in practice. In the following sections, the different types of collaborations are portrayed in more detail.

2.4.1 Three Forms of E-E Collaboration Arrangements

In chapter 2.1, Entertainment-Education was defined as "a theory-based communication strategy in which educational and entertainment professionals purposefully embed prosocial issues in the creation, production, processing, and dissemination process of an entertainment program in order to achieve different stages of change either on individual, community, institutional or societal level among the intended media user populations" (reformulation based on Wang & Singhal 2009: 272-273). In order to purposefully embed prosocial issues and/or in order to apply theoretical notions[41] (chapter 2.2) in an E-E intervention, partnership arrangements have to be made. In this theoretical section, these forms (E-E co-productions, E-E inscript participations, E-E service) and in the next section, the stages of E-E collaborations are briefly described. In part II of the thesis, both the collaboration forms and stages are researched, analyzed and depicted in detail with respect to the German context.

E-E co-production as defined according to Bouman (compare 1999: 123) is 'a formal transaction between a prosocial organization and either a broadcasting organization or a production company to design, produce and broadcast a new entertainment program for prosocial communication purposes'. An example of a co-production from a western country is the television program *Sesame Street* (as mentioned in Bouman 1999: 270), which was primarily designed to educate children in deprived neighborhoods. Lesser (1975) and Bouman (1999) say that a curriculum was developed, translated into story line ideas, and pre-tested with formative research to make sure that the resulting entertainment program has great potentials to reach and educate the young audience members. Further examples are the Dutch drama series *Villa Borghese*, which promoted healthy lifestyle issues (Bouman & Wieberdink, 1993; Bouman 1999: 244), and the internet drama series *Sound* (van Empelen, 2009; Bouman & Hollemans, 2008; Bouman et al., 2009; Bouman, 2011a; Bouman 2011b) that aimed at preventing hearing damages.

---

actual 'producer', the prosocial organization has full authority over all stages of the production process, from reading the first scripts to directing the last cuts". In E-E productions, the prosocial organization mostly does not succeed in 'selling' its entertainment program to a broadcasting organization and thus it is not broadcasted to a mass media audience. As the research interest of the thesis exclusively focuses on entertainment programs and the behind-the-scenes collaboration processes, which are broadcasted to a mass media audience o television (see chapter 1 and 5), E-E productions are not further elaborated here.

[41] The application of these theoretical notions serves a purpose as well, in a sense of the expectation of higher quality and increased effectiveness, if a theory-based approach is used.

E-E inscript participation is here defined by Bouman (compare 1999: 123) as 'a formal transaction between a prosocial organization and either a broadcasting organization or a production company to use *an already existing entertainment program* as a carrier of prosocial communication purposes'. In this E-E collaboration arrangement, both sides are involved in the design, production and broadcasting of the television episodes with the specific prosocial content. An example from the Netherlands is *Medisch Centrum West*, which tackled the topics of organ donation, women with heart failures and cardiovascular diseases in several episodes (Bouman, 1995; Bouman et al., 1998; Bouman 1999: 248-249). Another example is the drama series *Costa!*, in which HIV/AIDS protection messages have been incorporated (Bouman, 2004).

As Bouman (1999) points out in both co-production and inscript participation arrangements, prosocial and television professionals share a financial budget for integrating health, social or environmental themes into a *new* entertainment format (co-production) or an *existing* one (inscript participation). By sharing a financial budget, prosocial content professionals, in return, take an active part in the decision making process according to the program content. A high amount of energy and time commitment might be involved from both collaboration sides as well as challenging negotiation processes and potential power struggles that may result from the different aims of the two collaborating parties (Bouman, 1999: 130-132 and 184-185).

E-E service[42] should be defined here according to Bouman & Brown (2011) as "a strategy of prosocial organizations to facilitate ([through] factual and timely information, contacts with experts, shooting locations, etc.) broadcasting organizations, [production companies] or independent producers in dealing with a prosocial communication in their entertainment programs". For example, Hollywood, Health & Society (see chapter 4.2) successfully introduced health themes (e.g. HIV/Aids, diabetes, obesity, cancer) in US prime time entertainment programs, such as *The Bold and the Beautiful, Emergency Room* and *Grey's Anatomy* (Beck, 2004; Kaiser Family Foundation, 2008) through their specific E-E service approach. Other service collaborations from the German context took place in the episode *Suche Klima, biete Schutz* from *Lindenstraße* (introduction of climate friendly lifestyles) or in several episodes of *Gute Zeiten, Schlechte Zeiten* (introduction of drug prevention and healthy lifestyle issues) (Lubjuhn & Pratt 2009; Lubjuhn & Reinermann 2010). Bouman (1999: 122) notes that, "because there is no formalized agreement to collaborate, one is dependent on the good will of the other party".

---

[42] As mentioned above, E-E service was in former times named E-E lobbying. The author thinks that the term E-E lobbying is not an adequate expression to fit in collaboration arrangements. She has the opinion that every collaboration form incorporates 'lobbying' activities for prosocial themes from the health, social or environmental partner side. Some of these activities can have a stronger intensity in some collaboration types (co-productions and inscript participations) than in others (E-E service).

This goes with the portrayal of E-E collaboration stages in the next section 2.4.2, where the E-E service collaborations do not implement E-E contracts (on the program development), E-E briefings or establish an E-E team in the crystallization stage. Furthermore, and in contrast to the co-productions and inscript participations, both parties do not share a financial budget in service collaborations, and the prosocial content experts are not involved in the decision making process of the program content. Figure 2.3 sums up the different collaboration forms in E-E partnerships.

Figure 2.3: Collaboration forms in E-E partnerships

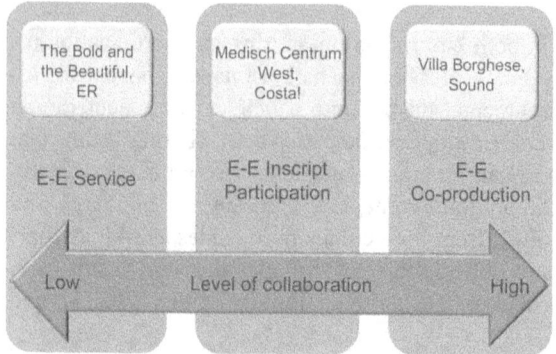

Source: Own illustration after Bouman & Brown (2011: 10)

The collaborative basis for all parties involved is quite different in each of the three collaboration forms. The question of which one is the most suitable depends on the specific prosocial organization and its resources, but also on the strategy of the collaborating broadcasting organization and/or production company. In addition, it depends on the cultural and media context, in which the partnership is created (see chapter 4.2 and 4.3 and part II of the thesis). In order to weigh the different pros and cons of each partnership form, Bouman (1999: 124) established a list with some points of references: capital investment, expertise, manpower, contract, corporate identity, time investment, research and follow up. According to Bouman (1999: 124) "*capital investment* means the amount of money the (…) [prosocial] organization has to invest in the partnership in order to design, produce and broadcast the E&E television programme. The funding may vary from federal government and private foundations to commercial sponsors. *Expertise* means the topical expertise: the amount of professional knowledge regarding the (…) [prosocial] issue. *Manpower* stands for the human resources involved. *Contract* refers to the possibility of signing formal agreements between partners [which refers to TV program issues]. *Corporate identity* means the amount of exposure and control of one's own 'name and frame' in the television programme. *Time investment* refers to the amount of time that needs to be spent during the collaboration. *Research* refers to the possibility of formative [process] and summative evaluation. *Follow-Up* means the possibility of planning additional supporting activities [e.g. workshops, events] during or after the broadcasting of the programme". The relative weighting of the factors is indicated and explained in the legend of table 2.1.

Table 2.1: Collaborations in E-E partnerships

	Co-production	Inscript participation	Service
Capital Investment	XXXX	XXX	X
Expertise	XXXXX	XXXXX	XXXXX
Manpower	XXXX	XXX	XX
Contract	+	+-	-
Corporate Identity	+	+-	-
Time Investment	XXXX	XXX	XXXXX
Research	++	+	+
Follow up	XXXX	XXX	X

XXXXX = a great deal
+ = yes or possible
X = hardly any
- = no or not possible
Source: Adapted from Bouman (1999: 124)

2.4.2 Stages of E-E Collaboration

Beside the different forms of E-E partnerships (co-production, inscript participation, service), it is important to differentiate between stages of collaboration.[43] Bouman (1999: 124 and 151-162) distinguishes between four stages: (1) orientation, (2) crystallization, (3) production and (4) implementation (see figure 2.4).

---

[43] Like the partnership arrangements, the different stages in collaboration may serve as a static and linear framework. They support analysis of the collaboration processes on the 'place of gift exchanges' in part II of the thesis. In practice, these stages sometimes blur, overlap and are more dynamic.

Figure 2.4: Stages of E-E collaboration

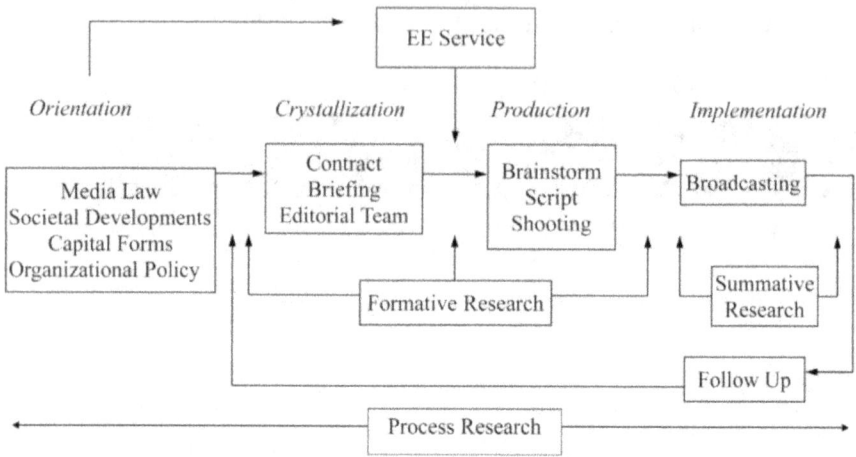

Source: Bouman (1999: 125)

When prosocial organizations consider using television as a part of their media policy, and embedding a prosocial issue in an entertainment television format, they have to follow different stages. In the following section, the E-E collaboration stages will be described according to Bouman. Furthermore, her work will be used to connect the different collaborative forms of E-E co-production, E-E inscript participation and E-E service to the stages of collaboration.

In the **orientation stage,** the form of E-E collaboration needs to be decided upon. Partners choose between creating and implementing a new television program (co-production), an already existing one (inscript participation) or a service collaboration (Bouman 1999: 125-127; Bouman, 2004). Prosocial change organizations and television organizations need to take both external and internal conditions into account when planning to collaborate. *External conditions,* for example, can comprise (inter-)national media law, specific societal developments or the culture and history of the country in which the partnership takes place. *Internal conditions* can, for example, refer to *capital forms* the partners have (Bouman 1999: 125-127). Bouman's work (1999) is essentially built on the capital forms of the different partners, as described by the French sociologist Bourdieu (Bourdieu, 1993; Bourdieu, 1991; Bourdieu, 1984). In her analysis, Bouman (1999: 126) uses Bourdieu's differentiation between economic (e.g. money, stocks, property), cultural (e.g. cultural competencies, qualifications, talents, skills) and social capital (e.g. image, goodwill, networks) as a central internal condition not only in the orientation stage, but also as a feature which can play a role in all stages of collaboration (see chapter 7.2.3). *Organizational policy* can also be an important internal condition. For example, is the prosocial organization willing to experiment with an affective communication approach to reach specific target group members, or do they stick to a more cognitive one as was the case in former times? And are the TV makers willing to discuss and share their thoughts with prosocial content experts? The specific conditions and characteristics for German E-E collaborations, which play a role in the orientation stage of collaboration, will be described in detail in chapter 6 and 7. In the orientation stage, the first steps of *process research* are also introduced (see below).

After these initial steps have been taken to design an E-E program, *contracts* need to be negotiated between the potential partners. This takes place in the ***crystallization stage***. Bouman (1999: 127) states, "These contracts have to lay down conditions for effective collaboration, such as the money involved, the time of payment, channel and time slot for broadcasting, the responsibilities of the editorial board, who has the final right to intervene and decide, agreements about additional sponsors and the sharing of revenues, names on the credits, spin-off activities, and public relation agreements". After finishing the contract issue (or during that period), *E-E briefing(s)* can start serving as a basis for the program production. Specifically from the point of view of the prosocial experts, the E-E briefing is an important and strategic stage in the collaboration process, because with it they can position themselves within the development of the program content. Bouman states that (1999: 127), "the briefing document contains the background, specifying objectives, target group and other relevant information". In some cases the briefing document is added as an appendix to the formal contract. Another feature of the crystallization stage is the formation of an editorial team, which Bouman calls an *E-E team*. In E-E team meetings, professionals from both sides meet to discuss collaboration issues (ibid.). Along with the crystallization stage, the initial planning for the *formative research* (see below) is done and, if used, the theoretical framework (section 2.3) of the television program is defined and brought in.

As figure 2.4 also indicates, the crystallization stage is a specific stage implemented in co-productions and inscript participations. As the prosocial experts do not share a financial budget with the TV makers in service collaborations and as they are not a part of the decision making process on the program content, there is no need to develop contracts according to the TV program; briefings and the formation of an E-E team to develop the program is also not necessary. This is why E-E service collaborations skip the stage of crystallization in Bouman's model.

In the ***production stage***, the program itself is developed. For this reason, the work on the *script*, the *shooting* and the editing all play a constitutive role and "the framework of the briefing and the contract serve as the arena for the development of the programme" (Bouman 1999: 127). As a first step, Bouman (ibid.) describes the jointly-implemented *brainstorm*. In this session, knowledge, ideas and suggestions are shared to create the best possible format for both partnering sides. According to Bouman (ibid.), "in practice, a brainstorm is sometimes hard to distinguish from a briefing. The important difference, however, is that a briefing is done from the perspective of one of the collaboration partners [which is in the majority of cases the prosocial side], and has a closed structure: the information to be transferred is fixed in outline or even detail. A brainstorming session includes both partners and has an open structure".

In all three processes (i.e. scripting, shooting and editing), many different people from the media field work together. In E-E collaborations, the producer, director and the head writer are most important from the point of view of prosocial experts, because they make the decisions that affect the final product (Bouman 1999: 128; Kauschke & Klugius, 2000). The producer is responsible for handling all the business details of the production company (crew management, finding financial resources, administrating the budget), and he ensures that production operations run smoothly and on time. As a head producer, he also makes final decision on the program content. Overall, being the head of the production company, he keeps an eye on everything. The director usually establishes and maintains stylistic conventions. Virtually, every stylistic decision begins and ends with the script (sets, costumes etc.). So for the prosocial experts, it is also important to communicate and stay in close contact with this person. The head writer establishes the style of the television program and has control over the story development. When the scripts are finalized, it is difficult to make corrections or adaptations (see Bouman 1999: 128; Kauschke & Klugius 2000). Thus, if possible, prosocial experts also should stay in close contact with the creative team right from the start of the collaboration.

Depending on the *collaboration form*, the brainstorm, the scripting, shooting and editing are jointly organized by the television side as well as the prosocial side, as is the case in E-E co-productions and lesser in E-E inscript participations (as described above). In the case of E-E service collaboration arrangements, the prosocial experts have the role of advisor with regard to the program's content (e.g. whether a portrayal is authentic and accurate). Regular brainstorms are not implemented and the television professionals alone are in charge of the scripting, shooting and editing. In this context, the prosocial experts take the role of an advisor with regard to the program's content (e.g. on whether a portrayal is authentic and accurate) (Lubjuhn & Reinermann, 2010).

After the production stage, the **implementation stage** starts, in which the program is broadcasted. Follow up activities (belonging to the program) usually take place. As Bouman (1999: 128) points out, most E-E television programs are part of a multi-media (or in today's terms crossmedia or transmedia) campaign. As soon as the TV program is aired, the follow up activities can start. The prosocial organization therefore often combines mass media with interpersonal communication strategies. For example, in the case of crossmedia or transmedia approach the prosocial experts use an interactive blog on the internet or they create discussions or events together with the television makers, all of which aim at involving the people into participatory exchanges on the prosocial issues depicted in the program. During the implementation stage, summative research is implemented (see below).

Summarizing, figure 2.4 shows the stages of orientation, crystallization, production and implementation. These four stages are characteristic of E-E co-productions and

E-E inscript participations. Both the prosocial organization and the TV broadcasting organization or production company *jointly design and implement the stages* in these two collaboration forms, as described by Bouman (Bouman 1999: 151-162). In E-E service (formerly E-E lobbying) the stages differ, as Bouman's model in figure 2.4 also indicates. The partners go through the orientation stage, skip the crystallization stage and then go through the production stage together, though not in the same way as they do in co-productions and inscript participations. As mentioned above, they do not share a financial budget with the TV makers and they do not participate in decision-making processes on the program development. The TV makers design and implement the program and the prosocial experts provide advice.

2.4.3 Research Conducted During the E-E Collaboration Process

Section 2.3 describes the theories related to the creation and implementation of an E-E intervention. In addition to the theoretical notions, there are different types of research methodologies that can be applied to an E-E intervention. In the following paragraphs, formative, process and summative research are described briefly in the context of E-E projects. For this portrayal, Bouman's theoretical framework of stages in E-E collaboration (figure 2.4) is also used.

2.4.3.1 Formative Research

Formative research, or pre-production research, is carried out before media programs are produced. As its name suggests, it helps in the formation of television programs. It aims at determining the communication needs, desires, behaviors and media usage of the target group (see section 2.7) in order to develop understandable, high quality, culturally appropriate characters, storylines and messages (Nariman, 1993). Sabido (section 2.2.3) was one of the first to deal with the involvement of formative as well as other research types in E-E programs. He developed different formative research methods, which support the creation of an E-E media format, as described in the following (Singhal & Rogers 1999):

- *Identification of the core educational value* in the program. Sabido developed a *value related grid* with specific statements on the prosocial issue that should be depicted in the TV program (worded as "It is good that..." and "It is bad that..." regarding, for instance, the status of the woman or family harmony).[44] Furthermore, he organized workshops with television professionals, health and environmental experts, policymakers, commercial sponsors and others to discuss the value grid and to reach a consensus on the *moral framework* of the program, which these relevant leaders were asked to sign in order to indicate their support. This necessary moral framework is not only based on the opinions of the involved E-E partners, but furthermore on legal documents, such as national constitu-

---

[44] For further details see Nariman (1993). The value related grid is primarily applicable for non-western countries and therefore not in the scope of the thesis.

tions, policies and laws (Poindexter, 2008). The identification of central educational values serves to define 'prosocial' topics for the E-E program.

- *Evaluation of television's role in society* (broadcasting facilities, role of public and commercial broadcasters, influence of the government, availability and appropriateness of commercial advertisers) so that it is clear, which stakeholders need to be included in an E-E intervention and to have previous knowledge on what their roles and aims are in the television field.
- *Evaluation of infrastructure*, which supports the prosocial issue to make sure it is adequate to reach as many media users as possible.
- *Assessment of the appropriateness* of the E-E format against the background of the demographic and socio-cultural characteristics of the audience.
- *Assessment of the physical characteristics* of the intended audience to design characters, sets and costumes close to reality.

Sood et al. (2004) argue that participatory forms of formative research in particular (e.g. audience discussion groups, participatory sketching and audience scriptwriting) appear to be the wave of the future for Entertainment-Education.[45] Singhal, Wang & Rogers (2011: 14) add that the positive deviance[46] approach (see chapter 9.3.2.2) can effectively serve as a part of formative research, and the findings then can be incorporated in the design process of the messages in order to create role models that exemplify positive deviance behaviors on an E-E narrative.

Usually, the formative research process starts in the orientation or crystallization stage, and it ends after the production stage (see figure 2.4). Furthermore, formative research is typically applied in co-productions and inscript participations (Bouman & Hollemans, 2008; Draaisma & Bouman, 2005; Lubjuhn & Bouman, 2009; Rijs et al., 2007, Bouman & Hollemans, 2012). The prosocial experts design and implement the formative research activities and then later use the results for the creation of the TV program content in collaboration with the entertainment makers to better meet the needs of the audience members. By contrast, specific formative research for the program is usually not applied in E-E service collaborations (Beck, 2004; Kaiser Family Foundation, 2008; Lubjuhn & Bouman, 2009), although the prosocial organizations certainly do have an in-depth knowledge of their different target groups and can incorporate this in their script advice. This is for several reas-

---

[45] If so, participatory forms need more research, and if it turns out to be fruitful, it should be, as a consequence, increasingly integrated in the design of E-E interventions, also with respect to Germany.
[46] "Positive deviance (PD) is an approach to social change that enables communities to discover the best practice and local wisdom they already have, and then to act on it. PD is an assets-based approach, identifying what's going right in a community in order to amplify it, as opposed to focusing on what's going wrong in a community and fixing it" (Singhal, Wang & Rogers 2011: 14). People, who are "positive deviants" are called like that because "their behaviors are not the norm and "Positive" as they model the desirable (...) behaviors" (ibid.: 15).

ons: as mentioned above, the important difference between the co-productions/inscript participation and service is that in co-productions/inscript participation, both sides work together to design and implement the program, whereas in service collaboration, the prosocial experts advise the TV makers and they are not involved in the creative and development process of the TV program. So one main reason why prosocial organizations usually do not invest in formative research when implementing a service collaboration is that there is very little chance that the research results will find the way into the program. The prosocial experts do not have the possibility to take part in decisions on the program content, as is the case in co-productions and inscript participations.

2.4.3.2 Process Research

Process research assesses the implementation of the intervention (also compare Linnan & Steckler, 2002). In literature, there is not an ultimate definition of what can be considered as process research and often times process research has been described as a part of formative research. However, for the purpose of this thesis process research will be used as follows: as the term indicates, it ensures that various activities involved in implementing the E-E intervention are carried out as planned (Berkowitz et al., 2008: 226). Process research also indicates to what extent the various steps were effectively designed and implemented to achieve the desired goals. For example one central goal of process research can be to gather ongoing feedback about the execution and evolution of the E-E intervention (ibid., see for example the process research report the Sound effects campaign from Jurg & Bouman, 2009). As with formative research, this research type is usually applied in co-productions and inscript participations and less in service collaborations, because in co-productions and inscript participations there are much more different collaboration stages and decisions to make.

2.4.3.3 Summative[47] Research

Summative evaluation research seeks to answer questions about the effectiveness of the intervention: was the intervention successful in reaching and communicating with the target audience and did this influence the level of knowledge or the attitude and behavior of the target audience? This refers back to the E-E definition, most specifically the objective "*to achieve different stages of change either on individual, community, institutional or societal level among the intended media user populations*" which was elaborated on in section 2.1.

Summative research aims at finding the overall impact on the media users. It is also called post-production research, and it determines whether and to what extend the aims of the program (namely to bring about visible and measurable effects in prosocial education) are fulfilled. Summative research methods measure the effects of the E-E program by, for instance, using pre-post control group design (prefer-

---

[47] The term ‚summative research' can be used as a synonym for ‚effect research' or ‚impact research' and these different terms are applied in this thesis.

ably with a control group) or doing a case study on one of the areas in which the program had strong effects (Papa et al., 2000). Most of the effect research measured the short-term impact on audience members (Sood et al., 2004) and long-term studies are still rare.

As figure 2.4 indicates, the summative research takes place before (baseline measurement) and after the implementation stage of the collaboration. In contrast to the formative and process research, it is applied in co-productions, inscript participations and in service collaborations (Hether et al., 2008; Lubjuhn & Bouman, 2009; van Empelen et al., 2010). If it is applied in E-E service, the baseline measurement before the implementation stage of collaboration is regularly not implemented (see chapter 4.2).

An updated version of Bouman's model of stages in E-E collaboration (1999: 125) is presented in the following. It considers two additional aspects: (1) that co-productions/inscript participations and service collaborations differ from each other in the production phase (working together on the program content versus prosocial experts offering advice/service to it) and (2) that co-productions/inscript participations usually conduct formative, summative and process research on the E-E program, whereas service collaborations (if there is possibility to do research) apply summative research only. It is for these reasons that an updated portrayal of the theoretical model of the stages in E-E collaboration was chosen.

Figure 2.5: Stages of E-E collaboration (updated version)

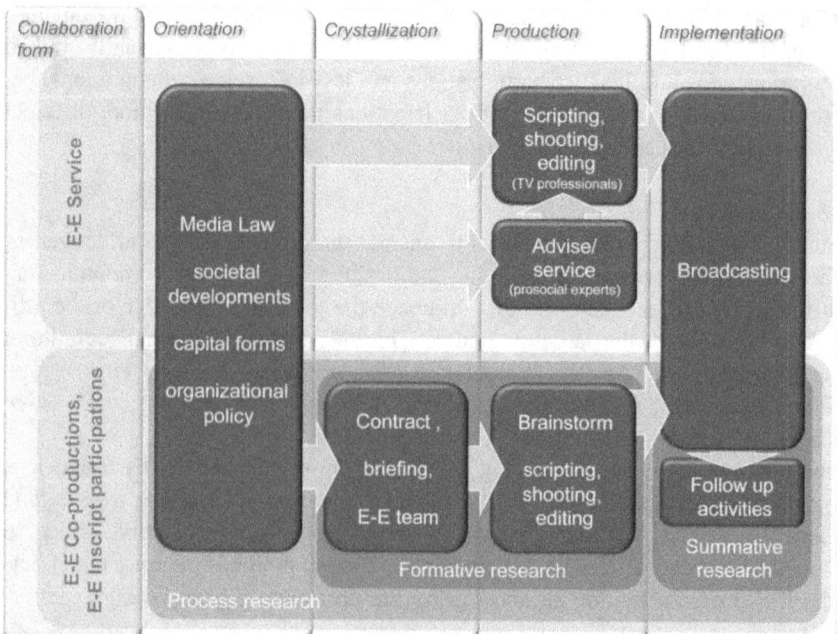

Source: Own illustration based on Bouman (1999: 125)

2.4.4 E-E Collaborations from the Perspective of Complexity Science

Prosocial change organizations working with health, social or environmental themes use different approaches on television and other mediums to reach media users with prosocial issues (Jordan et al., 2009). Bouman (1999) stresses in this context that prosocial change organizations frequently use an approach, which appeals for changes on the individual level. This, for example, means advocating a healthier lifestyle (doing sports, cooking and eating healthy meals, etc.) or living an environmentally friendly life (using as little energy and resources as possible, buying organic food and using public transport, etc.). Therefore, it is closely related to the social marketing approach[48] (section 2.3.1), which also promotes changes on the individual behavior level.

When collaborating with TV makers in different collaboration arrangements (section 2.4.1) and going through various stages of collaboration (section 2.4.2), Singhal (2008a) stresses that the prosocial organization brings a specific scientific perspective into the collaboration. He advises (1) to envision this issue and (2) on how to handle this perspective from the viewpoint of complexity science, so that the collaboration process itself runs smoother. Singhal (ibid.) argues that prosocial organizations orient themselves according to a perspective, which primarily focuses on knowledge, attitude and especially behavior change. In this context, the experts are regularly trained to believe that they can control, predict and achieve change in linear steps, often with a high degree of certainty (Papa et al., 2006) when they provide messages to the audience members. Singhal (2008a: 1) adds that "this (…) mind set – 'if we do this to people, they will behave this way' – is a result of the overwhelming dominance of Newtonian thinking that spilled over to social science and was reified over decades without much questioning".

This also means that experts working in governmental authorities or universities might oftenly portray prosocial problems as they work like 'machines' or 'clocks': when twiddling on two or three set screws, they expect a more or less certain outcome. For raising awareness among prosocial change experts that their mindset according to 'behavior change' can be to some degree challenging in an E-E collaboration, Singhal (2008a) suggests applying the discipline of *complexity science*. Complexity science "provides new insights into how social systems self-organize, evolve, and adapt as a result of interactions between its constituent elements" (Singhal 2008a: 3). The discipline pays special attention to highly planned cause-and-effect approaches to prosocial change, emphasizing the quality of interactions, mutual causality, non-linearity, outliers and contradictions (Papa et al., 2006; Singhal, 2008a; Waldrop, 1992; Zimmerman et al., 1998).

---

[48] This individual approach is very compatible with advertising issues. For example, 'where to buy' is mentioned in a television program on healthy food, or 'what to wear' is mentioned in a program for a successful workout. Thus, the approach has been criticized for making money with 'good things' and mixing up social and psychological theories with marketing and advertising principles (see criticism of social marketing, section 2.3.1).

Complexity theory is divided into three kinds of systems: (1) simple systems, (2) complicated systems and (3) complex systems. An example of a simple system is baking an apple cake. We know the ingredients like sugar, flour and eggs. We know how to cut and place the apples on the cake and we also know how long the cake needs to stay in the oven so that it tastes delicious. In simple systems, it is easy to agree on the outcome and they are highly predictable. An example for a complicated system is building a car with the help of a blueprint. Similar to simple systems, there is a very high degree of agreement about what to do, and a high degree of predictability about what the outcome will be. Social problems (like a 'recipe' of raising a child or living in a fulfilled partnership) (see Singhal 2008a: 3) and especially prosocial change issues are complex systems. There is a low level of agreement about what to do and a low level of certainty about what the results will be. Singhal (2008a) proposes that prosocial change organizations have frequently approached and treated 'change issues' through media television as being simple or complicated, but not as being complex. Given this background, Singhal (2008a) suggests characteristics of prosocial change organizations working with health, environmental or other social themes in E-E partnerships:

1. ***Be a creator***: Experts from prosocial change organizations or from the research field may create conditions which unleash the power and the talent of engaging dialogue and interaction among the audience members. Thus, they are more in the role of a creator, cultivator or initiator and less of a controller. This is especially true for collaborations in the television field. Even if the experts feel comfortable with the outcome of the produced TV messages, they cannot control or predict the effect on the audience. But what they can do is, for example, try to **stimulate interpersonal communication and dialogue among** the audience (e.g. fostering blogs or web-chats with soap stars regarding prosocial issues) or **participatory activities** (e.g. creating workshops with soap stars and audience members that focus on an exchange about health issues, or workshops that allow the audience members to be producers of prosocial storylines by telling about their 'real life experiences'), both of which are related to the E-E program.

2. ***Strengthen personal interaction and relations***: On the one hand, prosocial experts may find ways to enhance the quality of interaction between themselves and the audience (e.g. via telephone hotlines or live internet chats after the program). On the other hand, they may also place a high value on developing and strengthening personal relations with TV professionals. A relationship-centered practice (openness, diversity, authenticity, integrity) strongly influences the adaptability and creativity. Thus it is more likely to create prosocial change.

3. ***Small changes with ripple effects***: Prosocial experts may be aware that their television project may not have a big influence, but that it could rather be the input for small changes that create a ripple effect, much like the extra snow-

flakes which cause a whole avalanche.[49] This also means that a social change implication with a non-linear prerequisite does not necessarily need a 'big' solution.
The complexity discipline draws attention to the perspective that unknown aspects, dialectical tensions (Papa et al., 2006 as well as chapter 4), contradictions and sometimes messiness are essential for prosocial change issues. This especially applies to media messages motivating people to change. When looking at the position of prosocial experts collaborating with television professionals, this should not be regarded as a call for an attitude like 'letting everything go' because 'anything can be controlled'. Complexity science suggests rather taking another perspective or framework into consideration. This framework (1) supports the treatment of social problems as complex (not simple or complicated) ones in an E-E project and (2) allows experts from prosocial change organizations to be aware of the high importance of their role as a creator and as a strengthener of deep and interpersonal communication among audience members and in their relation to TV professionals for promoting prosocial change. These perspectives should be kept in mind when dealing with an E-E collaboration environment, and this is also why this thesis has dealt with the framework shortly.

2.5 Results and Critical Reflections of Entertainment-Education in Non-Western Countries

Now that the definition, the diffusion of Entertainment-Education and the theoretical aspects of the strategy have been depicted, the following question should be raised at this point: what are the results and criticisms in Entertainment-Education? This section aims to answer this question by briefly discussing both aspects of the E-E field. This discussion on results and achievements on the one hand, and criticisms on the other hand will be illustrated for non-western (2.5) and western (2.6) settings. However, the main bulk of literature on both results and criticisms has been derived from non-western counties so far.

2.5.1 Results in Non-Western Countries

As mentioned before, the E-E strategy has its origin in non-western countries. E-E scholars conducting research in these settings demonstrated substantial changes in

---

[49] Two more examples for these 'small changes' shall be provided here. The first is Rosa Parks' refusal to give up her seat in a segregated bus. Other Afro-American people did this several times before, but her refusal led to a cascading of events that eventually led to the Civil Rights movement in the United States. The second example is the E-E radio soap opera *Taru*, which promoted equal gender rights in India (Singhal et al. 2004; Papa & Singhal 2008). In the show the protagonist Taru initiated a birthday celebration for a young girl. In reality, girls' birthdays are traditionally not celebrated in Bihar, the area where the radio soap was broadcasted. After this particular episode was aired, several villages reported the celebration of girls' birthdays (Singhal et al., 2006), and this became a part of the everyday life in this area, which can be considered as one step further on the way to equal gender rights.

knowledge, attitude and behavior on numerous occasions (see Bouman, 1999; Brown & Cody, 1991; Chatterjee et al., 2009; Dura et al., 2008; O'Leary et al., 2007; Kiruswa, 2004; Lacayo & Singhal, 2008; Papa & Singhal, 2008; Ryerson, 2008; Ryerson, 2010; Singhal & Greiner, 2008; Singhal, 2004; Singhal & Rogers, 1999; Singhal & Rogers, 1989; Usdin et al., 2004; Vaughn et al., 2000). They have used a wide range of data-gathering types (surveys, focus groups, case studies, field experiments, content analysis of episodes and letters regarding a series, telephone calls, etc.) and exposure measurements (self-reported survey items, observation data, audience ratings, etc.) to analyze the E-E programs and their effects.[50] Bouman (1999: 106-108) gives an overview on multi-method data collection strategies used in E-E interventions. Sood et al. (2004) found out that more than 28 E-E programs from 1990 to 2002 had a (fairly) strong influence on the audience's knowledge, attitude and behavior.[51]

One key finding in recent effect research is that E-E messages serve as a catalyst, triggering interpersonal peer communication to change the social discourse of the audience members.

1. E-E programs can spark *interpersonal conversation* among audience members about the prosocial issues that are addressed in E-E television programs[52] leading to dialog, decisions and individual or collective actions (Arendt, 2008; Brown, 2008a; Lampert, 2007; Papa et al., 2000; Singhal & Dura, 2008; Papa & Singhal, 2008; Sood & Rogers, 2000; Valente et al., 1996; Valente & Saba, 2001).

2. E-E programs can spawn changes in the *external environment* of audience members by interpersonal communication and growth in efficacy (also see 2.3.2, collective efficacy)[53] (Brown & Cody, 1991; Chatterjee et al., 2009; Singhal & Rogers, 1999; Singhal et al., 2005; Papa & Singhal, 2008; Usdin et al., 2004).

---

[50] Singhal & Rogers (1999, in chapter 8) gave a broad overview of methods in use for measuring effects in Entertainment-Education.

[51] Bouman (1999: 111 and 252-268), Singhal et al. (2004) as well as Singhal & Rogers (1999) give a detailed overview regarding the results of E-E projects and case studies from non-western countries.

[52] In the Tanzanian radio soap *Twende na Wakati* (*Let's Go with the Times*), the dominant influence for the adoption of safer sex practices was stimulating interpersonal communication about HIV/AIDS, as also occurred in the case of family planning. Singhal & Rogers (1999: 168) state "of the 61% of 1,018 listeners in 1995 who talked with others, 55% reported talking to friends; 37% to spouses; and 8% to other individuals. Those who talked with each other were much more likely to adopt an AIDS prevention method (92%) than listeners who did not talk with others (69%)".

[53] The popular African television series *Soul City* serves as an example for how behavior change can be socially supported. In 1999 the series modeled a new collective behavior to portray how neighbors might intervene in a domestic violence – that is, by gathering around the abuser's residence and collectively banging pots and pans. Pot banging to stop partner abuse was reported in several locations in South Africa after broadcasting the series (Soul City, 2000; Usdin et al., 2004).

Mayer (2008) proposes that it is not the E-E message itself, which leads to behavior change, but the ***participative process***, that the messages or the whole program can initiate. A study by Chatterjee et al. (2009) states that the participative process and the interpersonal communication between people may be the key element leading to prosocial behavior change. Importantly, recent scholars highlight the significance of ***dialogue*** for changing behavior (Anderson et al., 2004; Gergen et al., 2004; Hammond et al., 2003; Papa et al., 2000; Zoller, 2000; Zoller, 2004).

These findings enable new theoretical delineations. One significant work in this context is the one of Papa & Singhal (2008). They reveal four components of dialogue that are central to the relationship between the media stimulus provided by E-E programs and their effects on the audience. The first dialogue type is the ***stakeholder dialogue*** between television professionals, prosocial research experts and the potential audience members in order to develop storylines and characters during the crystallization and production phase of collaboration. After the E-E program is broadcasted in the implementation stage of collaboration and follow up activities are put in place, three other forms of dialogue can have effects on the audience: (1) ***internal dialogue*** (section 2.3.4), (2) ***interpersonal family dialogue*** and (3) ***community dialogue*** (Chatterjee et al., 2009; Singhal & Dura, 2008). Nonetheless, the interpersonal effects of peer group, community and other forms of 'human-to-human' dialogues have not been investigated in detail yet. While communication scholars have revealed that these dialogue forms occur, it is still open as to how these dialogues emerge, and how they influence people to change their thinking and behavior. Recent E-E effect research mainly uses the parasocial interaction and the identification of the viewer with positive and transitional television characters (see section 2.3.4).

In summary, Entertainment-Education has proven itself as a strategy for influencing the knowledge, attitude and behavior of people. Nonetheless, the lessons from unsuccessful projects must not be ignored but rather we must learn from them as well (see section 2.5.2). The main strength of the strategy lies in its insights into problems and themes (e.g. those in the health, social or environmental field). E-E programs promote dialogues among the mediated role models, which lead to reflections of the viewers' own behavior and to conversation between them. Therefore, according to Lampert (2007), the strategy can be used as a prerequisite for a potential change in behavior.

2.5.2 Critical Reflections in Non-Western Countries

Besides the promising possibilities, the E-E strategy also has its limitations. In the sections before, several critics were mentioned in terms of methodological criticism (section 2.4.3.3; less long term effect studies available), theoretical criticism (section 2.3; some theories have not been updated for a while), ideological criticism (section 2.2; 'banking education approach'). This section will add to the discussion of E-E critics three more issues: the unintended effects, different potential challenges when designing and implementing an E-E intervention and the issue of transferability to western countries.

Critics of the E-E strategy point out that E-E programs do not always produce the desired effect. This is also known as the **unintended effects discussion**. Nariman (1993), Singhal & Rogers (1999), Slater et al. (2006), Yoder et al. (1996) and other communication scholars refer to several effects of E-E programs that have failed to reach their original aim. An example is the character Bhagwanti in the Indian soap opera *Hum Log (We People)*. Bhagwanti was designed to be a negative role model for female equality. She submissively allowed her husband and mother-in-law to berate her for her unknown family lineage, her lack of cooking skills and so forth. Nonetheless, summative analysis of Singhal & Rogers (1999: 92) showed that "some viewers sympathized with Bhagwanti's character, viewing her as a positive role model for tolerance, compromise, and patience". To minimize unintended effects, formative research and pre-testing of E-E messages are important (section 2.4.2).

Besides the unpredictable effects, Singhal & Brown (1999) identify six potential challenges through conducting summative research mainly in former non-western E-E projects:

1. **Social structure of communities**: E-E programs set boundaries when heterogeneous values and beliefs exist in the community (chapter 3.4.3.6 'the sociocultural equality dilemma').
2. **Social conflict**: E-E can also raise social conflicts. This was proven by the impact research on the family planning soap opera *Tushauriane* in Kenya. The soap opera kindled the salient social conflict regarding the primacy of sons over daughters.
3. **Organizations that control information**: such as political leadership, those in control of development capital, the pool of technical expertise and the availability of policy-makers for strategic planning, etc.
4. **Media environment**: such as media access, source credibility of media and the credibility of media personalities promoting prosocial messages. For instance, E-E music video campaigns in the Philippines were released to promote sexual responsibility, while many audience members did not have telephones to call the toll-free hotlines to talk with counselors.
5. **Language**: The example of the popular television series *Superbook*[54] helps to understand this issue. When *Superbook* was translated into Romanian by Romanians living in Belgium, the audience in Bucharest and Hungary complained about the Transylvanian accents.
6. **Infrastructure limitations**: Infrastructure limitation can occur when exclusive social networks limit the audience members' contact with change agents or literacy rates are low in rural areas where educational print materials are distributed.

Alongside unpredictable effects and the above-mentioned challenges, which are

---

[54] *Superbook* is an anime television series produced by a Japanese producer in conjunction with the Christian Broadcasting Network in the USA.

mainly confirmed for non-western countries, another group of boundaries can be summarized as the field of *transferability* (see section 2.6). As pointed out before (section 2.2), the E-E strategy has a long tradition in designing and implementing projects in non-western countries where most of the programs and evaluation studies have been conducted (Ryerson, 2008; Ryerson, 2010). Given this background, effect studies for western countries had to start from the very beginning to investigate the impact on knowledge, attitudes and social behavior change.

The last field to visibly limit E-E programs, is the field of moral criticism (is E-E manipulation or is it not?). These and other *ethical considerations* will be depicted in detail in chapter 3 (section 3.4). The main reason for not describing the ethical considerations here but in chapter 3.4 instead, is that they should be discussed in relation to Germany and its television culture. These considerations and critics are very much linked to the misuse of *entertainment television* for propaganda purposes.

2.6 Results and Critical Reflections of Entertainment-Education in Western Countries

Now that the results and critical reflections on the E-E strategy in non-western countries have been discussed, this section addresses the question which research results are available from western countries. Since the 1970s, a small number of effect research activities have been conducted in the field of Entertainment-Education in western settings. Effect research has mainly investigated impacts on the individual level by focusing on short-term changes in knowledge, attitudes and behavior. Furthermore, the focal point of these research studies has been on determining whether effects occurred, rather than on providing theoretical explanations of the process how audience members changed their perception, attitude and behavior as a result of their exposure to E-E programs.

Clearly, the design of effect research in E-E strategies in western countries differs from that in non-western countries, because the prerequisites are different, as is the environment for implementation. This is outlined in the next paragraph (2.6.1). Afterwards, some results from the USA (Hollywood, Health & Society) and the Netherlands (Center for Media & Health) will be portrayed (2.6.2). These US and Dutch research centers have been two important players in the study of E-E effects. (Effect) research activities of both centers will be presented, as will be differences in the methodology to research. Lastly, the question about which steps Germany has made so far according to E-E effect research will be raised.

2.6.1 A Media-Saturated Environment

Communication scholars have discussed the effects of Entertainment-Education on a broad basis (for examples see Bouman & Brown, 2008a; Lampert, 2007; Sherry, 2002). All of them agree that the promising results confirming knowledge, attitude and behavior change in non-western countries cannot be transferred to western countries as implied above (problem of transferability).[55] Why is that? One difference between both settings seems to be quite obvious: non-western countries provide a much smaller range of media compared to western countries.[56] Sherry (2002) and Greenberg et al. (2004) have referred to this problem in discussing the topic of 'Entertainment-Education in media-saturated countries'. They criticize the lack of consideration for typical factors that play a role in western societies, like the diffusion of competing media messages. Sherry (2002), for example, suggests that the consistency of messages, the repetition in various media channels and the reliability of the message sources are factors to influence the potential effectiveness of E-E messages. Another problem in media-saturated countries lies in the fact that the audience has access to a variety of media and can therefore consume a huge amount of prosocial messages (via TV, radio, web 2.0, etc.). Consequently, the omnipresence of these messages can lead to circumstances where the audience is overwhelmed with prosocial messages (Sherry, 2002: 220).

In addition, prosocial messages can be presented in terms of content that is either *(1) conflicting* or *(2) inaccurate*. An example of conflicting messages may be messages designed to promote low-fat diets to reduce heart disease versus messages stating that fat promotes the absorption and retention of calcium and therefore reduces the incidence of bone disease, including osteoporosis. Another example focuses on the discussion about climate change in the media. While some formats report that climate change is caused by anthropogenic CO_2 emissions, others reject that viewpoint. For example, there are some populist TV formats, such as *RTL Extra Special* (RTL) named *Climate Fake,* which give skeptical opinions about anthropogenic climate change.[57] Beside conflicting messages, inaccurate messages may also be broadcasted. One example is a storyline from *Eli Stone*, a US drama series (Kornblum, 2008). Before the broadcast of one episode, US research institutions and health organizations were calling on broadcaster ABC to cancel it, arguing that the storyline leaves the audience with the destructive idea that vaccines cause autism. They insisted that it provides incorrect information from an academic standpoint and cannot be shown to the public. ABC rejected the request. Instead, they reminded the viewers before the show that it is fictional format. Additionally, ABC referred viewers to the website of the Centers for Disease Control and Prevention, a governmental health institution, where viewers could get further information.

Given this background, Sherry (2002) concludes that E-E programs in media-saturated countries require in particular a careful integration of planning, research, pro-

---

[55] Bouman (1999: 110-111) provides in this context an overview of differences between non-western and western country settings.

[56] Thus, for example, the program *Soul City* from South Africa reaches 80% of its target population. In western countries, this is not possible, because there are too many program options for the audience to choose from (Usdin et al., 2004).

[57] To solve this problem, Parrot et al. (2002) suggest training the audience in media literacy. Media literacy makes individuals aware of the persuasive intent of media content so that they recognize the inherent strengths and weaknesses associated with the messages.

duction and evaluation with regard to prosocial issues in the program. These messages need to be shown realistically, differentiated and consistently. This is equally true in non-western settings.

However, Sherry's argumentation cannot be broken down into a practical implementation standard. In western countries, such as Germany and Great Britain, various media legislations exist which, for example, make it difficult for prosocial experts to be a part of the decision making process on program content at all (Forster & Knieper, 2005; Griffin, 2005). In addition, in countries where the television field is wealthy, mighty and at least fully commercial driven, like in the USA, the 'small financial support' coming from the prosocial side is not an incentive to approve steering power on the program content (Epstein, 2005). It is clear that strategies for E-E collaboration practice and its research need to be found. These strategies should strongly take the country-specific media system, legislations, the historical background of the country into account, e.g. dealing with entertainment media in a culturally sensitive manner, or the topic of persuasion via entertainment formats. In other words, when E-E co-productions/E-E inscript participations (section 2.4.1) are difficult to create and implement for more than one reason, other arragements such as the E-E service collaboration (section 2.4.1) may be applied and specific features need to be developed that fit the legislative, cultural and societal background of the western country setting.

2.6.2 Results in Western Countries: the USA, the Netherlands – and Germany?

Although challenges and critics (section 2.5) are involved when designing and implementing Entertainment-Education in a media format, the effort to do so seems worthwhile. Specifically, television can be characterized as a significant medium for providing prosocial issues to its users. The following paragraphs will argue that, according to recent studies, viewers in western countries use entertainment television as an important source for gaining prosocial knowledge and also as a crucial incentive for changing their attitudes or even behavior. The following three paragraphs therefore sum up some research results of E-E interventions in the USA, in the Netherlands and some of the first steps being made in Germany in this context.

2.6.2.1 Hollywood, Health & Society, the USA

One main bulk of literature research[58] on E-E effects in US television programs comes from communication scholars at the University of Southern California working with the Hollywood, Health & Society (HH&S) program. They have provided a number of studies that show the prosocial effects of E-E programs on

---

[58] Literature research on US E-E effect studies was conducted from September to November 2008 during a research visit at the University of Southern California, Los Angeles. Many papers and background details regarding the studies only were available on site. Thus, only research studies published by November 2008 were taken into consideration in this context.

the audience members' knowledge, attitude and behavior (Kaiser Family Foundation, 2008; Hether et al., 2008; Porter Novelli et al., 2000; Porter Novelli et al., 2005; Kennedy et al., 2004; Morgan et al., 2009; Movius et al., 2007; Murphy et al., 2008; O'Leary et al., 2007; Scales et al., 2006; Valente et al., 2007; Wilkin et al., 2007; Whittier et al., 2005). Appendix 1 gives an overview of the findings. In many of these studies, researchers investigated *single E-E storylines* with summative research regarding the effects on the audience. All of them indicate the crucial role of entertainment television programs when disseminating health themes, and furthermore they show clear evidence that self-reported changes in knowledge, attitude or even behavior occurred among the US audience members. One example of effect research that indicates changes in knowledge and behavior is depicted in the following, illustrating that Entertainment-Education turns out to be an effective strategy as proved by University of Southern California research team.

Based on a collaboration of health experts and Hollywood professionals brought together by the HH&S program (chapter 4.2), Morgan et al. (2009) used an online survey to investigate the impact of organ donation storylines in four television dramas (*CSI: New York, Numb3rs, House* and *Grey's Anatomy*) on viewers' knowledge and behavior. Results revealed that viewers acquired knowledge from the content of each drama. Viewers who were not organ donors prior to exposure to the dramas, were more likely to decide to donate organs, if the drama explicitly (1) encouraged donation, (2) portrayed characters revealing how they had become donors and (3) discussed the merits of donating (see role-modeling issues in Bandura's Theory, 2.3.2). Viewers were also more likely to become an organ donor, if they were emotionally involved with the narrative character. Furthermore, 10% of the non-donors who saw the respective episode of the US crime series *Numb3rs* decided to become a donor.

To sum up, through the HH&S program and the collaborating reseachers from the University of Southern Califorina in the USA, several results proved the success of E-E service collaborations (chapter 4.2) in fostering health changes in knowledge, attitude and behavior experienced by the audience members.

2.6.2.2 Center for Media & Health, the Netherlands

Unlike in the USA, in the Netherlands effect research is generally not done on single E-E messages and storylines broadcasted in entertainment TV formats. The Dutch research regularly provides results about (most of the time newly) produced TV formats as well as about the whole underlying health campaign.[59] The majority of Dutch interventions take place in E-E co-productions and E-E inscript participations, and they involve not only summative research, but also formative and process research activities (section 2.4.2). Bouman provides an overview (1999: 239-251) on several Dutch E-E interventions and their results. Most of the conduced E-

---

[59] The reasons for the differences between the USA and the Netherlands will become clearer in chapter 4.

E research comes from the Center for Media & Health (CMH) (see chapter 4.3).[60] Through their projects, the CMH provided several effect results on E-E interventions that have proven a change in knowledge, attitude and behavior towards healthy lifestyles (for examples see Bouman & Draaisma, 2006; Eiling et al., 2006; van Empelen, 2009).[61]

In the following, the example of effect research of the *Sound-Effects* campaign is given to illustrate in which context the CMH effect research (as well as formative and process research) is conducted (Bouman et al., 2009; Lubjuhn & Bouman, 2009; van Empelen et al., 2010, see chapter 4.3.5). The *Sound-Effects* campaign was designed and implemented by the Center for Media & Health in collaboration with the *Public Health Service of Amsterdam (Geneeskundige en Gezondheidsdienst (GGD) Amsterdam)*. The Sound Effects campaign aimed to prevent hearing loss among youngsters (16 to 30 years) in Amsterdam who frequently visit music and dance avenues. The Center for Media & Health developed a theoretical framework for the campaign based on extensive formative research (chapter 4.3.5.2). A central element of this theoretical framework is the Elaboration Likelihood Model, which describes different routes (a peripheral and central route) for persuasive information processing (compare section 2.3.7, theoretical foundation of the Elaboration-Likelihood-Model). For the peripheral route the CMH decided to apply the Entertainment-Education strategy and designed and implemented an E-E drama series named *Sound*, which is broadcasted on the internet. As project partners they involved TV professionals from *Endemol Productions*, who developed and produced a compelling, entertaining and educational script for the series. The target group was invited by various publicity activities in the media to visit the website www.sound-soap.nl where they could watch the *Sound* drama series. On this website with the drama series (peripheral route), the visitors could directly click to another website www.gooutplugin.nl where more factional background information was given about the topic of hearing loss prevention measurements (central route).

The effect study of this *Sound Effects* campaign, of which *Sound* was part of, was based on a pre-post control design study. The results showed that the prevention messages regarding hearing loss had a positive impact on the attitude and self-efficacy of the target group members (Bouman, 2011a; Bouman, 2011b; van Empelen, 2009; van Empelen et al., 2010). Beside extensive formative and summative research, the campaign also carried out a process research study, in which the hindering and facilitating factors of the design and the implementation of the campaign were analyzed and described (Jurg & Bouman 2009).

In summary, in the Netherlands Entertainment-Education is mostly based on an integral campaign approach which can involve co-productions/inscript participations. This integral campaign approach also makes use of formative, process and sum-

---

[60] The review of effect research at the CMH took place from May 2008 to June 2008 and in February 2009 during two research visits. It comprises an in-depth look at the project's effect research results.

[61] Some of these studies and projects will be depicted in chapter 4.3 in detail.

mative research. The results of this research into the Entertainment-Education strategy show that it has the potential to influence prosocial knowledge, attitude and behavior of media users.

2.6.2.3 Germany

Scholars in Germany have not been able to provide detailed information about the effects of E-E interventions – regarding either single messages or whole campaigns – with the amount of coverage the USA or the Netherlands has. However, four studies deserve mentioning, as they may provide (some) first hints about audience members and positive effects:

- Gassmann et al. (2003) did a study on an episode of the German hospital drama series format *Schwarzwaldklinik*. They wanted to know whether it was possible to positively influence the willingness of audience members to become organ donors by exposing them to a fictional entertainment format. The result was that after viewing the program the audience members were influenced positively in their attitudes and willingness to act. Gassmann et al. conclude: "The hitherto negligence of the persuasive impact of entertainment programs in the focus of scholarly interest was obviously a missed opportunity. In general tendencies it is clear that beyond information and educational programs, socially relevant themes, social values and positive behaviors can be transmitted through the media" (Gassmann et al. 2003: 493).
- Reusswig et al. (2004) found out that the entertainment television movie *The Day after Tomorrow* stimulated learning processes among the German audience with regard to climate change topics. After seeing the movie, the audience was more willing to change on a personal level as well as to request political action for the climate change problem.
- Schwender et al. (2008) revealed in their studies on prosocial episodes of the entertaining knowledge show *Welt der Wunder* that at least half of the episodes involved audience members in a positive, emotional manner. This was considered to be a crucial condition for conveying environmentally friendly messages to them and to initiate changes in their knowledge, attitude and behavior (ibid.).
- A study by Witzel et al. (2008) found out that hospital drama series (produced in the USA) like *House* or *Grey's Anatomy* influence the German audience and that the audience applies the storyline messages to their everyday life.

Generally, the German studies hint that popular entertainment television can be a crucial transmitter for conveying prosocial messages to audience members, although the above research studies, apart from Schwender et al. (2008), were not implemented in the context of a 'marriage' between prosocial experts and entertainment TV makers, but relate to productions created by TV makers only. Thus, it might be interesting to raise the question of whether future research can detect even more positive effects on audience members when also experts from prosocial change organizations add their input for accurate and authentic portrayals.

In conclusion, the findings on Entertainment-Education from the USA, the Netherlands and the first steps in Germany show that E-E research in a western setting is still in its infancy. Even so, summative research data demonstrates changes in knowledge, attitude and behavior, both in the USA and the Netherlands. Furthermore, several studies used (1) formative research to make the prosocial messages fit very well to the media users and to enhance the probability of effectively reaching them and (2) process research to evaluate the E-E interventions through the whole process of design and implementation. In Germany, only first hints exist so far. However, the positive results from the USA and the Netherlands may be used as an incentive for German stakeholders to deal with E-E collaborations and to increasingly apply research activities in the future.

2.6.3 Critical Reflections in Western Countries

The methodological, theoretical and ideological criticism, which was mentioned in section 2.2, 2.3, 2.4.2 and 2.5.2 is also applicable for western countries, as is the unintended effects discussion (see 2.5.2). One of the most famous examples for **unintended effects** comes from a western setting. It is the television character Archie Bunker from the US television series *All in the Family*. Archie Bunker was originally designed as a negative role model. With the help of humor he was intended to raise awareness regarding ethnic prejudices. In fact, it was shown that especially prejudiced audience members identified Archie Bunker as a likeable, honest and down-to-earth person (Singhal & Rogers, 1999, Brown & Cody, 1991).[62] It should be also mentioned here that *All in the Family* was not originally designed as an E-E intervention. More generally spoken, the discussion around unintended effects in western countries lacks in richness of data and examples according to programs designed as E-E interventions.

Furthermore, the **six challenges** described in section 2.5.2 (social structure of communities, social conflict, organization that control information, media environment, language, infrastructure limitations) need to be investigated more in detail in western countries, i.e. questioning these challenges for each specific country.

Due to the media-saturated environment and the specific media culture and media legislation (some more liberalized, others not), the challenges and critics might differ immensely from each other (see part II of the thesis). As the situation is a completely different one, the **transferability** of effect results is indeed not possible in any case (see 2.5.2).

Some more critics suggest that Entertainment-Education will never be that effective in western countries. They argue that (1) the messages cannot get through because of the media-saturated environment, (2) the audience will see through it (sophistication of the audience), (3) the broadcasting stations (more the commer-

---

[62] The so-called 'Archie Bunker effect' is defined as the degree to which certain audience members identify with negative role models in E-E interventions (Singhal & Rogers, 1999).

cial than the public) will not risk losing audience share for even prosocial reasons, (4) there is a fear and resistance from TV makers at being 'told what to do', (5) there is a scant evidence about the effectiveness of long-term impacts (almost no overtime follow ups) and (6) effects are not foreseeable (mixed evidence success – some E-E programs succeed while others fail).

These critics stand against some positive results, and indeed, it becomes clear that further research is needed on the E-E strategy and its appearances in western settings, so that researchers can formulate more concrete results and criticisms for different western countries.

2.7 Who watches E-E Television Formats? A localization of Target Groups

Section 2.3 describes which theories and concepts are applied in the E-E strategy. Many of them focus on psychological factors, which play a decisive role in influencing the audience knowledge, attitude and behavior in terms of a prosocial change. Besides psychological factors, all (prosocial) communication is connected to the social environment in which it takes place. From this premise Morell (2001) identifies several social factors, including age, gender, educational background, social status, language, power and social relations. Thus, in the wider environment of the public, many social factors impact, whether a media user is reached by a prosocial message or not. In the field of prosocial marketing, health and the field of environmental communication, these factors are taken into account in targeting communication campaigns or TV formats in depth. For instance, a communication campaign promoting climate-friendly lifestyles and focusing on a target group[63] of eldery people (65 and older) is different from a campaign addressing young people. Or a campaign for eldery people coming from higher socio-economic milieus is different from a campaign for elders coming from lower socio-economic milieus. The more specific differentiated the definition of a target group, the more differentiated the aim for the target group can be worked out (Lehmann & Sabo, 2003). Indeed, by focusing on target groups, the number of people that are addressed decreases (see also chapter 3.4.3.4), but Corcoran (2007) and Lehmann & Sabo (2003) make the point that with a focus on specific target groups and correlating communication strategies, people are both better reached and addressed. Specifically in health communication, but also emerging in environmental communication, the E-E strategy is used internationally by governmental (related) and research organizations to mainly address people coming from *lower socio-economic milieus* –

---

[63] The term 'target group' derives from and is used in communication science, consumption theory and advertising. A target group can originally be described as a group of people who should be reached with specific issues through marketing or advertising goals. For instance, marketing experts focus on a target group to increase the market share of a product or they want the target group to donate money for a 'good project' (Behrens et al., 2001). In the field of health and environmental communication, the term target group is used to describe the media or campaign users to be reached with the prosocial messages.

or the so-called *mainstream milieus* (Schwender et al., 2008) – as well as *children* and *adolescents* (Bouman, 1999). For the research purpose, that is to learn from E-E theory for the German context, it might be useful to deal with the target group members more in detail, also with the specific focus on Germany. These target groups are depicted in the following two sections.

2.7.1 People from Lower Socio-Economic Backgrounds: the Mainstream Milieus

This section will argue why it makes sense to use an E-E strategy for addressing lower socio-economic backgrounds or mainstream milieus. Therefore two perspectives will be taken into consideration, relating to the research interest (chapter 1): the health communication perspective and the environmental communication perspective. Both have received a lot of attention in scholarly and also public debates over the last decades, and they have been discussed in the context of the question of how to reach mainstream milieus. The discussions will be shortly pinpointed.

2.7.1.1 Health Communication Field

Since the 1970s a shift has been taking place from disease prevention towards health promotion (compare Bouman 1999: 19). First international reports referring to this change were the *LaLonde report* from Canada (1974) and the *Black Report* from the UK (Townsend & Davidson, 1982). The *LaLonde* report talked about health promotion and described health in more than biological terms. The *Black Report* emphasizes that health can be associated with differences in the socio-economic status of people. This triggered an international discussion about health inequalities and how to prevent and reduce them. Health inequalities have been discussed among health communication experts, politicians, medicine experts and scholars from different scientific communities since the late 1980s and early 1990s. According to Bouman (1999: 27), "there is an urgent need to develop new health communication strategies to bridge the gap in health inequalities in society".

In Germany (but also in other countries), socio-epidemiological studies have pointed out that health inequalities are strongly related to the socio-economic status (Altgeld & Hofrichter, 2000; Elkeles & Mielck, 1997; Geene et al., 2001; Helmert et al., 2000; Mielck, 2002): people with a higher socio-economic status are, on average, healthier than people with a lower socio-economic status (Bouman 1999: 27). Thus, it is clearly recommendable to focus on mainstream milieus, which are on average less healthy than other societal milieus (ibid.). For explaining these health inequalities, the literature provides manifold models (Mielck, 2003; Richter & Hurrelmann, 2006; Siegrist & Marmot, 2006; Whitehead & Dahlgren, 2006; Wilkinson & Marmot, 2003). In these models, four elements usually emerge: (1) living conditions (such as working conditions or health forehandedness), (2) health relevant behavior (such as nutrition, smoking, compliance), (3) health conditions (such as morbidity and mortality) and (4) social disparities (such as differences according to education, professional status and income).

With these elements in mind, some examples of health inequalities are provided here. A study conducted by the German Federal Ministry of Labour and Social Affairs (2003), for example, states that less than one third of the unemployed people are of very good or good health, whereas more than a half of the employed people are of very good or good health. The educational background serves as another example. The share of healthy or very healthy people comprises the highest German educational group and is around two times higher than the lowest educational group (BMAS, 2005), which is due to several reasons not further mentioned here. In other words, people with a lower educational background live much more unhealthy lives than better-educated people. For instance, they smoke more often (without having any intention of stopping) or they do fewer sports than better-educated people.

There is an urgent need to focus on these lower socio-economic groups in Germany (and also in other countries) because the number of people belonging to these 'risk groups' is increasing (BMAS, 2005). In 2005, around 13% of the German population lived beneath the poverty level, which means that one out of eight people in Germany can be considered as poor (BMAS 2008: 24).[64] Additionally, more than 36.4% of the German population has an income that belongs to the low wage labor market (BMAS 2008: 12).

Given this background, several recommendations were given by health scholars and others for reducing those inequalities in Germany. These measures specifically fit target groups from the lower socio-economic milieus (BMAS, 2005; BMAS, 2008; Mielck, 2003).[65] One of the measures is to design and implement public communication campaigns with the help of mass entertainment media (BMAS, 2005; BMG, 2007; BMG, 2008). Nonetheless, only a few governmental (related) authorities have followed this recommendation so far (Clobes & Hagedorn, 2008; Lubjuhn & Reinermann, 2010).

2.7.1.2 Environmental Communication

Scholars and practitioners first used the term environmental communication in the late 1960s. Jurin, Roush & Danter (2010: 12-14) divide environmental communication activities in three big waves, one from 1969-1974, the second from 1989-1994 and the third from 2000 and onward. Characteristically is, as they state, that the amount of environmental communication activities increased, as did the different topics addressed in this field. Since its early years, environmental communication has been applied to principles, approaches, strategies, techniques and models of

---

[64] In Europe, a solitary person is considered poor when she or he has less than 781 euros (net) available for living expenses each month (2008: 24).
[65] In this regard, the German Federal Centre for Health Education (FCHE) launched, for instance, a nation-wide platform for supporting health promotion in lower socio-economic milieus in 2007. More than 1100 offers and measures are described there to give a national overview concerning the topic (ibid.).

communicating environmental protection (Cox, 2010; Jurin et al., 2010). Flor (2004: 20) stresses that one essential aspect of environmental communication is the "efficiency in using media for social agenda setting".

How to reach different groups in societies with environmental consumption (e.g. resource or energy efficient) messages in media has been debated in scholarly literature and practice for a longer period of time in Germany and beyond (Kuckartz et al., 2002).[66] Some decades ago, the bulk of scholars and other societal stakeholders were confident that a 'crisis scenario communication' supported by communicating facts, figures and sophisticated elaborations may convince people from different milieus to behave in an environmentally friendly way, whereas more recent findings have proven that this approach failed (Lichtl, 2007; Kuckartz et al., 2002; Schwender et al., 2008).

Several years ago, environmental communication research became increasingly aware of and interested in target groups and how to address them through media or campaign messages (Buba & Globisch, 2008; Wippermann et al., 2009). For example, Liedtke et al. (2007) distinguish between *environmentally conscious* and *environmentally friendly behavior*. Environmentally conscious behavior arises, when media users reflect that, on the basis of facts, figures and sophisticated elaborations, it is necessary to protect the environment. These environmentally conscious media users usually come from higher socio-economic milieus and like to watch high quality documentaries and read high quality magazines, which help them form a differentiated opinion on environmental issues (Wippermann et al., 2009: 37). People behaving in an environmentally friendly way regularly do not feel responsible for their environment, and they have not internalized norms in order to promote environmental issues. If they change their lifestyles towards more environmentally friendly ones, they do so unconsciously (ibid.). For example environment-friendly behaving people are not necessarily interested in saving the environment as, for instance, when they abstain from a plane flight not for reasons of environmental protection, but for the wish to save money.

In German television, there is a visible trend towards serving those target groups who behave in an *environmentally conscious* way (i.e. people who have a high(er) educational background). On a regular basis, for instance, 3sat, ARD, SWR, WDR, ZDF doku, EinsPlus, National Geographic Channel, Discovery Channel and ARTE have implemented formats or sometimes whole shows/programs which offer many factual information and sophisticated elaborations, especially designed to appeal to higher socio-economic milieus, or the so-called 'information elite'. Indeed, envir-

---

[66] As Michelsen (2007: 25) argue in this context, the term environmental communication has been replaced by the term sustainability communication because the question of communicating environmental issues should be integrated in the concept of sustainable development. As will be outlined in chapter 5, this thesis argues for the German context (part II of the thesis) that the discipline of sustainability communication comprises not 'only' environmental components, but also health and social communication ones. It is quite a new discipline, for which study courses, university departments and occupational images do not yet exist on a broader basis and need to be established.

onment-friendly behaving people (or the mainstream milieu members, see Wippermann et al., 2009) are much less targeted by TV formats sending environmental messages and there are much less entertainment or 'human interest' shows, involving environmental issues balanced and accurate in their stories. The Netherlands and other countries portray how this could work (Lubjuhn & Hoffhaus, 2009; Pratt et al., 2010). In Germany, for reaching these lower socio-economic target groups with environmental messages, an entertaining approach should be preferred (Clobes & Hagedorn, 2008; Pratt et al., 2010).

Great potentials are in storytelling (Glathe, 2010; Lubjuhn & Pratt, 2009, Schwender et al., 2008) to get environment-friendly behaving people more consciously involved in environmental issues. In environmental and sustainability research, this group of people is also considered to be the 'unmanageable, unsustainable consumers' who are hard to address (Schwender et al., 2008; Reisch et al., 2006). The suggestions offered through storytelling should (1) help them save money, (2) be easy to integrate in their everyday life, (3) be easy to remember and thus (4) be easily discussed with friends, family and community members (participative function).

In summary, the need has been identified to experiment and specifically address mainstream milieus with environmental messages with the help of affective orientated and entertaining strategies. Entertainment-Education though has not been recognized and appreciated very much so far in Germany (also see chapter 6.2.2) and further steps and research in this direction need to be designed and implemented.

2.7.1.3 Conclusions

To conclude, reaching lower socio-economic groups has been considered a challenge in health and environmental communication. They were found to be very hard to address. The health communication field, however, has dealt with this challenge much longer than the environmental field. The problem of addressing people from lower socio-economic milieus is rooted in several barriers (Dervin, 1974, 1976). According to Steele et al. (2007), lower socio-economic groups have

1. Accessibility barriers: They cannot afford, for example, healthy or organic products, or they have problems with things such as child care or scheduling.
2. Acceptability barriers: They prefer to manage themselves; think nothing more can help; don't know how or where to get help; are afraid to ask for help because of what others would think; do not get around to it; do not bother or they have language problems when confronted with 'cognitive information'.
3. Availability barriers: Professional help is often not available in their area, or professional help is not available at the time required, or the waiting time is too long for them.[67]

---

[67] Some of the barriers can be especially applied to people with a migrant background. They need to be taken into consideration as a special group among the lower socio-economic milieus.

The existence of myriad barriers has created a need for mass media communication strategies, especially those involving the E-E strategy in attempting to reach lower socio-economic milieus.

For health and environmental organizations, it was and nowadays still is not easy to reach lower socio-economic groups with lifestyle themes. It seems that the traditional background and their approach to spread messages in an 'object-orientated' manner (using facts and figures, sophisticated and elaborate explanations, etc.) (Bouman, 1999: 29) does not fit in with these milieus.

That is to say, people from lower socio-economic groups have less or no 'reading culture', and they use more audiovisual media like television instead of print media (Bouman 1999: 29; Statistisches Bundesamt, 2006; Haas, 2007). Studies in this context emphasize that preferences for entertainment television genres are related to a lower educational level in the audience. For example, the studies of Porter Novelli et al. (2000; 2005) illustrate that lesser educated people prefer to watch light entertainment programs (game shows and reality shows) or dramas (daily soaps, telenovelas) in comparison to more highly educated people and that they are much more likely to change their knowledge, attitude and behavior through entertainment TV formats.

In consequence, Entertainment-Education can be considered as a useful strategy for reaching lower socio-economic groups by responding to their needs. Firstly, entertainment television is based on a popular and emotional culture. Secondly, it is more people (or human interest) than object-orientated. Thirdly, it enhances the participatory exchange of audience members (with their family, neighbors and friends) regarding the issues that are shown on TV (Gray, 2008). In Germany, first steps need to be made to experiment with Entertainment-Entertainment and with how the mainstream milieus can effectively be reached.

2.7.2 Children and Adolescents

The general inequalities between higher and lower socio-economic milieus described in the health communication section, and the attributes for reaching socio-economically weaker groups with environmental messages can also be transferred to the situation of children and adolescents.

Young people living in families that come from higher socio-economic groups are, on average, healthier than young people who are raised in a lower socio-economic environment. In addition, the studies from Paus-Hasebink et al. (2007) and Lubjuhn & Liedtke (2008) emphasize in this context that parents from lower socio-economic milieus usually have less educational competencies to foster environmentally friendly and healthy consumption behavior patterns in their children, and often times they serve as a 'negative role-models' for their children.

The increasing number of people in German society living under fairly poor circumstances (as well as people in other western countries) illustrate that also children and adolescents are much affected by poverty. Of the 10.6 million German people living under poor conditions, 1.7 million are children and adolescents under sixteen (Statistisches Bundesamt, 2006). This means that the families of every sixth child younger than seven years is supported by social welfare, and more than 14% of all children can officially be considered poor (Deutsches Kinderhilfswerk, 2007). The rather bad financial situation of the family is mostly related to bad educational conditions and an unhealthy and environmentally unfriendly lifestyle (Deutsches Kinderhilfswerk, 2007).

Children and young people growing up in lower socio-economic milieus basically adopt the media habits of their parents and other family members at an early age (see section 2.6.1): they (1) regularly develop a non reading culture, (2) they have a greater affinity for audiovisual media than printed media and (3) they consume a lot more television than young people from higher socio-economic groups (Kuchenbuch, 2003; Paus-Hasebrink et al., 2007). Therefore, Entertainment-Education can be reasonably used as a strategy to especially reach these children and young people with health or environmental messages.

Besides the use of Entertainment-Education as a strategy to sensitize adults, adolescents and children living under difficult socio-economic circumstances, scholars and media professional discovered high effects of the E-E strategy on the target group of ***children and younger people in general*** (Arendt, 2008; Bouman & Hollemans, 2008; Bouman et al., 2009; Lampert, 2007; Schwarz, 2004; Singhal & Dura, 2008). This also includes children and young people from higher socio-economic and educational groups. So why does Entertainment-Education bear great potentials to address children and adolescents independent of their socio-economic/educational background?

Children and young people generally like watching more entertainment than information programs in comparison to adults, as Paus-Haase & Wagner (2001) argue. In addition, they usually have a wider understanding of information than adults: they use their favorite entertainment programs not only for amusement, but also to orient themselves and gain information in their everyday life (Lampert, 2007). Barthelmes (2001) adds that the topics shown on television have a close connection to the real lives of young people, especially when they involve entertaining storylines. More than half of the youngsters between 12 and 19 years talk to their friends regarding the topics they have seen in TV programs (JIM, 2006). These topics can be, for instance, listening to music or wearing trendy clothes. Furthermore, they can also serve as a catalyst for discussing delicate issues such as HIV/AIDS, smoking or environmental behavior (Lampert, 2007).

In consequence, Entertainment-Education seems to be a useful strategy for sensitizing knowledge, attitude and behavior of young people regarding prosocial issues.

2.8 Summary

For reaching people from lower socio-economic milieus as well as children and adolescents with prosocial messages, communication strategies need to take a more affective rather than cognitive approach into consideration. Research suggests that prosocial change organizations working with health, social and environmental themes should do detailed analysis on their campaign's target group as one key for effective and efficient communication strategies in reaching the public with prosocial issues. When deciding to involve entertainment media, research furthermore shows the importance of letting activities be guided by a theoretical approach (2.3 and 2.4).

The E-E strategy is based on an interdisciplinary, theoretical framework. Professionals working internationally in the research and the governmental field started using different theories and concepts originated in psychology, communication and social science as well as social marketing and advertising as a solid foundation for their prosocial projects. Besides the integration of academic studies, they have increasingly involved formative, process and summative (effect) research when collaborating with entertainment TV makers. This process can serve as a starting point for Germany in contrast to the USA and the Netherlands, where it has already been practiced for several years.

Many discussions and questions have been raised regarding how effective the developed E-E strategy is. Critical reflections and results of the strategy have been depicted. Some critics suggest that Entertainment-Education will never be that effective in western countries. They argue that (1) the messages cannot get through because of the media-saturated environment (2) the audience will see through it (sophistication of the audience), (3) the broadcasting stations (more the commercial than the public) will not risk losing audience share for even prosocial reasons, (4) there is a fear and resistance from TV makers at being 'told what to do', (5) there is a scant evidence about the effectiveness of long-term impacts (almost no overtime follow ups) and (6) effects are not foreseeable (mixed evidence success – some E-E programs succeed while others fail).

Regardless of these, positive results have demonstrated that Entertainment-Education can serve as an effective media strategy for influencing audience members' knowledge, attitude and behavior, especially when the strategy is combined with other communication methods like participative or interpersonal communication approaches. This does not only go for non-western countries, but for western ones as well. Finally, the chapter dealt with mainstream milieus, children and adolescents as being crucial target groups who may be receptive to the E-E strategy.

3. Entertainment Television, Entertainment-Education and Prosocial Themes

> "Television teaches. If it didn't, there would be no commercials on the screen, because advertisers want people to learn a behavior, to learn to buy their products. Television can also teach people to plan their families, fight poverty, continue studying as adults, care for nature and respect their own bodies. We should use television to save life on earth".
>
> - Miguel Sabido, 2010[68]

Chapter 2 illuminated theoretical debates in the field of Entertainment-Education in order to learn from them for Germany's collaboration practice. The status quo regarding theories in use was pointed out, as were the results, critical reflections, effects and target groups that an E-E strategy preferably can reach. This chapter will shed some light on the field of entertainment television and its relationship to the E-E approach. But why focus on this field? E-E collaborations take place in the field of entertainment television. In the collaborative process, prosocial themes are detached from the sophisticated academic background in which government (related) and research organizations regularly use them. Stripped to simplicity, they become part of the storylines, which are broadcasted to mass media audience and they play a crucial role during the follow up activities related to the television program. As mentioned before, television can influence the public agenda, and German prosocial change organizations have started experimenting with Entertainment-Education as a practicable communication approach for spreading respective concerns. In addition, effect research on Entertainment-Education (chapter 2.5 and 2.6) has shown that the audience appreciates perceiving prosocial messages on entertainment TV and that these messages foster learning processes and interpersonal dialogues – both of which are important prerequisites for behavior change.

To understand how accurately and authentically depicted prosocial themes can be a part of the program and to understand how the audience can be informed, educated and motivated to make a choice for a prosocial life, it is essential to grapple with the field of television, its role and its function in society. This chapter aims to touch some elements of the television field, its history, research approaches, genre types and ethical considerations. Each paragraph is discussed according to the potentials and limits of Entertainment-Education and prosocial themes, as well as their potential for spurring knowledge, attitude and behavior change. Apparently, as with any medium of communication, television has its own advantages and boundaries, especially when prosocial concerns are involved.

---
[68] Retrieved from www.miguelsabido.com (15th April 2010).

3.1 Approaches at the Interface of Television and Society

Specialists and laymen have debated interrelations between television as a mass medium and society for several decades. Firstly, it is hard to draw a clear line between theory about television and theory about society (Bouman, 1999; McQuail, 2005; Severin & Tankard, 2001). Following Gehlen[69] (1972), McQuail (2005), Reichertz (2000 and 2007b) and Reichertz & Iványi (2002), television is a 'social institution' within society, with its own rules, practices and orientation offers for audience members. Television is ultimately dependent on society, although it has some scope for independent influence. It may be gaining some measure of autonomy as its range of activity, economic significance and informational power grows. McQuail (2000: 5) adds that "this is a potentially spiraling and self-fulfilling process, driven by ever-increasing estimation of their [the mass media] significance by political and cultural actors".

The interrelationship of television and society is omnipresent (i.e. other sections as well as chapters of the thesis will touch several of its aspects in addition to the following one). For instance, one recent academic debate about television facing society deals with the blurring of boundaries in entertainment and information programs (section 3.3). Another discussion refers to the increasing growth of entertainment and narrative storytelling (also see chapter 6.2.1). The following section will deal with important theoretical debates at the interface of television and society (also see Bouman, 1999: 42-43). In this context some perspectives give more credence to the argument that television influences society through its 'manipulative power', while other perspectives argue that it is the other way around, i.e. audience members are being emancipated through television.

3.1.1 Different Perspectives on Television and Society

A culturally critical perspective of television has been prominent since the appearance of the medium in the mid 1950s. The **Frankfurter School** was one of the early critical approaches. Leading scholars were Adorno, Horkheimer and Marcuse. In the view of this research tradition, television manipulates the audience because it does not show the real world. Instead of seeking information about 'real things', it creates a form of 'pseudo-reality' or a 'pseudo-legislation' for reality is-

---

[69] The anthropologist Arnold Gehlen laid the cornerstone for understanding the functions and transformations of social institutions with his book *Der Mensch. Seine Natur und seine Stellung in der Welt* (1972). In his anthropological approach, he argued that people are 'Mängelwesen' (incomplete creatures) because they need stabilizing institutions to survive. In his view, it is the ability of social institutions to provide their members with a firm, all-encompassing set of orientations and stabilizations. Institutions enable people to take action without reflecting and asking for a deeper meaning over and over again. In this regard, policy agencies, companies and families are institutions. Furthermore, everything (e.g. a stapler, a rubber or a university ID card) can be an institution in Gehlen's theory when they facilitate people's living conditions in a cultural environment.

sues (Marcuse, 1964). Hardt (1992) adds that their attack on television criticized the uniform worship of technique, monotony, the escapism and the production of false needs, the reduction of individuals to consumers and the removal of ideological choice for the audience. Another critical influence on the audience covers the standpoint that television – and especially entertainment television – is an 'addictive drug' which can be used as an ideological instrument (Adorno & Horkheimer, 1973; Adorno, 1957). Even if new critical approaches reflect the role of television in current times, the Frankfurter School still plays an important role in ongoing discussions in terms of the use of television by ideological organizations.

Later developments of the critical cultural perspective came up in the mid 1960s with the approach of the **Birmingham School**, which deeply influenced the academic discussions about the role of television. Their leading scholars were Hall, Hoggart and William. The Birmingham School approach was primarily responsible for a shift from the question of ideology embedded in media messages to the question of how this ideology might be 'read' by the audience. In this regard, Hall (1973) proposes the model of 'encoding-decoding media discourse'. He argues that media messages are always polysemic (having different meanings), open and that they are only understandable with reference to the cultural background of each viewer, as she or he receives the message. Hall's model locates the media messages between its producers, who frame or 'decode' the meaning in a certain way, and the audience, who 'encode' the meaning according to their rather different social situations and frames of interpretations. Furthermore, Hall suggests three basic codes in circulation. The first one is associated with 'power'. The second one refers to the code of 'negotiation', which is essentially the code of the media in their role of neutral and professional carriers of information. The third code is linked to 'opposition', which is available for those who choose or are led by circumstances to view messages about reality differently, and who can 'read between the lines' of official versions of media events. This simple model recognizes that the ideology, as sent by television, is not the same as the ideology, as understood by the audience.

Conclusively, television is no longer understood as being an almighty manipulative instrument. Following the view of the **Birmingham School**, media messages of producers can be highly manipulative, but these manipulative aspects are mostly compensated for by the 'emancipation' of the viewers, who actively perceive, interpret and reframe the message. With the argument on empowerment on the side of the audience, television has lost its enormous power and influence.

Thus, approaches related to television and society can be differentiated according to two different models of media power (see figure 3.1). The *dominance model* may be characterized by the Frankfurter School, which considers the media, and more specific television messages, as being 'almighty' or having a direct influence on the audience members. This perspective is closely linked to sender-orientated media approaches (section 3.1.2). The *pluralism model* sees the audience in an emancipated role, as it is the case with the tradition of the Birmingham School: various factors in the media user's cultural environment affect whether or not a message reaches her or him. This perspective closely relates to media debates about receiver-orientated approaches (section 3.1.2). So in short, communication theory provides very heterogeneous views of media power. For instance, one extreme is to argue that the audience is not emancipated, but passively receptive (*dominance model*) and another extreme is to follow the idea that audience members are completely emancipated, powerful, active, distanced and receiving (*pluralism model*). In-between these poles, there are several different strata of media power.

Figure 3.1: Ideal type models of media power

	Dominance Model	Pluralism Model
Societal Source	Ruling class or dominate elite	Competing political, social, cultural interests and groups
Media	Under concentrated ownership and of uniform type	Many and independent of each other
Production	Standardized, routinized, controlled	Creative, free and original
Content and World View	Selective and described from 'above'	Diverse and competing views, Responsive to audience demand
Audience	Dependent, passive, organized on a large scale	Fragmented, selective, reactive and Active
Effects	Strong and confirmative of established social order	Numerous, without consistency or predictability of direction, but often no effects

Source: McQuail (2005: 70)

Another approach that illustrates the power and the authority from the viewers' standpoint is ***postmodernism*** (see Bouman, 1999: 43). McQuail (2000) argues that it shapes the contemporary 'zeitgeist' in a way that we no longer share fixed beliefs or commitments. According to McQuail, there are increasing tendencies towards hedonism, individualism and living in the present moment. Grossberg et al. (2006) even equalize postmodernism with the commercialization of everything, emphasizing the pleasure connected with watching TV and not the useful purpose behind. The work of Baudrillard (1983) helps to understand the postmodernism development as it relates to television. In his 'simulacrum concept', he argues that differences between an image and the reality are no longer important for the audience: "the mass media provide an inexhaustible supply of images of pseudo-reality that serves instead of experience and becomes for many hard to distinguish from reality itself" (Baudrillard cited after McQuail 2000: 115).[70]

The appeal of the postmodernism concept helps to sum up the essence of the media's own logic. It is also useful, firstly, when connecting diverse social changes, for example the fragmentation of the class structure. This fragmentation plays a decisive role for Entertainment-Education, because it can be tail-ored specifically to lower socio-economic milieus or to younger people/children (chapter 2.7) who should preferably be reached through the messages in the program and the related follow up communication activities. Secondly, it facilitates the blurring of the entertainment and information genres (section 3.3.2), and this seems to support the introduction of E-E programs in the television landscape (see Bouman, 1999: 43).

Clearly, when looking at the above contrasting theoretical perspectives in the field of television and society, the exact role the media takes up, the levels of influence it exerts and how much the audience members might or might not free themselves from its influence depends on the theoretical viewpoint. Given this background, the importance of effect research on audience members becomes even more evident as being a crucial instrument for determining the precise audience exposure to specific television programs. From the perspective of theories about the interface of television and society, it might also make sense to apply and foster research activities on prosocial messages as well as on E-E collaboration processes in Germany.

Moreover, Hall (1973) argues that television is an instrument of ideological representation. Thus, prosocial change organizations, which want to use television to get prosocial messages out, become players in the game of ideological representation by adapting its rules and conventions. As will be made clear in chapter 4.2, 4.3 and 6.1, prosocial change organizations have to play this game differently according to the characteristics and legislations of the media system in each country. The role might range, for example, from a pure 'supplier' of health, social and environmental themes for TV makers (chapter 8.4), to an advisory or service role (chapter 2.4.1, E-E service collaborations), to an even more active role as being a part of the 'cultural power' of dominant media ideology (chapter 2.4.1, E-E co-productions/ E-E inscript participations).

3.1.2 History of Impact

The effects of television as a mass medium are strongly shaped by the historical circumstances of time and place (also see Bouman 1999: 45). Those factors are, for instance, the interests of governments, changing technologies, the activities of pressure groups and even the findings in fashion and society. In this regard, McQuail (2005) differentiates between four phases that mass media effect research has been going through, starting with an emphasis on sender-centered communication models and later developing more receiver-centered communication models (also see Bouman, 1999; Fasel, 2001; Reichertz, 2010).

---

[70] This idea is well exemplified in the film *The Truman Show* (1997), a film in which the whole plot turns on the situation of a real person who lives his life within the plot of a long running soap opera dealing with an imaginary environment.

In the first phase (1900-1930), mass media were seen as an 'all-powerful' tool, having a considerable power to shape opinions and beliefs, to change habits of life and to mould human behavior to the will of its controllers (Bauer & Bauer, 1960). Scholarship in this period produced a lot of literature regarding the power of propaganda (Grossberg et al., 2006; Lasswell, 1927; see also section 3.5.2). Concerns were often raised in a progressive, reformist way and were aimed at harnessing media to some desirable prosocial goal (education, combating prejudice or increasing public information).

In the second phase (1930-1960), mass media as an 'almighty instrument' were under scrutiny. Initially, researchers began to differentiate the possible effects according to the social and psychological characteristics of the audience, taking variables like personal contacts or the social environment into consideration. In any case, only a very limited number of effect studies were conducted at this time. In general, the era was marked by expressions of disillusions about the effects of powerful mass media. Klapper (1960: 8) concluded about this research phase that "mass media communication does not ordinarily serve as a necessary or sufficient cause of audience effects, but rather functions through a nexus of mediating factors".

The more 'modest role' of the media was changed and revised to a more 'powerful' one in the third phase (1960-1980). One reason for that was the introduction of television, which was believed to attract a large audience and have the power to change their belief, attitude and behavior (Bouman 1999: 45). Effect research of this period borrowed many concepts from behaviorism and (social) psychology, like the theories of cognitive dissonance (Festinger, 1957) or the elaboration likelihood model (Petty & Cacioppo, 1986b; chapter 2.3.7).

The fourth phase (1980 - present) can be characterized as the negotiation of mass media effects according to its media content, its audience focus, and the media organizations (such as commercial and public broadcasters as well as collaborating prosocial change organizations). According to Bouman (1999: 45), McQuail (2005) and Severin & Tankard (2001), this contemporary phase is also characterized by the approach of 'social constructivism'. With this approach, it has become more meaningful to focus on qualitative methodologies to investigate 'meaning structures' of people and organizations who/which are involved in or exposed to television issues (Jankowski et al., 2000; Ratner, 2005).

The different phases demonstrate that the power (potential effect) of media may indeed be seen according to historical conditions (Rosengren & Windahl, 1989). In consequence this would mean that today's television, especially interactive television or internet protocol (IP) TV, provides a content and a social experience unlike at any other time in history before.

In all, it is fair to say that television research does not assume that television has a universal impact. On the contrary, television effects can differ enormously according to the 'coding' of the medium as a 'transmitter'. This 'coding' includes the format (such as broadcast television or IP television), the program (entertaining or informational) or its content (health, social or environmental issues). Television can also differ according to the 'decoding' environment of the audience (such as individual attributes like demographics, age, interpersonal communication possibilities, etc.). Obviously, the results, from the perspective of television and society, suggest applying research activities to Germany's prosocial collaborations. Only with these research activities, it will be possible to learn more about Entertainment-Education in Germany and its detailed effects.

3.2 Entertainment Television Research

Three international trends exist that fuel the growing use of (television) entertainment in the field of prosocial communication. The first trend has been the decisive growth of entertainment media worldwide during the last two decades. The second one is the global expansion of communication systems and technology. The third trend refers to the increased competition between public and commercial broadcast organizations, which smudges the lines between traditional education and entertainment programs. These trends seem to be some of the reasons for the growing interest for prosocial change organizations in entertainment television as a part of their public communication agenda.

Nowadays not only are more people producing and consuming more entertainment media, but there are also more ways to access entertainment media products in more places in the world than in any other time in history. The expansion of global television networks, the coverage of the internet with music, films and TV programs and the diffusion of new communication technologies like mobile phones and i-pods are creating a tremendous burst in the production of entertainment media. Zillmann & Vorderer (2000) call present times the 'entertainment age'. The following sections will briefly depict two issues. Firstly, the main research traditions on television are illuminated to get a more holistic picture of the subject. Secondly, entertainment theories in particular are illustrated, both according to their linkages to E-E formats and with perspectives for implementation strategies in Germany.

3.2.1 Television Research

Television research tries to give answers on a variety of questions both prosocial change organizations and TV makers have. For example, 'How does television influence audience knowledge, attitude and behavior?' 'Which factors make people watch television programs?' or 'What are the audience ratings?' The kind of questions, methodologies and methods used for answering them are very much dependent on who is interested in the results of the television research and the amount of financial, human and time resources available (also see Bouman 1999: 45).

As the analysis in part II of the thesis suggests, Germany's prosocial change organizations such as governmental (related) authorities, universities or other social research institutions may have different roles in designing and implementing prosocial television projects, and they may ask different research questions. The answer to the questions is often only possible to find through research activities. The research, which the prosocial change organizations design and implement (formative, process and summative research), was described in chapter 2.4.3. For example, a prosocial change organization is involved in an E-E co-production, and they want to know more about the impact of an E-E television program. Therefore, they implement effect research (see chapter 2.4.3.3). Or a prosocial organization is involved in an E-E service collaboration and then creates and implements a follow up activity (e.g. an event, discussion roundtable or a blog) relating to the prosocial television program. Then they want to do research on the interpersonal communication measurements elicited by this follow up activity.

Looking at the television field, TV organizations indeed ask different questions and thus use other research methods. An example would be that a commercial broadcasting station or a production company wants to know the latest audience ratings for a primetime television show. This is important information for them, because the higher these ratings, the higher the advertising they can ask for. To answer this question some broadcasters have their own research section for conducting audience related information. Other broadcasters engage private media market research institutes (such as Nielsen or GfK Consumer Group) for getting the information they need. These research questions are answered by electronic data ratings and it is the simplest kind of research (also see Bouman 1999: 45).

Clearly, the two collaboration sides have different interests and, accordingly, conduct research on the entertainment program and their follow up activities. In figure 3.2, the different stakeholders who may have an interest in conducting entertainment TV research are depicted.

Figure 3.2: Different agents from the prosocial and TV field conducting entertainment TV research

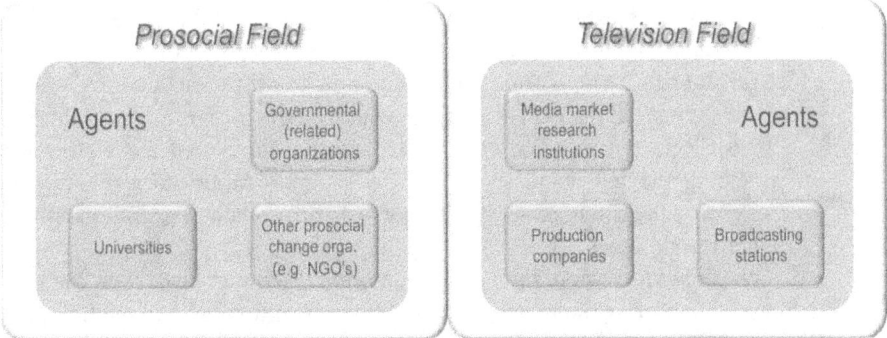

There are many television research traditions in use (Dickson, 2000; Grossberg et al., 2006; McQuail, 2005; Perry, 2002; Sayre & King, 2003; Severin & Tankard, 2001; Wimmer & Dominick, 2000), and they are not easy to strictly separate (i.e. several of them have overlapping elements). The following paragraph briefly describes striking traditions and their methodologies and methods used (1) by prosocial change organizations and (2) by television makers.

When looking at prosocial change organizations, their main research traditions in use are the following (Bouman, 1999; McQuail, 2005):

- *Social behavioral tradition*: The social behavioral tradition asks how certainly TV programs, storylines or specific messages influence audience knowledge, attitude or behavior. Most of the E-E effect research that has been conducted belongs to this research tradition. The methodologies and methods in use are very broad, i.e. they range from qualitative (e.g. in-depth interviews or experiments) to quantitative (e.g. regression or causal) analysis.
- *Critical tradition*: The critical tradition is an examination and critique of society and culture in which media scholars consider the structures, themes, symbols and meanings of media messages.[71] Here, the focus is more on the message analysis itself rather than on the generated effects. Some methods in use are message system analysis and traditional rhetorical analysis.
- *Cultural studies tradition*: According to the cultural studies tradition, communication researchers investigate how people use television according to their social needs. Questions are raised including 'How are norms, values and attitudes defined in society?' and 'How are they depicted in television programs?' Most of the research conducted in this tradition is qualitative (e.g. in-depth interviews, case studies, field experiments) and often includes a pre- and post testing design.
- *Structuralism and semiology tradition*: In the structuralism and semiology tradition, scholars look at television from a linguistic point of view, examining the text and language structures television refers to. Questions are raised like 'Which symbols, rules of grammar and syntax are used in television messages and which effect do they have on the audience?' This research tradition preliminary works with quantitative methodologies.
- *Uses & gratifications tradition*: The uses & gratifications tradition wants to find out what the audience 'does' with the television messages (chapter 2.3.6). Relevant questions are 'What was the motive of the viewer for watching the television show?' or 'What gratification does the viewer seek from the TV messages?' Scholars use both qualitative and quantitative methodologies.
- *Agenda setting tradition*: The agenda setting tradition deals with the representation of media messages and their transfer to mass and public agendas. Scholars pose questions like 'How often is a message represented in television?' and 'What influence does the frequency of presented messages have on the audience and the public agenda?' This tradition has often been used in the field of political advertising and campaign research using primarily quantitative methods.

---

[71] This tradition is very well associated with the theorists from the Frankfurter School (section 3.1.1).

In comparison to the prosocial change organizations, the television field is especially interested in conducting the following research:

- *Audience research*: This research perspective investigates how many audience members watch a single TV show and to which kind of audience segments they belong. Questions are answered such as 'How many viewers watched the program?' 'What were their demographic and ethical characteristics?' and 'What did they like in the episode and what did they not like?' The results of these investigations are put together to rating indexes. TV stations and advertisers are interested in this data to enhance and specialize their performances and adapt them to the main target groups of the audience.[72]
- *TV content research*: This research perspective focuses on the content shown on television. For example, 'What kind of content is broadcasted and how?' or, in the case of prosocial themes, 'What kind of prosocial content is broadcasted (i.e. is it content related to rare diseases like black fever or frequent ones like diabetes)?' or 'Which characters having which socio-demographics (e.g. ethics, age) get which diseases on TV programs, and how are they treated?' 'Which characters having which socio-demographics do actively save the environment and how is this depicted?' The outcome of this research could, for example, be that Hispanic characters suffer more often from diseases in TV shows than black or white people, and they less often receive proper treatment. Or perhaps elderly people fight for environmental protection in soap or telenovela plots more often, whereas younger people do less so.[73]
- *TV advertising research*: The TV advertising research perspective investigates the advertising shown on television. From this perspective, researchers ask questions like 'How much money was spent on advertising?' or 'In which advertisements could the target group of the program be interested in?'

Depending on the specific research interest, regularly quantitative methods are used in the research that the TV field conducts, or a mixture of quantitative and qualitative methods. Figure 3.3 is an extended version of figure 3.2, not only displaying the different agents conducting TV research but also the core research traditions they are deploying.

Figure 3.3: Different agents from the prosocial and TV field and entertainment TV research traditions in use

---

[72] The prosocial change organizations are also interested in this research tradition, as it is an important success factor for their E-E collaboration.

[73] TV content analysis is at least commonly interesting for prosocial change organizations to conduct (Murphy et al., 2007) and might give them hints about which prosocial content is depicted in entertainment television and how.

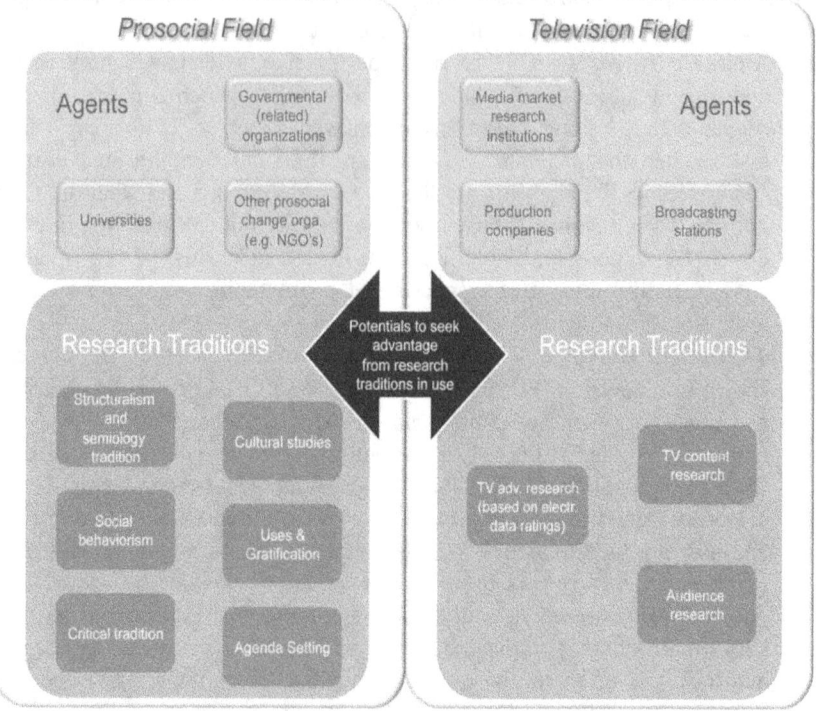

3.2.2 Entertainment Theories

The findings from the field of entertainment theories could be an initial help for designing and implementing E-E collaboration projects in Germany. Consequently, this paragraph briefly introduces important results and links them to E-E television interventions.

As stated before, "entertainment – not autos, not steel, not financial services – is fast becoming the driving wheel of the new worlds economy" (Wolf 1999: 4). With respect to our expanded leisure time activities, researchers not only agree that entertainment is what most people are looking for (Zillmann & Vorderer, 2000 for an overview), but some even predict that "entertainment will define, more than ever before, the civilizations to come" (Zillmann 2000: 18).

From a critical viewpoint, scholarly investigations may analyze and interpret what entertainment movies, programs and texts might stand for, but as an academic field, entertainment research does not yet exist (Vorderer, 2003). Furthermore, Vorderer (2003: 131) adds that "there has been a certain lack of empirical, that is, systematic research on the uses and effects of entertainment, within the United States as well as in Europe".

Vorderer (2003) argues that there is not 'the' single entertainment theory in academic research. He refers to many theoretical assumptions, models, hypotheses and theories, which have been established during the past 30 years primarily by Zillmann (Zillmann, 1988; Zillmann, 1994; Zillmann, 2000) and by Zillmann in cooperation with his colleagues (Zillmann & Cantor 1977; Zillmann & Bryant, 1986; Zillmann & Bryant, 1994; Zillmann & Vorderer, 2000). Three main concepts of entertainment theory will be described here shortly: (1) the mood-management/the selective-exposure theory, (2) the affective-disposition theory and (3) the excitation-transfer theory.

The *mood-management/the selective-exposure theory* investigates how and why people seek entertainment. Their holistic assumption is based on media users who are hedonistically orientated.[74] According to this theory, the audience members maintain and engage their positive moods, and they alter their negative moods by choosing TV programs that best serve these interests. Vorderer (2003) proposes that the audience members benefit from their own previous experience with different media products by using the media as a 'full advantage tool'. Thereby, they behave rationally, and in most cases, they are unaware of the underlying psychological processes involved.

From an E-E standpoint, the theory emphasizes that messages need to be chosen carefully in order to facilitate 'good mood experiences'. For example, a daily soap may engage the audience's positive mood by giving them the feeling that the characters are experiencing even worse things in the narrative plot than audience members are in real life. The positive mood can be turned negative, when messages are distributed with a moralized undertone or by wagging the forefinger at the audience (i.e. the educational purposes of the prosocial change organizations 'shines through intensively' in the storyline).

The *affective-disposition theory* focuses on the process while the audience is being exposed to the media. Following Zillmann's understanding of empathy (2003), the audience members first perceive, then access and then morally judge with regard to the characters shown in the entertainment television program. Consequently, the audience members agree or disagree with the characters' behavior, and they develop positive or negative impressions, which lead to emotions like fear or hope about the outcome of the story in which their beloved protagonist and the disliked/hated antagonist are portrayed.[75] A prototypical entertainment experience like suspense or hope can be considered a direct consequence of affective dispositions. As a result, this theory does not only describe the process of the exposure, but even more, it specifies the relations between the narrative characters, affective dispositions and

---

[74] This can be considered a characteristic for the majority of mainstream milieus (chapter 2.7).

[75] This theory is reminiscent of Bandura's social cognitive learning theory (chapter 2.3.2). The difference between Bandura's theory and the affective-disposition theory is that the latter theory focuses on audience involvement on an affective level according to the characters and the feelings arising as a result (fear, hope, love, etc.). The social-cognitive theory in contrast focuses on the modeling character of the protagonists' and antagonists' behavior, and this leads the audience members to re-model the shown positive behaviors they can affectively relate to in their everyday life.

the experience of entertainment. From an E-E perspective, this theory demonstrates that prosocial messages can have an impact on the audience, especially when they are exposed to narrative characters who deploy (dis-)affections and emotions like fear, anger, happiness or sadness.

The *excitation-transfer theory* aims to explain the primarily physiological processes, which take place at the end of or subsequent to the exposure. According to this theory, media users will not only experience an immense relief, but also gain positive or even euphoric gratification through observing the resolution of a character's distressing situation in the course of the narrative (such as considerable challenges, danger, despair or hopelessness). The more distressing the situation, the more intense are the feelings of relief and gratification after the exposure. From an E-E standpoint, collaborators should pay attention to highly distressing or controversial situations in the narrative plot, especially for the characters modeling prosocial behavior positively. This increases the likeliness of the audience to adopt the prosocial knowledge, attitude and behavior patterns.

3.3 Theories in the Field of Entertainment Television Genres

E-E collaborations between prosocial change organizations and entertainment TV makers use different TV genres for sending health, social and environmental messages. Messages have been sent, for instance, in daily soaps, reality or quiz shows. In each genre, collaborating partners as well as audience members are confronted with the specific genre features. For example, the daily soap content is based on melodramatic archetypes, a non-narrative closure and the distinction between the main and sub-plots, whereas the quiz show content is based on the thoughts of participators in competition. In this section, several insights about different entertainment genre features will be given by briefly outlining their historical development, the audience purposes that they fulfill and their potential for sending prosocial messages through taking advantage of collaboration (also see Bouman 1999).

3.3.1 Defining and Classifying Genres

Definitions and classifications of mass media help to explain their roles and functions in society in general. On a lower level, features of television programs facilitate the understanding of what the viewers 'do' with (entertainment) television. In this regard, genre theory provides a framework for categorization. Its origin comes from rhetoric and literary theory and has expanded to include media theory in recent years. In academic literature, there is often considerable theoretical disagreement about the definition of genre. "A genre is ultimately an abstract conception rather than something that exists empirically in the world" (Feuer, 1992: 144). Bordwell adds that "any theme may appear in any genre" (Bordwell, 1989: 147).

A genre can refer to any kind of mass media content category (film, television, print, radio, etc.). Following Bordwell (1989) and Fiske (1987) categorizations can be made according to the country of origin (a German program), the director, producer or broadcaster (a CNN program, a Spielberg film), the technical process (cinema scope), the cycle (the 'fallen women'), the style (the Golden Age), the structure (narrative), the ideology (Third Reich), the purpose (information, entertainment or sub-variants), the audience (children, adults, teens), the subject or theme (a nature program), the form (lengths, structure, place, language) and the meaning (reality reference).

The genre can be seen as "a means of controlling demand" (Neale, 1980: 55). The relative stability of genres enables producers to predict audience expectations. In this regard, Gledhill states that "differences between genres meant different audiences could be identified and catered to (…). This made it easier to standardize and stabilize the production" (Gledhill, 1985: 58). In relation to mass media, the entertainment television genre is part of the process of targeting many different market sectors and audiences. In this context, various entertainment programs were targeted to reach a special focus of viewers coming from lower socio-economical classes as well as children and adolescents (chapter 2.7).

3.3.2 Genres in Entertainment Television

In recent years, it has become quite obvious that there are huge interfaces between information and entertainment genres. Hybrid and overlapping forms seem to be increasingly rising. Abercrombie (1996: 45) proposes in this context that "the boundaries between genre are shifting and becoming more permeable". This blurring has made the question of role of television in society even more interesting. Kolandai-Matchett (2008), Lampert (2007) and Schrob & Theunert (2000) state that with the blurring of these borders, information and entertainment seem to have become one. On the one hand, viewers can be informed and educated by entertainment programs, and, on the other hand, information programs can entertain them. These developments are affirmed by recent studies which argue that audience members enjoy being informed and entertained at the same time (Kennedy et al., 2004; Schwender et al., 2008; Wilkin et al., 2007). To understand the specific characteristics and features of entertainment television genres and to explore which genres are suitable for dealing with prosocial themes, four main genres are presented for this purpose here: (1) children's television, (2) reality TV/talk shows, (3) drama – daily soaps/telenovelas, detective drama and comedies as well as (4) game and quiz shows.[76] The tendency of genres to blur in information and entertainment television can be found in figure 3.4.

---

[76] These genres are picked, because several of them had been used in E-E collaborations – some with greater success than other – as the analysis will reveal.

Figure 3.4: The blurring of the genres

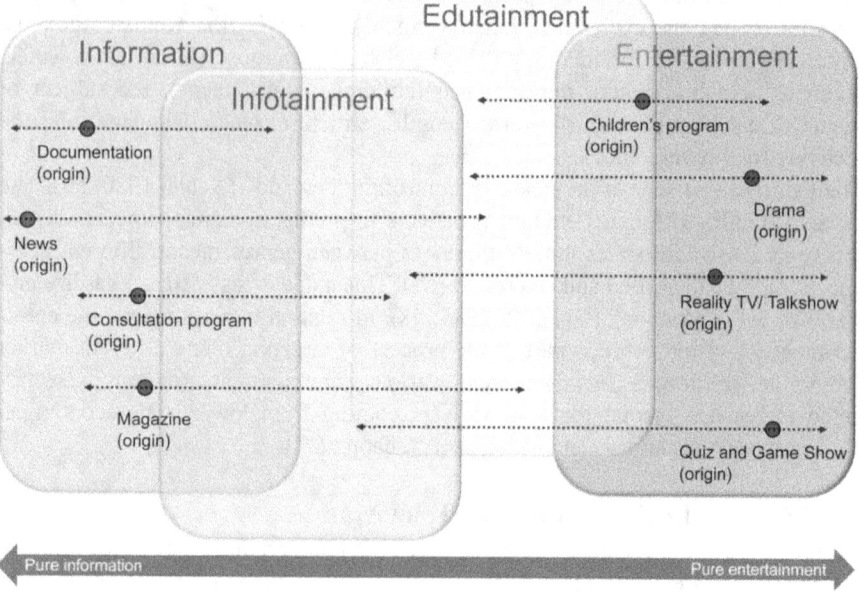

3.3.2.1 Children's Television

Children's television is an unusual genre, because it is defined not by the characteristics of the 'text' but, by the audience who watches it. The natural opposite of a 'children's' genre ought to be an 'adult's' genre. Messenger-Davis (2001: 96) sees in this a definition shift stating, "adult programming now usually means sexual or pornographic".

Thus, one obvious definition of children's television as a genre is that there will be no sex in it. This kind of protectiveness is institutionalized in regulatory documents dealing with possible 'harm' for children and youngsters (for example see European Parliament & Council of European Union, 2007; Landesmedienanstalten Deutschland, 2000).

Outside the regulatory protected children's grouping, many scholars put forward the criticism that children's programs are exploited to an extreme extent for lucrative commercial propositions, like the *Teletubbies* or the toy- and merchandising-linked cartoons such as *Smurfs*, *Ninja Turtles* (USA) or, more recently, *Pokémon* (Japan). Scholars such as Kenway & Bullen (2001) and Kline (1993) have questioned the effect on narrative quality when merchandising becomes the primary focus.

Labeling a genre as belonging to its viewers, as in the case of 'children's', is a reminder for producers and writers as well as collaborating prosocial authorities that they are in a special cultural sphere, telling stories to a specific audience who are likely to be influenced, inspired or disturbed by what the actors on screen do. In terms of sending prosocial messages with the help of E-E collaborations, the genre has been successfully used so far in western countries (Röll, 1999; DBU & KI.KA, 2003; Singhal & Rogers, 1999).

3.3.2.2 Reality TV/Talk Shows
Reality TV
The term reality television is used to depict a variety of programming, starting with docusoaps (e.g. *The Super-Nanny* or the show *"Erwachsene auf Probe" (Adults on Probation)* to talk shows (see next paragraph) and more recently many versions of talent contest shows (e.g. *Germany's Next Top Model, Germany's Next Superstar, The Musical Casting Show*), which are popular all over the world. Reality TV is a hybrid form, drawing on (and re-establishing) genetic codes and conventions derived from numerous other sources like game shows, soap operas or documentaries. This genre is generally thought to have emerged in the late 1980s in the USA and then very quickly established itself within mainstream popular programming in 1990s. One of the key elements is the juxtaposition of the 'everyday' or banal with the unexpected and the bizarre.

The idea that television can bring us closer to reality is not – in itself – new. Gripsrud (1998) suggests that television established itself from the outset on the premise that it is the medium that is closest to 'the real'. He goes on by stating that the 'everydayness' of using the medium at home functions to convey a sense of the ubiquity of television along with its capacity for the transmission of reality. This explains, following Gripsrud (1998), the apparent demand for 'reality' in modern societies.

Scholars and the public have intensively discussed the effects of reality television. Critics on this medium can be broadly divided into two main positions. The first position criticizes the ***shock value***, arguing that television professionals pander to the lowest common denominator in parading the less pleasant side of contemporary life as voyeuristic spectacle. In this body of literature, researchers claim that reality television does 'harm' to viewers (Casey et al., 2008).

The second position takes the oppositional view to the first body of literature. Researchers and pundits have been keen to cite reality TV as an example of '***democratainment***'. Some of those "pro-reality TV" sources emphasize that people can very well model the shown behavior in their own lives, because it is so close to their own reality (Andrejevic, 2004; Hill, 2005). Indeed, the social cognitive learning theory of Bandura (chapter 2.3.2) makes the point that viewers can best learn from role models, when the shown behavior is very closely related to the audience's real life. Thus, reality TV seems to be a genre with great potential to broach the issue of prosocial messages. This is also true for reality TV shows that not only show the life of normal people, but also those of celebrities (Cooper, 2008). In recent years, governmental (related) authorities and TV professionals interested in prosocial themes have discovered and used this potential by embedding prosocial themes in (celebrity) reality TV. Examples are the Dutch celebrity reality show

Echt Elly (Lubjuhn & Hoffhaus, 2009), the New Zealand reality show *Wa$ted* (Pratt et al., 2010) as well as the British reality show *Outrageous Wasters*. All three shows portray sustainable consumer lifestyles to make the audience members learn from them, change their attitude or behavior. For example, ways of saving energy and resources are depicted, as is the use of public transport or a bicycle instead of a car, or eating less meat. For the actors of the reality show, some prosocial lifestyles were very challenging to practice in everyday life. For instance, for the Dutch celebrity Elly Lockhost, the main character in *Echt Elly*, it was challenging to reduce her meat consumption or to go by public transport and not by car. In general, these formats show the challenge of living a prosocial lifestyle, and they leave the audience members with the message that they do not need to change everything – especially those things which are very hard for them to change. They show that the audience members are responsible for their environment and that they can practice prosocial behavior in their everyday life without it taking much effort. In Germany, reality shows sending prosocial themes in collaboration with prosocial change organizations have not been introduced so far.

Talk shows
Talk shows are a genre of explicit conversation, dialogue and discourse overseen by the host of the show. Marshall & Werndly (2002) and Casey et al. (2008) outline the distinction between two categories, which are significant to consider for E-E formats: celebrity and confessional talk shows. **Celebrity talk shows** have their origin in vaudeville and variety radio, and they have been a constant fixture of light entertainment, starting in the USA and Great Britain in the 1950s. The programs often have the name of the host in the title (like the German shows *Johannes B. Kerner, Beckmann* or *Harald Schmidt*), and both the host and the celebrity guest(s) usually "consume light refreshments while engaging in light banter" (Casey et al. 2008: 278).
The celebrity talk show could be very useful in terms of sending prosocial messages via the celebrity guests or the host of the show. As described in chapter 2.3.5, there is a body of literature making clear the positive impacts celebrities could have on audience knowledge, attitude and behavior. In this respect, the messages have the limitation that the celebrity can only 'talk' about her or his prosocial activities. A modeled behavior, like it is shown in narrative plots, does not follow the main genre characteristic. In any case, showing modeled behavior would be a more effective condition for influencing the viewers (Morgan et al., 2009).[77]
The **confessional talk show** established in the 1980s and 1990s with the increasing

---

[77] A successful example for implementing sustainable consumption messages in a celebrity talk show was the German show *Johannes B. Kerner* (named after the host), which was broadcasted on 12th March 2009. In collaboration with the sustainability platform utopia, *Johannes B. Kerner* implemented a show with lesser light in the studio, thus saving 200 times the energy compared to regular programs. The invited celebrities arrived by public transport, were catered to with eco-food, wore eco-fashion and talked about their experience concerning living a sustainable lifestyle.

popularity of daytime television shows like in Germany *Hans Meiser, Illona Christen* and *Arabella Kiesbauer*. Central for those programs is the participation and the contribution of 'everyday people' whose experience and narratives make up the content of these shows. Shattuc (1997) describe a gradual shift in talk shows towards the end 1990s; they began to move away from being concerned about personal issues related to social justice and to focus more on interpersonal conflicts. This involved confrontation, aggression, emotional outbursts, crises and an attempt at resolution.

An ongoing discussion among communication scholars focuses on talk shows as a medium for learning behavior patterns (some negative, but also positive prosocial behavior patterns) (Shattuc, 1997; Weintraub Austin et al., 2000). Nevertheless, with respect to the shifting paradigm in talk shows towards interpersonal conflict and sensation, talk shows can been seen as a genre with lower potential for integrating prosocial messages. There is no familiar example demonstrating proactively integrated prosocial themes in confessional talk shows.

3.3.2.3 Dramas: Soap Operas/Telenovelas, Detective Dramas and Comedies

The drama theory of Bentley distinguishes between five different theatre genres: tragedy, comedy, tragic-comedy, farce and melodrama (Nariman, 1993). Drama, in theater or television, which has the core purpose of entertaining the audience, embodies the ancient art of storytelling and oral history. In this sense, it provides a natural frame for combining entertaining and educating elements. For entertainment television purposes, three popular subgenres, soap operas/telenovelas, detective dramas and comedies, are outlined in the three following sections.

Soap Operas/Telenovelas
The main differences between a soap opera and a telenovela (or the television novel) are in their origins. The telenovela has its origin in Latin America where it came up in the early 1960s (Creeber, 2001), while the soap opera has its roots in the USA. Moreover, both genres differ in their formats. On the one hand, the telenovela begins, builds up to a climax, concludes and ends. The whole narrative story focuses primarily on one or two actors and their environments. On the other hand, the daily soap is a continuous series, which means that it has an indefinite run and therefore does not feature a final episode in which the narrative is closed or resolved. It is a never-ending format.[78]

Beside those two main differences, the soap opera and the telenovela are very similar in their ways of narrative storytelling. As the soap opera is much more prominent and often used for E-E purposes, it will be described in the following section. The term 'soap opera' was coined in the USA in the 1930s when the sponsors of

---

[78] For example, Germany's first telenovela *Bianca – Wege zum Glück (Bianca - Ways to Fortune)* was aired on the pubic broadcaster ZDF from November 2004 to November 2005 with a closed story, whereas the most famous German weekly soap, *Lindenstraße*, has been running since December 1985.

these daytime broadcasts were detergent companies like *Procter and Gamble*. Since then, daily soaps have been very popular. For instance in 1996, top German daily soaps such as *Gute Zeiten, Schlechte Zeiten (Good Times, Bad Times)* (RTL) and *Verbotene Liebe (Forbidden Love)* (ARD) had more than three million viewers each and every weekday. Some communication scholars have pointed out the social function of soaps as being a 'talking point' for people. Through them, viewers are able to communicate with others, share information, feelings and views about both people and social issues (Paus-Haase et al., 1999; Simon, 2004). Thus, daily soaps have an extreme participative function among the audience.

From an E-E standpoint, critical opinion can generally be summed up using the differentiation of Singhal & Rogers (1999: 60), who distinguished between a conventional soap opera and an E-E soap opera and suggest four main differences between both (see table 3.1).

Table 3.1: Comparison of conventional soap operas and E-E soap operas

Conventional Soap Operas:	Central and Secondary Plot	Entertainment-Education Soap Operas:
1. Entertaining	Continuing Story	1. Entertaining and Educational
2. Morally Incoherent (value erosion)	Low Production Costs	2. Morally Coherent (value reinforcement)
3. Unrealistic	High Ratings	3. Realistic
4. Atheoretical Development	Commercial Sponsorship	4. Theoretical Development

Source: Own illustration based on Singhal & Rogers (1999: 60)

1. *Entertainment vs. Entertainment-Education*: The primary purpose of conventional soap operas is to attract a large audience, often depicting undesirable values like violence, greed, excessive sex and materialism. In contrast to that, E-E soap operas are mainly designed and implemented to reinforce prosocial beliefs and values.[79]

2. *Moral confusion versus coherence*: Many of the conventional soap operas are morally incoherent, as no clear distinctions between good and bad behaviors are made (Simon, 2004). Good moral characters frequently violate social norms and values, or bad moral characters are portrayed enhancing prosocial norms. This con-

---

[79] One example of an E-E soap is Miguel Sabidos progam *Acompaname (Accompany Me)*. The soap illustrated in rather dramatic terms and over the course of the nine-month series (five days a week during Mexican prime time during 1977-78) the personal benefits of planning one's family by focusing on family harmony.

fuses the audience about what constitutes good versus bad. E-E soap operas seek to avoid sending those confusing signals to their audience.

3. *Unrealistic versus realistic*: Alexander (1985), Casey et al. (2008) and McCarthy (2001) suggest that conventional soap operas display inaccurate portrayals of life, and thus they are mostly experienced as unrealistic among the audience. E-E soap operas try to be as close to reality of the audience as possible. A great amount of research has been done about the messages in E-E soap operas, and this research supports close-to-reality depictions of life (see chapter 2.4).

4. *Atheoretic versus theoretic*: This is the most striking point in the distinction. Conventional soap operas have no theoretical foundation, whereas E-E soap operas include a theoretically grounded framework of communication theories (see chapter 2.3).

In comparison to other entertainment genres, soap operas have been successfully used to spread prosocial messages among the audience (Bouman, 1999; Lubjuhn & Pratt, 2009; Singhal & Rogers, 1999). They are very useful for including health, social and environmental messages, because they engage the audience's participatory processes like talking to family members, friends and colleagues about the issues in the soap. Thus, the soap opera can be considered as a useful and promising genre for reaching viewers with prosocial messages. In western countries, many soaps have been used to promote prosocial themes in one or several episode(s) in which TV makers have collaborated with prosocial change organizations. The co-production of a new E-E soap opera, such as described by Singhal & Rogers (1999) above, is a characteristic phenomenon for non-western countries, but also for the Netherlands (chapter 4.3).

Detective Drama

The detective drama has been one of the most popular genres on television with some series proving so successful that they have retained a presence in the schedule for decades.[80] Detective drama started as live programs, recycling prose fiction, movies and radio shows in the early 1950s. Cooke (2001) divides detective dramas into two approaches. The first one is the ordinary uniformed policeman. The second one is the skilled plain clothes detective. Both of them set a pattern for the genre. Rogers (2008) describes the detective drama as a case in point, encompassing programs about amateur sleuths, private eyes, professional crime fighters, and real life crime depiction. She emphasizes that this genre is limited by dealing with the specific actions of police officers. What makes the detective drama so interesting is its eternal struggle between good and evil.

---

[80] A famous German example is the detective drama *Tatort (Crime Scene)*, which has been aired on the public broadcaster ARD since 1970. *Tatort* is the most popular detective drama in Germany. Klein (2008) points out that in 1980 it had one of the highest market shares ever with 24.39 million viewers. This was more than a quarter of the whole population. In 2007, the average viewers number was 7.1 million viewers (Klein, 2008), which is still very high for Germany.

In research, the detective drama is analyzed in terms of its history (Moran, 1992), textual structures (Thompson, 1996), form and ideology (Buxton, 1990), criticisms on the depiction of violence (Brunsdon, 1998) as well as moral considerations and effects on the cultural discourse (Stark, 1997; Nelson, 1997). In the field of impact research, scholars argue that it engages clear universal concerns of law and order, the good and the bad, crime and punishment and the intersection between the public and the private sphere very well. For example, Delaney (2007) claims that the genre has consistently explored social mores, attitudes and popular concerns. This makes the detective drama a genre with the potential for dealing with prosocial issues in the storylines in order to show modeled behavior and initiate interpersonal discussions among the audience. For example, German detective stories have been used as E-E collaboration genres several times to promote ethical themes such as human trafficking.[81]

Comedies
The discussion of the television comedy genre has been categorized in fits and starts, exploring a diverse range of concerns, and arising out of conflicting histories and methodologies. This lack is due to a congruence of factors. Most visible, comedy's status as 'low culture' means that academics have chosen to focus on more 'serious' concerns. In addition, humor is, on the whole, popular and popularist, and, although there are academic aims to broaden analysis out to popular forms, it is obvious that work needs to be done to develop 'quality' tests.
Comedies are built on the focus of dilemma resolution, as well as on caricature and stereotypes. The field of comedy is enormous, covering comedy formats like sketch shows and sitcoms (situations comedies), advertising and animation, as well as the role of comedies in other genres like news or magazines (Hartley, 2001; Neale, 2001).
Following Hartley (2001), comedies evoke confusion, disruption and reconciliation. Hartley (2001: 66) states that "one of the pleasures of watching sitcoms was to observe how bizarre some of the family set-ups were, no matter what their surface 'smileyness' suggested about 'family values'".
Thus, a comedy portrays personal happiness as more important than public achievement, values, norms or orientations. With the help of friends and family, problems are worked out and the story has a happy ending. In recent years, comedies involved more moral and ideological issues, dealing with homosexuality (see Feuer 2001 about 'gay sitcoms'), political controversies or racial tolerance. Furthermore, according to Mills (2001), comedies trivialize, they are superficial, sensational, ambivalent and ambiguous. This genre seems difficult to use for E-E purposes. Prosocial messages could suffer, if the overall goal is to satisfy the personal happiness of the viewers. The US comedy *Mr. Lopez*[82] is one of only a few ex-

---

[81] Due to the anonymous status, which was guaranteed to the study participants, the name of the format and the organization involved are not mentioned here (see chapter 5).
[82] Hollywood, Health & Society (see chapter 4.2) brought the TV producer of *Mr. Lopez* to-

amples familiar so far that promote prosocial lifestyle issues.

3.3.2.4 Quiz and Game Shows

Quiz and game shows have proven to be an ever-present part of television scheduling. This genre is a boon to television networks which are keen to win high ratings, because they are cheap to produce and popular among different cultural audiences. Thus, quiz formats produced in one country can be easily adopted worldwide. The quiz show has its origins in radio shows. According to McQueen (1989), the earliest quiz show ever shown on TV was *Spelling Bee*, aired by the BBC in 1938. Quiz shows can be characterized according to the type of knowledge required and their social power (Fiske, 1987). Some of them are targeted to special audiences (e.g. housewives or retirees) and placed in daytime slots five days a week, while others appeal to the youth and older children coming from school and thus occupy the afternoon hours. The most elaborate and expensive shows are shown in the evening hours on prime time program; a good example is *Who Wants to be a Millionaire?*, which is licensed in more than 120 countries worldwide (Hochmuth, 2008). Despite their popularity – or maybe because of it – many quiz and game shows have a low cultural status. Many scholars have been critical of the genre, particularly when identifying the ideological function it has in sustaining the value of competitiveness and social mobility, both of which are central to the maintenance of capitalist societies (Fiske, 1987). Despite ideological considerations, the popularity of quiz shows suggests that the viewers take some pleasure in the format and harsh conditions of the game. Additionally, viewers enjoy identifying with the winners of quiz shows, urging them on to achieve success. Several sources suggest learning effects that quiz shows can have on the audience (Cooper-Chen, 1994; Hallenberger, 2008; Panyr et al., 2004). The most important seems to be that the audience has a user value, because they have the 'feeling' that they learn something (Hochmuth, 2008). In this respect, Hallenberger & Foltin (1990: 163) point out a user value which makes quiz shows more entertaining than films or other programs: "Audiences enjoy entertainment the most when they feel they are learning something from it and benefitting themselves in some way". This makes quiz and game shows a genre with the potential for dealing with prosocial messages which reach the audience. Some recent examples from the Netherlands address healthy lifestyle issues in quiz and game shows (Bouman, 1999: 54; Stivoro, 2008) that have high audience ratings. In Germany quiz and game shows have not been used so far to promote prosocial topics through collaboration with prosocial change organizations. In conclusion, some entertainment genres have greater potentials to effectively involve prosocial messages (i.e. change the knowledge, attitude and behavior of audience members) than others. Prosocial change organizations and TV makers should be aware of the pros and cons of each genre before they decide for an E-E

---

gether with health experts from governmental authorities and research institutes to actively promote accurate diabetes messages (e.g. what the disease can do to the body, how to prevent it and how to support people who are affected).

co-production, E-E inscript participation or an E-E service collaboration. The following table 3.2 gives an overview of the genre potentials for E-E programs, and summarizes which of the E-E TV formats have been implemented on the elaborated genres using prosocial collaborations in Germany, the USA and the Netherlands.

Table 3.2: E-E potentials for different TV genres and their tendencies to use the genre in E-E collaborations

Genre	Children's TV	Reality TV / Talk Shows				Dramas			Quiz and Game Shows
Subgenre		Talent contest shows	Docu-soaps	Repres. Talks	Live Talks	Drama/ Soap Opera/ Telenovela	Detec. Drama	Come-dies	Quiz and Game Shows
Potentials for E-E in general	+++	+/-	++	+	+	+++	+++	+	+++
Germany: So far tendency to use the genre in an E-E collaboration	+++	-	-	-	-	++	+	-	-
USA: So far tendency to use the genre in an E-E collaboration	++	-	-	-	-	+++	-	++	-
The Netherlands: So far tendency to use the genre in an E-E collaboration	++	-	+	-	-	+++	-	-	++

+++ = high   ++ = middle   + = less   - = no or not known

3.4 Ethical Aspects and E-E Television

Entertainment-Education involves various ethical considerations in theory and practice. Thus it is striking to examine these considerations, especially in the entertainment TV context, where several ethical questions and dilemmas can arise when experts from the prosocial field and TV makers team up. Ethics is a branch of philosophy that studies the principles and implications of right and wrong in human conduct and they are very complex.[83] Many tensions can arise when it comes to questions like 'Should entertainment be used to persuade?' 'How is prosocial defined?' 'Who decides what E-E messages are promoted?' 'How subtle should the message be?' 'How much should one compromise about her or his own professional standards?'

Interestingly enough, rarely do genetic scholars worry about the ethics of cloning methods, which may save lives. It is equally rare to find social workers who worry about the ethics of introducing family planning methods. Or environmentalists who worry about the ethics of promoting climate protection strategies to convince people to individually protect the environment because climate change is caused by

---

[83] In Entertainment-Education, the collaboration partners have to deal with, for example, (1) diverse disciplines (theories, methods, settings), (2) vulnerable groups (drug dependent, marginalized, stigmatized, those suffering from health inequalities or poverty or lack of rights) and (3) a challenging field of work that requires partnership with other professionals.

human beings (Singhal & Rogers, 1999). Most of the criticism comes from 'outside', and this is where tensions arise (Brown & Singhal, 1997; Singhal & Rogers, 1999).

Obviously, Entertainment-Education can do good, but it can also be misused. What are the core ethical struggles E-E implementers are confronted with when they work together in collaborations? To deal with this question, the first section gives a brief overview of ethical approaches (i.e. the 'meta ethics' or moral frameworks which can be used in Entertainment-Education). Here it is clarified why communitarianism (i.e. focusing on the community and the context as an ethics of duty) is the best theoretical approach for Entertainment-Education. Furthermore, a differentiation between three ethic levels is made. After that, the second section gives a short description of persuasion, manipulation and propaganda and their relation to entertainment TV and Entertainment-Education is given. Also, these terms are reflected in relation to the Nazi regime, as being striking for the German context. Finally, the third section illustrates the ethical dilemmas that experts from prosocial change organizations and TV makers have to deal with while collaborating.

This chapter does not aim to give answers to the ethical struggles in Entertainment-Education; indeed, it raises even more questions than answers in discussing them.

3.4.1 Theoretical Approaches

Bouman & Brown (2008b) identify three ethical approaches that have been used in the context of E-E collaborations: utilitarianism, contractarianism and communitarianism.

The ***utilitarian approach*** was primarily used in the 20th century. The philosophy of utilitarianism is based on the values of consequences. Following the British philosophers Jeremy Bentham (1748-1832) and John Stuart Mill (1806-1873), who mainly influenced this approach, right and wrong are seen as what leads to good and bad consequences (Bouman & Brown, 2008b). The utility is the ultimate appeal of all ethical decisions. In short, this approach emphasizes that the end justifies the means, if the end is good and useful and contributes to man's happiness. The most ethical decisions are those resulting in the greatest good for the greatest number of people. Interestingly, utilitarianism says that everyone must aspire to the greatest good for the community (Bouman & Brown, 2008b). This brings up one of the more striking critiques of the approach: why should an individual aspire to the 'greater good' for the community? From logical standpoint, there is no reason that people serve the 'greater good' in any situation for many reasons. Take, for example, a family-planning campaign that follows the higher good of reducing the HIV/AIDS rate in India. E-E implementers who have been working in the communities know how much this 'higher good' differs from people's reality. Religious issues, tabooing and stigmatizing HIV/AIDS as well as low levels of education lead to conditions where people abandon acting according to the 'greater good'. Conclusively, this approach broadly ignores the ***community context in which ethical decisions are made*** (ibid.). Additionally, the utilitarian approach follows the logic that the greatest good for the greatest number means, in consequence, that 'the good' is distributed. But this argument significantly changes depending on the viewpoint. For example, the German government promotes communication campaigns against domestic violence, because they believe in the 'greater good' of gender quality, human rights and not to harm others. By way of comparison, in Saudi Arabia it is within a man's right to control his wife, even if that control includes violence against her. He is allowed to abuse her, if he thinks that this is justified. People from a western cultural background consider this as a clear signal of gender inequality and negligence of human rights.

The second approach, the *contractarianism*, focuses on the right to equal liberty, which is considered greater than the autonomy of individuals. Primarily advocated by John Rawls (1999), it emphasizes the intrinsic value of rightness over the notion of consequences for the common good (Feinberg, 1980). Using this ethical approach in E-E projects does not seem to make much sense, because Entertainment-Education aims to change individual behavior, but also tries to initiate a social change in society (Bouman & Brown, 2008b). Thus, an ethical approach should recognize the value of the individual and the social context in which people live and interact. Nonetheless, the *contractarian* approach ignores the context of community decision-making (ibid.).

The ethical approach that is particularly advocated in E-E interventions is the *communitarianism* (Bouman & Brown, 2008b). It stresses the relationships and interdependence of people, giving preference to values like peace, fairness, solidarity, honesty, justice, reciprocity, stability and sympathy (Bouman & Brown, 2008b; Christians, 2006). The approach is based on the ethics of duty and not on ethics of consequences (see contractarian approach) or rights to equal liberty (see utilitarian approach). This means that the communitarianism judges on what is right and wrong on the basis of ***external values existing within a society or community frame*** (Bouman & Brown, 2008b).

In recent years, these external values have been used as so called *core values* (chapter 2.4.3.1) when prosocial change organizations and TV makers team up for a 'greater good'. Setting E-E core values – such as the depiction of gender equality or the respectful treatment of the environment by showing characters going by bike or recycling waste – ***means balancing individual and community needs and responsibilities***. Entertainment-Education wants to provide prosocial information and static assumptions of increasing knowledge. But furthermore, it aims to create personal involvement, emotion, empathy and dialogue with the community members. The communitarian approach takes both aspects – the increase in knowledge and the interpersonal involvement – into account and it has gained support from several communication scholars working in the prosocial field (Bayer et al., 2003; Bouman & Brown, 2008b; Callahan, 2003; Callahan & Jennings, 2002; Etzioni, 1998; White & Popovits, 2001). They argue that the communitarianism follows the ethical logic that prosocial decisions are adopted, rejected or reinvented in community and interaction forms.

Bouman & Brown (2008b) point out that there is lack of theoretical models, which help E-E implementers apply the communitarian ethics to prosocial campaigns and collaborative work. Thus, future research may provide assistance by investigating these models.

Following Coady & Bloch (2002) the theoretical ethics or meta ethics described in the last section can also be characterized as a '*code of ethics*', because they portray principles comprising values and visions. Furthermore, and apart from this theoretical level of the ethical discussion, the authors compile a second ethical level: normative ethics. These are guidelines or procedurals such as professional codes or research guidelines, often described as '*codes of conduct*'. This normative level can be considered an applied ethical level. Furthermore, a third ethical level exists, and this is micro ethics in practice (i.e. raising questions such as, 'Can I change the message's appeal/effectiveness through the use of fear?'). This level can be summarized as '*codes of practice*' and is most relevant for appliance in reality. An overview of Coady & Bloch's three different ways of defining ethics as well as their frameworks and code forms is given in the following table 3.3.

Table 3.3: Ethics, their frameworks and codes.

	Ethics form	Ways of defining ethics	Legal/ Governance framework	Sociological/ cultural framework	Forms of codes
Broad	Meta ethics (Theory)	Moral frameworks/theory • Utilitarism – Focus on consequences autonomy • Contractarian – Focus on rights to equal liberty • Communitarianism – Focus on community and context and ethics of duty	Principles	Values & norms	Code of ethics
	Normative ethics (Applied)	Procedural/guidelines • International charters • Professional codes • Research guidelines • Policy and procedures	Policies	Norms & attitudes	Code of Conduct
Specific	Micro ethics (Applied)	In practice (i.e. bioethics) • Can I have a control group that does not receive the E-E message? • Can I persuade with this fear message appeal?	Rule	Behaviors & action	Code of Practice

Source: Illustration based on Brown (2008b) and Coady & Bloch (2002)

According to Bettinghaus & Cody (1994), E-E implementers should constantly work on different ethical aspects by (1) creating ethical standards guiding their behavior, (2) knowing all they can about persuasion models and their effects, (3) establishing criteria for decision making, and (4) relating to reliable resources of messages. Coady & Bloch (1996) add that the legislative authorities should take care of discussing and establishing these codes with E-E implementers (ibid.). Examining how far developed the just-described recommendations are and to which extent they are applicable within the German collaboration context might be an issue to discuss in the part II of the thesis (chapter 9).

3.4.2 Persuasion, Manipulation and Propaganda

As outlined above and in chapter 2.1, Entertainment-Education is a form of persuasive communication.[84] Furthermore, Entertainment-Education might even be considered in terms of "indirect communication", or even manipulation and propaganda. For example, one pillar in the ethical discourse about Entertainment-Education refers to 'making propaganda in disguise' and 'manipulating the audience' with TV messages. This is especially true for the German context, as further explanation will reveal. For a more balanced discussion, it may be useful to look at the definitions of the terms persuasion, manipulation and propaganda, and to find intersections and differentiations among them. In this way, it may be possible to clarify some of the aspects brought up in the ethical discussions on Entertainment-Education and collaborations issues. In the following sections, the terms persuasion, manipulation and propaganda will be outlined more in detail.

3.4.2.1 Discussion of the Three Terms

Regarding the definition of persuasion, Bettinghaus & Cody (1994: 5-6) propose the following: "As a minimal condition, to be labeled as persuasive, a communication situation must involve a conscious attempt by one individual or group to change the attitudes, beliefs, or behavior of another individual or group of individuals through the transmission of some message".

Persuasion implicates that the receivers of the message go through a ***change voluntarily***, without putting them under pressure or limiting them to other choices. They have the choice to change, and it is up to them, whether and when the time is 'right' for a change. Hence, the audience has the choice to watch the program, and they decide whether the shown messages affect them in their everyday life. In general, persuasion can be considered as a principle of human action that has been practiced since the early days of human history. Bettinghaus & Cody (1994: 29) add that "we all attempt to control the environment around us. We couldn't be living organisms if we didn't, and persuasion is but one way we use to fit ourselves into our society". Nonetheless, persuasion can have a negative connotation, especially if it is related to advertising issues, which is most applicable for the German context (Volpers et al., 2008).[85] A reason for this kind of negative connotation

---

[84] According to Severin & Tankard (2001), the major models of persuasion are McGuire's (1968, 2001) information processing theories, the dual-process models like Petty and Cacioppo's (1986) elaboration likelihood model and the Chaiken, Liberman & Eagly's (1989) heuristic systematic model (see chapter 2.3.7).

[85] Communication scholars discuss the placement of persuasive messages for commercial products in TV programs under the term product placement (Johansson, 2001; Müller, 1997). While product placement is legally allowed in the USA or in the Netherlands for a longer time, in Germany it had been forbidden for decades. However, due to several reasons (chapter 6.1), product placement has been legal in Germany since April 2010. In addition to

might also be that, from a literary standpoint, the border between persuasion and manipulation is often unclear. Communication scholars have broadly discussed whether the use of persuasion leads to manipulation. On the one hand, academic discourse refers to manipulation as a tool, whereby there is a conscious attempt to change behavior, and thus persuasion conclusively results in manipulation (Bettinghaus & Cody, 1994). On the other hand, scholarly discourse makes a clear distinction between persuasion and manipulation. From this point of view, ***manipulative communication*** is encouraging people to change or to do something on behalf of the ***selfish and advantage-taking nature of the sender*** of the message and ***not on behalf of the best interest of the receiver*** (Brown, 1958). Reardon (1991) adds that manipulative communication can be distinguished from persuasive communication in that the manipulative message includes *false promises*.

The use of the word manipulation has come to have a very negative meaning. Rorty (1982: 204) calls this communication research field the "dark side of social science". As discussed, the literature refers to clear differences between persuasion and manipulation; nonetheless, in their everyday use, the terms are often applied interchangeably since many people are not well aware of their distinctions.

While the word 'persuasion' may be negatively perceived when associated with the word 'manipulation', it is even more negatively perceived in connection with the word 'propaganda' (Dillard & Pfau, 2002; Severin & Tankard, 2001). However, scholars find clear differentiations in academic discussions. According to Petty & Cacioppo (1981), ***propaganda*** is used to refer to an attempt by one individual or agency to change the view of others in order to ***further one's own cause or damage an opposing one***. In short, when an act of sending media messages benefits the source, but not the receiver, this can be called propaganda. Usually, propaganda promotes a particular ideology (Bettinghaus & Cody, 1994). In practice, there have recently been several attempts to label another groups' persuasion campaign or TV formats as propaganda. These include using expressions such as 'pro-life distortion campaigns' or 'pro choice propaganda piece'. Nonetheless, from a scholarly standpoint, propaganda is used to bias information, withhold information that harms one's own view, teach nonfactual as true information or make an opinion appear as facts (ibid.).

---

product placement, the topic placement is currently a grey zone in Germany's media legislation. For example, what if a company does advertising on a theme (e.g. a country or the topic of resource efficiency) and relates this (subtly) to their product or service? Or, to put the question another way, what if the prosocial theme is considered a product by the implementers and thus legitimized through the legislation of product placement? These issues have not been well regulated yet and, regarding the discussion around product and topic placement, some of the German E-E interventions for prosocial purposes had been lumped together with other commercial forms communicating persuasive messages (Holzapfel, 2007; Johansson, 2001; also see chapter 6.1 and chapter 8.2.5). In any case, these developments make the discussion regarding Entertainment-Education even more interesting and worth examining, both in terms of reflecting the lessons learned and in making recommendations for future practice (chapter 9).

At this point it should have become apparent that there are differences between the three terms: persuasion covers a 'voluntary change', manipulation includes advantages for the senders, it is not in the best interest of the receivers and false promises are given, and propaganda damages the receivers' view. Nevertheless, there is *no absolute criterion to draw a clear line* between these communication forms – it is rather a judgment someone makes.

As hinted above, the linked association between propaganda, manipulation and persuasion is especially true in German culture (O'Brien, 2004). When German people hear the word propaganda, they are likely to associate the word manipulation or even persuasion. This fact colors the ethical discourse of Entertainment-Education and prosocial collaborations for Germany even more.[86] Clearly, Entertainment-Education is a form of persuasive communication and should normally be used to do good and no harm. However, entertainment media – and especially entertainment TV – have been misused many times in history before to spread false information or damage audience members' views under the guise of 'educating' people. This happened especially under the Nazi regime in Germany, which is one of the main reasons why the ethical discussion is so sensitive in German society. For many Germans, there is a clear line of association from persuasion (Entertainment-Education) to manipulation or even to propaganda. This tendency is a part of the culture, the collective memory or zeitgeist of the Germans (also see chapter 7.4), which needs to be discussed and handled very carefully in the field of governmental or prosocial communication (chapter 7.3). As part of being a crucial prerequisite for understanding how sensitive the German discussion around the E-E strategy as a persuasive communication method might be, it is important to understand more about Germany's past and the use of entertainment in fictional formats for the purpose of influencing people during the Third Reich. Therefore, some of the activities of the Nazi regime – namely their misuse of entertainment TV to promote their inhuman ideological worldview – will be briefly touched upon in the next section. This may give hints into why the approach of prosocial organizations collaborating with TV makers is, to some degree, a sensitive topic in public (see also chapter 7.3).

3.4.2.2 Relations to the Nazi Regime

The Nazis extensively used entertainment films as 'educating pieces' to glorify the regime and 'teach' the audience lessons. Following Bramsted (1956), propaganda messages that 'successfully reached' the audience are based on two striking conditions which are similar to many other governmental propaganda approaches (e.g. those seen in Stalin's Soviet Union or the Mao's China). Firstly, the Nazis had essentially a communication monopoly. Secondly, the propaganda was wedded to terror and backed up by force.[87] Joseph Goebbels, the Nazi minister of propaganda, is

---

[86] How the collaboration partners handle this issue is depicted in depth in part II of the thesis.

[87] For example, if one's neighbor expressed a dissenting view, he could disappear from his

reported to have said, "a sharp sword must always stand behind propaganda if it is to be really effective" (Bramsted, 1956: 450). Sadly enough, the Nazis were very aware of the impact narrative storytelling can have on people, and they misused it for their regime purposes. Some scholars argue that the Nazis were in a unique position of using entertainment television for spreading their 'toxic' ideology, because the TV was a new medium at that time and people related to it as a 'magical tool' which they believed in almost without question (McQuail, 2005, see section 3.1.2). According to O'Brien (2004) and Staudenmaier (1996), the Nazis used the following techniques in their entertainment messages to reach the audience in front of the television:

- Positive and negative role models for identifying and modeling the behavior in everyday life,[88]
- Selective forms of realism in portraying heroes,
- Showing exaggerated, unrealistic situations and the reactions of characters,
- Optimistic portrayal of the world,
- Transporting universal Nazi values,
- Intensively involving health and environmental issues by (1) glorifying the nature of the 'Vaterland' (home country) and (2) showing strong, tall and blond Aryan character stereotypes. Environmental messages were used to emotionally connect people to the beauty of the 'Vaterland' and its sustainable preservation. Health messages were utilized to communicate a healthy lifestyle and a good body shape for protecting the 'Vaterland' against the 'enemy'.

The misuse of entertainment television during the Nazi regime still has striking influence in Germany's culture. Given this background, German society is justifiably more critical when it comes to the use of media entertainment in terms of 'persuading' people to 'change their attitude and behavior' than, for example, in the USA or in the Netherlands. Conclusively, the ethical discussion must stand at the forefront when German E-E projects and partnerships are designed and implemented; likewise, a detailed reflection on which collaboration form to choose, etc. should take place (part II of the thesis).

---

home during the middle of the night, never to be seen again.

[88] One example is the famous piece by Leni Riefenstahl called Olympia, which portrayed the Olympic games in 1936 as a media event of unparalled propaganda value. A second example is the film Wunschkonzert (Request concert). In Wunschkonzert the characters of Inge Wagner (Ilse Werner) and Herbert Koch (Carl Raddatz) served as 'positive role models'. They meet at the Olympic ceremony, have several romantic trips in nature environments like the Berlin Wannsee and marry afterwards. When Herbert is called to serve the country in the war, Inge accepts her patriotic duty to endure separation stoically without knowing its purpose. At the end they are rewarded. Inge and Herbert are the typical war role models: she waits patiently for her man, remaining loyal to him while he puts his military duty and honor above all personal desires (O'Brien, 2004). 'Negative role models' are represented by those trying (but ultimately failing) to harm the regime (ibid.).

3.4.3 Ethical Dilemmas

With the help of Entertainment-Education, audience members should be persuade to change their knowledge, attitude and behavior voluntarily. For picking up and dealing with this issue of 'latently persuading people', the E-E strategy has undergone several proactive steps to be ethical over the past decades. As depicted in chapter 2.3.3, Sabido has established a moral framework to ensure that the values promoted are preserved in the countries' constitution and legislation. In this context, agreement on the program's value grid signed by the involved stakeholders – broadcast media officials, government officials, commercial sponsors, etc. – guides the process of producing the program. Sabido has also suggested involving local producers and scriptwriters to work on the program, ensuring that it is culturally sensitive, authentic and incorporates local language. Subject matter specialist in health, social and environmental issues should additionally insure the accuracy of the shown program content. Moreover, formative, process and summative research helps (1) to analyze and anticipate the viewer's needs and desires (2) to produce programs that fit to the audience's real life experience and (3) to understand the program's effects. By portraying positive, negative and transitional role model behavior and realistic consequences, the audience members can draw their own conclusions, reinforced by the epilogue of the program.[89] Furthermore, the suggestion was made in section 3.4.1 to involve a code of ethical practices and a code of conduct to strengthen the ethical discussion in Entertainment-Education.

Those proactive measures in ethics do not seem to be sufficient enough to dissolve the discourse, specifically when taking into consideration that the latter ones were primarily designed for non-western country settings. Clearly, when trying to convey them to western countries, the situation completely differs, especially in Germany where media legislations demand that TV makers may not be influenced by external entities (see chapter 6.1). Therefore, it is necessary to reflect on these details, as will be done in part II of the thesis. Nonetheless, E-E research brought up and discussed different ethical dilemmas which not only count and might be applied in non-western country settings, but which the implementers of E-E collaborations in media-saturated countries are also confronted with and must at least be aware of (Bouman, 1999; Bouman & Brown, 2008b; Brown & Singhal, 1990; Brown & Singhal, 1993; Brown & Singhal, 1997; Singhal & Rogers, 1999). These eight dilemmas are outlined as follows.

3.4.3.1 Prosocial Development Dilemma

The most important ethical dilemma reflects the fundamental question of whether it is right to use the mass media as a persuasive communication tool for helping

---

[89] Sabido makes these suggestions within the frame of designing and implementing E-E collaborations in non-western countries. As chapter 4 shows, approaches from western countries have reframed Sabido's suggestions and have developed several new strategies, which tackle E-E collaborations and the confrontation with ethical considerations in their specific context.

people change in terms of prosocial issues. However, critics who argue it is not right should acquiesce to the fact that it is *virtually impossible* to produce value-free entertainment messages. In this context, the *MINTIFF* program[90] (Falkenroth, 2010) found out that the latter argument plays a crucial role in ethical discussions in Germany, especially when arguing for an increased application of the E-E strategy. Entertainment messages in daily soaps, reality or quiz shows tell the viewer stories about what can be considered as right or wrong, good or bad (Bettinghaus & Cody, 1994; Gottberg, 2007; Guttman, 2000; Linssen, 2008; Samaniego & Cortés Pascual, 2007). Making the point that persuasive communication is unethical and should therefore be avoided denies the media reality. Bettinghaus & Cody (1994) suggest that persuasive communication cannot be purged in a democratic society. In this regard, arguing that it is unethical to promote prosocial behavior in media formats like television or radio seems inconsistent with democratic freedom in society. A serious attempt to dissolve the dilemma would be to take into consideration not communicating at all. Watzlawick et al. (1969) make the point that even communicating nothing means taking position towards an issue and can be value-laden.

This dilemma is not easy to solve, because what is prosocial or what can be considered prosocial behavior depends on the nature of the behavior being promoted and on who decides whether a behavior is prosocial. In general, E-E programs have focused in past years on unquestionable values such as sexual responsibility, disease prevention, environmental protection, saving energy and resources. Who wants people to be infected with diseases? Who wants to live in polluted environment? No one would disagree. However, the acceptance of the prosocial messages depends on various factors, such as the exact prosocial theme or the context, in which it is communicated. For instance, everyone would agree that living a healthy lifestyle or refusing domestic violence is a reasonable expectation in western country settings. There is also general agreement about protecting the environment, but disagreements might arise, when more specific issues are promoted such as the use of renewable energies like solar or wind power (also see Lubjuhn & Pratt, 2009). Here, the range of acceptance of what can be 'prosocially promoted' to the German society seems to be narrow and need to be carefully reflected (also see chapter 7.2).

3.4.3.2 Prosocial Content Dilemma

The prosocial content dilemma raises the question of how to differentiate between prosocial and antisocial behavior. Some viewers might perceive prosocial what other individuals would sense as antisocial. Pro-euthanasia groups, which support the choice of terminally ill human beings to control their deaths, consider a media messages about euthanasia as prosocial. Anti-euthanasia groups that support the rights of each human being to stay alive regardless of the status of her or his disease consider such a message as antisocial. Another example comes from the field of avoiding HIV/AIDS and pregnancy. In the past, the Catholic Church considered

---
[90] For more information on the program see chapter 8.3.1.1.

any HIV/AIDS and unplanned pregnancy campaign for young women which promotes the use of condoms as 'unethical', 'antisocial' and 'not sustainable'. For them, a prosocial campaign would have primarily encompassed the promotion of sexual abstinence.[91]

Labeling an issue means doing a value judgment. In various countries, stakeholders such as policy makers have a lot of power to control and frame these issues. They can, depending on the country, have a strong part in the decision making process, especially in terms of what can be considered as pro- or antisocial. This leads to the next dilemma.

3.4.3.3 The Source Dilemma

The third dilemma deals with the question: who decides what is prosocial, which audience should be targeted and which messages should be sent? In the past, national governments have played a core role in conveying messages in E-E interventions, especially in non-western countries. Likewise, in the Netherlands the national government is involved in this context. When raising the question in Germany about who decides whether the message is a pro-social or an anti-social one and if and how it will be aired, the definite answer is that the TV makers decide. They have to decide according to the law and on the principles of freedom of the press (and without being influenced by other parties) which message content they send. So the source-centered dilemma about who decides what is a good or bad, a prosocial or antisocial message is a central one (see also part II of this thesis) because at this point it comes to the question of which rights the TV makers and the prosocial stakeholders have by law to decide on and influence the program content. This issue will be an interesting point when it comes to the focus of Germany's E-E collaborations. Another question is what assurance is there that the government leaders or TV makers and journalists would use this approach appropriately? There is no guarantee on these issues, and several cases of misuse have been documented in the literature (Holzapfel, 2007; O'Brien, 2004; Volpers et al., 2008).

3.4.3.4 The Audience Segmentation Dilemma

The audience segmentation dilemma reflects the E-E strategy in terms of targeting the prosocial message towards a specific audience. Audience segmentations are made (see section 3.3.1) in order to reach a relatively homogeneous group with the media message. For example, the Dutch celebrity reality show *Echt Elly* (Albeda College, 2009; Lubjuhn & Hoffhaus, 2009), which deals with sustainable consumption patterns, was targeted to societal groups with low educational backgrounds, having an immigrant background and living in the suburbs of Rotterdam. The implementers of the show specifically wanted to deal with their problems and show alternative action strategies in the field of prosocial consumption. However,

---

[91] Recently, under Pope John Paul II., the Catholic Church has changed their stances on this, indicating that condom use to prevent HIV prevention is acceptable for those who choose not to be abstinent.

segmenting the audience for educational reasons may mean to exclude other important audience segments like adolescents, people having a higher educational background or people living in rural areas and facing maybe some similar problems.

3.4.3.5 The Oblique Persuasion Dilemma
Singhal & Rogers (1999: 220) note about this dilemma "the Entertainment-Education strategy takes an oblique route to persuasion by sugarcoating the lessons in part to break down the individuals' learning defenses to the educational messages". In fact, subtly learning about prosocial issues while being entertained is one of the key elements of Entertainment-Education. The implementers of E-E programs are sometimes criticized for using subtle messages and 'playing a game' with the viewers whom they influence, often without their conscious knowledge. However, recent studies point out that (1) viewers realize, the messages are entertaining and educational at the same time and (2) that viewers prefer to lean some lessons while they are entertained (Kaiser Family Foundation, 2008; Kennedy et al., 2004; Morgan et al., 2009; Movius et al., 2007; Whittier et al., 2005). The foremost indicator for viewers' enjoyment of E-E programs is the ***audience ratings***. For example, *Grey's Anatomy, Desperate Housewives* and *Private Practice* have implemented various E-E messages on HIV/AIDS, sexually transmitted diseases, organ donation and cancer in their storylines (see chapter 4.2), and the ratings of these shows are constantly high regardless of their 'embedded' E-E messages.

3.4.3.6 The Socio-Cultural Equality Dilemma
This dilemma debates the question of how to ensure that prosocial television maintains socio-cultural equality among audience members. Following Gudykunst & Kim (1984) socio-cultural equality means reading each social and cultural group with the same value or importance. In countries with a high degree of homogeneity, there is high consensus concerning a society's normative beliefs and behaviors. For example, Japan has a high cultural homogeneity (around 99%), which means that they have fewer problems agreeing on what is prosocial and prosocial behavior than people coming from the USA and Australia where the homogeneity index is lower (Kurian, 1984).
Ensuring socio-cultural equality through prosocial television is especially important in countries with a long immigration tradition or where people from various ethnicities, linguistic and religious backgrounds live together (e.g. in India).

3.4.3.7 The Unintended Effect Dilemma
The seventh dilemma refers to unintended effects. It takes into account that a prosocial development is a complex phenomenon whose consequences are not always foreseeable. Those undesirable effects often result from the diffusion of messages. Several examples of unintended effects are given in chapter 2.5 and 2.6.

3.4.3.8 Professional Role Dilemma

The last ethical concern refers to the paradox of the professional standards of the collaboration partners. Prosocial experts working with health or environmental issues tend to neglect and thus violate the standards of the television professionals in the collaborative process (Bouman, 1999; Bouman & Brown, 2008b). One dilemma they have to deal with is how to overcome or close the gap between their respective goals, which are, on the one hand, to inform, educate and motivate viewers to make a choice for prosocial lifestyles and on the other hand, to get high audience ratings by telling entertaining and 'real life' stories. For experts from governmental (related) agencies, this goes with an understanding that entertainment television will never adapt their agenda one-to-one in their storylines. Beck (2009) suggests that for collaboration issues these experts should learn and understand the 'rules' of the television field and, with this background in mind, they have a more realistic view of what the 'possible' goals and outcomes of the collaboration can be.

3.5 Summary

This chapter has presented the field of entertainment television. The focus had been on theoretical and practical perspectives in this field when promoting prosocial issues through E-E collaborations.

In the beginning, the role of television as a 'social institution' was discussed from several viewpoints. The culturally critical perspective of the Frankfurter School relates to television as a tool of almighty ideological influence. The Birmingham School emphasizes that the medium still gains manipulative power, but the audience is pushed into a more active position, as emancipators of a critical mass, interpreting and giving their own meaning to the TV messages. Postmodernism shows the medium using a hedonistic view, where audience members play an emancipator role in interpreting messages according to their individual background.

Television has changed its meaning and purposes according to the historical and societal developments that occurred over decades. Recent developments point at a globally drawn 'entertainment era'. It has become obvious that, from a TV research standpoint, no clear cause-effect statements can be made about the impact that entertainment TV has on audience members. Consequently, it is strongly recommended to ***investigate the E-E television formats*** according to the collaboration form (chapter 4.2.1), its targeted audience members, its genre and several other components (e.g. broadcasting time, etc.) that may play an important role.

For investigating the impacts as well as the prosocial content or messages, experts from prosocial change organizations use different television research traditions when implementing their research on E-E programs: the social behavioral tradition, the critical tradition, the cultural studies tradition, the structuralism and semiology tradition, the uses & gratifications tradition as well as the agenda setting tradition. In contrast, TV professionals are primarily interested in research relating to audience ratings and they apply audience, TV content and also advertising research with the primary purpose of keeping these ratings high. The research conducted in the TV field bears a great potential also for the purposes of prosocial change field when specifying E-E contents in order to reach audience members effectively.

Different genres and their potentials to illustrate prosocial issues were also illuminated in this chapter. Analysis revealed that especially drama (e.g. daily soaps and telenovelas), game and quiz shows, detective programs and children's programs have great potential for portraying E-E topics aimed at changing behavior and spurring interpersonal communication. Comedies or talk shows have less potential in this regard.

Thus, both results from TV research traditions and genre analysis give useful hints for future E-E collaborations in Germany according to (1) how E-E research can be conducted and (2) which entertainment TV formats might be useful for promoting prosocial issues.

Finally, the ethical aspects prosocial change organizations and TV professionals have to be aware of when implementing Entertainment-Education in television programs were discussed. Germany's specific historical background, especially the Third Reich era, has a strong influence on how Entertainment-Education is perceived in society and among E-E implementers. It will be one of the tasks in part II of this thesis to cover this issue more comprehensively.

4. Good Practice Examples of Two Media Centers in the USA and the Netherlands

The first chapter dealt with basic principles of the thesis. Firstly, a research gap in the field of Germany's E-E collaborations was identified. Secondly – and based on this – the core research question (framed by the conditions and forms of German partnerships) was introduced. Finally, central definitions were presented.

The second chapter discussed the theories involved in Entertainment-Education as well as the societal groups, which are open to receiving affective-orientated messages. The third chapter debated the theoretical notions from an entertainment television perspective. Therefore, the entertainment television field and its potentials and pitfalls for sending prosocial messages were illuminated from different perspectives (societal approaches, entertainment television research, theories in the field of entertainment television genres as well as ethical approaches).

The following chapter presents theoretical aspects of E-E collaboration. Furthermore, the chapter analyzes the world's two most significant media centers, both of which create and implement E-E collaboration models in western countries (one in the USA and the other one in the Netherlands). Both the theoretical collaboration notions as well as the lessons learned from the media centers will be incorporated in the German analysis in part II (chapter 5.3.5).

The international centers make use of theoretically founded and research-based strategies while carrying out collaborative work. The core of these strategies comprises

1. using specific E-E partnership arrangements (E-E co-productions, E-E inscript participations, E-E service),
2. using strategic collaboration activities (such as briefings and consultations, section 4.2 and 4.3) to bring the prosocial and the entertainment side together,
3. doing formative, process and summative evaluation (see chapter 2.4) and
4. using E-E theories (see chapter 2.3) to reach media users with messages (specifically in the Netherlands).

For describing the two E-E media centers and their approaches, Papa, Singhal & Papa's (2006) theoretical concept of dialectical tensions for prosocial change will be used. The first section will examine **why this theory is beneficial** in outlining the two centers. Secondly, the media institutions will be presented according to **three dialectic tension fields**: (1) steering power and emancipation, (2) fragmentation and unity, (3) dialogue and dissemination. At the end of presenting each of the three dialectical tension fields, **insights are summarized**, which may contain fruitful advices and suggestions for the German E-E collaboration practice and which need to be scrutinized in depth in part II of the thesis. The chapter ends with a **summary of results**.

4.1 Theoretical Notions from the Dialectical Tension Concept for Prosocial Change

E-E collaborations take place in an environment of changes. These changes occur on two different levels. The first level refers to the changing effects the messages can have on the audience. Hence, the audience may be engaged to change their knowledge, attitude and behavior related to the prosocial issues on television. The second level of changes alludes to the collaboration process in which the partners are involved. An E-E collaboration may be considered a changing process itself – a process in which both sides explore 'new horizons' while they are working with each other. They are confronted with dialectics, contradictions and tensions along their joint way (Bouman, 1999; Bouman, 2004; Papa et al., 2006; Singhal, 2008a). For example, the collaborative partners frequently recognize how difficult it is 'getting connected' with the other side and that changes have to occur for both the partners and themselves when aiming at a win-win situation. This, for example, is especially challenging in the USA where the E-E partner serves as a resource to the TV partner who makes all the decisions about content.

One of the core goals when establishing E-E collaboration approaches in the USA and the Netherlands has been to reduce the dialectic tensions in the collaborative process and to contribute to a better understanding among the partners. The E-E approaches in use are based on the assumption that the collaborative partners have to (more or less) change something when they work together. As this is not an easy process, the E-E collaboration centers guide and advise both sides in their changing processes, and they develop and implement tools for building bridges between them. In the USA and the Netherlands, it was a journey of exploration, inconsistencies and tensions until effective and successful models were established. Furthermore, the approaches are in a continuous process of development and improvement (Beck, 2004; Bouman, 1999). Researchers and practitioners are constantly working to find additional collaboration methods for reducing dialectics and tensions between the collaboration partners and thus contribute to an even more advanced strategy for both partner sides.

Given this background, some theoretical notions from the dialectical tension concept (Papa et al., 2006) may incorporate useful components for analyzing the approaches of the media institutions in the USA and the Netherlands. Papa, Singhal & Papa (2006) discovered during their investigations on four different institutional settings for prosocial change that many dialectic tensions surface. Based on their analysis, they argue that these dialectical tensions are central to the process of organizing a prosocial change.

This thesis suggests that the two pioneering media centers can be related to these institutional settings for the above-mentioned reasons. In this chapter, the media centers will be portrayed according to three dialectical tensions (following Papa et al., 2006): (1) steering power and emancipation; (2) fragmentation and unity (3) dissemination and dialogue.[92] Figure 4.1 gives an overview over the dialectical tensions in E-E collaborations.

Figure 4.1: Developing and implementing E-E collaborations embody multiple, co-existing dialectic tensions

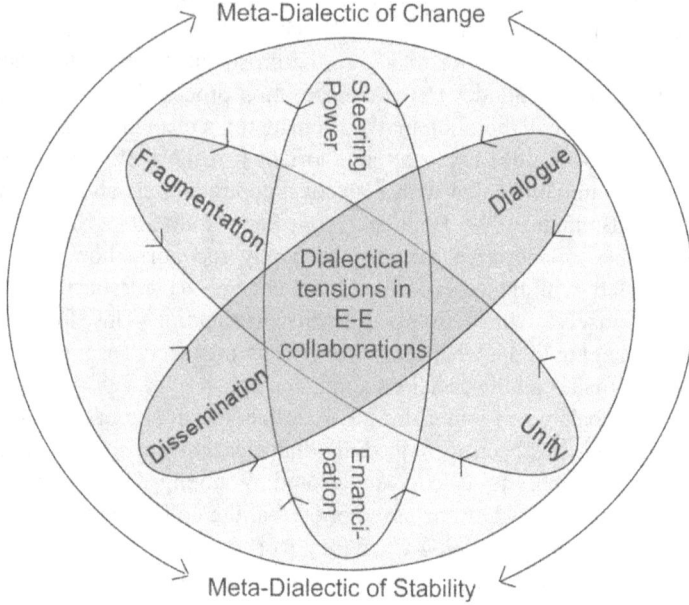

Source: Own illustration according to Papa, Singhal & Papa (2006: 61)

Obviously, the theory was chosen to put the focus on dialectic tensions, inconsistencies and contradictions, which are a central component when designing and implementing E-E collaboration models.

4.1.1 The Dialectic of Steering Power and Emancipation

The tension between steering power and emancipation is adequate for describing the *environment and the group of agents* in the collaboration field.

The E-E media centers do not exist in a vacuum where they connect the prosocial and the TV side. In both countries, there are different groups of agents (e.g. governmental (related) organizations, media stakeholders, research institutes, universities or NGOs) that interrelate with or are part of the media centers. Their legislative and societal roles have a huge impact on how the collaborations work. For example, from a legislative perspective, the prosocial organizations might not be al-

---

[92] The dialectical tensions used for the portrayal of the media centers are reframed and fitted to the specific context.

lowed to share a financial budget with the TV makers, which would have an immense impact on how collaborations are established and practiced. This also clarifies that some stakeholders can have more steering power than others and, furthermore, some can be in a more 'emancipated' role. For instance, Hollywood producers can steer the collaboration with health experts because they are comprised of powerful private industry companies with a vast amount of financial resources available (section 4.2.3), whereas the situation in the Netherlands is different (section 4.3).

4.1.2 The Dialectic of Fragmentation and Unity

In both the USA and the Netherlands, the media centers and their collaboration approaches came into existence according to a specific *history of events*. A tide of events took place leading, step-by-step, to the development and the implementation of the centers. Most of these events have been initiated consciously (e.g. through the prosocial organizations, universities and private stakeholders like consultants). Therefore, it may make sense to talk about an *agenda setting process*. For instance in the Netherlands, it was mainly due to the Center for Media & Health that the Dutch E-E collaboration approach established (see section 4.3.4). In the USA, the federal government's Centers for Disease Control and Prevention (CDC) was unique in developing an E-E collaboration to address a broad spectrum of disease and injury topics, with an agenda to design an E-E program for public health (see section 4.2.4).[93] Nonetheless, these processes have been full of tensions because multiple voices and interpretations on how to initiate and implement such an E-E collaboration agenda were continuously present. Thus, the process of 'agenda-setting' occurred with many fragmentations. On the one hand, these many voices may be necessary to preserve diversity in the creation process of the model. On the other hand, these differences may create tensions, separating people rather than unifying them and thus also creating risks. Both dialectical sides may be a reason why the agenda setting processes in the USA and the Netherlands frequently seem to proceed in intricate developments (i.e. going two steps forward and one step back). The people who worked on establishing an E-E agenda had to overcome many of these fragmentation struggles, and they had to find ways for unifying the different voices to ensure that the collaboration was beneficial for both sides and across all funding agencies.

4.1.3 The Dialectic of Dialogue and Dissemination

The tension between dialogue and dissemination is beneficial for clarifying the centers' *collaboration models* and their *activities, projects and tools*.
The Dutch and the US media centers have applied several activities to bring the health and the entertainment television sides together. A core activity of their

---

[93] Other federal government organizations attempted similar E-E collaborations, but with a much more narrow agenda, restricted by a single health theme and a single funding organization.

everyday business is to disseminate information and to initiate dialogue. Dialogue involves sharing information, ideas, stories and experience and thus serves to validate knowledge and resources through an interactive learning process. Dissemination, in contrast to that, mainly comprises situations in which information (such as tip sheets, see section 4.2.5) is handed over to the partner side. The partners then can get involved and reflect on their own. The relationship of dialogue and dissemination is also of great interest. Borders between both can be fluid. In this part, questions according to the proportions of both dialectics are raised. These include: when a health expert and a TV producer make use of a collaboration activity which promotes dialogue (e.g. a telephone consultation) (see section 4.2.5), is there also an element of dissemination? If so, how is it involved? And, if comprehensible, how did this develop over time? For example, maybe originally an activity was exclusively designed to evoke dialogue, and later disseminating elements were added. Clearly, a dialectical tension between information dissemination and dialogue is very much present in the context of the collaboration activities and will be examined more in depth. The following figure sums up the approach for this chapter:

Figure 4.2: Analytical framework for illustrating the E-E media centers and their collaboration approaches

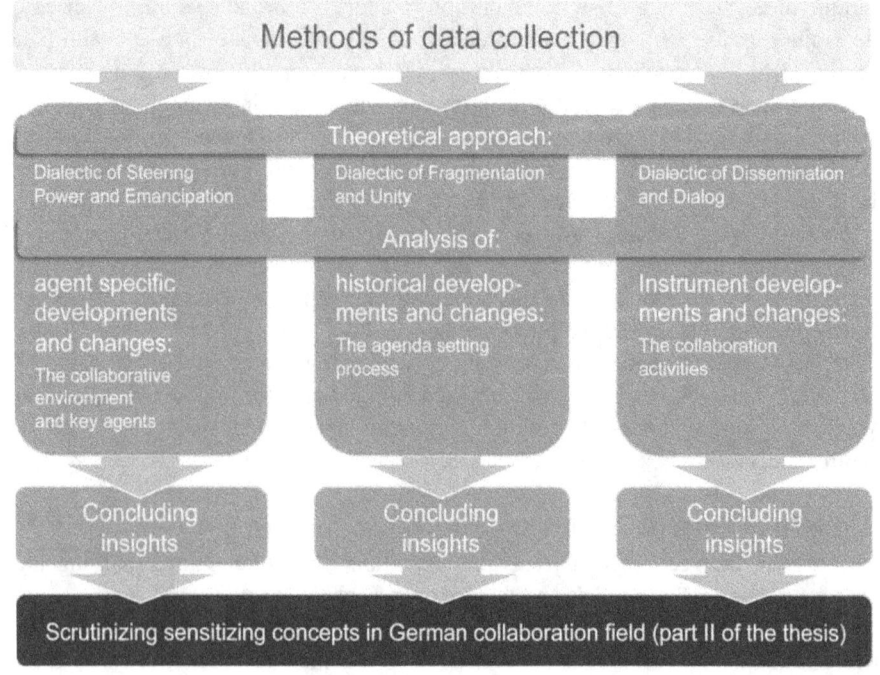

4.2 Hollywood, Health & Society Program, USC Norman Lear Center, Los Angeles, USA

"Before coming to Hollywood, Health & Society I worked in developing countries, where we had funding to produce or co-produce entertainment programming. This gave us control from beginning to end. Hollywood, Health & Society is a completely different model. It flips the model upside down on its head. Hollywood, Health & Society focuses on providing accurate, up-to-date health information to Hollywood's scriptwriters and producers to inspire TV health storylines. We do not produce and we do not pay for it. The reason why the model works is because we are a free, on-demand resource. We don't tell writers what to write. This is important to clarify. We respect writers as fine artists and master storytellers. What we do provide them with is inspiration and "real stories of real people" through expert consultations. We make it easy for them to access accurate information".

- Sandra de Castro Buffington, 2008

Analyzing Data

Readers may note that in both media center contexts of organizing for social change explored in section 4.2 and 4.3, the same approach of data analysis was used. For reasons of efficiency, this data analysis process will only be illustrated in this chapter and not in chapter 4.3.

The data collection through participant observation, interviews, informal conversations, literature and material review was analyzed in a continuous, cyclical process using Morse (1994) and Morse & Field (1995). They suggest applying a four stage-conceptualization of qualitative data analysis: comprehending, synthesizing, theorizing, recontextualizing. Comprehending comprised the selection of the most appropriate methodological approaches (i.e. entering the field, learning what is going on, trying to make sense of the data and identifying when enough data is gathered to offer a rough description of the research phenomenon). In the synthesizing stage, the field notes, summaries and transcripts were analyzed to get a sense of what is typical about the phenomenon when putting introductory pieces together. After preliminary readings of the material, codings of the content were conducted and dominant themes were suggested. Then, an intensive reading began, where the codings and the dominant themes were put together in context and where they were re-defined. In the end, a framework for large order and small order themes emerged from the data. After this stage, it was possible to make some general comments on the research topic. This eventually led to a latter stage of data analysis, theorizing and recontextualization. The theorizing process can be considered as a „constant development and manipulation of malleable theoretical schemes until the 'best' theoretical scheme is developed" (Morse, 1994: 32). During the theorizing process, alternative explanations and phenomena under study were developed, and then these explanations were examined to determine their fit with the data. The next step of data collection includes a recontextualization. This involved finding ways in which theoretical explanations can be applied to other contexts, i.e. organizing the design and the implementation of E-E collaborations when comparing the Netherlands with the US results and coming up with insights for the German study (part II of the thesis).

4.2.1 Methods of Data Collection

Using the theoretical notions of dialectical tension of social change, this thesis interprets the approach of the Hollywood, Health & Society (HH&S) program, which is based at the Annenberg School for Communication's Norman Lear Center,[94] University of Southern California (USC). In order to do this, this thesis integrates (a) a study on materials (such as information brochures, leaflets, presentations, minutes and transcriptions of events, meetings and discussions rounds) and scholarly literature on the HH&S program (e.g. Arango & Stelter, 2009; Beck, 2000; Beck & Pollard, 2001; Beck, 2004; Beck, 2009; Lubjuhn & Bouman, 2009; Parvanta & Freimuth, 2000; Pollard & Beck, 2000; Salmon, 1994; Salmon, 2000; Stolberg, 2001; Wilson, 2002); (b) field studies (observations and interviews) of the HH&S program involving a total time period of twelve weeks (September 2008 - November 2008); (c) the communication with team members, researchers and practitioners working with HH&S, including two interviews with Vicki Beck, former director of HH&S (2002 - 2007), and Sandra Castro de Buffington, current director of HH&S (since 2008); and (d) video material on HH&S events and prosocial TV storylines which have arisen from the E-E collaborations initiated by HH&S.

Five current and former HH&S team members, four health experts and four Hollywood TV professionals in Los Angeles and bordering cities were interviewed in this matter. Three out of 14 interviews were done via telephone (two with health experts and one with a Hollywood producer). The face-to-face interviews with the team members and the HH&S partners were conducted in their workplaces. These included the HH&S office, the offices of health organizations, Hollywood production sets and private homes.[95] Pictures from important events and gatherings were

---

[94] The Norman Lear Center is a nonpartisan research and public policy media institution that studies the social, political, economic and cultural impact of entertainment on the world. The Lear Center was officially launched January 24, 2000.

[95] An overview on the interview partners is given in appendix 2.

taken, as were notes from significant conversations. All narrative, in-depth interviews were tape-recorded and analyzed by clustering important experiences and topics. At the end of several days, there was the possibility to discuss the impressions in informal settings with the team members and the collaborative partners of HH&S.

In addition to the personal and telephone interview previously described, the researcher, during various field visits, met informally with 22 E-E researchers, practitioners and pioneers working with HH&S. Thus, the analysis draws on data collected from approximately 36 people.

4.2.2 E-E Partnership Arrangement of Hollywood, Health & Society

Before describing the results from the dialectic change analysis in more detail, a short theoretical presentation of HH&S shall be given according to the E-E partnership arrangements. HH&S is an E-E service collaboration program. In chapter 4.2.1, E-E service collaborations were defined as 'a strategy of prosocial organizations to facilitate (through factual and timely information, contacts with experts, shooting locations, etc.) broadcasting organizations or production companies in dealing with a prosocial communication in their entertainment programs.' HH&S offers different *outreach activities* (section 4.2.5) such as tip sheets, expert briefings, panel presentations at writers' events, newsletters and the HH&S website to the TV writers to support them in their scripting process. The health topic experts with whom HH&S is collaborating play the role of advice-giving professionals for the scripts. As an outcome of the advice, the TV makers broadcast accurate and authentic health storylines. HH&S collaborates with PhD students and expert faculty to conduct summative research on the key health messages, and to implement other research features that are described in detail in chapter 2.4.3.3. An interesting issue comes up when looking at the structural setting of HH&S. The program does not only collaborate with one entertainment company or one health organization in a specific time frame, but they simultaneously work with a variety of TV shows, executives, writers and storylines, as well as a variety of health topic experts, communication researchers and funding agency staff. The professionals from both sides who are connected through HH&S collaborate whenever it is necessary for an indefinite time frame. Since they collaborate on a variety of topics, the model of HH&S can be considered a constant E-E service approach (compare chapter 8.3.1.1) (multiple collaboration partners and funders, ongoing time frame of collaboration, variety of health topics and themes).[96]

In the following, the dialectics of steering power and emancipation are described in the light of the *collaborative environment and key agents* of HH&S (4.2.3). Through the support of the dialectic of fragmentation and unity, the *agenda setting*

---

[96] In contrast to that, the occasional E-E service approach is merely a one to one collaboration, usually for a specific time or project frame focused on one specific health theme, like it is practiced in Germany (chapter 8.3.3).

process of HH&S will be described afterwards (4.2.4). Lastly, the dialectic of dissemination and dialogue will give insights into *the collaboration activities* HH&S creates and implements (4.2.5).

4.2.3 Dialectic of Steering Power and Emancipation

In this section, the dialectic of steering power and emancipation in organizing for social change is used to analyze the ***environment and the key agents*** HH&S is collaborating with. Therefore, the theoretical concept of concertive control (Barker, 1999; Papa et al., 1995) is applied here as well as to the analysis of steering power and emancipation mechanisms of the media center in the Netherlands (section 4.3.3). Barker (1999: 40-41) states that "concertive control (...) presents a general conceptualization of the complex ways through which we become willing participants in and creators of a system that controls our own behavior. It is a powerful and persuasive system that demands our obedience, and we obey because the system reflects our own work values. (...) Team members will create their own discursive formations, they will identify strongly with them, and the formations will persuade them to create meanings that will very effectively control their own behavior".

Both collaboration centers established in the USA and in the Netherlands follow these principles as became clear through the analysis. The core rationale for selecting this theoretical notion to describe the dialectic of steering power and emancipation in the USA is that HH&S personnel is simultaneously using elements of 'restricting and empowering' while they collaborate with the health and entertainment side. This is significant for concertive control contexts and will be outlined in the following.

Digression: Concertive Control

The theory of concertive control is primarily practiced in organizational settings where interpersonal relationships and teamwork are used to create a shared reality relating to values of the organization.[97] Concertive control exists when control is embedded in lateral, mission-centered, highly coordinated actions (Tompkins & Cheney, 1985). Papa, Singhal & Papa (2006) conceptualize the theoretical concept of concertive control according to three pillars:
Empowerment: Empowerment is central for control contexts. For instance, when members of an organization experience empowerment, their commitment to that organization becomes stronger and they are more likely to internalize the control mechanism. In HH&S, the process of empowerment evolves as Hollywood producers and health experts collaborate with one another to uplift their own goals (i.e. telling good stories [the TV makers] and conveying educational messages [the health experts]).

---

[97] An extended version of the theoretical approach is depicted in Barker (1999) as well as in Papa, Singhal & Papa (2006).

Identification: For effectively regulating the behavior of members and partners, they must identify with a set of organizational values and factual premises that guide their decision-making and their activities (Barker & Tompkins, 1994). *Discipline*: Concertive control situations are often characterized by micro-techniques of discipline to regulate and normalize individual and collective actions.

4.2.3.1 The Role of HH&S Personnel

HH&S's core mission is to increase accuracy and frequency of TV health content and maximize the impact of health storylines in entertainment television so that the audience can learn from it and change their attitude and behavior. Its mission is strongly influenced by its funding agencies, including the Centers for Disease Control and Prevention (CDC, see section 4.2.3), as well as, in recent years, the Bill and Melina Gates Foundation. With the Bill and Melinda Gates Foundation, HH&S is increasingly focusing on global health themes. Since 2008, the funding base has tripled and has become quite diversified. HH&S's primary health content goals are at first sight not compatible with the purpose of the entertainment industry, which wants to tell compelling stories and achieve high audience ratings.[98] HH&S is well aware of the fact that Hollywood is not a 'health educator', but they recognize the power of TV health storylines to entertain and educate viewers. Therefore, they *frame* their program's mission for the entertainment side. The reframing strategy includes promoting themselves as a credible, accurate and timely resource for health storylines. When they work together with the entertainment makers, they behave like one of the entertainment professionals, speaking their jargon and being aware of their cultural capital (Bouman, 1999; Bourdieu, 1993; Bourdieu, 1998). They frame themselves as ***service providers*** for the television professionals. One employee of HH&S says that she "calls the TV show or writes them and says, 'hey, we have a great expert about child violence, you know, and your show is all about children. This is a great topic for you to address. So I would love to bring this guy [the health expert] in [the writer's room] to talk to you and share stories with you'" (personal interview, August 11, 2008).

To be a good 'framer', HH&S personnel needs to have a specific educational background. They usually have a scientific background in public health and they additionally have experience in working with the entertainment industry. As a result, they can easily switch from the public health communication environment (communicating with health experts) to the entertainment environment (communicating with TV makers). They are also effective at bringing them together for collaboration. During their work, HH&S staff members interact in three different communication frames:

1. In the ***health frame*** they communicate with health experts and the program funders.
2. In the ***entertainment frame*** they communicate with Hollywood professionals.

---

[98] The higher the ratings, the more money the shows receive for advertisings.

3. And in the *mixed frame* they guide the collaborative process of health experts and Hollywood professionals.

The analysis showed that HH&S has a high interest in keeping these communication frames stable and non-mixed. For example, HH&S tells health experts not to give their contact information away to the Hollywood professionals. One staff member explained that they "want to stay in the loop and the health experts shouldn't be bugged by the writers all the time" (personal interview, November 11, 2008). This is a strategy of gaining and maintaining steering power on the collaborative processes and the communication frames they interact in.

HH&S team members not only invest time in bringing both sides together in the *mixed frame*. They also spend very much time doing grass roots work in the *health* and the *entertainment frame* with only one side of the collaboration partnership. But what is that good for? Working in these two separate frames primarily aims at keeping both collaboration sides interested in an enduring partnership. Therefore, HH&S adapts the rules and norms of each frame when communicating with the health or the entertainment side, supporting the behaviors and principles the professionals are used to.

Interestingly, when the HH&S team members connect the health and the entertainment side in the *mixed frame*, they empower Hollywood writers to use the rules and norms of their *entertainment frame*, and the health experts are trained by HH&S to adopt basic principles of the entertainment frame when communicating with the TV professionals. For HH&S, this is a way to effectively get health messages through to Hollywood and to make them identify with the program.

4.2.3.2 The Role of Health Experts

Health experts can act freely when communicating with HH&S in the *health frame*, whereas they are more guided when interacting with the TV professionals in the *mixed frame*. The underlying principles that analysis has revealed are presented in the following sections.

Health Expert Empowerment

HH&S team members work with more than 500 health experts (they call them subject matter experts) like doctors, researchers and health consultants from the CDC and other leading health institutions in the USA. Health experts who frequently collaborate with HH&S often have a good reputation in their fields of expertise. Becoming a health expert for HH&S first means receiving communication training and then collaborating with Hollywood in the mixed communication frame (i.e. interacting with TV makers via email, telephone or face-to-face). By observing and guiding the health expert, HH&S staff members quickly realize which communication form best fits the expert in order to effectively have an impact on the Hollywood producers, and they discuss this issue with the health expert. HH&S team members encourage health experts to share information in a variety of communication formats, since writers may become interested in a topic after they have heard about it. This is especially helpful when interacting with writers before or during the writing stage (production stage, see chapter 2.4.2) of the storyline. When health experts participate, they may discover that a specific communication form becomes their preference. For example, one doctor was guided in a field visit to a writer's room in Hollywood, where he told entertaining stories with key health messages. He enjoyed this form of communication with the TV makers, and after this briefing he clearly expressed his preference for doing this kind of consultation in an informal face-to-face talk. Another health expert stressed in a telephone interview that his preference is not to communicate face-to-face, but via email: "They [the writers] send an email to someone at HH&S and then in turn that question is forwarded to me. So I never deal directly with the writers. I send my response back to HH&S and they forward it to the writers. (…) What is verbal – they do not really understand what I'm saying, because, you know, I say this with medical terminology (…). I like to write things down so they can really understand" (telephone interview, 27 October, 2008).

Consequently, by letting the health experts choose their 'own' communication channels, they feel more comfortable and will make themselves more available to communicate with Hollywood professionals. HH&S team members support the decisions of the health expert, and this contributes to trust in the relationship between the both of them.

Identification and Discipline
The analysis of the data collected on health experts suggests that the experts have a high level of identification with the HH&S program, as they share its aim to increase accurate and authentic health information in US television – information that will help audience members to learn, and/or to change their attitude and behavior towards healthier lifestyles. One HH&S employee explained: "First we tell them [the health experts] about who we are and what we do because lots of times they just think the show is calling them. (…) 'We are here to help the writers as a resource', and then the experts know: 'ah, I'm doing this as a good thing, I'm helping to ensure accuracy in TV because people learn from it'" (personal interview, November, 11 2008). Thus, HH&S team members can convince health experts quite immediately to collaborate with them, because of their shared aims and vision. However, there was one issue which, in the analysis process, first seemed to be a hindering factor to get health experts working with HH&S. It is routine that the professionals volunteer their time, energy and expertise to work as "**unpaid technical consultants**" (personal interview with a health expert, October 21, 2008) for HH&S. Sometimes a health expert invests a lot of time and effort with a TV writer in Hollywood without knowing if the given information will have any impact. There is never a guarantee that the TV makers will integrate the health information in their storylines. In addition, a health expert has to be very *flexible* during the working day and sometimes in the evening hours, because Hollywood may call and need information quite fast. There have been cases where HH&S personnel contac-

ted a health expert on Friday afternoon for consultation on a storyline which had to be finished on Monday morning. The health experts show a *high level of discipline and tolerance* while collaborating with Hollywood. They do it, because they are led by idealistic motives that they can influence a mass audience with their information. In fact, there has been only one case where the border of discipline and tolerance was crossed, and a health expert was not willing to collaborate. The reason was that the health expert could not see the 'greater health good' anymore. In this case the health expert, who was taking part in a telephone consultation (section 4.2.5), was asked by Hollywood writers to 'plug in' the name of a specific parasitic disease into an already-completed storyline. The health expert explained that the show "wants somebody [a character] who has got some kind of parasite in the blood that would then show that this person has been in this remote area of South America, you know, five years earlier. If you could find the parasite in the blood, it would connect them to a crime that had happened there. (...) That is ridiculous" (personal interview, November 21, 2008). As a result, the health expert declined to consult on this story. Usually, health experts show a high level of discipline and tolerance when they collaborate with Hollywood, but they can be discouraged, just as HH&S team members are discouraged, when the writer has already written a storyline with no expert input. But staff and the majority of experts know that providing even plug-in information builds trust and relationship with writers. Therefore, the TV professionals are more likely to request help much sooner the next time, and to return for repeat consultations thereby increasing the chances of accuracy and social value of TV health storylines.

Paradox of Sociality and Control

There are two paradoxes, the paradox of sociality and the paradox of control (Papa et al., 2006; Stohl & Cheney, 2001), which can be found in the practices of health experts. Firstly, the *paradox of sociality* is related to the intensity of health experts in terms of their commitment to achieve the mission of HH&S. Health experts feel, on the one hand, pride in helping Hollywood to 'improve' their storylines. Nonetheless, to accomplish the mission of HH&S, they sacrifice unpaid consultation hours during their regular working and sometimes spare time. Secondly, health experts experience a *paradox of control* (Papa et al., 2006; Stohl & Cheney, 2001). This paradox surfaces when, on the one hand, they experience a perceived freedom and empowerment as they communicate with HH&S staff members in the *health frame.* On the other hand, they experience less freedom within the *mixed frame*, because there the health experts have to concentrate on the wishes of the TV professionals and codetermine with the HH&S staff members to 'latently' reach the TV makers with health messages. Indeed, this communication strategy is far different from the way they normally communicate their health aims in other projects or contexts (health communication campaigns, etc.). It is also worthwhile to note that some experts are more amenable to working with writers than others, because they have a better understanding of creative needs and television demands.

4.2.3.3 The Role of TV Professionals

HH&S has primarily collaborated with prime-time TV shows, including medical shows like *Emergency Room* (ER), *Grey's Anatomy, Law & Order Special Victims Unit (SVU)* and *Dr. House,* and also with a wide range of daytime dramas, children's programs and Spanish-language telenovelas. These shows reach on average 7 to 20 million people. In the medical shows, some research personnel and writers have a professional background in medicine or public health. But these people are usually not specialists in a wide range of topics and they do not have enough time to permanently help all of the writers on the show. To ensure the accuracy of information according to specific health topics (e.g. obesity or a sexually transmitted disease), HH&S offers Hollywood a good solution.

One goal of the Hollywood professionals is to depict, where possible, accurate and authentic health information. Why is this so and how has this developed? On the one hand, with the rise of HH&S and other smaller-scale health groups, some famous Hollywood professionals like Neal Bear (the executive producer of *Law & Order SVU*) modeled accuracy in the writing in his shows, especially in *Emergency Room*. The show received extremely high ratings. Other shows realized that **the more accurate, the more compelling the story**.[99] On the other hand, analysis also reveals **strong tendencies among TV makers to free themselves** from these standards, because the 'cultural capital' of the **entertainment frame** works against any ambitious plans to be accurate and authentic; the time pressures to write and produce an episode are very high: deadlines need to be met in time, and furthermore, quick direction changes and (emotionally based) decisions are made. Writers with a medical background especially have to struggle with their colleagues when steering mechanisms (of accuracy) and emancipation mechanisms (to overlook accuracy) create tensions. One medical writer of *Grey's Anatomy* pointed out that other TV makers on her show say that "only 2% of the people are going to know that this [a depicted health storyline] is even wrong". She went on, stressing: "And then we had another storyline where we had a psychiatrist, and one of our executive producers is very into the art of psychiatry, and she got very mad about how we were going to tell the story, the psychiatry story. And I said, 'see? 2% of the people will know that that's wrong'. And she said, 'oh, I get it'. You know, after five years of me fighting for the 2% of people who will know, we've finally reached an impasse now where we know it's very important, and that 2% of people is important. But we also know that we compress things" (field observation, October 2, 2008).

So, when it comes to Hollywood collaborations with HH&S, the writers and producers overcome the struggles in their **entertainment frame** and decide to invest (more) time to get accurate information as well as (new) ideas for compelling everyday stories.

---

[99] Aiming for accurate and authentic depictions is a trend which has also been picked up by German entertainment TV professionals (see part II of the thesis).

Hollywood Professionals having a High Level of Steering Power
The analysis of the entertainment television professionals clearly shows evidence that how the collaboration approach works in the USA very much depends on the ***media legislation***.

Characterization: US television system

The US television system is characterized by economic interest, deregulation, privatization, commercialization and a high rate of advertising (Hilmes, 2003). With the scope on broadcast network television, there always has been an oligopoly. Beside other cable and satellite networks, NBC, CBS, ABC and Fox can nowadays be considered as the 'big players' in the field of television broadcasting (Gomery, 2008). According to Discovery Communications, the four-network broadcasters shared 45% of the viewers in 2002 (Jack Myers Media, 2002). Regulating broadcast TV has a long history in the USA and goes back to the 1930s. Since its establishment, it has been critically discussed in policy, in science and by the public. The main point of critics is that the governmental agency Federal Communication Commission (FCC), which is responsible for 'serving the public interest', primarily enacts rules and regulations, which are more advantageous rather than disadvantageous for the commercial broadcasting stations (Gomery, 2008). One example is the protracted television station licensing freeze and its termination of insurance in 1952. The lifting of the licensing freeze opened floodgates to television's commercial expansion (Hilmes, 2003). Other examples are the FCC rules of 1996 and 2003. With the Telecommunication Act in 1996, the network's owned-and-operated (O&O) affiliated stations reached 25% of TV homes. Under the rules of 2003, these stations carried the Big 4, NBC, CBS, ABC and Fox to 39% of households (Alexander et al., 2003).

Attempts to create a stronger lobby for the public broadcasting system in the USA failed and more than 70 years of experience with regulation of the TV industry has proven, if nothing else, that the public interest is an elusive concept on the US television market. The most significant reality is the fact that TV broadcasting in the USA is particularly an economic business, and it generally can provide greater services to the public "when the business is good. Thus, economic issues historically have been part of [government's] Commission's Allocation" (Alexander et al., 2004: 64). The TV lobby has a huge influence on policy activities (McChesney, 2008). Gomery describes it in other words: "Members of the congress know the score, they need the TV to help them getting reelected" (Gomery, 2008: 220).

In addition, advertising times does not come under any kind of legislative regulation. In essence, this means that TV advertising never became a political issue. In recent decades, debates were simply centered on the idea that there might be too much advertising, so the Association of Broadcasting (NAB), the central media lobby organization, added limits to its self-regulated industry code. However, according to Nielsen (2007, 2008), a constant growth in TV advertising has taken place during the last years. Advertising revenue is the fuel that drives the economics of broadcast television in the USA. For instance, Procter & Gamble spent more than 2.6 million US dollars for advertising in the first quarter of 2008 (NMR, 2008).

Hollywood professionals only have few restrictions from the legislative side, and when they do not follow the rules, there are no real sanctions for punishing them. Applying this to the collaboration field, Hollywood has the autonomy to behave within the collaboration as a privileged actor. The Hollywood professionals have the power to decide what they want and do not want to send and, in addition, they have enough financial resources available. So trying to have steering power on health content by handing out financial resources, for instance, would not work out.

In the US collaboration example, HH&S team members and health experts have to take the mighty position of the Hollywood industry into account. The key to success for conveying health content to them is to keep the TV professionals satisfied. Nonetheless, on a broader level, the overall power of Hollywood could have an explosive character, because there are no strong legislative authorities exercising control over the commercially driven entertainment industry. The analysis revealed examples where Hollywood sent storylines with inaccurate health information (e.g. that vaccines lead to autism) or they depicted specific societal groups like homosexual or retarded people inaccurately.[100] This is a field where a lot of tension has arisen in recent years between Hollywood and advocacy groups – the so-called Hollywood lobbyists – which are advocating for an accurate depiction of specific societal groups and topics. Some cases have been documented, where Hollywood lobbyists started up campaigns to boycott films or series, because they feel Hollywood hurts the interests of their group, and thus they wanted to put pressure on the Hollywood professionals.[101] In the view of the fact that many of the Hollywood lobbyists work in the health field or are health experts themselves, it led to TV makers being critical of health experts in general.

Because of these tensions it can also be challenging for HH&S to convince Hollywood professionals of their collaboration approach, especially when writers and producers have only recently heard of and started working with them. HH&S does not collaborate with advocacy or special-interest groups and does not push a single agenda. According to the director of HH&S, Sandra de Castro Buffington, the program upholds Hollywood's creative freedom above all. The analysis shows clear evidence that HH&S distinguishes their approach from the Hollywood lobbyists

---

[100] All of the major broadcasters (non cable) have Standards and Practices Offices that monitor shows and storylines for questionable content, i.e. smoking, sex and inappropriate language and depictions. If there is a question, the writer or producer gets a note and the content is negotiated. These network executives are aware of advocacy issues, but are unable to cover the whole scope of potential inaccuracies.

[101] A case from a movie storyline was told as an example where a character in the film *Tropic Thunder* said: "you didn't play the full retard and you didn't get the Oscar". The lobby group for retarded people protested, called for boycotting the movie and insisted on an official excuse from Hollywood (personal interview, October 23, 2008).

very well when communicating with TV makers in the *entertainment frame*. They do so by stressing that they are an *overall resource and provider for health information* and not an advocacy group or media watchdog for specific health topics. In other words, HH&S builds up trust within the relationship, and they want to show the TV makers that the program is something very unique. They differentiate themselves from other organizations that are media watchdogs and may suggest a 'negative experience' for the writers.

In essence, figure 4.3 sums up insights for the German analysis resulting from the agent specific analysis of HH&S.

Figure 4.3: Insights for the German analysis from agent specific change analysis of Hollywood, Health & Society

> (1) Being a service provider and not a promoter for health themes:
> HH&S staffers support the collaboration process by positioning themselves as facilitators between the health and the entertainment side and by offering services to the TV professionals. Advocating for the health themes would be counter-productive.
>
> (2) Having no or little steering power on the program content:
> Because of the US-specific media environment and legislations HH&S has no means to have steering power on the program content. One option to increase their steering power would be to hand out financial resources (which would be allowed by US media law), but for the Hollywood professionals this is not an incentive, because they have enough financial resources available for their productions.
>
> (3) Using a constant E-E service approach in E-E collaboration:
> HH&S is focusing on constant collaborations with professionals from different TV broadcasting and production companies and health organizations at the same time. The time frame of collaboration is indefinite and HH&S includes a variety of health themes in their consultations (see chapter 8.3.1.1).
>
> (4) Working within three separate communication frames:
> HH&S staffers interact within three different communication frames to spur an effective collaboration and to reach their organizational aims:
> a) the health frame (communication between HH&S staffers and health experts => behaving as one of them),
> b) the entertainment frame (communication between HH&S staffers and TV makers => behaving as one of them),
> c) the mixed frame (in which HH&S staffers bring the TV and the health side together to collaborate).

4.2.4 Dialectic of Fragmentation and Unity

Dialectic notions of fragmentation and unity are used here for providing a framework to explain the historical changes of the HH&S service model. HH&S members and their partners often were confronted with fragmentation and unity processes while the program was being designed, implemented and further developed. What this means will be elaborated in this section in detail.

4.2.4.1 Fragmentation Among CDC Workers

The main effort of establishing the HH&S program goes back to the Centers for Disease Control and Prevention (CDC). The CDC is an agency of the US Department of Health and Human Services with the core purpose of protecting public health and safety by providing information that enhances health decisions.

Before establishing HH&S, many Hollywood producers used to contact the CDC in order to receive health information and to get inspirations for their storylines from 'credible experts' (Beck, 2004). The CDC recognized the great potential for providing the entertainment industry with accurate health information. But how could they *effectively* provide health information to the Hollywood producers and writers? How could they promote accurately depicted health topics in television storylines in order to raise awareness among the media users or, even better, change their attitude and behavior towards healthier lifestyles? The initial approach of the CDC was to initiate outreach activities to the entertainment industry by topic-specific health campaigns in the field of HIV/AIDS, obesity, sexually transmitted diseases, etc. These outreach activities were practiced by single CDC departments which established networks and contacts to Hollywood. However, their gathered information was not disseminated CDC-wide for further use.[102]

Vicki Beck, who took the position at CDC that focuses on establishing lasting partnership structures with Hollywood, says that "all these different campaigns across CDC were paying contractors to come in and help them [the CDC] with all kinds of activities, and they would go out and get a couple of contacts in Hollywood and do something and then, when the contract was over, everything disappeared. And I just saw that it was unfortunate, because we should be developing lasting relationships, sustainable programs. If [the] HIV/AIDS [department] does it, the people over in [the] vaccines [department] can use those contacts for their campaigns" (personal interview, October 27, 2008).

Dialectically speaking, a long-lasting approach to reaching Hollywood was missing, which led to fragmentation processes among the CDC workers. For instance, the obesity department was planning a campaign, and they invested many of their working hours to establishing networks within the entertainment industry. Later the workers found out that the same activities took place before in other campaigns, and so the contacts were established before, but the information disappeared, usually with the contractors who established the networks and who were paid for short-term efforts. For the involved workers this was quite a frustrating experience. It resulted in workers in different departments being unaware of what their colleagues might have achieved, and having to track down past contacts and lessons learned. The CDC management identified these fragmentation processes among their employees in an early stage, and they started to think about another communication approach for connecting with the entertainment industry. One core prerequisite for such a new approach was that it should be based on more coordinated outreach activities, taking advantage of the contacts and successes of different CDC departments and topics for other CDC staff. The CDC came up with the idea and strategies for an approach which does not couple activities to single health

---

[102] There are many coordinating departments and sub-departments responsible for different health topics in about 25 buildings with around 7000 workers just in the city of Atlanta, Georgia, the headquarter of the CDC (Etheridge, 1992). In addition, the agency has a major presence in nine other US cities and in 54 countries around the world.

campaigns. In 1994, the HIV/AIDS program at the CDC consulted with a group of communication and entertainment industry experts who recommended a more proactive, coordinated role for the CDC when working with the entertainment industry. At that time, international research projects had demonstrated the impacts of health messages in television and radio E-E soap operas (Singhal & Rogers, 1999). The panel of invited experts recommended supporting the establishment of an E-E function of the CDC, and with this the foundation for what would become a ***national E-E collaboration model*** was laid (Beck, 2004).

4.2.4.2 Unifying Efforts – The E-E Pilot Project

The first step on the way to a collaboration model was the establishment of an E-E pilot project in 1998 with its headquarters in Atlanta. Its coordinator at the CDC was Vicki Beck. Beck positioned the project as an agency-wide effort to create and maintain structures for outreach to the entertainment industry. She talked to CDC team members from different departments and to Hollywood producers, and she came up with a strategy for enhancing social capital[103] among the different people. CDC personnel and Hollywood professionals should connect with each other more frequently and develop strong and trusting relationships through continuously having a central office and contact staff from the CDC side. Throughout initiating this process there were many hurdles to overcome in (1) ***intra-group communications*** (in the interaction among the CDC workers on their part and the Hollywood TV makers on their part) and (2) ***inter-group communications*** (in the interaction between the CDC staff and the Hollywood TV writers and producers).

On the level of intra-group communication, fragmentation among the CDC workers, but also among the Hollywood producers arose, because some people on both sides were not convinced that a collaborative approach would be profitable for their work. So one goal was to unify and to gain trust among these different voices on the side of the CDC as well as on the side of the Hollywood professionals. On the inter-group level, tensions arose when CDC workers and entertainment professionals communicated with each other. This led to processes disconnecting them from one another. For example, TV producers emphasized that they did not want to work with the health experts, because they had the prejudice that the health experts were just pushing their health agenda. Or the health experts thought that the TV producers were only interested in entertainment value and the audience ratings without being aware of the responsibilities they have when they tell stories.

In essence, the 1998 launch of the CDC-wide E-E pilot project made the first steps to ***unify inter- and intra-group communication processes***. How the pilot project did this is described in the following sections.

---

[103] Social capital can be defined as the building of interpersonal networks between people so as to enhance social trust, foster reciprocity, and facilitate coordination in order to benefit the collective (Preece, 2002; Putnam 1986; Wallis et al., 1998). It is enacted through patterns of engagement, trust and mutual obligation among people (Bellah et al. 1985; Kawachi, Kennedy, Lochner, 1997; Kawachi et al., 1997; Portes, 1998; Taylor, 1989).

4.2.4.3 Building Long-Lasting Networks

The primary objective of the E-E pilot project was to foster structures for a long-lasting exchange between the CDC and Hollywood. In the beginning, *credible health materials* were provided in the form of information binders. The pilot-project managed an *exchange* of CDC experts, providing technical assistance when a scriptwriter asked for help. Public health speakers made presentations at conferences and participated in panel discussions attended by scriptwriters, and Beck submitted questions for a health survey to find out about the characteristics of entertainment television viewers.

Additionally, CDC staff worked together to establish an award program to recognize exemplary accomplishments of daytime dramas that inform, educate and motivate viewers to live safer and healthier lives. The establishment of the award was one important step on the way to unifying the intra-group communication among the CDC workers from different departments and across different topics. They came together to join the award committee and to discuss how they could create the award. By doing so, they could exchange and discuss the perspectives of the E-E pilot project in general. They created the structural judging procedures as well as the guideline the judgers should use. Beck remembers (Beck: 2008, personal interview) that it was a difficult process to get everyone from different CDC departments working together. However, in this way, the 'voices' at the CDC became more unified, and people got a sense of what could be achieved by a collaboration approach. The committee participants worked out the award program and shortly afterwards the award was launched.

In addition, Beck worked on unifying the different 'voices' on the side of the entertainment industry, convincing them of the benefits of collaboration. Therefore, she met with key agents from the entertainment industry like Neal Bear. He was very interested in the collaboration approach and he started advocating for it. Beck emphasized that while it is not easy, it is important to "find someone in the entertainment industry, who understands what you are trying to achieve. Work with them, get some good examples and then start running around to the other shows saying: 'look, this is what Neal Bear has been doing with us.' And then Neal would tell people, 'call Vicki and her staff. You know, get their help'" (personal interview, October 27, 2008).

4.2.4.4 Succeeding in the Unification

The E-E pilot project has shown promising results since its inception in 1998 (Beck, 2004). Credible health materials were established, panel discussions and an award program were launched and impact studies from a survey showed that entertainment television is a credible health source for audience members in the USA from which they can learn and take action for healthier lifestyles. Finally, the exchanges about the E-E project among the CDC workers as well as among the Hollywood professionals (intra-group communication) created a promising frame for strengthening and deepening the collaboration activities (inter-group communication). According to Beck (2004: 217-218) in "2001 the CDC recognized the early successes and limitations of the Atlanta-based pilot effort and announced a request for proposals from outside the agency to establish an E-E program for public health. The result was a cooperative agreement partnership with the University of Southern California's Annenberg School for Communication's Norman Lear Center. The Norman Lear Center offered a Los Angeles base, health communication theory and research expertise, and E-E experience. In 2002 Hollywood, Health & Society was launched as a USC/CDC collaboration, based in Los Angeles". Since then, the program has established a lasting network for leaders in Hollywood's entertainment industry and in the health field, using members from the CDC as well as other health leaders (e.g. doctors, professors and researchers). Some of them were unified in the advisory board of HH&S. In addition, a key alliance with the Writers Guild of America West (WGAW)[104] was established. The Writers Guild provided an excellent network of Hollywood TV makers and it functioned as another entertainment industry advocate for the E-E approach. For example, when panel discussions or the Sentinel for Health Award took place, the Writers Guild offered their rooms and they invited the Hollywood professionals to participate in the events. Since 2002, HH&S has expanded its E-E collaboration model by implementing several collaboration activities (such as briefings, consultations, tip sheets, etc. see section 4.2.5) and using summative research on the prosocial messages. Figure 4.4 sums up the insights from the historical change analysis of HH&S.

Figure 4.4: Insights for the German analysis resulting from historical change analysis of Hollywood, Health & Society

---

(1) Ideationally and financially investing in an E-E collaboration pilot
(e.g. a project, or activities such as round tables, award ceremonies and media research etc.).

(2) Looking for key agents:
One or two advocating opinion leaders from the health and the entertainment side can help to promote a partnership approach.

(3) Developing and implementing strategies to overcome fragmentation
- intra-group communication (among health experts on their part and entertainment professionals on their part) and
- inter-group communication (between health and entertainment television professionals).

(4) First strengthening intra-group, then inter-group communication:
Before deepening the collaboration activities between health and entertainment professionals, it is important to increasingly unify voices on each side for the benefits of collaboration activities.

---

[104] Writers Guild of America West (WGAW) is one of the biggest US labor unions, representing writers of television and film and employees of television and radio news. The 2006 membership of the guild was 7,627 (www.wga.org).

4.2.5 Dialectic of Dissemination and Dialogue

In this section, the theoretical notions of dialectics of dissemination and dialogue are used to depict the *changes and developments in activities (projects or tools)* of the HH&S. This goes with asking the question: 'Which activities, projects or tools has HH&S created since its foundation?' The most striking collaboration activities will be analyzed in this section according the HH&S's four main model pillars: outreach activities (4.2.5.1), events (4.2.5.2), evaluation (4.2.5.3) and advisory board (4.2.5.4). Moreover, at the end of this section, some more developments are portrayed, which took place after the phase of data collection in 2008 and afterwards.

4.2.5.1 Outreach Activities

The outreach model of HH&S is based on different activities to support TV professionals in the production stage of collaboration. The activities are a mixture of dissemination and dialogue evoking methods, which accommodate the writers and producers with health information. In 2000, the outreach model started with a simple binder for Hollywood professionals (see above). HH&S team members took the binder to meetings in Hollywood. This was the first time that information was strategically disseminated to the TV makers with background resources for health information and contact details for any further questions. The first versions of the *tip sheets* were also integrated in these binders.

Tip Sheets

Tip sheets include basic information and case examples for storylines and additional resources on health topics. They are phrased in a way that is typical for the entertainment industry (e.g. easy language, short sentences, storytelling components). For example, tip sheets answer the following questions regarding specific health topics: 'What's the problem?' 'Who is at risk?' and 'Can it be prevented?' Moreover, tip sheets comprise case examples for storylines. In years right after the start of HH&S as a pilot project in 1998, tip sheets were created on the basis of CDC campaign topics with input from a TV producer who had worked on daytime and primetime shows. Later the topic variety was expanded.

Tip sheets are created in a dialogue process between the HH&S and health experts from the governmental agencies CDC and the National Cancer Institute (NCI), both funders of HH&S. The first tip sheet draft and with it the majority of content is developed by HH&S team members and it is then passed onward to their funding institutions for minor changes, while in former times it was more often the other way around. This development demonstrates that the dialogue process came about from a higher level of CDC/NCI involvement (designing the first tip sheet draft in earlier years) to a lower one (commenting on the HH&S's first tip sheet draft nowadays). Analysis suggests that this might be a sign that trust between the governmental agents and HH&S has improved over the years.

Tip sheets are disseminated to entertainment professionals through different communication channels. They are (1) available on the web page of HH&S (more than 60 tip sheets), they are (2) used as disseminating health material when HH&S and a health expert visit Hollywood professionals in the writers' room (see expert briefing), they are (3) sent via e-mail to Hollywood TV makers as introductory information before they are connected with a health expert on the telephone (see telephone consultation) and they are (4) included in the HH&S newsletter Real to Reel (see newsletter) with a linkage to the web page.

Expert Briefing
Another central outreach activity is the ***expert briefing***. It is used as a dialogue-evoking instrument to give Hollywood suggestions for accurate depictions of health topics when writers are at the stage of collecting ideas for storylines. The stories and experience shared with HH&S personnel and health experts provide affirmation that briefings are a very effective activity for providing writers with health information, because in the stage of doing a briefing with writers, they are open-minded about integrating suggestions instead of having a fixed storyline in their mind or on paper. In a briefing, HH&S team member(s) and a health expert visit Hollywood people in the writers' room. The health expert tells compelling stories and by that tries to get health messages through. She/He does this by telling entertaining experiences from her/his everyday life (e.g. working in a hospital). Before starting this 'performance', the HH&S employee briefly introduces the expert. Furthermore, an ***info package*** is handed out. The info package aims to give the TV makers disseminating information, which can be useful after the briefing. In this context the info package comprises

1. ***information on HH&S*** (e.g. brochure, newsletter, etc.) with contact data, their main goals and achievements,
2. ***biography*** of the health expert to show that she/he is a trustworthy resource for health information and has a high reputation,
3. if available, one or two ***academic articles*** on the health topic, often published by the health expert her-/himself,
4. ***tip sheet(s)*** on the discussed health topic(s),
5. ***newsletters*** for TV shows HH&S has consulted on. Newsletters are derived from newspaper sources like *USA Today*. They are short, they sum up facts, contain some pictures of the shows and they have vivid headlines like 'Are Medical Shows Good for Our Health?' or 'Grey's Study Shows Viewers Remember TV Health Messages'.

In the pilot project phase of HH&S (1998-2002) and in the earlier years after HH&S's official affiliation in 2002, there was an emphasis on expert panel discussions and not so much on expert briefings. After a couple of years HH&S realized that the panel discussions were very well-attended though not by current Hollywood writers. As a solution HH&S came up with the strategy to do fewer panel discussions and more expert briefings. Therefore, they started collaborating with health experts in Los Angeles as well as CDC and other funding agency experts who visited Los Angeles for meetings and conferences several times a year. Thus, HH&S expanded the collaboration to include *local experts* at USC and UCLA[105] medical schools who were easily available to do briefings in Hollywood.

When identifying experts and topics, HH&S strategically looked at those prime-time shows that had the highest audience ratings. Then, they investigated which ethnic groups (like African-Americans or Hispanics) and which age groups watched the shows and which health topics were important for these groups to address (see 'evaluation, TV monitoring'). Given this background, HH&S arranged, for instance, to brief TV makers using a health expert who could give good examples and ideas for obesity storylines, especially for a Hollywood show which was particularly watched by African-Americans, who were at a high risk for obesity.

In summary, the analysis showed so far that the expert briefings are one central **dialogue-evoking collaboration** activity. They can be considered a key instrument for reaching writers with new ideas and topics. Frequently, they can open doors for working together with new writers who may not yet be collaborating. When a briefing has been successful for the producers and writers, it is quite likely that they will contact HH&S later on to ask for help and further information. The basis for that is provided by a disseminating activity which is the info package described above.

Telephone Consultation

The telephone consultation is an outreach activity, in which the TV writers play the proactive part in initiating the dialogue with HH&S and the health side. The telephone consultation serves for the writers as '*first aid*' for getting missing health information for an existing storyline to 'plug in'. When writers have spent quite a lot of time developing a storyline, everything needs to happen very fast. The storyline is produced shortly afterwards, and there is no time left for big changes. In such a situation, Hollywood writers call HH&S to receive support. In one observed analysis case, a writer for *Private Practice* called a HH&S employee to inform her that they were doing a storyline on a woman who is six months pregnant and involved in a heavy car accident. The writer wanted to know as fast as possible about what kind of pre-birth damage the accident could cause for the unborn baby. In the next step, the HH&S team member investigated her database (with more than 200 health experts) to find a person specializing in pre-birth damages. After finding the adequate expert, she tried to get connected with him to fix an appointment for a consultation for the same or the following day.

Analysis revealed that connecting both sides on the phone can sometimes be challenging, because the writers as well as the experts are very busy. Cases were observed where an appointment was cancelled and renewed several times a day before the consultation finally took place in the evening. In the *Private Practice* case,

---

[105] UCLA is the abbreviation for University of California, Los Angeles.

the health expert (a hospital doctor) consulted Hollywood professionals on the telephone before, so there was no need for the HH&S employee to prepare him additionally for the talk. In the consultation, the health expert explained specific examples and surgeries he did in cases of pre-birth damage in the last trimester of pregnancy. For instance, if there was a heart defect, a physician might insert a balloon inside the baby's heart to treat the defect. The writer might then follow up with more questions. For example, the writer might ask when a doctor could diagnose this heart defect. During the consultation, the HH&S employee stays on the telephone line writing down keynotes on all information that has been exchanged so that later she can determine which consultation has led to which storyline on television. One reason the staff stays on the phone for a consultation is to ask the doctor if there are any key messages that are important to convey. This is usually covered in an earlier conversation with the expert, when they are reminded to write down 2-3 key messages for the phone conversation, but experts can forget to tell the writer. Some writers are more receptive to this type of information than others, but there are some who will even ask what is important to convey. Another reason why the team member **constantly stays on the phone** is to prevent situations of misunderstandings. For her it is important to 'jump in' anytime she thinks it is necessary to build bridges between the dialogue partners.

During the time when HH&S ran as a pilot project and in the early years of its affiliation at the USC Norman Lear Center beginning in 2002, the number of telephone consultations was not as high as in recent years. For instance, in the early years 2001/2002, before team members were hired, HH&S did around 15 consultations; in 2003/2004 HH&S did 22 telephone consultations a year (Hollywood, Health & Society, 2007). In the following years, with more staff and more outreach, the inquiries of TV writers increased to 243 in the years 2004/2005 (see Hollywood, Health & Society 2007). The stories shared with the Hollywood professionals suggest that a core reason for why they called HH&S for consultations on the phone is because credible information had been passed on to them (in form of a recommendation of colleagues) or simply because they received the newsletter from HH&S with the telephone consultation number, so they thought they would see whether HH&S could be an additional support. Thus, based on the disseminated information (e.g. the newsletter), a dialogue (telephone consultation) was initiated between the entertainment and the health side, and the TV writers were satisfied with this dialogue. This eventually led to (1) further dialogue with the health side working together with HH&S and (2) disseminating positive information and recommendations among TV colleagues regarding the work of HH&S.

Newsletter and Website

HH&S has two other information-disseminating outreach activities. These are the Real to Reel newsletter and the HH&S website. The 5-Year summary of HH&S from 2002 until 2006 (Hollywood, Health & Society, 2007) shows that the first **Real to Reel newsletter** was sent out to writers in 2003. This is an endeavor with a much shorter history than expert briefings, telephone consultations or tip sheets. The idea of doing a newsletter was based on the concerns that the writers do not call HH&S, because they never saw anything from them on paper. HH&S had the idea to send out updates on a regular basis (news at CDC, NCI, links to the tip sheets, something the writers may have read in the newspapers). When visiting Hollywood professionals in the writers' rooms, HH&S personnel realized that they used so-called news clips to get ideas for their storylines. So HH&S decided to support them in this context, preparing news in a more interesting and appealing way for them. The newsletter is sent out three times a year, each time two months before the shows begin their rating periods[106] in November, February and May. Introducing a newsletter as an additional dissemination activity was very useful for the TV makers and, furthermore, it kept the funding governmental agencies satisfied because they saw that information of their agencies was being spread.

HH&S also uses its *internet page* to provide important information to writers and producers. Material with information about the program can be found there. HH&S gives some insights into their main activities, and they prominently provide a hotline to TV makers which they can dial any time they need support regarding health information. Since documenting the monthly average web hits starting in 2001, the hits have grown from 549 in the years 2002/2003 to 1889 monthly web hits in the years 2005/2006 (Hollywood, Health & Society 2007). This indicates that the webpage is an undertaking with growing importance.

Transmedia

In 2005, HH&S staff started working with TV network website managers to provide links to health information when a health storyline appeared. The link to the health information of a funding agency or health agency partner was posted on the TV show's website. Web tracking data was collected by CDC and NCI to document the surge in hits when a storyline appeared and viewers followed the link on the TV website to seek more information on the topic (Le et al., 2009).

Since then, transmedia has been a growing outreach activity and according to Sandra de Castro Buffington (2011) can be considered as the "biggest focus (...), which links TV health storylines to health content on TV show websites, links to credible sources of information, Facebook, Twitter, home videos by actors and more". Transmedia refers to "storytelling across multiple forms of media – TV, film, Web pages, Web video, social networking sites, blogs, comics, even books – with each form offering unique elements of a story to enhance a user's experience and immersion in the story. Hollywood, Health & Society's Transmedia Outreach aims to extend the impact of the informational resources".[107] HH&S offers televi-

---

[106] Rating periods are periods of time (about three weeks) in which the shows try to push out all their promotion for their programs, because in these periods audience ratings are measured. The number of audience members measured in this rating period will then determine how much the shows can ask for advertising.

[107] Retrieved from http://www.learcenter.org/html/projects/?&cm=hhs/transmed (28th Febru-

sion writers and producers to embrace this new media model. One recent example of the transmedia approach is the collaboration of HH&S with TV makers from the show *Army Wives*, Lifetime Television and the CDC on the topic of traumatic brain injury. In the three-episode arc one of the main characters, Joan, learns that she is suffering from a traumatic brain injury. "Besides serving as subject matter experts for the on-air program, CDC experts also drafted language and provided links that wound up in an informational page on the *Army Wives* official site".[108]

4.2.5.2 Events

Another group of collaboration activities can be summarized under the topic 'events'. They can be considered as foremost *dialogue-evoking activities* and they are *follow up activities* to the advisory work on the TV program. These activities inform Hollywood writers, and they honor those that use accurate health information portrayals in an entertaining and innovative way.

HH&S looks back at a long history of implementing *panel discussions*. Their discussions feature health experts who talk about the challenges of addressing difficult health issues that are of interest to TV professionals. Writers and producers who have grappled with these topics talk about the challenges and responsibilities they face when bringing them to the screen.[109] In the early stage of the HH&S, the program collaborated with health NGOs to implement these panel discussions. This was especially important in times where financial support was low. By sharing a financial budget with NGOs, HH&S had been able to keep panel discussions ongoing since 1998, which is when the pilot project was introduced. Since 2008, HH&S does not collaborate with NGOs on funding of panel discussions. They have diversified their funding and tripled the funding since then. HH&S also has redesigned the panel discussions and now offers them four to five times a year. They now serve to inspire and inform writers and producers, and to reinforce the creative partnerships between scriptwriters, health experts and HH&S. Thus, panel discussions are a dialogue-evoking activity with a long tradition.

Another event activity is the *Sentinel for Health Awards*. The awards recognize exemplary achievements of TV writers who inform, educate and motivate viewers to make a choice for healthier and safer lives through storytelling. For the awards CDC communication staff (as well as representatives from academic, public health, entertainment and advocacy organizations) offer advice to the annual award activities and assist with judging activities in two different judging rounds. From 1999 until 2003, HH&S collaborated with another organization, Public Communication International, in the so-called Soap Submit to present a health award. 2004 marked

---

ary 2011).
[108] Retrieved from http://www.learcenter.org/html/projects/?&cm=hhs/transmed (28th February 2011).
[109] Past topics have included bioterrorism, the impact of television on kids, the uninsured, youth mental illness, disease detectives and the role of nutrition in preventing diseases like cancer.

the first year that HH&S implemented its own prime-time and day-time drama awards in the Writers Guild of America West (WGAW) in Los Angeles. This award was a great success, so HH&S decided to extend the awards strategy by adding more categories for health storylines for writers (e.g. the category 'Spanish-language telenovela' was added in 2005 and 'children's program' in 2008)[110] as well as a global health award in 2009. In addition to offering four to five panel discussions a year at the WGAW, it offers an annual Sentinel for Health Awards ceremony followed by a panel discussion with winning writers to share their stories.

In sum, the activities like 'panel discussions' and 'award ceremonies' usually serve to evoke dialogue between the health and the entertainment side. They are supported through the dissemination of material and sheets to inform the involved health experts and TV professionals about the proceedings of the events or to clearly instruct them during the judging process and the award ceremony.

4.2.5.3 Evaluation

Through evaluation research HH&S recognizes the importance of demonstrating the effectiveness of their work by conducting content and effect studies (summative research) on TV health storylines (Beck, 2004) after the program has been broadcasted. These activities are *foremost disseminating activities*. For example, they investigate audience impact on storylines, TV viewing habits and TV content analysis. But why is it important to investigate the health messages on TV? HH&S team members know that the success of their program is closely related to the issue of whether audience members learn or maybe change their attitude and behavior when watching health messages on TV and maybe later discuss them with family members and friends. If they can prove that the messages reach the audience members, it is more likely that they receive further funding for their service program. So, one of the first things that HH&S implemented after the affiliation of the pilot project was a representative and self-reported survey called ***HealthStyles***, which focuses on the target groups of both daytime and primetime entertainment audience members. Analysis of data from the HealthStyles survey indicates that over half of regular viewers report learning processes about the depicted health storylines in daytime/primetime drama. After seeing the health storyline in a drama, one third of the regular viewers described taking action, while nearly two-thirds of the regular viewers described having learned something (Porter Novelli et al., 2000; Porter Novelli et al., 2005). Thus, with the HealthStyles survey, HH&S team members made an important step in extending the financial and ideational support of their program, because they could argue to (potential) funders that people learn from the broadcasted messages and also want to take action after watching them.

Moreover, ***TV content and viewing habits analysis*** provide HH&S with important facts and figures about how health content is portrayed and, for example, which

---

[110] With the strategy to expand the awards, the entries for storylines from writers increased. For example, in 2001/2002, HH&S counted three entries. In 2005/2006 that number had increased to 30.

characters (e.g. an African-American) suffer from which diseases, and, if the characters get better, which strategies are depicted for a recovery in the storyline (e.g. going to a doctor or asking friends for support). Analysis showed, that audience members tend to identify greatly with characters, who have the same ethnic background (Murphy et al., 2008). So in a show like *Mr. Lopez*, where the main character is a Hispanic and the show is often watched by Hispanics, it makes sense to identify and address health topics and problems such as diabetes or high blood pressure, which are typical for Hispanics. Clearly, these research results are important when justifying the HH&S program activities to their funders. Since 1998, more than 20 studies have been conducted in this field, and many of them have led to academic publications.[111] Additional research projects tracked information about how viewers sought for additional health information when storylines were aired in TV shows, as noted in the previous section. If the viewer wanted more information, they checked the website of the TV show where a link was provided by HH&S staff. They could click on the link which would take them directly to a health agency site, such as the CDC, NCI or other health agency (Le et al., 2009).

4.2.5.4 Advisory Board

HH&S established an advisory board consisting of entertainment industry insiders, public health leaders and academic experts to guide the program in all phases. The advisory board idea was born shortly after the official establishment of HH&S in 2002. In the first year after establishing the HH&S at USC/Norman Lear Center, staff members persuaded Neal Bear to be the co-chair of the board. Additionally, they confirmed Victoria Riskin as a co-chair. At that time she was the president of the WGAW. After two years, she left her position and the Writers Guild board voted that the new president of the WGAW would continue as co-chair of the HH&S board, so it has been passed from one president to the next. This was a meaningful decision for HH&S, because from this point on they partnered with the WGAW, the industry organization that represents TV and film writers in their contract negotiations with TV and film producers.

In essence, having the advisory board has been an important ***dialogue evoking activity*** for unifying voices in the entertainment industry and health organizations behind HH&S and to give HH&S recommendations for their program. In 2008, the program had 44 board members. One central board element is the annual advisory board meeting where health and entertainment experts discuss developments and perspectives of HH&S. This takes place on the same day that the Sentinel for Health Awards are accepted at the WGAW. In the annual board meeting, HH&S team members give updates on grants, milestones and future development opportunities. This is followed by a strategic discussion and advice round by the board members. For example, questions are discussed such as 'How do we frame issues of social determinants and global health as storytelling?' or 'Do we try to move with the program into reality shows?' The results out of this discussion serve as a

---

[111] Several of these studies are mentioned and explained in chapter 2.6.2.

basis for orientation at HH&S until the next board meeting takes place.

2008 and afterwards
After the time of data collection, several aspects have changed over the last three years. As Sandra de Castro Buffington stated "funding sources have diversified (...). We have funding for special projects. Our work has become international, working in India, South Africa, Latin America and the Middle East with multiple global partners such as the UN and The World Bank. We are taking writers and producers of television and film on research trips overseas to India and South Africa. We are conducting story-bus tours of inner city Los Angeles" (De Castro Buffington, 2011).
Moreover, HH&S is planning to expand into the field of climate change themes. Sandra de Castro Buffington explains in this context: "I have a mandate this year from the CDC, one of our partners, to address climate change. I'm thrilled. The main thing is we need funding from a climate group – it has to be a foundation or a government source, because we don't take funding from any special interest groups – for me to really develop this into a full-blown program. We need climate change to be something that writers are addressing on a regular basis. If we had full funding and I could have a team focused on nothing but climate, that's exactly what we'd see".[112]

Figure 4.5 outlines which insights derived from the analysis of activities of HH&S and what can be recommended for the German field.

Figure 4.5: Insights for the German analysis resulting from instrumental change analysis of Hollywood, Health & Society

(1) Providing a flexible mix of activities for TV makers:
Different activities should be offered for TV makers which fit their needs in various situations (e.g. a briefing when storyline ideas should be collected or telephone consultations when the storyline has already been developed and further advice is needed).

(2) Combining dialog evoking and disseminating information activities:
Collaboration activities are successful, when dialog evoking and disseminating information features are mixed up (as in the case of the briefings or award ceremonies).

(3) Starting the collaboration approach with outreach, event and evaluation activities in a combination:
Briefings and tip sheets (outreach), impact research (evaluation), award ceremonies and panel discussions (event) are a promising combination for getting E-E collaboration activities successfully started. On this basis, further activities may be added for a long-term strategy.

(4) Activities run side by side as a part of an E-E service strategy not limited to a specific project period:
On this basis the decision is to be made, which activities are striking to emphasize, to scale down, or to bring in as new ones.

---

[112] Retrieved from HH&S webpage - interview with Sandra de Castro Buffington: www.learcenter.org/html/projects/?&cm=hhs (8th March 2011).

4.3 Center for Media & Health, Gouda, the Netherlands

"The aim of the center is to collaborate with the media; you can say to bridge the gap between social change institutions, health institutions and media professionals to really work together to make a better society. E-E collaboration is a kind of marriage, and in a good marriage you respect each other, you support each other and you try to develop the best in each other's characters to really create a successful relationship. And with Entertainment-Education it is more or less the same. Sometimes of course you fight. There is tension, which is very natural, and I think the ingredient of respect, of really being interested in the drives and in the motives of the other helps you to create a good E-E format and good E-E results".

- Martine Bouman, 2010

4.3.1 Methods of Data Collection

This thesis also interprets the approach of the Center for Media & Health (CMH) by using the theoretical notions of dialectical tension of prosocial change. Using methods of data collection similar to those employed with HH&S, the thesis integrates *(a)* a study on materials (such as information brochures, leaflets, presentations, minutes of events, meetings and discussion rounds) and scholarly literature on the media institute (e.g. Bouman & Houten, 1993; Bouman, 1999; Bouman & Hutten 2001; Bouman, 2002; Bouman, 2004; Kremers & Bouman, 2004; Bouman, 2005; Bouman, 2006; Bouman & Brown, 2008a; Lubjuhn & Bouman, 2009; van Empelen, 2009), *(b)* field studies (observations and interviews) of the program involving a total time period of ten weeks (eight weeks from May 2008 – June 2008 as well as another two weeks in February and March 2009); *(c)* the communication with team members, researchers and practitioners (net)working and collaborating with the CMH, including one interview with Dr. Martine Bouman, founder and director of the CMH; and *(d)* video material on events/conferences and prosocial TV storylines which arose from the E-E collaborations initiated by the CMH.

As in the USA, the focus on agent-specific, historical and structural changes of the CMH as experienced by team members and their collaborative partners since the foundation of the center is of core interest. In this matter, three CMH team members, three health experts, one international E-E collaboration expert and three TV professionals were interviewed in Gouda, Utrecht, Den Haag, Rotterdam and Hilversum. Three out of ten interviews were done via telephone (all three with TV professionals). The face-to-face interviews with the team members and the CMH partners were conducted in their workplaces (i.e. at the CMH office, at health organizations, at TV production offices, during traveling hours via train and in official places such as cafés and restaurants).[113] Pictures from important events and gatherings were taken, as were notes from significant conversations. Like in the case of the USA, the narrative, in-depth interviews were tape-recorded and investigated by clustering important experiences and topics. At the end of many days, there was also the possibility of discussing the impressions in informal settings with the team members and the collaborative partners of the CMH.

In addition to the personal and telephone interviews previously described, the researcher talked to different scholars, practitioners and pioneers to get more insights into the E-E field.

4.3.2 E-E Partnership Arrangements of the Center for Media & Health

This section serves to embed the approach of the CMH into the theoretical aspects of E-E collaborations depicted in chapter 2.4. The main partnership arrangements, which the CMH creates and implements, are *E-E co-productions* and *E-E inscript participations*. *E-E co-production* was defined according to Bouman (1999: 123) as 'a formal transaction between a prosocial organization and a broadcasting organization or a production company to design, produce and broadcast a new entertainment program for prosocial communication purposes'. *E-E inscript participation* was defined as 'a formal transaction between a prosocial organization and a broadcasting organization or a production company to use an already-existing entertainment program as a carrier of prosocial communication purposes' (ibid.). Beside these partnership arrangements, the center has been increasingly designing and implementing *E-E service* activities[114] in recent years (section 4.3.5). One reason for this development has been a change in Dutch media legislation in 2008 (section 4.3.3). The rules for co-production have been sharpened. In these times national (health) organizations, which receive financial support from the government, are no longer allowed to spend their budget on co-production collaborations with the public broadcasting television industry. The rationale for this is that the public broadcasting organizations already receive financial support from the government and this would be doubled should they also receive financial support from government-related national health organizations. It has also been proved that in the past some co-production agreements led to questionable practices. In some cases the results were not worth the money invested, due to a lack of proper monitoring and a clear understanding of the purpose and aim of the co-production agreement. With this restriction in the Dutch media legislation of 2008, it is no longer possible for health organizations and TV entertainment professionals, working in public broad-

---

[113] Appendix 2 gives an overview on the interview partners.
[114] In chapter 2.4.1, Bouman & Brown (2010) defined E-E service as 'a strategy of prosocial organizations to facilitate (through factual and timely information, contacts with experts, shooting locations, etc.) broadcasting organizations or production companies in dealing with prosocial communication in their entertainment programs'.

casting organizations, to share a financial budget in broadcasted mass media programs which is, as explained in the theoretical chapter 2, a core characteristic of co-productions and inscript participations. This and other developments (section 4.3.3) led, in recent years, to a growing interest from the CMH in exploring possibilities in *social media and web 2.0 formats* (and not in broadcasted TV programs) for designing and implementing effective E-E co-productions (in which both parties can still share a financial budget) or even E-E independent productions, where the CMH owns and controls the whole process and product. An E-E production is defined by Bouman (1999: 123) as 'an initiative of a prosocial organization to act as an independent producer and design and produce one's own entertainment program for prosocial purpose and 'sell' it to a broadcasting organization'. In the case of web 2.0 formats (also called webisodes) it is not sold to a broadcasting organization, but uploaded to the internet via You Tube or special websites. Being now the actual 'producer' the CMH has full authority over all stages of the production process, from reading the scripts to directing the last cuts.

In the following, the dialectics of steering power and emancipation are used to highlight the collaborative environment and key agents of the CMH. Using the support of the dialectic of fragmentation and unity, the agenda setting process is portrayed afterwards. And at last, the dialectic of dissemination and dialogue will illuminate the collaboration activities, which the CMH creates and implements. Together with the outcome of the US media center, the results of the Dutch collaboration context will serve to establish a higher sensitivity[115] for the German analysis in part II of this thesis.

4.3.3 Dialectic of Steering Power and Emancipation

In this section the dialectic of steering power and emancipation is used to analyze the CMH and its *environment and key partnering agents*. In this context, the theoretical concept of concertive control has been of additional help in understanding some of the underlying principles involved (see section 4.2.2). The rationale for incorporating theoretical elements of the concertive control concept is mainly that both the CMH and the collaborating health and TV professionals emancipate themselves in the collaboration process. Also, they are affected by the steering power mechanisms of their partners. Both issues are very characteristic of environments enacting concertive control. Some points will be discussed in the following to explain what this means.

4.3.3.1 The Role of CMH and Collaborating Health Experts

In this section the question is tackled which role the CMH and their partnering health organizations take over in the collaborative practice, particularly with regard to the positions they undertake in relation to each other as well as to their partners from the entertainment field. The CMH has an approach that differs from the HH&S when working together with entertainment and health partners. The CMH is

---
[115] Chapter 5.3.5 defines the term 'sensitivity' in detail.

an ***independent research expertise center*** (and not an E-E program based at a university like HH&S). With a combination of research grants and NGO support, the CMH works with a network of universities, higher educational institutions, producers, creative artists, health communicators, NGOs, and government officials to design, implement and evaluate entertainment-education media programs and lifestyle campaigns. Its core mission is to develop media interventions based on the Entertainment-Education strategy, which contribute to health and quality of life and to social change in general. The CMH is the first media center worldwide to carry out in-depth research into E-E collaboration processes for western countries. The CMH needs to constantly apply for research grants so that it is able to fund its various projects. One of its core project funders is the Netherlands Organization for Health Research and Development (ZonMw).[116] Thus, the E-E interventions developed and implemented by the CMH (section 4.3.5) take place within the framework of the various E-E project grants. For each project, they usually work together with partners from the health and the entertainment television field.

The main purpose of CMH projects is to create prosocial entertainment media content which is guided and ensured through research (1) on the E-E collaboration processes and (2) on how to effectively reach media users. In terms of the creation and implementation of E-E co-production/inscript participation interventions/and independent E-E productions, the CMH conducts the majority of its project work in a very different manner to HH&S. In these types of collaboration the CMH plays a ***health promoter*** role. However it also has several E-E service activities where it operates in a role similar to HH&S by serving as a ***service provider*** for its collaborating partners (section 4.3.5). As the CMH has a lot of experience with co-productions/inscript participations, the focus will be on these collaboration forms in the next paragraphs (which shall also make the contrast to HH&S clearer).

For creating and implementing co-productions/inscript participations, the CMH applies for grants. When successful, it invests the financial resources (in addition to investments for research activities) in a TV-format (and nowadays also in web 2.0 formats), and in this context the CMH shares a financial budget together with the TV professionals to create a prosocial TV program or episode. Clearly, this implies that they are a part of the decision making process with regard to the program content. They have, in comparison to HH&S, more steering power in the collaboration process. Having the role as a ***health promoter*** in co-productions and inscript participations, the CMH itself ***takes over the role as health communication expert*** in facilitating prosocial themes to the TV professionals. They can make use of their ***steering power*** to create TV entertainment formats together with TV professionals. As already described, for HH&S it was only possible to conduct summative research because of the E-E service collaboration context, mainly resulting from the

---

[116] ZonMw is a national organization that promotes quality and innovation in the field of health research and health care through initiating and fostering new developments. The majority of ZonMw's commissions come from the Ministry of Health, Welfare and Sport (VWS) and the Netherlands Organization for Scientific Research (NWO).

US media environment and legislations (section 4.2.3). Conversely, the CMH operates in a different (public) broadcasting media environment and finds itself thus in another situation. Because of its stronger involvement in the decision making process with regard to the program content, there also exists greater possibilities to conduct (beside summative also) formative research, the results of which can be incorporated in the TV program. Thus, the CMH has more possibilities to ensure that the creation of prosocial content fits with target audience members. Before going into more detail with the Dutch approach, it may be first important to sum up the crucial differences between the Dutch and the US media center. The following table 4.1 clarifies the differences between the models.

Table 4.1: Differences in the E-E media center approaches of CMH and the HH&S

E-E Media Center	Main collaboration form(s)	Main role in collaboration	Implementation	Research	Steering power in the format
CMH	E-E co-production E-E inscript participation	Health promoter	• invest financial resources in the production of the format => sharing a financial budget • design and implement the format together with TV professionals in a creative process	Formative, process, summative research	higher
HH&S	E-E service	Services provider (bringing health experts together with TV professionals)	• no financial investments in the TV production (no need) • train health experts and use specific strategic tools to "get messages through" to TV makers • no guarantee that they pick up the health messages	Summative research	lower

Media Legislation Rules and Changes for E-E Co-productions/Inscript Participation Practice

According to the former Dutch media law, prosocial organizations could share a financial budget with TV makers in order to produce a new format together (E-E co-production) or to create prosocial content in an existing format (E-E inscript participation). As a result the CMH could have an active part in the decision making process with regard to the TV content, and it could have a higher level of steering power than HH&S has within the E-E service program.

Three legislative issues were striking to consider for creating and implementing E-E co-productions/inscript participations:

1. **Financial budget**: Prior to 2008, the CMH, other health experts and TV professionals could share a financial budget. Nonetheless, the TV makers should be the holder of at least 51% of the shared financial budget. The steering

power of the CMH and other health institutions is regularly related to the extent of financial resources they invest when sharing a financial budget. For example a 10 percent contribution to the budget would offer less scope for steering power than a 49 percent contribution.
2. **Responsibilities**: The TV professionals by media law have the final say when making decisions regarding the program content in the production stage of collaboration.
3. *Informing audience members*: Before and/or after broadcasting the TV program in the implementation stage of collaboration, the audience should be informed that the program was made possible with the financial support or funding by authorities from the prosocial field.

The latter rule especially has caused challenges in the practice of co-production/inscript participations, as noted by several interview and conversation partners, because TV professionals feared they would lose audience members by making it public that a governmental (related) authority was involved with the creation of the program. In this context, a health expert from a partnering CMH institution described a difficult situation that she experienced in her E-E co-production: "There is no program in Holland that is fully funded by the government. In our case, the public broadcasting channel put more money in it [the program] and then the government said, 'You have to do this, you have to do that' and they [the TV makers] really didn't like it. That was a struggle (...). [In compliance with the law of informing the audience] At last the TV channel gave in and wrote 'this program is also funded by ...'" (personal Interview, 25 February 2009). In this example, the health communication expert explained a co-production case where controversies arose regarding whether audience members were informed about the health organization participating in the program or not. Nonetheless, the Media Law was followed at the end. In contrast to that, several other cases were reported in which TV makers ignored the rules (i.e. they took the liberty to not inform the audience members that a health institution was involved in the broadcasted program). This was one of the main reasons why Dutch politicians decided to change the rules according to the collaboration in E-E co-productions/inscript participations. From August 2008 onwards, as described earlier, health communication experts from governmental (related) authorities and institutions – this includes the CMH and most of their partnering organizations from the health field – are no longer allowed to share a financial budget for a television program which is broadcasted by a public broadcaster. The CMH and other health communication experts stressed that with the new rule they lose *the opportunity to reach target groups coming from lower socio-economic milieus*. They are afraid that these rules probably will not be changed in the foreseeable years to come.

In essence, the CMH and other health institutions received a high level of steering power in the process of designing and implementing an entertainment TV program in E-E co-productions and inscript participations. By sharing a financial budget with TV professionals, they could emancipate themselves and, for example, correct scripts which did not accurately depict health issues. With the *new restrictive rules on co-production in the Media Law health experts have lost an essential steering mechanism*. Bouman (2009) suggests a solution by pleading for a way in-between the current and the old co-production media rules. The idea is that a *media committee* could be assigned which supervises co-production and inscript participation partnership activities in a review process (approval, funding issues and rules related to informing the audience about the partnership, etc.). The months and years to come will indicate which developments will arise. Nonetheless, it may be important to emphasize that the new legislation does affect broadcasted TV formats, but not the web 2.0 television and other formats on the internet. Out of this and for several other reasons (e.g. the growing interest of target group members in internet formats), the web 2.0 can be considered as an upcoming and effective medium for implementing E-E formats in the Netherlands (see the *Sound* project in section 4.3.5) and beyond.

Paradox of Sociality and Control
Two types of paradox are also linked to the practices that the CMH and its health partners are involved in. Firstly, there is a *paradox of sociality* (Stohl & Cheney, 2001). The CMH and its partnering health organizations are aware of the tremendous power that entertaining media content can have on the audience members. So they know that by collaborating with TV professionals the chance is high that they can get prosocial issues conveyed to a mass audience. Nonetheless (and herein lies the paradox), the collaboration energy they spend on the partnership is often high as well. In a situation similar to the USA, health communication experts involved in an E-E collaboration accrue many additional (and unpaid) working hours to keep the collaboration working, especially in the hot times when the TV episodes are produced. In this context, they need to completely assimilate to the logics, rules and norms of the television field. One health communication expert involved in an E-E co-production for example states: "In the evenings you are going to the studio and you are doing a lot of extra hours (...). The big part of your work is targeted at the television programs. It must be established in three months because then they have to broadcast it and you want quality. So, you have to invest (...). You have to fit in their steps and appointments" (personal interview, June 21 2008).

The CMH and its partnering health organizations are also confronted with a *paradox of control* (Stohl & Cheney, 2001). This paradox surfaces when, on the one hand, they perceive the freedom that comes with creating their own steering mechanisms (e.g. making corrections and changes in the storylines, developing criteria for the TV makers, creating a briefing document, etc.) in co-productions or inscript participations. On the other hand (and paradoxically), the CMH and its health partners can also experience less freedom in the collaboration, especially with regard to how their steering attempts on the program content may be limited by the TV maker's emancipation of themselves (e.g. by rejecting or ignoring the CMH team members' contributions or by depicting health issues in the program different to what they had previously agreed upon in the joint script version). The following story shared by a health communication expert collaborating in a co-production shows the control paradox explicitly: "She [the actress in a storyline] went on her motorcycle and she was driving straight forward. And she wasn't looking like she drank a lot, you know, very focused. When I saw that I felt like 'wow, that is like a detail, but from our point of view, we want to tell something about alcohol and drugs (…)'. And that wasn't correct. But at that stage it was too late. We read a scenario before, which said 'she gets on the motorcycle and she is staring all the way, looking drunk'. And then you see the episode and you see their interpretation of drunken (pause). It is very difficult (pause). There is no clear line. We needed to tackle this kind of incorrect things" (personal interview, February 5, 2009).

4.3.3.2 The Role of TV Professionals

The analysis put forward in this dissertation supports the idea that, there were in the past very few Dutch TV professionals *who were interested in creating a format in a joint process* (i.e. putting oneself into the position of the other and to be open-minded to learning something from the collaboration partner) (personal interviews June 21, 2008 and February 5, 2009). This fostered strong tensions between both sides. The TV professionals usually acted like 'peacocks' in collaborations (Bouman, 2004; Bouman, 1999); they acted arrogantly and were not open to an exchange with the health side. Furthermore, many of them were convinced that they did not need help with the health content in their storylines. Thus, a collaboration was very challenging to design and implement, because the TV professionals only very rarely were ready to create a joint frame of reference in the collaboration, often telling the health experts that they 'know better'. In recent years, changes have become observable as can be withdrawn from the data.

Characterization: Dutch television system

The Dutch broadcasting system can be characterized through a mixture of public and private entities. From their inception, public broadcasting channels in the Netherlands have been shared by different broadcasting organizations. In this unique 'pillarized' system, different religious and political groups used to have their own broadcasting organization, supported by paying members. The more members, the more broadcasting time an organization got on the available television channels and radio frequencies. To prevent them from only advocating their own issues, the Media Act requires the public broadcasting organizations to provide a 'full program' with a reasonable ratio of culture, information, education and entertainment.[117] Throughout the seventies the TROS, a non-religious and non-

---

[117] Under the Media Law of 1988, the ratio has been 20% for culture, 25% for information, 5% for education, 25% for entertainment and 25% has been non-allocated Also at least 50% of the programs had to be locally produced. In 1991 the requirements were reviewed: 30% for education and information, 20% for culture, including 10% for art, and the rest was non-allocated (Bardoel & Bierhoff, 1997).

political public broadcasting organization, recruited enough members to get broadcasting time. The tros was the first organization to put more emphasis on entertainment (often programs imported from the USA), a phenomenon much debated in Dutch society that became known as 'vertrossing' (Bardoel & Bierhoff, 1997; Manschot, 1993).
Until 1987 there were only two public broadcasting networks in the Netherlands. Transmission was accomplished by individual or central antenna systems: aerials for receiving satellite television channels were still a rarely used novelty, and there were no Dutch satellite channels. After 1987 television programming expanded, however, mainly due to the introduction of a third public network in 1988 and four commercial networks since 1989 (RTL-4; RTL-5; Veronica; SBS6) (Bardoel & Bierhoff, 1997). The growth of new delivery systems, particularly cable (and to a lesser extent, satellite and VCR) provided even more opportunities for viewing (Frissen, 1992).
The start of commercial broadcasting in the Netherlands has drastically changed the television landscape. Due to the strong competition for viewers between public and commercial broadcasting organizations, all public broadcasting organizations have now shifted their programming towards more (light) entertainment (Bardoel & Bierhoff, 1997; Frissen, 1992; Manschot, 1993). Because of the diffusion of viewers over more channels, viewer rates have declined dramatically since the introduction of commercial broadcasting. Hence there is strong competition between public and commercial channels for the public's favors.
Source: Bouman (1999: 19-21).

In general, the Dutch TV market can be considered a liberalized market. Much as in the USA, producers can use the opportunity of product and topic placement to finance their TV programs with additional money. Furthermore, the influence of Dutch politics on TV programs tends to be viewed less critically in the Netherlands than in Germany (see part II of the thesis).

Changes in Mind-Set and increased Awareness of Responsibility
The stories shared by TV professionals collaborating in E-E interventions of CMH projects uncovered that the interviewed professionals have experienced a **change in mind-set**. One TV producer explained: "In the beginning [of working in E-E collaborations] I thought, 'oh Jesus, I don't want them to tell me how to tell a story because they do not know things'. I think I was quite arrogant. And I thought they wanted boring things. They don't like drama - they only like their messages. That was the first thing I thought. Especially because of the stories from the soap examples in South Africa [referring to the E-E program *Soul City*] I thought, 'well, maybe there is really something we can learn from health research and there are a lot of people who know a lot about human beings and behavior, and we can really use it to make better stories'. So that was a great change for me" (personal interview June 26, 2008). In addition to stories of mind-set changes during the involve-

ment in E-E interventions as exemplified by the above TV producer, TV professionals also describe a *process of becoming increasingly aware of the responsibility they have* when telling stories, particularly due to the exchange with health experts. One TV professional, for example, said that with every told story, a sense of what can be considered as good or bad is transported. This means that stories are highly value-laden. She additionally stressed that they can have an enormous influence on the audience members' everyday life and that this is also very important when depicting health issues on television. This increased sensitivity specifically arose from the E-E collaboration experience she made and from which she really learned something (personal interview March 18, 2009).

In essence, the CMH could introduce some awareness raising processes among the TV makers with whom it collaborated in co-productions and inscript participation interventions through offering help with its different activities (section 4.3.5). The openness and the willingness to fully engage in a process of reciprocal (ex)change of perspectives, which is a prerequisite for changes in mindset and behavior, can be considered a central achievement in the Dutch collaboration environment.

The following figure gives an overview on significant insights from the analysis of the collaborative environment of CMH.

Figure 4.6: Insights for the German context resulting from the agent specific change analysis of the Center for Media & Health

(1) Being a health promoter
is the core role of the CMH and the basis for their success. Furthermore they also increasingly act as a service provider in E-E service collaborations. This can also be considered as promising partnership arrangement for the Dutch environment.

(2) The health promoter role is related to co-productions and inscript participations having a high steering power on the TV program:
As a health promoter, the CMH shares in the majority of their projects a financial budget with the entertainment TV makers (and also other health partners). Here, the steering power level within the TV format can be considered as high (in comparison to E-E service, see HH&S).

(3) Media legislations and the cultural/media environment are core prerequisites for steering power in the collaboration:
The media legislation and the cultural/media environment determine to a high degree to which kind of extent health communication experts can have steering power on the TV format. In co-productions/inscript participations this level is high; in E-E service it is lower.

(4) Making TV professionals aware:
Through a long history of collaboration projects and events, the CMH has raised awareness for health themes among several TV makers and partnering with them has become less difficult.

4.3.4 Dialectic of Fragmentation and Unity

The theoretical concept of the dialectics of fragmentation and unity is used in this section to analyze the historical changes of the CMH.

4.3.4.1 First Unifying Efforts of Martine Bouman

The main effort of establishing the CMH goes back to a history of unifying efforts of Martine Bouman. As a health communication specialist, she started working at the Netherlands Heart Foundation in 1983. Her task was to design and implement health education projects for the general population. At that time the Netherlands Heart Foundation had a strong medical emphasis focused mainly on secondary prevention strategies. Because most of these organizations were founded by biomedical or medical specialists, health problems and their solutions were defined more in medical and technical terms than in terms of social behavior, and the focus was often more on content, rather than communication strategies. In her working context, Bouman realized that the traditional communication methods used at that time by the Netherlands Heart Foundation such as brochures, telephone help desks and topical events and exhibitions, had a high focus on cognition and rationality and did not reach a lot of less well educated audiences. These traditional communication methods were particularly motivating to people who already had cardiovascular diseases and who were already interested in health issues, but not for people who were young and healthy and who were not spontaneously interested in disease prevention and a healthy lifestyle. Bouman discovered a more effective way to address her target group. She realized that the messages of the Netherlands Heart Foundation had to compete with thousands of other communication messages. As the attention of the target audience needed to be caught and held, and especially for audiences that were not spontaneously interested in health messages, it was no longer sufficient to rely solely on the rationality of the message: other, more emotionally appealing and popular communication methods also needed to be brought into play. Through her in-depth research she learned more about the Entertainment-Education strategy and became more familiar with it.

The concept of Entertainment-Education for promoting healthy lifestyles and prevention was something completely new at that time, and for the Netherlands Heart Foundation, it was uncommon to experiment with such popular communication strategies and methods. When Bouman introduced the E-E strategy to colleagues, at first they were critical and resistant. Bouman sensed at that point that it would take quite an effort to unify these critical voices behind her innovative ideas. As a part of her strategy, she did more research and she wrote a report to the directors of the foundation in order to get funding to experiment with Entertainment-Education. After some time and several arguments, she succeeded and the first E-E project, *Villa Borghese,* was designed, co-produced and implemented. With that intervention the first step was made to start the experiment with the E-E strategy at the Netherlands Heart Foundation on a broader basis and to use the research results of the project to unify some critical voices behind her. Because *Villa Borghese* was the first E-E project ever recorded in the Netherlands and because it revealed positive outcomes on the audience members, Bouman and her colleagues promoted *Villa Borghese* as an innovative communication strategy at conferences and in publications. Through these first unifying efforts, Entertainment-Education gradually became a new idea not only at the Netherlands Heart Foundation but for the whole health communication field in the Netherlands.

4.3.4.2 Strengthening Unification Efforts

After *Villa Borghese* proved itself through formative, summative and collaborative process research results, through lessons learned and through reasonable audience ratings, several critical voices became increasingly convinced that Entertainment-Education could be a feasible strategy for reaching target group members from lower socio-economic milieus with healthy lifestyle messages.

As a next step Bouman and her colleagues implemented the second E-E project. This time they collaborated with TV professionals from an existing, well-known hospital series named *Medisch Center West*. By sharing a financial budget, they designed and implemented several storylines together with TV makers (e.g. on organ donation, heart failures among women and diets to minimize the risks of cardiovascular diseases). The summative research on the messages in *Medisch Center West* showed positive effects on the audience members, and this convinced even more critical voices to take Entertainment-Education seriously. At this point in time Bouman decided that she should spend more time and energy on the topic. She made the decision to deepen her knowledge of the E-E strategy and collaboration processes within the framework of a PhD research. In 1994, Bouman left the Netherlands Heart Foundation and started her PhD at the University of Wageningen, and in 1998 she finished her PhD and published her book *The Turtle and The Peacock* on the results, thus making them available to a broader public and specifically to health communication and TV professionals. The outcome of her work created publicity in the Netherlands because one of Bouman's main arguments was that entertainment with an added value can also be something from which the general public can learn. This was a new thought, because former scientific articles tended to support the idea that popular entertainment generally had little practical value or as Neil Postman (1986) said 'we are amusing ourselves to death'.

The interest in Bouman's research and its relevance and innovation created a starting point for her to apply for more funding for new E-E projects. Bouman was reflecting at that time whether to choose an academic career, but at the time there was not an E-E department or even an E-E curriculum at any of the universities. So she took the decision to create some kind of new discipline herself. In 1999 she started a research organization named Bouman E&E Development which, after growth in both its projects and team members, became the Center for Media & Health in 2007. Bouman emphasized in this context: "The Center for Media & Health is more or less a kind of organic follow up of my earlier work at the Netherlands Heart Foundation and my dissertation at the University of Wageningen. While doing research I wanted to continue exploring and working with the whole concept and idea of Entertainment-Education, and [I thought that] since there was no other place to do it, I would do it myself. So I see the CMH more or less as a private communication department and academic media center" (personal interview September 29, 2009). Since the start of Bouman's first E-E project, *Villa Borghese*, the strategy has been a success developed in the Netherlands. Through research results Bouman could prove that E-E is a strategy which can influence the audience members' knowledge, attitudes and behavior and thus engage in healthier lifestyles. In addition to the research results leading to more advocates and to more funds to work with the strategy, another important event supported Bouman (1) in expanding activities in the Dutch E-E field and (2) in becoming more visible to the international research community. In 1997 Bouman visited the second conference on Entertainment-Education in Ohio, USA. The idea was born there to bring the next international E-E conference to the other continents. The organizers of the conference saw the innovative developments in the Netherlands, and they thought it would be interesting to explore them in-depth. As a result, in 2000 the third international conference on Entertainment-Education was held in the Netherlands and hosted by the Netherlands E-E Foundation of which Bouman is the CEO.

Consequently it is very true for the Dutch history of Entertainment-Education that the development and expansion of the strategy goes primarily back to the pioneering work of Bouman who succeeded in unifying voices behind the strategy. A central difference between the history in the United States and in the Netherlands is that the developments in the Netherlands are even more related to a personalized success story – Bouman's. She did not stay in established organizational structures with the goal of changing them (such as in the case of Vicki Beck with the Centers for Disease Control and Prevention) but she created a completely new organizational structure on her own which should empower different stakeholders to design and implement Entertainment-Education and prosocial change through media formats.

Figure 4.7: Insights for the German analysis resulting from historical change analysis of the Center for Media & Health

---

(1) Funding a first experimental project on E-E
and guiding it with research activities regarding the impact on the audience members as well as on the collaboration process.

(2) Using research results for receiving more research grants:
Based on the first E-E research results, proven changes in knowledge, attitudes and behavior of the audience members lead to further funding for new E-E projects.

(3) E-E research results help to create a vast body of knowledge on the theme
and they can help to overcome fragmentation processes

(4) Based on research results individually creating innovative and new organization(s)
which support(s) the process of strengthening E-E activities and which fit the need for advanced developments of the E-E strategy country-wide.

4.3.5 Dialectic of Dissemination and Dialogue
In analogy to the US media center, the dialectic of dissemination and dialogue is used to illuminate the processes of organizing prosocial change at the CMH. In this section, the developments and synergies of the different collaboration activities the CMH has implemented and improved since its start are depicted according to the main emphasis of the center's approach to Entertainment-Education: (1) consultancy activities, (2) evaluation and methods as well as (3) education.[118]

4.3.5.1 Consultancy Activities
Although the core focus of the CMH lies on designing, implementing and researching E-E projects (see next paragraph), consultancy projects are also an important pillar. The CMH supports health organizations with strategic advice on how to effectively initiate and establish E-E co-productions and inscript participations. Usually the health field engages the CMH to benefit from their E-E expertise because they themselves are less experienced. The CMH gives advice in various contexts and during different stages of collaboration in order to support institutions from the health field to successfully create E-E interventions (i.e. helping them to reach their aims and objectives). These different contexts and stages of collaboration will briefly be described in the following paragraphs to get a clearer picture of how the CMH supports other health organizations through its E-E expertise.

In the *orientation stage* (chapter 2.4.2) of a co-production/inscript participation, the health institution that seeks the advice of the CMH has some ideas about the E-E program it wants to create, but its ideas are not yet concrete. Therefore, the CMH advises them in the initiation of an E-E intervention. For example, they discuss and implement workshops on (1) the program and how to set up a campaign around it, (2) the options for accompanying research on the program and the campaign (see below), (3) financial issues or (4) how to get the TV makers on board. In the *crystallization* and/or in the *production stage* (chapter 2.4.2), the CMH can play a role in doing outreach to TV professionals as a part of their consultancy work. This means that it initiates the contact with them and, together with the health organization, creates a frame for exchanging program contents (creating a briefing document for the TV makers in the crystallization stage, doing a brainstorm in the production stage, etc.).

The popular youth drama series *Costa!* serves as an example of the advisory activities the CMH provides. The consultation by the CMH aimed to support the E-E inscript participation of the health organization *Stichting Soa Bestrijding* (Sexually Transmitted Disease Foundation), which collaborated with the TV professionals from *Costa!*. The *Stichting Soa Bestrijding* asked the CMH for advice to support the E-E inscript participation. The *Stichting Soa Bestrijding* wanted to influence the norms and values of audience members regarding safer sex through a popular entertainment television program, and it was willing to experiment with an E-E intervention. As the *Stichting Soa Bestrijding* had less experience in that field, it

---
[118] An appendix 3 CMH project overview is provided.

called on the CMH as an expert to support them with the initiation and implementation of the intervention. The outcome of the consultation was an E-E collaboration in the context of an inscript participation in six out of ten episodes of *Costa!* in 2001, which promoted entertaining safer sex messages. On behalf of and together with the *Stichting Soa Bestrijding,* the CMH set up initial meetings with the producers and writers of *Costa!* to discuss prerequisites of a potential collaboration. They also created a briefing document and helped to negotiate and coordinate other conditions with the TV makers such as the financial production support and the role of the health side in the decision making process, especially with regard to how to depict the health content.

In the end, the advising activities contained both disseminating and dialogue evoking components. From the dialogue evoking perspective, the interaction between CMH and the health organization asking for advice plays an important role. Furthermore, the interaction processes is significant, which the CMH tries to initiate between the health partner and the television organization. Beside the dialogue evoking components, disseminating elements are also used. This is applicable, for example, in the dialogue processes with the health partner, in which the advice-giving talks are supported through advisory reports, files and data that depict crucial theoretical considerations from the research point of view as well as outcomes from CMH project work. In addition the TV makers receive disseminating information through, for instance, the briefing document.

The CMH team members also made clear that the activities involved when giving advice should be attuned to the specific needs of the partnering health organization. So before starting a consultation, they investigate in detail the principal organization, including its approaches, aims and working environment.

4.3.5.2 Evaluation and Methods

Alongside the consultancy, **evaluation activities** also have a long tradition at the CMH, and they have comprised the majority of the project work since its inception in 1999. Usually, the CMH conducts research involving formative, process and summative measurements (see figure 4.1) for the E-E TV program as well as its communication campaign. The research results are used by the CMH to effectively set up, guide and finally examine the E-E intervention they launch.

Alongside evaluation, the CMH designs and experiments with new communication and research **methods**. These activities contribute to the design, modeling and implementation of innovative collaboration forms and enhance the quality and effectiveness of the E-E collaboration for both partner sides. In consequence, method activities can be introduced in co-production/inscript participation partnership arrangements, E-E service arrangements or even to experiment with new forms in order to find innovative and effective ways of collaborating.

In fact, both activities (evaluation and method) have been developed for and applied in specific project contexts. Thus, if and how long they are applied in practice is very much dependent on the duration and funding of each project. Two project examples will briefly be depicted here to show how evaluation and method activities work in practice in CMH projects.

Sound Effects campaign – Evaluation through Formative, Process and Summative Research
Using the example of the *Sound* Effects campaign (2006-2009), the CMH and the *Public Health Service of Amsterdam (Geneeskundige en Gezondheidsdienst (GGD) Amsterdam)* received a grant from the governmental organization *ZonMw* to design, develop, implement and research a campaign for preventing hearing loss among young adolescents (16-30) who frequently visit discotheques, dance events and other music venues. In order to reach the target group with an effective approach and to evaluate it, the CMH did formative, process and summative research. When applying *formative research*, the CMH first investigated, through collecting both qualitative and quantitative data (MSN chatinterviews with youngsters and personal interviews with stakeholders), which communication and media channels young people use and what their prior knowledge, attitude and behavior was regarding the hearing loss issue. Based on these results, the CMH decided among others to design and implement an E-E drama series named *Sound*, which is broadcasted on the internet. The CMH and the *GGD Amsterdam* created a briefing document and collaborated with TV professionals from *Endemol Productions*, to develop and produce a compelling, entertaining and educational script for the series. The storylines were pre-tested among the target group members. For example they were asked if they could relate to the story and the content. With the results of this pretest, the content was further (re)designed to enhance its potential to reach younger people, with hearing loss prevention messages.
The theoretical foundation of the campaign of which the *Sound* drama series was part of was the Elaboration-Likelihood-Model (see chapter 2.3.7). To persuade youngsters to seriously deal with the problem of hearing loss, the CMH designed and implemented a campaign using two routes: on the 'peripheral route' the target group was directed to a website where they could watch the *Sound* drama series (www.sound-soap.nl). Directing the youngsters to the website was made possible by using online and viral marketing strategies.[119] On the 'peripheral' website with the drama series, it was possible for visitors to use a direct link to another website (www.gooutplugin.nl). Here the central message of the campaign and background information was given about the topic of hearing damage and prevention measurements.
Also part of the whole research of the campaign was an extensive *process research* study, in which the hindering and facilitating factors and all the decisions that had to be made during the process of the design and the implementation of the campaign were analyzed and described (Jurg & Bouman 2009). For this purpose all the

---

[119] The postcards were central for addressing the youngsters to go to the web page and see a recent episode. In this context slogans have been used like "love makes blind, love makes barren - See you @ www.sound-soap.nl".

minutes of the campaign meetings and other reports were documented in a logbook, so that crucial decision making factors (why and how decision were taken) could be identified and used in the interpretation of the overall results at the end of the campaign several months or even years afterwards.

After the implementation of the whole *Sound Effects* campaign of which the *Sound* drama series was part of, the CMH in collaboration with an external university-based researcher used **summative research** based on a pre-post control group design, to investigate the impact and change on the target group. The summative research showed changes in knowledge in many youngsters, and several mentioned attitude and behavior changes with respect to the hearing damage issues (Bouman et al., 2009; van Empelen, 2009). These changes included taking preventive measurements in discotheques through the use earplugs or not standing in front of the speakers any longer.

By sharing the research results with other professionals via articles, conference presentations and making them available on the internet, the CMH **disseminates** them further into the scientific field. Based on the results of former projects, new E-E projects are granted to the CMH. Furthermore, the (formative) results are used to *initiate dialogue* between the CMH and its collaborating TV professionals, and they serve in these conversations to underpin (legitimization and justification) the importance of offering accurate and authentic depictions of the prosocial program content.

Tips for Scripts – Developing innovative Methods for E-E Collaborations
The idea to design and implement *Tips for Scripts*[120] as an innovative E-E method was inspired by a similar project of Hollywood Health & Society and was borne out of the results from a former project of CMH named *Health on Screen* (Bouman E&E Development, 2005). The *Health on Screen* project investigated the prerequisites of an effective information exchange process between TV and health communication professionals. In this research project the TV makers indicated that they like to receive background information from health experts for their storylines. Today they mostly use the internet to search for more factual information, however often they get lost in the enormous amount of data and find it difficult to choose from the overload of information. So when receiving help and additional information, they were confronted with two problems: (1) health organizations could not deliver adequate information as fast as the TV makers needed them and (2) the advice given on the internet regularly comprised a huge variety, was not clearly arranged and was not recent at all.

To overcome these two challenges, the CMH developed a method of reaching script and scenariowriters through an E-E service approach: the initial project *Tips for Scripts* was funded by the governmental organization *ZowMw*. For implementing *Tips for Scripts* the CMH has worked together with various other health organizations and EndeMol TV production company. *Tips for Scripts* is an online-data-

---

[120]*Tips for Scripts* is a project implemented in 2009/2010 (www.tipsvoorscripts.nl).

base platform providing Dutch TV makers with timely, brief and accurate information, which is specifically adapted to their needs. As a first step, the project designed criteria for an effective portrayal of health information on the platform (e.g. a selection of interesting health topics and case descriptions for storylines). The pilot version of the database was then evaluated to measure whether the online platform was friendly to use as well as interesting and manageable for TV makers. Based on this pilot test some adaptations were made.

In summary, the CMH involves both *information disseminating and dialogue evoking elements* when designing and implementing innovative methods within the frame of their projects.

4.3.5.3 Education

The last group of activities illuminated here belongs to the field of *education activities* for Entertainment-Education. The CMH follows two main tracks in this field: the first track includes workshops, presentations and other events which help to spur the exchange of information and the harmonization between health communication experts and TV entertainment professionals so that they can learn from each other. The second track includes activities which may spur and sensitize (health) communication and media students to engage themselves in the E-E strategy. Applying both tracks goes with more recent developments: the CMH started their first activities in this field in 2004, five years later than the consultancy and evaluation/method activities. One core reason for that lies in the fact that evaluation results from former E-E projects emphasized the need for educational E-E activities through (a) implementing discussion forums for exchanges between TV makers and health communication experts and (b) sensitizing media and (health) communication students regarding E-E issues. Thus, the CMH started planning project activities in this context and the education field. In the following, two important project examples shortly for the tracks (a) and (b) will be illustrated. Specifically, these examples are the *Day of the Soap* for track (a) and the *Teaching Modules* for track (b).

Day of the Soap

The *Day of the Soap* is an annual event to spur an effective and fruitful exchange between health and TV professionals. The CMH implemented this forum for the first time in 2004. Just as HH&S is partnering with the Writers Guild of America West, the CMH has collaborated with the Media Academy in Hilversum where the discussion forum takes place annually.[121] The reason for this partnership is obvious: like the Writers Guild of America West, the Media Academy also has a high reputa-

---

[121] The Media Academy has been the core training institute in the Netherlands for broadcasting companies and the audiovisual industry. Their aim has been to provide quality training for radio, television (regional, national and international) and new media in the field of both programs and facilities. In 2009, the partnership ended, because the Media Academy went bankrupt.

tion among TV makers, and when they implement and advertise an event like the *Day of the Soap*, the probability is quite high that TV makers trust the recommendation and, as a result, participate in this forum. The core approach of the *Day of the Soap* is showing audience members from the prosocial and the entertainment media field how E-E collaboration may effectively work. On each annual *Day of the Soap* forum, **effective collaborations are presented** by giving (on average four to five) good practice project examples from the national as well as the international context. This concept is successful as data analysis emphasizes that Dutch TV makers in particular take what they have learned from the good practice examples and apply it to their working practice. These examples have sensitized Dutch TV makers to partner with experts from the prosocial field. Lebo Ramafoko, program manager at the South African drama series *Soul City*, presented one of these approach examples at the Day of the Soap in 2008. The series *Soul City* is collaborating with the *Soul City Research Institute*, which evaluates the prosocial messages in the drama. As a result, they can measure which of the depicted stories has had a high change impact on the audience members. Ramafoko, for instance, presented a specific storyline about domestic violence.[122] She showed an example clip in which neighbors collectively decide to break the ongoing circle of spousal abuse in the neighborhood. They gathered around the abuser's residence and collectively banged pots and pans, thus censuring the abuser's actions. This episode had one of the highest audience ratings, and after the episode was broadcasted, pot and pan banging to stop domestic violence was reported in several areas in South Africa.

Besides the 'pure presentation' of the E-E collaboration examples, the international and national presenters are asked to give an **inspiration session**. This means that they are asked to explain more about the backgrounds and prerequisites leading to the successful implementation of the good practice example. This inspiration session plays a central role in the course of the *Day of the Soap*, because here, after disseminating information has been given to the audience members in the presentation, dialogue is encouraged between the audience and the presenters. Usually, the *Day of the Soap* is then closed with a *final reflection* and discussion on future perspectives of E-E collaboration in the Netherlands and worldwide.

In essence, the *Day of the Soap* mixes **disseminating and dialogue evoking elements** to spur discussion and create a common frame of understanding.

Teaching modules

The teaching modules project offers tools for sensitizing media and (health) communication students for E-E issues. Therefore, the CMH has set up a collaboration framework with six different educational institutions.[123] The CMH designed a tail-

---

[122] This storyline modeled new collective behavior, and it demonstrated how neighbors might intervene in a domestic violence situation. The prevailing cultural norm in South Africa was for neighbors, even if they wished to help an abused woman, not to intervene in such a situation.

[123] The six institutions are the University of Amsterdam, the University of Maastricht, the

or-made teaching curriculum for each institute and evaluate it. The activities, for example, comprise:

1. Developing a *curriculum* for Entertainment-Education, including theoretical work (e.g. term papers) and practical exercises (e.g. designing an E-E intervention as a project assignment, producing an E-E clip or an episode of a reality show).
2. Team members from the CMH give *guest lectures* in seminars in which they reflect on and discuss health and mass media issues, collaboration issues and the E-E strategy in general.
3. The CMH has implemented a *database together* with the educational partners in order to create an E-E community of young talented professionals (LinkedIn group etc.). Using this database, students can get and exchange information about Entertainment-Education in the Netherlands through an *interactive platform* and, for example, talk job prospects for the future.

Thus, here are also both *disseminating and dialoguing activities* in use which strengthen E-E perspectives for future generations working in the media as well as in the health field.

In essence, figure 4.8 outlines insights derived from the analysis of instrumental changes of CMH.

Figure 4.8: Insights for German E-E collaboration practice resulting from instrumental change analysis of the Center for Media & Health

> (1) Providing a flexible mix of E-E activities:
> An E-E collaboration model is successful when it offers different activities for both collaborating sides that fit their needs in various situations.
>
> (2) Combining dialog evoking and information disseminating elements:
> An E-E collaboration model is successful, when dialog evoking and information disseminating activities are combined in projects.
>
> (3) First putting the emphasis on E-E consultancy and evaluation/method activities,
> then additionally introduce E-E education activities:
> This can be considered a success strategy for constantly fostering Entertainment-Education in the Netherlands.
>
> (4) Activities (consultancy, evaluation/method, education) run in specific project periods:
> Usually the CMH implements one activity (sometimes two) in a single project context (co-production/inscript participation or service), for which they have to apply in a grant process. When receiving the grant, they can start designing and implementing the activity limited to a specific project period.

University of Twente, the Media Academy, the Stenden University in Leewarden and the Netherlands School of Public Occupational Health. Additionally, the project is evaluated by the Education Technology Expertise Centre (OTEC) of the Open University of the Netherlands.

Analyzing the two most significant E-E media centers in western country settings from the viewpoint of three different organizational change perspectives will play a central role in insights for the German analysis in part II of the thesis.

4.4 Summary
4.4.1 Dialectics of Steering Power and Emancipation
By using the approach of dialectics of steering power and emancipation, we learned from the analysis of the collaborative environment and the key agents that in the USA and the Netherlands *different approaches* are implemented.

HH&S uses a *service provider* approach. They frame themselves as facilitators between the health and TV sides, offering services to the TV professionals which completely fit their needs. They clearly distinguish themselves from 'health advocates'. HH&S is a specific program for an *E-E service* collaboration approach. By being the service provider they try to get adequate and authentic health messages through to the TV makers and thus to the audience members, but there is not a guarantee that this will happen at all, because the TV professionals have the final say on what to portray. This also means that, on the other hand, HH&S and their collaborating health content matter specialists have little influence when it comes to the process of what will be broadcasted and what not. For Hollywood TV makers, it is not an incentive at all to receive additional financial support from the health side, because they are not dependent on this money. When the strategy of financial support does not work out for structural market reasons, HH&S took the decision to frame itself as a collaboration process facilitator acting like 'one of them', adapting to their needs and wishes and being there as a reliable and a on-time resource for health information. This can be considered as the most effective strategy for having the highest impact on the produced prosocial entertainment television content, when taking into account the cultural and historical background, the media system as well as the media legislation of the country.

In the Netherlands, the CMH's approach of a *health promoter* is very effective. Furthermore, they are also increasingly filling a role through being a *service provider* similar to HH&S. In their main role as a health promoter, the CMH mostly creates and implements *E-E co-productions* and *E-E inscript participations*. As a service provider, they design and implement E-E service collaborations. This specific role is made possible by and related to the media system and the cultural environment. The TV makers are interested in receiving additional financial resources for their production and sharing a financial budget together to produce a format 'with an added value'. Both the TV and health professionals are part of the decision making process with regard to the program content. Co-productions/inscript participations were possible in public broadcasted TV programs until 2008. Since this time, two important developments have taken place: first, for several reasons, the CMH became increasingly orientated towards creating co-productions/inscript participations in social media/web 2.0 formats. Second, they increasingly explored and experimented with E-E service approaches.

In co-productions/inscript participations, the CMH finally has a higher level of steering power on the program content than in an E-E service collaboration, where they simply act as a service provider.

For Germany it is obvious that the media law and the developments in the media (specifically in the TV environment) are essential prerequisites, which need to be analyzed in detail. Furthermore, the different *roles* of the media centers and the *related forms of E-E collaborations* are connected to each other. While the E-E service collaboration is linked to a service provider role and less steering power, the E-E co-productions/inscript participations are linked to a health promoter role along with a higher level of steering power. These are important aspects of Germany's E-E collaboration practice. The analysis in part II of the thesis will specifically take these points into account.

4.4.2 Dialectics of Fragmentation and Unity

By using the approach of dialectics of fragmentation and unity, we learned from the analysis of historical changes in both the USA and the Netherlands that (1) *fragmentation processes must be overcome* and (2) voices have to be *unified behind an E-E program.* In the USA, Vicki Beck was the pioneering person dealing with this context. In the Netherlands, it was Dr. Martine Bouman. The USA findings showed that looking for key agents who support the E-E pilot program right from the start might be very helpful. When an E-E pilot program has been established, analyses in both countries stressed that it is essential to *guide the pilot activates with research*. If there are positive outcomes, it may be a reason for enlarging the pilot activities.

For Germany, we can conclude that the results from the two media centers also strengthen the insights from the theoretical chapters (specifically chapter 2). They assert that E-E pilot activities are very effective when *evaluating statements* can be made (a) about the collaboration approach itself and (b) about how effective the approach is to positively impact knowledge, attitude or even prosocial behavior of media users. In short, this means that when *investing in an E-E pilot, it is essential to focus on research activities*.

4.4.3 Dialectics of Dissemination and Dialogue

By using the approach of dialectics of dissemination and dialogue we can infer from the analysis of E-E activities that both the USA and the Netherlands use *information disseminating and dialogue evoking activities in a flexible mixture*. This can be considered as a key success factor in both countries. The US model suggests that outreach ('briefings' or 'tip sheets'), events ('awards ceremony' and 'panel discussions') and evaluation activities (impact research) in a mix provide an effective starting point. The model in the Netherlands suggests first implementing consultancy activities (for partnering health experts) as well as evaluation/method activities. As a next step, educational activities can be created and implemented.

According to their organizational structure and approach, HH&S and the CMH introduce their activities differently. The activities of HH&S run side by side as a part of the E-E service strategy, which is *not limited to a specific project period*. Consequently, HH&S receives funding money for the whole program and the staff members decided in consultation with their funders which activities are vital to emphasize, to scale down or to expand by bringing in new ones. In the Netherlands, the CMH runs its *activities in specific project periods*. Usually, the CMH implements one activity (sometimes two) in a single project context for which they have to apply in a grant process. When receiving the grant, they can start the design and implementation stage.

The following figure 4.9 gives a short summary on insights that need to be taken into consideration for the German analysis.

Figure 4.9: Sensitizing insights for the German analysis

(1) Examining the *media legislation* rules and the *status quo of conditions (media system)* for E-E collaborations in detail.
How is both handled by the E-E implementers in practice?

(2) Analyzing to the *forms of collaborations*:
co-production/inscript participation and service and how far they are implemented in practice.

(3) Investigating whether there is/are *(an)other collaboration form(s) available*
apart from service, co-production and inscript participation.

(4) Analyzing the *facilitating role* and the *steering power* of the health experts within these forms of collaborations.

(5) Analyzing *which type of approach* may be useful when implementing an E-E media center in Germany.

(6) Investigating which *activities* may be fruitful
when deciding on the order for an effective German E-E approach.

Epilogue I
Conclusions and Lessons Learned

The purpose of this epilogue is to summarize some conclusions and lessons learned that answer the first two sub-questions of this thesis:

A1 *Analyzing theoretical debates*: What is the status quo in scientific debates in the field of Entertainment-Education and prosocial entertainment television and how might this provide hints for answering the main research question?

A2 *Analyzing significant E-E media center approaches*: Which insights can be composed from two significant international E-E media centers in order to get closer to the conditions and forms of E-E collaborations in Germany and effective future collaboration practice?

E-E Theory (Sub-question A1)
Chapter 2 outlined the E-E approach based on an interdisciplinary theoretical

framework (chapters 2.3 and 2.4). Governmental (related) organizations and scholars from universities working from outside Germany started using different theories and concept origins from the scientific fields of psychology, communication and social science as well as social marketing and advertising as a foundation for their E-E projects. They specifically want to find out how these theories can be used to reach audience members with prosocial content and thus change their knowledge, attitude or even behavior. Furthermore, theoretical aspects of E-E collaboration forms and stages were presented. For a collaboration in Germany, it may be useful to explore which possibilities can be developed from theoretical foundations based on the current practice situation, which will be examined in part II of the thesis.

Besides dealing with E-E theory, E-E effects (chapters 2.5 and 2.6) were also discussed. The outcome was that, on the one hand, there are critics for whom Entertainment-Education will never have the same effect in the west as it has had in non-western countries. On the other hand, there have also been achievements and positive results available for E-E interventions in western countries. For Germany and for the analysis in part II, it may be important to be aware of potential domestic criticism.

E-E Definition (Sub-question A1)

Using scholarly literature, the current definition of Entertainment-Education was presented. On this basis, a reformulated definition which fits into the research frame was established and is discussed over the course of this thesis: *"Entertainment-Education is a theory-based communication strategy in which educational and entertainment professionals purposefully embed prosocial issues in the creation, production, processing, and dissemination process of an entertainment program in order to achieve different stages of change either on individual, community, institutional or societal level among the intended media user populations"*.

This status quo of E-E definition includes the contention (1) that theory is involved in the E-E collaboration process and (2) that prosocial and TV professionals work together (with more or less the same involvement) in all stages of the design and implementation of the TV program. This definition can be considered as an ***ideal one***. It refers to ***E-E co-production/inscript participation*** partnership arrangements, where both conditions (theory involvement and partners who jointly work on the program content) are fulfilled. But as already discussed in chapter 2.4, there is another form of collaboration, E-E service, which varies from this definition in the sense that the prosocial side advises the TV makers on the program content, but they are ***not*** jointly creating and implementing it together in the different stages of the program development. This is also exactly the reason why no E-E theory is regularly applied in this form of partnership: the prosocial side does not play a proactive part in the different stages of decision making on the program content. In consequence, this means that there are collaboration activities in practice (see E-E service in chapter 2.4.1) which ***vary from the ideal definition of Entertainment-Edu-***

cation. But this variation makes the situation even more interesting and colorful. It shows that there are other activities and forms of collaboration, which can be considered as a less comprehensive ***version of the ideal definition***, but nevertheless can indeed be understood as an E-E activity in a broader sense.

How far the ideal definition is applied in Germany, and which variations exist (i.e. E-E service or maybe even another form or activity) will be addressed and discussed in part II of the thesis. After exploring these and other questions, it might be necessary to add some new components to the discussion about the ideal definition and its variations according to the results from Germany's collaboration practice.

Formative, Process and Summative Research (Sub-question A1)
One striking element of Entertainment-Education is to implement research during the collaboration process. In the Netherlands, the CMH's main collaboration arrangements created and implemented are E-E co-production and E-E inscript participation collaborations, in which a TV program is guided by formative, process and summative research for reaching audience members effectively. Both formative and process research is not easy to implement in western countries when it comes to programs broadcasted to a mass media audience. In the majority of cases, there is simply no time to do this type of research and to integrate the results into the TV program. Nonetheless, the Netherlands succeeded in implementing several of these research results based on mass television TV programs.

In the USA, where HH&S runs an E-E service collaboration program, the center team members conduct summative research. Formative and process research is usually not possible to implement. Summative research has been established as a very useful E-E research instrument for measuring the impact of E-E programs. Both in the USA and in the Netherlands, this is quite a common procedure. In Germany neither summative nor formative and process research is done in programs in which TV and prosocial professionals team up. Exploring the conditions for conducting further research in the E-E field is a central conclusion to be drawn for part II of this thesis. In this context, one of the important questions is to ask how far it is possible to introduce not only summative but also formative or process research related to E-E formats.

TV (Entertainment) Research (Sub-question A1)
From the standpoint of TV entertainment research, it became clear that the medium of television has changed its meaning and purpose regarding historical and societal developments over the last seven decades. Current literature refers to a global 'entertainment era' and thus it makes sense to focus on entertainment TV and its impact on audience members. TV entertainment research exists internationally, but it is a rare trend in Germany.

For investigating impacts as well as the placement of the prosocial content, experts from governmental (related) authorities and research institutions use different television research traditions (see chapter 3.2.1). Existing literature emphasizes in this context that no clear cause-effect statement can be made about the impact that entertainment TV has on the audience members. The research results may differ according to components such as (1) the targeted audience members, (2) the broadcasting time, (3) the complexity of the message or (4) the interpersonal communication measures for the audience members which can be engaged after they have watched the TV program. In consequence, this means that there is a need to introduce or strengthen both research and the theoretical groundwork surrounding E-E interventions in Germany. Part II of the thesis tries to contribute to and answer what possibilities may exist in this context.

Another important factor, which provides a hint for answering the main research question, is the genre discussion and the question about which entertainment genres are useful when incorporating prosocial content. The analysis revealed that drama (daily soaps and telenovelas), game and quiz shows, detective programs and children's programs have great potential for depicting E-E topics aimed at changing behavior and spurring interpersonal communication. This also should be taken into consideration in the German context.

The examination of ethical aspects in Entertainment-Education showed that they may play an important role when it comes to the implementation of E-E collaborations in Germany. Specifically the Source Dilemma in Entertainment-Education seems to be important (i.e. the question of who decides about what are prosocial and antisocial messages or what constitutes 'good or bad' and who decides what messages will be implemented). German TV makers have the sovereign power enforced by media legislation to decide what they want to send without being influenced by third parties (see chapter 6.1). This provides interesting perspectives on how E-E collaborations are practiced in Germany.

Insights from the Media Centers in the USA and the Netherlands (Sub-question A2)

In chapter 4 of the thesis, several insights were deduced by analyzing the two chief E-E collaboration centers in the USA and in the Netherlands.

One central outcome is that the E-E collaboration practice is strongly related to ***media legislation rules*** and questions such as: Are prosocial change organizations allowed to share a financial budget together with the TV professionals and to have steering power on the program content of a TV format? If yes, to what extent, and which practice developments can be observed? If not, what other practice is identifiable? Besides media legislation and questions predominantly deriving from it, the ***current developments in the TV market as well as the organizational developments in the prosocial field*** play a decisive role and need to be examined in detail. This touches questions such as: How do TV producers finance their TV formats and to what extent are they reliant on governmental (related) authorities as a financial resource? And what are the aims of prosocial change organizations when reaching specific target group members? Do they also focus on mainstream milieus in their approaches, and if so, are they open to experimenting with an affective instead of a cognitive communication strategy?

According to these prerequisites, the USA and the Netherlands implement different *forms of collaborations*. The US model involves a *service* partnership arrangement with a specific strategy for approaching TV makers. The Dutch model primarily uses *co-productions and inscript participations* when implementing E-E interventions. In recent years, the Dutch model has also increasingly included E-E service activities (specifically due to changes in the media legislation). In addition, during their respective collaborations both media centers play different *roles in the partnerships*. The center in the USA assumes a role as a service provider, 'moderating' between the health and the entertainment TV side in their E-E service program, whereas the Dutch center primarily interacts as a health promoter, bringing in their health communication perspective much more strongly, because they have more steering power over the program content.

In conclusion, based on the analysis of media legislation and current developments in the TV market, the question of which forms of collaborations and practices exist and how they can (or cannot) be related to the approaches in the USA and the Netherlands are raised regarding Germany. Furthermore, part II of the thesis poses the question, which recommendations can be given for a future media center approach in Germany.

The analysis suggests that on the way to greater E-E efforts (such as a pilot project program or the formation of a media center), *several processes of fragmentation* need to be taken into account. Both media centers needed more than one decade to overcome these fragmentation processes and to *achieve unifying efforts* by experimenting and finding strategies for an effective E-E approach. For Germany, the question is raised about the fragmentation processes which currently exist and to what extent it is useful to take the insights in the USA and the Netherlands into consideration when finding a strategy for the implementation of a pilot project or when looking for key agents supporting the E-E topic.

Both the USA and the Netherlands apply activities from their media center work such as outreach, event and evaluation (see USA) or consultancy, evaluation/method and education activities (see the Netherlands) to meet the country-specific needs of their funders and partners. Both activity strategies have in common that they provide a flexible mixture of *dialog evoking and information disseminating elements*. An examination of which activities have already been implemented in Germany as well as what activities may be useful to introduce and in which order will be touched upon in the part II of the thesis.

PART II

5. Research Methodology

> "If what is designated by such terms as doubt, belief, idea, conception, is to have any objective meaning, to say nothing of public verifiability, it must be located and described as behavior in which organism and environment act together, or inter-act".
>
> - John Dewey 1938: 38

Whereas part I of the thesis dealt with E-E theory and insights from international E-E media centers to find hints for significant conditions and forms of E-E collaborations in Germany, part II provides the answer to the main research question. In this chapter, the methodology of the empirical research into the E-E collaboration process will be presented. Before, a short digression will be given on the term 'sustainability' or 'sustainable development', and why using this term in part II of the thesis is preferable to 'prosocial change' (see chapter 1).

Digression 'sustainability'/'sustainable development'
With chapter 5, part II of the thesis begins and the focus is exclusively on the German E-E collaboration context. As explained in chapter 1.1, from here on the term 'sustainability' (and not 'prosocial (change)') will be used to describe themes, organizations and experts from the health, social or environmental field who want to achieve 'socially desirable' developments.[124] But why this change in terms of describing a socially desirable development? The term 'sustainability' is used in German scholarly literature to describe the socially desirable processes to which society should aspire (Grunwald & Kopfmüller, 2006; Schwender et al., 2008). 'Sustainability' or 'sustainable development' is reflected as an overall concept and a moral value (Grunwald & Kopfmüller, 2006; Hauff, 1987). It is also used by different societal stakeholders (government, research and science, media) as an 'umbrella term' to bring health, social and environmental themes together (Ali, 2002; Bundesregierung, 2004; Reisch & Bietz, 2006; Trojan & Legewie, 2001; Rat für Nachhaltige Entwicklung, 2006). In general, Germany can be considered a country in which the term is used and discussed in many social or cultural environ-

---

[124] Although the terms 'prosocial change' and 'sustainability'/'sustainable development' both describe socially desirable developments, the terms have different origins; they have been reflected and used so far in different scholarly traditions and cultural contexts, and these differences should be paid attention to. In scholarly discussions, the relatedness of the terms 'prosocial change (communication)' and 'sustainability (communication)' has not been reflected yet; no clear intersections or differences have been defined so far. Research is thus necessary to clarify where both the prosocial change and the sustainability communication fields have interfaces, where they do not and what they can learn from each other.

ments[125] and specifically among well-educated societal groups. Current academic discussions specifically reflect how people from lower socio-economic milieus can be reached with 'sustainability messages' to increasingly integrate sustainable behavior patterns into their everyday life (Liedtke et al., 2007; Lubjuhn & Reinermann, 2010; Reisch & Kreeb, 2007; Schulz et al., 2008; Schwender et al., 2008). The challenge is that in German academia the field of 'sustainability communication'[126] has not been reflected and explored so far with respect to the E-E tradition. One reason is that sustainability communication as well as Entertainment-Education are both new fields for German academic discussions which first need to be explored in communication science and research (Reinermann & Lubjuhn, 2011). Given the background on sustainability/sustainable development in Germany in this short digression, it makes much sense in the eyes of the author to build a bridge from the sustainability field to the E-E field and to bring both together in part II of the thesis.

5.1 Research Question

The main research question in this E-E research study is:
What are the conditions and forms for Entertainment-Education collaborations between entertainment television professionals and sustainability experts from governmental (related) authorities?
In total, the main research question consists of five sub-questions, of which the following first two sub-questions were answered in part I of the thesis:

A1 *Analyzing theoretical debates*: What is the status quo in scientific debates in the field of Entertainment-Education and prosocial entertainment television and how might this provide hints for answering the main research question?

A2 *Analyzing significant E-E media center approaches*: Which insights can be composed from two significant international E-E media centers in order to get closer to the conditions and forms of E-E collaborations in Germany and effective future collaboration practice?

Three further sub-questions (sub-questions B1-B3),[127] will be answered in part II:

---

[125] In the following, some examples are given to strengthen the argument: Germany, for example has a *Rat für Nachhaltige Entwicklung* (Council for Sustainable Development) or the German government publishes a national strategy for a sustainable development. There are many bottom-up movements in the field of sustainability, such as student organizations, consumer groups and so on. Furthermore, the *deutscher Nachhaltigkeitspreis* (German Sustainability Award) is awarded for businesses showing an excellent sustainability performance.

[126] Sustainability communication can be defined according to Michelsen (2007: 27) as a "Communication process which deals with a new, secure social development which is centered on the principle of sustainability. Values and norms such as inter- and intra-generational justice are included in it as is root cause analysis and the perception of problems as well as individual social action and design options".

[127] At this point it is important to stress that in this part II, it was originally planned to integrate a fourth sub-question, dealing with the description of Germany's status quo of E-E collaboration implementers: Which E-E collaborations exist in Germany's television field (i.e.

B1 *Researching conditional collaboration factors*: What are significant conditions (i.e. external and internal conditions as well as crucial characteristics) of present E-E collaborations in Germany which influence the collaboration process?

B2 *Investigating collaboration practices and their forms in depth*: Based on the conditions and characteristics, how can the present collaboration process between sustainability experts and television professionals in Germany be described in different forms and stages with regard to the development and implementation of collaborations?

B3 *Developing a theoretical concept and making recommendations for the future*: Based on the conditions, characteristics and forms, how can the theoretical concept of E-E collaborations in Germany be summarized and what are the best recommendations for the German collaboration context when managing E-E collaborations in the future?

Having answered these three sub-questions with the help of a qualitative study will lead to the answer of the main research question. The methodological reflections of the study are described in the following.

5.2 Introduction to the Data Collection and Analysis with the Grounded-Theory Methodology

This chapter aims at methodological, process-orientated and, as far as possible, chronological documentation of the study. After some general introductory remarks, the phases of data collection (section 5.3) and data analysis (section 5.4) will be described in detail.

The research of this thesis is based on the qualitative research approach of the Grounded Theory analysis of Corbin & Strauss (2008), who base their empirical data founded theory on the symbolical interactionism (Denzin, 1994). Corbin & Strauss (Corbin & Strauss, 2008: 1) define the Grounded Theory as a "specific methodology developed by Glaser and Strauss (1967) for the purpose of building theory from data". They use the term Grounded Theory in a generic sense to denote theoretical constructs derived from qualitative analysis (ibid.).[128] As a part of qual-

---

which organizations team up?). The answer to this question was given during the research process. The results will reveal that several E-E collaborations act in a difficult environment. Therefore, out of organizational and personal protection reasons, the researcher decided that none of the organizations (and by extension the names of the implementers) will be named in part II. Hence, the question regarding which partners team up was naturally answered in the data collection process (see below), but will not be elaborated here.

[128] The Grounded Theory has changed and developed further in its history. This thesis alludes to the more recent formulations (Corbin & Strauss, 2008; Corbin & Strauss, 1990; Charmaz, 2006). Using primary and secondary literature (Breuer 2009; Charmaz, 2006; Corbin & Strauss, 2008; Legewie, 1993), the current formulation can, as far as possible, be discerned from the depiction of commonly used terms in Grounded Theory (e.g. open, axial and selective coding, coding paradigm, theoretical sampling method of constant comparison, categories, dimensions, theoretical saturation).

itative research, the Grounded Theory allows the development of a theory or a theoretical concept to emerge from the data through constant comparison and by giving free space to those issues which may occur in the process of research (Berg & Milmeister, 2008). Thus, it stands in contrast to quantitative approaches, where a theory or hypothesis forms the start and the aim is to verify or falsify it during the research process.

By applying the Grounded Theory methodology, this study was incorporated in a research process, in which the researcher changes the research theme and the theme changes the researcher (Breuer, 2000; Mruck, 2000). Consequently, the outcomes of this study must be understood as a product of an *interaction process*.

But why is the Grounded Theory applied? And, more generally spoken, why is qualitative research used? Indeed, the answer to these questions is directly related to the main research question itself (Reichertz, 2007a). Responding to the latter question may be self-evident: as indicated in chapter 1, this thesis uses a qualitative approach, because the German E-E collaboration field has not been investigated yet. So this study aims to set some markers in a field which is still terra incognita by answering the main research question concerning conditions and forms for E-E collaborations (i.e. depicting the social actions of the different milieus, fields or worlds of sustainability experts and entertainment professionals TV during their collaboration process). Answering the question of why the Grounded Theory methodology is applied is a bit more complex. The Grounded Theory was found to best fit as a methodology for answering the research question after going through an in-depth examination of qualitative research tools. Reichertz and colleagues (Lüders & Reichertz, 1986; Reichertz, 2007a) have provided crucial guidance for the decision making process regarding the question of which methodology to apply to effectively answer the main research question. Reichertz and colleagues differentiate qualitative research into four 'big traditions of questions'. They argue that first, each qualitative research question (and interest) can be subordinated to these 'big traditions'. Secondly, they stress that with each 'questioning tradition' a jointly used portfolio of research methodologies and methods can be linked. Those traditions are the following: (1) the question according to subjective sense structures and actions, (2) description of social actions and milieus, (3) reconstruction of interpretation- and action-generating structures and (4) (re-) construction of historical and social pre-stylized interpretation work. The main research question posed in this thesis regarding conditions and forms of E-E collaborations clearly belongs to the second principle question; the *description of social actions and milieus*. In this regard, the goal is to describe and document various professional domains as well as to investigate different rules and symbols through the help of a specific tradition (e.g. interactionism, sociology of knowledge, etc.) (ibid.). As suggested by Reichertz (Reichertz, 2007a; Reichertz, 2008), the 'questioning tradition' of social actions and milieus revolves around applying the Grounded Theory and this study explicitly follows this direction.

5.3 Data Collection
5.3.1 Theoretical Sampling
The term theoretical sampling can be defined as sampling on the basis of the concepts derived from data (Corbin & Strauss, 2008: 65). In this present study, the theoretical sampling specifically focuses on the selection criteria of E-E collaborations based on which the collaboration examples were chosen, and on the interview partners who implemented these collaborations. Through the establishment of the criteria, it was possible to define E-E collaborations more in detail and compare them to each other. The methodological approach according to the selection criteria is outlined in the following.

As there is no status quo of E-E collaborations available in Germany from which potential study participants could be selected, the first and initial task was to conduct an appraisal on the status quo concerning E-E collaborations with the help of *selection criteria* that fit the focus of the research interest. After in-depth literature research, the following criteria were created based on (1) experiences made by the researcher in the Dutch and the US collaboration environment and (2) experiences with some German E-E implementers before the interviews and informal talks started (i.e. through field visits, participatory observations and workshops):

- *Collaboration partners*: Collaboration examples were analyzed in which governmental (or agencies working on their behalf) teamed up with entertainment television professionals in order to reach people with sustainability messages. This included ecological, health and social themes.
- *Communication in public/scholarship*: Examples were chosen in which the above-mentioned implementers communicated in any way to the scholarly environment or the public (e.g. at least through giving general information on their organizational webpage, in newsletters, etc.) that they were engaged in a collaboration by naming the partner side. (This effectively excludes those collaborations in which the implementers did not communicate the collaboration activities in any way).
- *Detectable timeframe*: Collaborations were included which took place before 2009 (according to the data collection period).
- *Mass media coverage*: Examples were selected in which the collaboration activities addressed a mass (mainstream) audience through the television format and not regionally/locally broadcasted TV programs, which are only able to cover a small segment of audience members.
- *Promote change*: Examples were included which preferably offer sustainable solutions and promote a change in knowledge, attitude and behavior through the collaboration.

On the basis of these selection criteria, *17 E-E collaboration examples* (in 17 different mass television formats) were selected as a *status quo*. The first examples were traced back to the early 1990s. Usually at this point, those collaborators should have been mentioned to give the reader a more transparent insight in the data collection process. This will not happen here in order to protect the study participants' anonymity as guaranteed. Only through this guarantee it was possible to conduct a comprehensive data collection of the E-E collaboration field at all.

After establishing a status quo, the collaboration examples were investigated more in depth as much as possible (through literature and internet research) to deepen the background knowledge on each collaboration and to find out some of their core characteristics. Therefore, a *desktop research* was undertaken and an analysis grid of each collaboration was developed. The aim of this research step was to become more familiar with each collaboration and its activities and procedures before talking to the study participants (also see Breuer & Lettau, 2009).

Afterwards, the study participants were contacted (see next section). The first interview was conducted with a sustainability expert and the second one with a television professional to not only compare and examine differences, but also to look at where connections are. Table 5.1 gives an overview of the number of study participants and the professional field they are from (sustainability, television entertainment and media legislation field[129]) who were interviewed and/or spoke informally with the researcher during informal talks.

Table 5.1: Overview of the study participants

	Interviews	Informal talks
Television professionals	13	7
Sustainability professionals	10	2
Media legislation experts	2	2
Total	25	11

As the table indicates, in total **25 interviews** and **11 informal talks** on E-E collaboration activities were arranged. The core reason for implementing additional informal talks was that, during the data collection process, it became obvious that several E-E implementers did not want to talk about (all) their experience when being tape-recorded, although their anonymous status was guaranteed. They preferred to meet with the researcher to informally talk about their experience without putting their voices or specific issues on tape.

Bringing the data collected from interviews and informal E-E collaboration talks together, all 17 collaborations that constitute the E-E status quo were covered.

---

[129] The media legislation experts were additionally consulted, because the media legislation turned out to play a crucial role in the German context (see section 5.3.5).

5.3.2 Contact Initiation

The contact initiation was generally carried out by e-mail through a standardized cover letter which contained background information on the study, the interview request to use a tape-recorder, the content of the questions, the style of the interview, the confirmation of anonymity and an announcement that the researcher will contact them by telephone. In the majority of the cases, the telephone conversation was used to discuss the question of the willingness to participate, an additional confirmation of the participant's anonymity and the scheduling of an appointment. In a few cases, the telephone call was used for further questions regarding the content of the study. In several cases the study participants wrote back via e-mail that there was no additional conversation on the telephone needed, and they suggested options for interview appointments.

Most of the contacted E-E implementers announced a high interest in the study and its results and agreed to an interview appointment, although no financial compensation could be offered. Two of the people contacted declined to be interviewed. One said that the reason for not wanting to take part was because there was too little time available, and the other mentioned that he had changed to a new organization since the collaboration had ended, and he thus does not want to talk about the issue anymore. The person, who said that he had little time, suggested answering questions on the collaboration process in written form, which the researcher agreed upon.

5.3.3 Interview Style

The qualitative literature comprises a confusing multiplicity of attributes which serve to typify interviews through their used form of negotiation (e.g. problem-centralized; theme-centralized; focused; narrative; standardized – partly standardized – non standardized; structured – non-structured; open – closed). The typology is heterogeneous and the borders between the different interview types are fluid. Flick (1995) focuses on a bi-categorized dimensioning and differentiates between narrative and guided interviews. Similarly, Breuer (1996) suggests the distinction of narrative and focused interviews. Schütze, Merton & Kendall described prototypes of those interviews very early (Merton & Kendall, 1979; Merton et al., 1956; Schütze, 1983). In the continuum between narrative, focused and guided interviews, this study maintained a position in-between the three poles with a strong affinity to the narrative interview style. During the whole data collection process, the researcher tried to follow the ideal model of an interested, though rather uninformed listener while the study participants had the position of an expert (Breuer, 1996). The researcher used a basic guideline, which was based on the insights from the international E-E field as well as on prior experiences and the knowledge established about these collaborations in Germany. The guideline was understood as a background tool not in a sense that it produced a standardized interview, but more in the sense that it limited the interview to a list of possible themes and questions. Furthermore, during the interview progress, the guideline was adapted according to the findings withdrawn from former interviews.

In narrative interviews, the first narration-generating question has an essential meaning for the interview process. It tries to generate a holistic and narrative perspective and also familiarizes the interview partner with the interview style. The researcher used a narration-generating question, which elicits a story of the collaboration, starting with the first developments and closing with what can be considered the collaboration's end. This question motivated the interview partners more prone to monologues, to tell their stories for about 90 minutes. In the case of the interview partners more prone to dialogue, the stories lasted around 10 minutes. This goes with the findings of Witzel (2000) that some interview partners prefer a more narrative style while others prefer an emphasis on dialogue. The interview partners guided as far as possible the course and progress of the exchange, which required a flexible adaptation on the part of the interviewer.

Literature describes a change during the interview when using qualitative interview techniques. Witzel (2000), for example, notes the development from questions generating narration to questions generating understanding. Schorn (2000) differentiates between horizontal (holistical) and vertical (deepening) questions, whereas Schütze (1983) describes an ongoing change between a narrative demand and questions regarding abstraction. In the interviews conducted, similar differentiations were pursued. Whereas in the beginning demands regarding open narrations were predominate, follow up questions according to the narrations were raised at an advanced stage.

At this point it should become clear that the author considered another option of data collection (beside interviews/informal talks), namely to conduct participatory observations as an 'embedded researcher' in organizations which designed and implemented E-E collaborations. Becoming a member of their field would have meant becoming one of them and thus learning in practice how they interact. This approach turned out to be not feasible, mainly for two reasons: firstly, in the time frame of data collection, there was no ongoing E-E collaboration the researcher could have used for participatory field observations. Secondly, it turned out to be a very difficult issue for a researcher to get involved in the field and to receive insider information first hand. As a result, the author decided to refrain from participatory observations while being aware of the limitations of this decision, i.e. through 'only' conducting interviews and informal talks, the study participants generate *self-reported data*. This means that the collected data only allows statements about what they said is the case in the field of E-E collaborations, but no statements about the interaction going on between the partners which would have been possible through participatory observations while working as a 'member' in the E-E collaboration field.

5.3.4 Course of the Interviews

The interviews were conducted in three different phases from May 2009 until February 2010. The first interview phase was implemented from May to July 2009 (four interviews), the second from September to mid October 2010 (ten interviews) and the third from mid November 2009 to February 2010 (ten interviews) until the categories in the data were 'saturated'[130] (Charmaz, 2006; Corbin & Strauss, 2008). The different phases served to iteratively implement the study (Berg & Milmeister, 2008). The time in between the interview phases was used for the first analytical steps. On the basis of these findings new interview partners were contacted. Interestingly, several of the interview partners not only referred to their collaboration partners as potential future study participants, but they also knew people who implemented other E-E collaborations and alluded to them.

The interview locations were selected according to the preferences of each study participant. Some asked the researcher to visit the working place and have the interview there (at a sustainability organization, at the production company or at the broadcasting station), while others preferred to meet in a more neutral and public environment, typically in a café.

The interviews usually proceed in terms of first asking the instructional question. After the first narration was finished, the researcher posed follow up questions regarding the conditions and the consequences of their experiences. In addition, the interview partners were asked in depth about contexts, which seem to have a great importance but which were only briefly mentioned in former narrations. After or in combination with these follow up questions, some of the points of the guideline came in to play. The interviews duration lasted from 25 minutes to 150 minutes. The majority of interviews were around 100 to 125 minutes. Five interview partners (three from the television and two from the sustainability field) asked to stop the recorder while the interview was happening and they advised the researcher to 'just listen'. Than a shorter phase of narration started.[131] After the points had been mentioned, the researcher was allowed to switch on the tape recorder again.

The informal talks lasted from 30 to 150 minutes. There were six interview partners who were engaged in an informal talk after the interview. For each informal talk, detailed *field notes* were taken which contain conceptualization and analytic remarks following the standards of Corbin & Strauss (2008: 123-124). Schatzmann & Strauss (1973) and Corbin & Strauss (2008) moreover differentiate field notes in more detail with respect to *observational notes*, comprising the description of the actual event, and *theoretical notes*, denoting the researcher's thoughts about the event to holistically comprehend the ongoing talk. Both observational and theoretical notes have been integrated in the data analysis process.

Beside the field notes on the informal E-E collaboration talks, a *field note* was cre-

---

[130] "Categories are 'saturated' when gathering fresh data no longer sparks new theoretical insights, nor reveals new properties of these core theoretical categories" (Charmaz, 2006: 113).

[131] The reader might note that these 'interruptions' in the interview were not additionally taken into account in the 13 informal talks mentioned above. Informal talks only include those people who (1) wanted to give information without being tape-reordered or (2) ended the interview with the researcher (a clear cut was made) and then started to tell more of their collaboration story.

ated from each interview (i.e. in this case an *observational note*, which also was integrated in the data analysis process).

5.3.5 Sensitizing Concepts

As mentioned above, the interviews were conducted with the narrative collaboration story of the E-E implementers in mind. During the follow up question part of each interview, several sensitizing[132] concepts were also addressed where possible. These sensitizing concepts were usually a part of the guideline (i.e. they were mentioned as part of the background information for the researcher). The sensitizing concepts were based on the experiences the researcher made in the international E-E field and the first experiences collected in the German collaboration context (1) through the desktop research as well as (2) through field visits, participatory observations and workshops with German E-E implementers (see section 5.3.1 for both). During the interviews, the sensitizing concepts were used as a reflective help for the researcher to holistically scrutinize and picture the research interest later on during the analysis. In the following, the sensitizing concepts are briefly depicted.

Figure 5.1: Sensitizing concepts

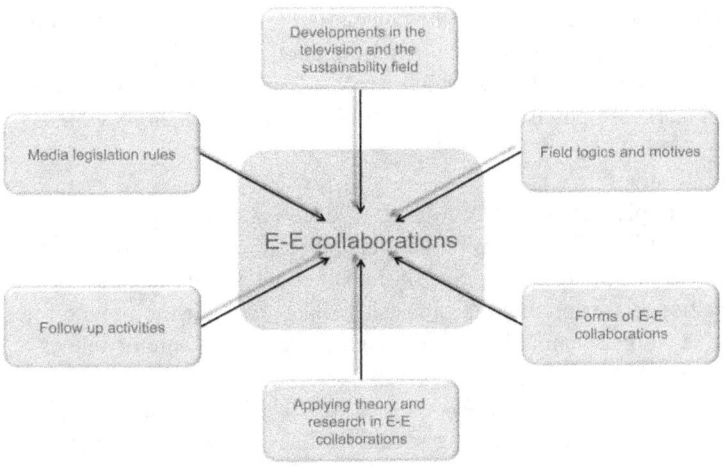

---

[132] 'Sensitivity' in the Grounded Theory methodology is described by Dey (1993: 63) (cited after Corbin & Strauss, 2008: 32-33): "there is a difference between an open mind and an empty head. To analyze data researchers draw upon accumulated knowledge. They don't dispense with it. The issue is not whether to use existing knowledge, but how". This quotation indicates that sensitivity stands in the Grounded Theory for insights and knowledge which existed before the data analysis starts and stand in an interplay with the data. „Sensitivity stands in contrast to objectivity. It requires that a researcher put him- or herself into the research. Sensitivity means having insight, being tuned in to, being able to pick up on relevant issues, events, and happenings in data. (...) insights into data do not just occur haphazardly, they happen to prepared minds during the interplay with the data" (Corbin & Strauss 2008: 32).

Media Legislation Rules
The examination and comparison of the Dutch and the US collaboration models indicated that E-E collaborations are very much dependent on the media legislation rules and the television system in which they are implemented. The researcher has kept this back in mind when she implemented the interviews. If participants raised the regulatory issue, they were asked to reflect on the theme in more detail (using their knowledge and experience) or the researcher raised the theme, when it turned out to have a possible importance in the collaboration process described by the participant. As media legislations turned out to be a crucial sensitizing concept, the researcher arranged additional interviews and informal talks with four media legislation experts.

Developments in the Television and the Sustainability Field
The description of the international E-E examples showed that current developments taking place in the sustainability and television field influence the E-E collaboration. Although this was a logical effect, the researcher made herself explicitly aware of this interrelation as a sensitizing concept. It further was a guideline through the whole data collection process. The researcher unobtrusively looked at the general developments and characteristics named by the participants in their own fields and how they interrelated to the counterparts' field. Relevant questions in this context were: 'Can you please explain more about the background on how entertainment media issues are dealt with in your field?' and 'Which developments on the television market might affect the collaboration with sustainability experts?'

Field Logics and Motives
The collaboration implementers act according to different field logics, and their main motives for getting engaged in the partnership result from this field logics. For instance, on the one hand, one motive of the Dutch television makers is to receive additional financial support from the sustainability side for the program development. On the other hand, this motive cannot be found among television makers in the USA.
Generally, the international E-E field showed that the field logics and the resulting motives of the partners lead to prioritizing specific collaboration forms (co-productions, inscript participations or service partnerships). Thus, during the interviews, the study participants were asked about their motives as well as their counterparts' motives for engaging in a collaboration. They were invited to tell more about their own professional fields as well as those of their partners. Besides, they were asked to find some characterizing words or metaphors in this context to get closer to the field logics and motives they are engaged in.

Forms of E-E Collaborations
Part I of the thesis also sensitized the researcher regarding different forms of collaborations. There are specific forms predominantly implemented in either the

USA or the Netherlands. This is due to the domestic television market and its regulations. In short, the forms must fit; otherwise it might become difficult to design and implement an E-E collaboration. The researcher refrained from posing questions regarding these forms and the stages of collaborations to the interview partners or prematurely trying to subordinate different German collaboration examples to various collaboration forms found in the international portfolio. The awareness of the different forms served more as a sensitizing concept for in-depth reflections of Germany's E-E characteristics. The international collaboration forms were kept in mind during the whole data collection and analysis process and the research constantly reflected to what extent the traced international E-E forms and their definitions were suitable for the German environment. Specifically, this means dealing with the questions of which forms can be adapted to the study findings and which must come in as new forms and components for the German collaboration context.

Applying Theory and Research in E-E Collaborations
In the Dutch and/or the US collaboration environment, E-E theory as well as formative, summative and process research is applied. During the interviews, it was essential for the researcher to experience whether the E-E implementers also applied theoretical notions and research, and why they did or did not so. Furthermore, by the end of the interview/informal talk, the researcher explained in several sentences how a collaboration form is practiced in the USA and/or the Netherlands and the participants were asked to briefly reflect on this.

Follow up Activities
As experienced in the international E-E field, theoretical notions and the practice of the media centers suggest follow up activities as a mechanism to spur interpersonal communication measures among audience members in addition to the television program. During the interviews it was critical to look on these follow up activities in detail and see which were implemented during the collaboration process. If not answered through the narration of the study participants, questions were raised such as: 'Who implemented the follow up activities and who was in charge of what?' 'What were the different tasks of you and your counterpart?', 'What happened in detail during the follow up activities?' and 'What has been important for you?'

5.4 Data Analysis
5.4.1 Transcription
The transcription of the interviews was implemented, if possible, directly subsequent to each interview. Out of the 25 interviews, six were transcribed with the help of an external staff member from a writing agency which specializes in interview transcriptions. The researcher transcribed the other interviews herself. Interview citations in the following depiction were often simplified, i.e. without using special characters or marks according to non-verbal or paraverbal information for

readability purposes. Breaks of two to five seconds were labeled with "..." and for breaks, longer than five seconds the expression "(lange Pause) (long break)" was used. For words or sentences that have been removed, the symbol "(...)" was applied. Moreover, to guarantee the anonymity of involved persons, the surnames of people as well as the places mentioned were alienated (see following chapters). Furthermore the interview quotes used in this thesis are the original text forms and no changes have been made. This in consequence could e.g. mean that the respondents did not finish a sentence, lefts it incomplete and starts with a new one.

5.4.2 Open Coding

After finishing the transcription, the data was openly coded, which is the first of three analytical steps in the Grounded Theory methodology (Berg & Milmeister, 2008; Breuer & Lettau, 2009). Corbin & Strauss (2008: 195) define the open coding procedure as "breaking data apart and delineating concepts to stand for blocks of raw data. At the same time, one is qualifying those concepts in terms of their properties and dimensions". Several qualitative researchers also applied metaphors for this analytical step. Bogdan & Biklen (1992) compare it to a big hall full of toys and the target is to categorize each toy to clusters which may show a sensible relation to each other. Kuckartz (1997) uses another metaphor. He notes that all citations should be classified into groups, much like drugs in a pharmacy, i.e. they need to be well sorted, labeled and put into drawers and shelves.

In the open coding process, Berg & Milmeister (2008) note that, during this first step of analysis, the researcher may have some hesitation and fear. These emotions develop during the work of the sense constructions, where an apparent tension between the reader and the text appears (Mey, 1999). The researcher puts her-/himself under pressure, because she/he aims at soon finding a category which provides orientation and security. The researcher does not want on the road of a 'perhaps-story'. Rather, she/he preferably wants to be on the safe side of it (ibid.). For resolving this pitfall Strauss (1987) gives four recommendations: (1) questions about the data should be easy and consistent with the research design, (2) in the beginning, coding should be meticulous, although in an advanced level the codes are reduced or summarized to sub-codes, (3) the coding procedure should be interrupted in order to write theoretical memos so that the original idea does not get lost and (4) traditional categories such as age, gender and social background should not be supposed right from the start. These traditional categories also have to work their way up to other ones. The researcher tried to follow Strauss' ideal description when implementing the open coding in this study. In the open coding phase, the researcher worked together with an independent coder[133] to, as far as possible, eliminate errors in this basic analytical step, but also to generate a reliable basis for the advanced stages of analysis (Corbin & Strauss, 2008).[134] The researcher printed out

---

[133] The independent coder had a psychological background and was familiar with the analysis procedure of the Grounded Theory methodology.
[134] Berg & Milmeister (2008) describe three essential advantages of such a teamwork in the

two hard copies from each interview transcript/field memo of the informal talks, and both the independent coder and the researcher manually and independently coded their own paragraphs or lines in the context in which they occurred. Afterwards, they met for coding sessions to compare and discuss the codes. Several times, different codes were used for describing the same paragraph or line. In these cases, the researcher and the independent coder discussed and agreed on whether multiple codes should be applied or whether the paragraph or line really can only be described through a single code. After each coding session, the researcher entered the agreed and recorded codes into the computer analysis program *MAXQDA 2007* (Corbin & Strauss, 2008). Furthermore, memos were generated on the codes in *MAXQDA 2007*, which resulted out of the discussions and reflections during the coding sessions. When the analysis team (i.e. the researcher and the independent coder) discovered paragraphs, lines and codes which seemed to have an essential meaning, extra sessions were scheduled with one or two other qualitative researchers to holistically reflect on their characteristics by comparing them to the existing codes (i.e. to find similarities and striking differences). The results of these sessions also were entered into memos in the *MAXQDA* program.

Thus, the first approach to a framework of categories comprised a progressing method of constant comparison of the existing codes and their relating memos. In this analytical step, there was no selection; each segment was coded at least once, but often multiple times and hence was subordinated to a contently suitable group, or it opened up a new group. This analytical step served, first of all, to exclusively accumulate codes without explicitly formulating categories.

---

document/segment: 16/26
respondent: SW
codes: Marktplatz (62), Tauschgaben (138), Finanzen (55), inhaltlicher Einfluss (132), Unsicherheit/Angst/Bedenken (19)
"Es ist von meiner Seite her natürlich erst einmal mit einer Angst verbunden, oder mit einem Misstrauen, dass man sagt, okay Leute, ihr packt uns jetzt zwei Millionen auf den Tisch (lange Pause), was wollt ihr dafür haben?"
This segment of the interview was open coded with five codes, because it referred to five different issues: 'market place', 'gift exchange', 'finances', 'influence on the program content' and 'insecurities/fear/doubts'.

---

document/segment: 12/14

---

coding procedure: Firstly, flexible role allocation is possible during teamwork. One person can be the other person's corrective. Secondly, teamwork initiates and slows down the interpretation process (i.e. the overhasty determination of categories can be avoided) and this process furthermore provides a rich environment for communication. Finally, through the exchange with others the story has its first target group. Although the story should make sense to the others, it can also fail. Thus, working with others is a good opportunity to test the involved stories.

respondent: WL
codes: Marktplatz (62), Tauschgaben (138), Schirmherrschaft (2), Tauschgaben ausbalancieren (2)

"Es wird ja immer schöner, weil die Szene war auch schon geschrieben. Wir hatten uns da ziemlich weit aus dem Fenster gelehnt, weil das mit dem Herrn Meffert [seinem Gastauftritt] so gut geklappt hat. Mussten das dann aber wieder rückgängig machen (...). Herr Breier hat gesagt ich komme für euch und mache die Eröffnung. Weil der Herr Meffert im Urlaub war zu dieser Zeit. In dem Moment, wo Herr Breier hörte, dass er bei uns nicht mitspielen darf, kam die Absage. Schirmherr ja, Präsenz [bei der Eröffnung] nein".

This interview segment was open coded with 'market place', 'gift exchange', 'patronage', 'balancing gift exchange'.

Both examples of the interviews contain the codes of 'market place' and 'gift exchange'. In subsequent data review processes, corrections, revisions as well as specifications of the existing codes mentioned above (and elsewhere) were made, and the first content related descriptions and categories were formulated. For making a possible system explicit in the data, the researcher also applied the explained method of constant comparison[135] to the first content-related descriptions and categories. This step resulted in a preliminary category system with 104 different single categories, which then were pared down to essential 39 ones, as it turned out that the other 65 were sub-categories, describing and representing a specific characteristic or dimension of the 39 essential categories. The preliminary category system is illustrated in appendix 4. At this point it was possible to start the discovery process of different properties and dimensions and formulate specific categories (see axial coding).

5.4.3 Axial Coding

While the open coding served to identify the initial preliminary (sub-)categories and concepts as well as their characteristics and dimensions, Corbin & Strauss (2008) note that in axial coding, the established preliminary categories or concepts are related to each other and scrutinized in depth. This leads to putting the data into a new order (also see Breuer & Lettau, 2009).

The first essential insight of the axial coding procedure was that the category 'license collaborations' may be a specific form in Germany's E-E collaboration environment and that this form stands with the three other collaboration forms of co-production, inscript participation and service on some kind of meta level above the preliminary (sub-)categories established in the open coding. Co-production, in-

---

[135] The method of constant comparison is significant in the Grounded Theory and particularly plays a role in open coding (Kelle & Kluge, 1999).

script participation and service also occur in the international E-E environment. However, the axial coding showed that they have other characteristics and dimensions in the German context (see chapter 8).

The second important insight when relating preliminary categories to each other was that initially **all collaboration activities** were linked to **gift exchange procedures**. In this context, the preliminary category of 'market place' was renamed the 'place of gift exchange'. Moreover, the strong relationship between this 'place of gift exchange' and the categories of 'common sense' and 'zeitgeist' could be clearly compiled through the axial coding. The 'place of gift exchange' refers to the field in which the E-E collaborations take place and 'common sense' refers to the field in which the collaborations are presented by the E-E implementers to the public. This creates a kind of two-fold standard and can be identified as an essential characteristic in the E-E collaboration context in Germany.

The third essential insight was that several of the categories clearly affect all forms of collaboration more or less intensively. For example the category of 'media legislations' has an influence on all collaborations, but implementers of co-productions and inscript participations in particular have to intensively deal with regulative issues on all collaborative levels.

The axial coding showed essential concepts of conditions and characteristics of E-E collaborations (see chapter 6). Following the example outlined in the open coding, the properties of the 'place of gift exchange' were analyzed using their properties and dimensions.

Category	Properties	Dimensional ranges
Tauschplatz	Tauschgaben	Gastauftritt
		Finanzen
		Einfluss auf das Programm
	Kooperationsformen	Co-Produktion
		Lizenzkooperation
	etc.	etc.

On the one hand, on the basis of the relation-making processes in the axial coding, the (sub-) categories grew, were deepened and extended through the analyzing procedure. On the other hand, some of the (sub-)categories also fell apart, because they turned out to be poor in data.[136]

---

[136] One sub-category of the 'gift exchange' was, for example, the 'physische Nähe' (physical closeness). It was used by two study participants to describe an additional reason why they chose the collaboration partner in a license arrangement. They explained that this physical closeness made things easy for them when they met to discuss details. However, the data analysis process showed that this sub-category was lacking a solid foundation. It was considered as not to be of importance and therefore fell apart.

5.4.4 Selective Coding

Selective coding can be considered as axial coding employed on a higher and more abstract level of analysis (Breuer & Lettau, 2009). Some Grounded Theory researchers even do not make a distinction between axial and selective coding: they subordinate selective to axial coding (Charmaz, 2006; Corbin & Strauss, 2008). In selective coding, one core category is chosen and systematically related to the other categories, validating these relationships and filling in categories that need additional refinement and progress (Strauss & Corbin, 1990). With the selection of the core category, the researcher decides on the architecture, the story line or central theme of the story, the depiction of the findings, the focus perspective of the theme's treatment; respectively the researcher decides for the theoretical concept grounded in data (Berg & Milmeister, 2008); Breuer & Lettau, 2009: 92). According to Strauss (1991: 67) this core category needs to include several aspects: it must refer to preferably many other categories, it must frequently occur in the data material, and it must be effortless to connect the core with other categories.

In the selective coding of this on hand study, the core category turned out to be 'the place of gift exchange'. In chapter 7 and 8 the 'story' of E-E collaborations with respect to the research interest is told in detail from this perspective.

5.4.5 Conditional/Consequential Matrix

When relating categories to a core category, the researcher applied the support by the means of a paradigm. Corbin & Strauss (2008: 89-91) suggest this support, because in advanced stages of analysis specifically, the data gets even more complex. The data consists of multiple concepts in complex relationships that are often difficult to tease out of the data. Corbin & Strauss (2008: 89) state that having a way to think about those relationships can be helpful, and therefore they offer the paradigm[137] as a tool which helps to identify contextual factors and then link them with the process. The basic components of a paradigm are conditions, inter/actions and emotions as well as consequences (ibid.). For making these components more transparent in the data, Corbin & Strauss suggest using a conditional/consequential matrix, which helps the analyst to sort through the range of conditions and consequences in which inter/actions and emotions are located and responded to (2008: 91). The matrix needs to be understood as a conceptual guide and not as a definitive procedure, and it should be modified to fit each study and data set (2008: 93). The researcher filled in the conditional/consequential matrix for the German E-E collaboration context as follows (also see Bouman 1999: 148):

---

[137] „The paradigm is a perspective, a set of questions that can be applied to data to help the analyst draw out the contextual factors and identify relationships between context and progress" (Corbin & Strauss, 2008: 89).

Figure 5.2: Conditional/consequential matrix for E-E collaborations in Germany

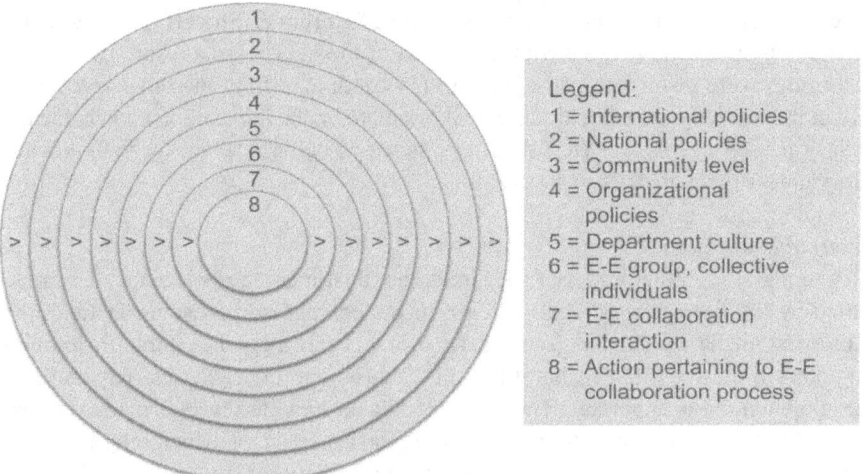

Legend:
1 = International policies
2 = National policies
3 = Community level
4 = Organizational policies
5 = Department culture
6 = E-E group, collective individuals
7 = E-E collaboration interaction
8 = Action pertaining to E-E collaboration process

Source: Own illustration using Corbin & Strauss (2008: 93)

Before the individual circles are described, some introductory remarks on the conceptual ideas of the matrix are given.

While applying this matrix[138], the researcher considered the matrix application ideas of Corbin & Strauss (2008: 91-93), and they served as a guideline:

1. Conditions/consequences do not exist in a vacuum. They are always connected through inter/action and emotional response, and the researcher tried to take this into consideration wherever possible.
2. The distinction between micro and macro is artificial. The researcher thus did not make this explicit distinction and was more interested in the interplay of micro and macro conditions.
3. The full range of possible interrelationships between micro/macro conditions are not always visible to the individual study participant. This is why the researcher listened to many voices when trying to understand the whole.
4. Conditions and consequences usually exist in clusters and can associate or co-vary in many different ways, both to each other and to the related inter/action. The researcher had this in the back of the mind when applying the matrix.
5. Inter/action and emotional responses are not confined to the individual. Therefore, the researcher considered the study participants as actors of representat-

---

[138] The matrix consists of a circle of concentric and interconnected circles with arrows going towards and away from the center. The arrows represent the intersection of conditions/consequences and the resulting chain of events. Conditions move toward and surround the inter/action to create a conditional context. Other arrows move away from the inter/action, representing how the consequences of any inter/action move from inter/action to change or add to conditions in often diverse and unanticipated ways (Corbin & Strauss, 2008: 93).

ives of sustainability organizations, production companies, broadcasting stations and media legislation agencies.

The researcher followed the recommendation of Corbin & Strauss (2008: 95) and studied any substantive topic within any area of the matrix. As a result, two essential issues were taken into consideration: (1) conditions from the outer levels will affect the more organizational individual orientated behaviors and (2) no characteristics (gender, age, power etc.) should be stated as being relevant for the evolving story unless there are data to support it.

International Policies

Beginning at the outer edges of the circle, the most macro area is situated, represented by the term international policies. In the context of the television field, the European media legislations (see chapter 6.1) serve as a good example for providing more room for E-E collaborations. In the sustainability field, international E-E developments are important. These developments include the E-E media centers (see chapter 4) as well as publications and reports in this area which refer to Entertainment-Education as a crucial communication strategy for sustainability change.

National Policies

In this second layer of the circle, the national policies, governmental regulations and cultural values comes in which are directly linked to the E-E collaboration issue. On the television side, national media regulations play a role. They only leave narrow space for specific collaborations forms (see chapter 8.2). In the sustainability field, there is no clear agenda setting so far to reach lower socio-economic classes with sustainability efforts through communication measures. According to cultural values, the critically viewed history of Germany during the Third Reich plays an essential role.

Community Level

The third ring includes the community related issues according to E-E collaborations. Corbin & Strauss (2008: 95) state that in this area all of the above-mentioned areas are included, but "they pertain to a particular community, giving it singularity among all the other communities". For instance in Germany, the sustainability field combines an E-E program with follow up activities for the target group. Even more, in some examples the E-E programs are part of a broader multi-media sustainability campaign to reach the target group in different settings (school, work, leisure time, etc.).

Organizational Policies

The fourth ring deals with the organizational and institutional background of the collaborating parties. Each has its own purposes, structures, missions, rules, histories, relationships and spatial features, all of which provide sources of conditions and consequences (Corbin & Strauss, 2008: 95). In the television field, the public and private broadcasters differ in their missions. While the public broadcasters are more into information and culturally attract people (though they also focus on entertainment), the private ones have a specific emphasis on entertainment and advertising and they completely function according to market principles. In the sustainability field, the collaborating organizations regularly have a bureaucratic and governmental background (or are supported by governmental institutions), and they involve more or less strong research activities.

Department Culture
The fifth circle refers to the sub-organizational level and thereby to the different departments that design and implement an E-E collaboration in both the sustainability organization and the broadcasting/production company.

E-E Group, Collective Individuals
The sixth circle comprises the personal and professional skills of the people involved as well as their expertise and knowledge for E-E collaborations. Firstly, this is important for the collaboration process itself (i.e. sustainability experts reflect messages from their research point of view, while television professionals translate sustainability issues in storylines), and secondly, it plays a crucial role in different collaboration forms.

E-E Collaboration Interaction
The seventh area represents the interaction between the television and the sustainability professionals in the collaboration process. Corbin & Strauss (2008: 115) state that this circle as well as the action level are the center of the matrix and play a crucial role.

Action Pertaining to the E-E Collaboration Process
This inner circle of the conditional/consequential matrix stands for action. When "applying this on E-E collaboration processes this encompasses the negotiations, discussions, legitimization of boundaries and so forth, that take place in order to arrive at and maintain an E-E collaboration and accomplish associated tasks" (Bouman, 1999: 149).

5.5 Summary

The Grounded Theory study in part II of the thesis aims at finally answering the main research question with the support of three different sub-questions the following chapters will explicitly address. Thus, the research aims to contribute to the development of E-E collaborations in Germany's E-E practice. Therefore, the last chapter depicts in detail how the researcher proceeded in the data collection as well as the analysis process. The following chapters will portray a reality-based description of the research field and develop a theoretical concept through qualitative data analysis. Indeed, after describing the E-E collaboration conditions, characteristics and forms, the research results may be useful in developing recommendations for future developments and strategies for the German E-E field (see chapter 9).

6. Conditions and Characteristics of Entertainment-Education Collaborations

> "Mister Heller and Mister Küfer were the involved parties [from the ministry] guiding the project. They were personally very engaged regarding the topic of how to communicate sustainability themes in an entertaining way. They said: 'We really need to do something new, because obviously, the old stuff is difficult in terms of reaching the target group [which consists of those from lower socio-economic milieus]'. And this has been... an extreme risk, mainly because we implemented the project not under... scientific 'laboratory circumstances', but let's say in a live-production where each week two million people are presented these things... you can imagine that this kind of sustainability communication [in entertaining formats] is not appreciated by everyone. Usually, they [the people in the ministry] expect something else. But they are not the target group of these programs. They more tend to watch TV channels such as Arte or 3SAT. They forget the simple principal that the bait must be attractive to the fish and not to the fisherman. Many of them [people in the ministries] have not come to terms with this yet (...). And it is difficult to make them understand that this is sustainability communication... many of them could not empathize with the everyday life of the target groups".
>
> - Communication scholar working on behalf of German Ministries, 2009

This chapter deals exclusively with vital conditions and characteristics that are important for the E-E collaboration process in Germany. It serves to answer the first of the three sub-questions in part II of the thesis:

B1 *Researching conditional collaboration factors*: What are significant conditions (i.e. external and internal conditions as well as crucial characteristics) of present E-E collaborations in Germany which influence the collaboration process?

This sub-question was answered with information collected from the interviews and the informal talks. In addition, some relevant background literature was considered and media legislation rules were studied to get a deeper understanding of what was said in the interviews (see also Corbin & Strauss, 2008).

In the following, significant conditions and characteristics (of present E-E collaborations in Germany) will be outlined based on the sensitizing concepts explained in chapter 5.3.5. Firstly, the *external conditions* of media legislation affecting Entertainment-Education (section 6.1) and current developments in the television and the sustainability field (section 6.2) are outlined. Secondly, *internal conditions* of field logics and collaboration motives (section 6.3) are illustrated.[139] Afterwards significant *characteristics* of E-E collaborations are described. These characteristics include forms of E-E collaborations (section 6.4), collaboration guiding research (section 6.5) as well as the follow up activities (section 6.6). The latter mentioned feature is specifically applied in the German collaboration context and thus should be discussed more detailed. The conditions and characteristics depicted in this chapter serve to answer the first part of the main research question regarding the *conditions* that have a crucial impact on German E-E collaborations.

6.1 Media Legislation Rules

In Germany, there are several media legislation rules which have an effect on E-E collaboration practices. The media legislation rules described in the following are the relevant ones.

6.1.1 Basic Law, Article Number 5: Freedom of Expression, Arts and Sciences

This basic law was enforced after the Second World War. Its 5th article emphasizes that every person shall have the right freely to express and disseminate his opinion in speech, writing and pictures and to inform her- or himself without hindrance from generally accessible sources. Freedom of the press and freedom of reporting by means of broadcasts and films shall be guaranteed. There shall be no censorship (Deutscher Bundestag, 2010). Clearly, this legislation stresses the importance of television makers having a free hand in the decision making process rather than being dependent to any other authority when deciding on their program content.

6.1.2 Media Independence from the Government

The first judgment of the Federal Constitutional Court (FCC) from 1961 (Bundesverfassungsgericht, 1961) also needs to be taken into consideration when looking at E-E collaborations in Germany. The background on the judgment came out of the attempt by former Federal Chancellor Konrad Adenauer to establish a German television organization in the hands of the state which should have broadcasted a second TV channel. The idea behind this proposal probably has its origins in Adenauer's desire to have a more government friendly reporting channel in contrast to the quite critical views of the first public broadcaster, ARD. The FCC judged that

---

[139] These conditions can play a role throughout the whole collaboration process, but they are usually most important in the orientation stage of collaboration (see chapter 2.4.2), where the potential partners reflect about their collaboration options.

this attempt was a violation of the 5th article in Basic Law (ibid.). They stressed the importance of the media independence from the government and drew parallels to the broadcasting act during the *Weimar Republic*. At that time, broadcasting was controlled and organized by the *German Reichspost*. This, according to the FCC, was instrumental in establishing the governmental steering power on programs and the later misuse of broadcasting for Hitler's propaganda during the Third Reich. This is why the government now feels it should focus on technical terms (i.e. providing the framework) instead of influencing content and cultural aspects (ibid.).

The first two pieces of media legislation clearly indicate that the responsibility of the *program content is the exclusive privilege of the television professionals*. No institutions (governmental or others) shall have a steering power on the content. The television makers are the people in charge of deciding what they want to present and how. They shall also decide what may be considered 'good and bad'. Hence, steering power from external stakeholders is generally viewed very critically, even if sustainability issues are addressed. One of the interviewed media legislation experts emphasized in this context: "With Germany's experience with regard to bad propaganda, there has been an eternal mistrust regarding policy steering power, of course rightfully, because what we have experienced in terms of bad shouldn't also be freely transmitted to the public in terms of good and prosocial issues".

Consequently, these two pieces of media legislation (sections 6.1.1 and 6.1.2) constrain the possibilities for creating and implementing E-E co-productions and E-E inscript participations in broadcasted mass media programs because, in both collaboration forms, the sustainability experts also play a role in the decision making process about the program content broadcasted on TV.

6.1.3 The Law regarding Advertising of a Political, Ideological or Religious Nature

Whereas the first two items refer to the *steering power on program content*, the next two presented legislations draw attention to the *financial resources* granted by organizations (including sustainability organizations) as a program support. The Interstate Broadcasting Treaty §7, para. 9 (ASMABG, 2010) prohibits the following advertising: "Advertising of a political, ideological or religious nature shall be prohibited. Sentence 1 applies to teleshopping accordingly. Public service announcements transmitted free of charge, including charitable appeals, shall not be considered as advertising within the meaning of sentence 1". First of all, this legislation makes clear that social or sustainability appeals transmitted *for free of charge* shall not be considered as 'advertising' and thus they are allowed, because they are supposed to contribute to a 'greater good'. Using *argumentum e contrario*, this means that political, ideological and religious advertising might include a payment and this type of advertising is forbidden, as the law indicates.

The prohibition of the political advertising is justified by a free, individual and official opinion making process. The reporting in television therefore should follow principles of equality and diversity (Volpers & Holznagel, 2009: 181). The aim is that all societal groups and opinions shall be depicted. Hence, it would be not acceptable if one single political or other societal group gained importance in the broadcasting sector simply because they had the wherewithal to pay for specific 'advertising' (ibid.).

Regarding the collaboration issue, this means that sustainability experts can collaborate with TV makers. Nonetheless, because the legislation explicitly mentions 'the free of charge' issue to secure the freedom of television makers, it gets *complicated as soon as financial resources are transmitted*. This may be seen as 'political advertising' independent of whether the collaboration serves a 'greater good'. When political advertising is prohibited while sustainability appeals for a 'greater good' transmitted free of charge are allowed, several interpretational questions may arise in E-E implementer's practice: 'Is E-E political advertising or a social appeal?' 'How can political advertising be exactly defined?' 'What can be considered a social appeal for the greater good?' 'What if, for example, the sustainability side wants to promote generally accepted climate protection messages such as 'save energy and save money', are these activities political advertising or social appeals for the greater good?' 'Does the differentiation between political advertising and social appeals only come with the financial resources (not) being contributed from the sustainability side, or are there other parameters indicating what constitutes political advertising or a prosocial appeal in both theory and practice?' The legislation does not give answers to these and other questions (also see Lubjuhn & Pratt, 2009), and it may cause problems in E-E collaboration practice when implementers try to figure out what they are allowed to do in terms of a partnership. The legislation only makes the distinction that political advertising is normally not free of charge whereas social appeals are and that former is forbidden while latter is not.

6.1.4 Sponsoring Law

With the sponsoring legislation, the situation gets even more complex and contradictory for E-E implementers who are looking for orientation standards, specifically in terms of whether the payment of financial resources in support of a TV program is allowed. In contrast to the political advertising law, the sponsoring rules emphasize that sustainability and other organizations *can financially support television makers* in their programs while sponsoring them (§2, 2 No.7 RStV, AS-MABG, 2010). Volpers & Holznagel (2009: 152) refer in this context to 'the principle of disclosure': when governmental, non-governmental or private organizations hand out sponsoring money, they need to be mentioned as *sponsor in the TV program*. Volpers & Holznagel (2009: 152) also clearly see a danger in this law, because with the consent to sponsor, not only for organizations which want to promote their products but specifically for those which want to promote issues, the dependency of the television makers on the sponsors increases as does 'the threat' of being influenced by them (also see Volpers et al., 1998: 138). In particular, when money is involved from social interest organizations or groups, the scholars stress that there is a high potential for the sponsors to become a part of the decision making process on how the theme is integrated into the storyline (ibid.). The reason for this is obvious: when a theme-promoting organization sponsors a television program, it is self-evident that they want 'something in return'; this may be the involvement on the decision making process on the program content (ibid., also see chapter 7.1).

Through allowing sponsoring activities, the sponsoring legislation indirectly opens a way for governmental, non-governmental or private organizations to be increasingly involved in decision making processes on the program content, and this clashes to some degree with the basic and the constitutional law mentioned above. Furthermore, it raises other important issues: Where does 'influencing or steering power on program content' start in practice and to what degree do the television makers act according to their own principles? To what extent does the sponsor influence the television professionals' decisions to depict what they otherwise would not integrate, because it would be against their principles? Obviously, where 'steering power' or 'influence' starts is a matter of the personal relation and cannot be comprehended by outside entities. It is a "subtle legal policy line", as one of the media legislation experts stated.

When summarizing the political advertising and the sponsoring law, some contradictions emerge for E-E professionals: while the political advertising rule allows sustainability appeals free of charge, it forbids political advertising, which includes the transmission of financial resources. The sponsoring rule allows money transfers to TV makers which, as has been pointed out, can probably lead to steering power on the program's content in return, specifically when the sponsor is an organization that wants to promote certain themes.

Interestingly enough, the interviews with media legislation experts also lead to two different interpretations of the legislative context regarding financial support on the part of sustainability organizations in an entertainment television program. While one expert said that financial support violates the broadcasting act, two other experts mentioned that paying money as a 'sponsorship' is allowed, though steering power on the program content in return is not allowed.

As the issue of supporting TV programs with financial resources and thus having steering power on the program only plays a role in E-E co-productions and E-E in-script participations, these two kinds of collaboration stand on shaky legal ground, and they seem to engender problems when E-E partners want to create and implement them in practice.

6.1.5 Product Placement Liberalization Law

In April 2010, Germany made a step towards an increasingly liberalized television market when the 13th version of the consolidated Interstate Treaty on Broadcasting (ITB) came into force (ASMABG, 2010). This version allows product placement in the formats of private broadcasters and product supplies in the formats of public broadcasters. This means that companies can pay private broadcasting stations to place their products in a storyline (product placement) or they can ask public broadcasters if they want to use their products in an episode without being paid for it (product supplies). Most importantly, the involved organization behind the product placement needs to be mentioned, while the program is broadcasted on television.[140] In addition, product placement is only allowed in so-called 'light entertainment formats' (Volpers & Holznagel, 2009; ASMABG, 2010), which excludes children's programs, news and consumer magazines as well as other information formats.

Product placement and supplies are regulated in the new version of the ITB, while *topic placement and supplies are not explicitly regulated*. The two interviewed media legislation experts as well as the literature (Volpers et al., 2008; Volpers & Holznagel, 2009) stress the importance of also regulating the latter, because with the current status of legislation, 'placements' make out a huge *grey zone* in media legislation. For instance, what happens, when a theme is advertised and it is related to a product or an organization? The connections between a product, a theme and the organization behind are central for future debates. Indeed, a company could promote a topic such as 'Turkey is a great holiday country' and link this message to their product/service with 'and if you want to visit Turkey, use our travel agency for booking'. The same goes with governmental organizations promoting sustainability topics as the interviewed media legislation experts specifically stressed. In general, while promoting a sustainability theme, such as the health message 'do not consume drugs', this message is, whether indicated or not, (in)directly linked to the organization which also benefits from it (e.g. the drug hotline of the organization is promoted in the storyline). These cases are not regulated by the new version of the ITB.

The new product placement legislation led to incoherences among participants of the present study while interpreting it. One group, which included members of the media legislation experts, framed the new legislation only in terms of its applicability to products, whereas another group of study participants interpreted this new legislation as a justification or a basic principle for doing 'topic placement' with private and public broadcasters. Some even considered it as a legitimation of implementing E-E co-productions and E-E inscript participations in which financial resources are exchanged for steering power on the program content (see chapter 8.2). This is mirrored in the following quote by a TV producer: "[Interviewer:] Topic placement is not implicated in this new law, and someone could argue (...) that environmental themes are part of a brand, and one could establish this brand and sell it to you and do something together. What do you say? [Producer:] I see that or I am 100% sure that people are thinking about doing this. Also from the production side [to approach sustainability organizations]."

---

[140] Germany is currently discussing the detailed rules on how to indicate that product placement is involved.

6.1.6 Wrap Up and Conclusions for Legislations affecting Entertainment-Education

The depiction of media legislations outlined that E-E service activities are compliant with media regulations. The problems start when designing and implementing E-E co-productions and E-E inscript participations. More specifically, this is (1) when the collaboration involves a sustainability organization which is part of the decision making processes and (2) when financial resources are handed over to television makers. In both contexts, the different pieces of media legislation are in *conflict* with each other. As an orientation for E-E professionals, they only serve to create contradictions. The comparison of the different legislations furthermore reveals a *grey zone* with a broader range of framing and interpreting space. In fact, no clear statements can be drawn from media legislations:

- While the political advertising rule forbids '(paid) political advertising', the sponsoring rule allows a 'sponsorship' by political or other stakeholders in which money is involved (handing out financial resources).
- While the German Basic Law and the Federal Constitutional Court emphasize the freedom and independence of television professionals on the one hand, the new product placement rule on the other hand gives way to increased liberalization processes and the involvement of third parties in the decision making process of the television program (involvement in the program content).

These contradictions mainly arise, because the legislations were instituted during different eras and were created according to national and global developments (see section 6.2). For example in former days, the media law reinforced the strict separation between advertising and content in broadcasted TV. According to recent media developments (for examples see Volpers, Bernard & Schnier (2008) it is challenging to draw a clear line between both and this is also mirrored in present legislation (product placement).

The following figure gives an overview of the media legislations which play a role for E-E collaborations. It illustrates their conflict areas to each other.

Figure 6.1: Conflicting pieces of media legislation which are relevant to E-E implementers

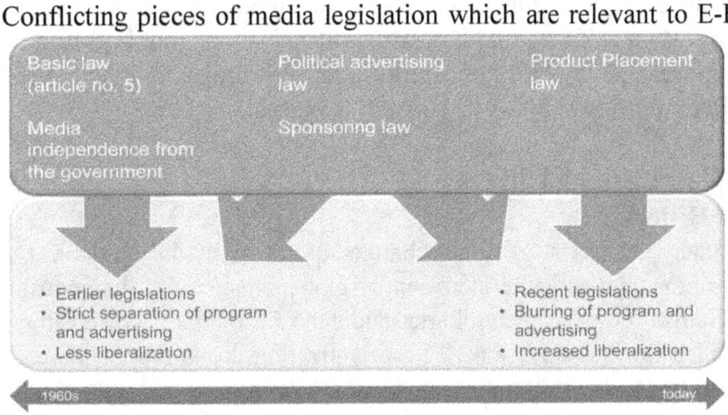

As the figure indicates, some of the legislations emphasize the separation of program content and advertising, and they intensively stress the freedom of television makers; others give way to a mixture of content and advertising. Consequently, this can increasingly lead to external parties being a part of the decision making process on the program content, which is in line with liberalization tendencies within the German television market in recent years (also see section 6.2).

Chapter 7 and 8 will elaborate in detail how both the sustainability and the television side interpret, frame and deal with the media legislation in practice.

6.2 Developments in the Television and the Sustainability Field Contributing to the E-E Collaboration Situation in Germany

In the following, the present situation in both the TV and the sustainability field is briefly described according to its relevance for the E-E collaboration process. The present developments in both fields are important conditions for initiating a collaboration, and they affect the action of the stakeholders as well as their decision making processes. They essentially contribute to the establishment and implementation of E-E collaborations, and they can thus be considered as crucial **external conditions** for E-E partnerships. The depiction is chosen from the perspective of the study participants of each collaborating side when asked about current field developments and characteristics related to their E-E practice. As mentioned in the introduction of this chapter, these results interplay with literature findings.

Firstly, a short background of the history of the TV field is given (section 6.2.1.1). Secondly, changes in the TV market are briefly outlined (section 6.2.1.2) and thirdly, the relationships between broadcasting organizations and TV production companies are portrayed (section 6.2.1.3). The study participants perceived the three issues as important conditions for E-E collaborations. Next, the sustainability field is briefly portrayed using the perspective of sustainability experts participating in the study but also taking the depictions in chapter 2.7 into consideration. Subsequently, the metaphor 'the bait must be attractive to the fish and not to the fisherman' is explained more in detail (section 6.2.2.1) and a background on criticism regarding affective and 'latently influencing' communication strategies is given (section 6.2.2.2). Both are central when reflecting conditions of E-E collaborations from the viewpoint of sustainability experts.

6.2.1 Television Field
6.2.1.1 History
In Germany the TV industry has changed dramatically during the last decades. One aspect of the change is the increasingly global character of this industry; another is the digitalization of its technologies and a third important aspect is the privatization of broadcasting organizations. The privatization drove the television landscape in Germany towards a 'dual system' in which both powerful public and commercial

broadcast organizations exist. On the demand side, they are competing for viewers and advertising, while on the supply side they compete for cable, satellite and terrestrial channels. Furthermore, there is competition in regards of the television content. The German TV industry is in two respects truly European. Firstly, the public broadcast organizations continue to be very important and secondly, the German television business is highly regulated by the government and public agencies. This includes not only the public, but also the commercial broadcasters (see last chapter 6.1 as well as Puppis, 2007).

The birth and growth of commercial television in the mid 1980s (Altendorfer, 2004) transformed the TV industry into a system with five significant players – two public (ARD and ZDF) and three commercial stations (RTL, Sat.1 and ProSieben) – ruling the market with a share of 54.7% in 2009 (Zubayr & Gerhard, 2010). While ARD, ZDF and RTL each have market shares of around 12%, ProSieben owns about 6% and Sat.1 holds 10% of the market share. The two public broadcast organizations together carry around a quarter of the German market share (ibid). Due to the misuse of a centralized broadcast system during the Nazi era, the Allies forced the German government to focus on a highly de-centralized and truly public broadcast system. This system was modeled on the BBC and is based on license fees keeping it quite independent from both the state and the influence of the market (also see section 6.1). In 1949, ARD (or more precisely, nine regional stations with the German public partnership) came into existence and was complemented by a second public broadcaster, ZDF, in 1961 (Puppis, 2007). Both developed into a public duopoly, providing non-commercial, informative and generally less entertaining television. This industry structure did not change until the beginning of the 1980s, when private broadcasting organizations were accepted due to the liberalization of the market, deregulation and the influence of big media conglomerates such as Bertelsmann and Kirch (nowadays RTL Group - Bertelsmann) and ProSiebenSat.1 Media. This led to rather new structural and institutional features, which emerged out of the television industry. Among these features were a high degree of economic concentration and thus sizable entry and exit barriers. These new features were produced and applied by the big five broadcasting agents. Another important feature concerned the program financing. While the public broadcast organizations are still mostly financed by a license fee (17.98 euro per month in 2009) regularly paid by everybody who has a television set or other transmitting mediums available in her/his household, commercial broadcasting organizations are allowed to intensively finance their programs with the help of advertising. The German media law also provides fewer obligations regarding program quality and coverage. Nowadays, the commercial broadcasters spend more than 20% of their total amount of airtime on advertising each year (Krüger & Zapf-Schramm, 2008). The public broadcast organizations are generally more confined by the media law, as advertising is restricted to only 20 minutes a day and only on weekdays before 8 p.m. (ASMABG, 2010 §16). When compared to the commercial broadcasters, the public broadcasters only spend around 1.5% of their total amount of airtime on advertising each year (Krüger & Zapf-Schramm, 2008). Hence, the public broadcasters can base their programming on criteria other than just quotas, which includes implementing their 'mandate of basic supply', which was enacted by the Federal Constitutional Court. The public broadcasters are 'protected' to not only function according to pure market rules as commercial broadcasters do. Their qualitative program orientation as well as their supply of a huge variety of opinions, values and norms serve as a legitimizing measurement of public broadcast stations when setting license fees.

6.2.1.2 Changes in the Television Market influencing E-E Collaborations – Trend Towards increased Economic Principles on the Television Market

Literature describes tendencies (Kiefer, 2007; Meyen & Riesmeyer, 2009) emphasizing that the economic market rules in the television sector have increased in recent years. The study participants from the television field also stressed this issue. Acting according to the television market means that the stakeholders are looking even more closely at audience ratings, market shares and money than they were several years ago. As the study participants from the television field emphasized, this is by trend not only valid for the private broadcasters, but also for public ones. One producer put this succinctly by saying, "The less money I have to pay for more audience members, the better it is". These commodification processes are interesting, specifically with regard to the public broadcasters, because they were involved in the majority of collaborations considered by the analysis. Usually, public broadcasters function according to other principles besides market rules (such as those described above). They receive license fees and thus they are regularly not reliant on the pure economic principles of the market. Nonetheless, study participants strongly believe that public broadcasters are increasingly ruled by a trend towards 'marketization', although in official terms it should not like that, because they are supported by tax payers' money. It seems that this money is not enough to ensure that public broadcasting stations do not act according to very competitive market principles (see paragraph below 'Relation between broadcasting stations and production companies').

Trend to Authentic Depiction of Entertainment Story Content
TV makers participating in the study explained that there is a trend to more authentic and accurate ways of depicting their stories. Data indicates that this trend derives from two significant developments. The first development arises from the requests made by the audience members. For instance, a scriptwriter of a daily soap shared the story about portraying a teenage character working as an intern and thus earning very little money. In one scene, he visits a café and orders a Café Latte, which normally costs two to three euros. When paying the bill, the character puts five euros on the table and leaves the café. Many young audience members wrote to the production company complaining about it. The scriptwriter added that these issues have happened gradually and more often during the last years, whereas more

than one decade ago, nobody would have paid much attention to it. The issues of authentic and accurate presentation is something TV makers pay close attention to, because less accurate and authentic depiction creates a barrier between the world of the TV story and reality, which the audience members view negatively.

In addition to audience members demanding accurate and authentic depictions, TV makers stated as a second development that they are influenced by the international standards on the TV market which clearly tend to display fictional formats more accurately and authentically. In particular, TV makers working for commercial broadcasters mentioned the US entertainment market as a role model in this regard (also see chapter 4.2.3).

Presenting sustainability contents authentically and accurately indeed plays an important role for television professionals. From the viewpoint of television makers, this goes with picturing 'both sides' of a sustainability theme. One television producer indicated that it is more authentic for the audience when the positive as well as the negative (i.e. the struggles) aspects of behaving in a sustainable manner are presented, and thus tension is created. For example when a teenage character is an environmental activist and classmates therefore tease him or his father is the owner of a nuclear power plant. For television professionals, these kinds of tensions constitute a good story. It is the duty of the TV makers to illustrate how the characters take action as a response to these tensions and come to solutions. Many entertainment professionals indicate that in this context it would be helpful to get advice and background information about sustainability themes that fit their needs of storytelling. However, the television professionals criticize while working with sustainability experts that they are generally only interested in showing the positive aspects of sustainability behavior in everyday life without referring to the struggles.

Growing Trend Towards Entertainment Formats
The growing trend towards entertainment television in Germany (and globally) has been pointed out by the television makers and has been discussed intensively in literature (Vorderer, 2003; Vorderer et al., 2004; Zillmann, 2000; also see chapter 3.2.2). Krüger & Zapf-Schramm (2007, 2008) give an overview of television programming separating between commercial broadcasting stations (RTL, SAT.1, ProSieben) and public broadcasting stations (ARD and ZDF) from 2001 to 2007. From their inception, the private broadcasters ocus on entertainment programs and, on average, the amount has increased over the last decade. The amount of non-fictional entertainment programs (like daily talkshows, quiz and games shows) has also grown. Comparing the years 2001 and 2007, the broadcaster SAT.1 raised the proportion of non-fictional entertainment programs by about one-fifth, from 25.9 to 31.1%. ProSieben enhanced its proportion from 15.4 to 17.6%.

Nowadays, the public broadcast stations invest fewer resources in high quality programs than back in the 1980s, when the public broadcast television ruled the industry. Nonetheless, a significant amount of money is still invested in these programs when taking into account the demands of the German audience watching TV at a high level (Zubayr & Gerhard, 2010). From 2001 to 2007, the total number of information and education programs broadcasted by ARD increased slightly from 41.3 to 43.1%, and this has not drastically changed since then. For ZDF, there are similar developments: the broadcaster boosted its information and education programs from 46.4 to 49.5% (Krüger & Zapf-Schramm, 2007; Krüger & Zapf-Schramm, 2008). Hence, many of the public broadcast stations invest in information and educational programs, and their total number of broadcasted programs in this field is about double of the amount of programs of this sort broadcasted on commercial broadcasting stations (ibid.).

Beside these developments, **public broadcasters** tend to *increase resources spent on (light) entertainment programs.* One reason for this development can be found in the global trend towards increasing the amount of entertainment media (i.e. audience members like to watch light entertainment) (Zable, 2009). Broadcasting these programs usually brings high market shares. Krüger & Zapf-Schramm (2007, 2008) found out that ARD in particular has raised the proportion of its fictional entertainment programming from 28.3 to 36.1% when comparing the years 2001 and 2007. ZDF increased this rate a little from 27.5 to 28.0%. In fact, both public broadcasters spent more airtime in 2007 sending fictional programs than the commercial broadcasters (RTL with 24.4% and SAT.1 with 26.0%). This trend towards increased (lighter) entertainment formats by the public broadcasters has been criticized in public debates quite often (Ouellette, 2002; Richter, 1989; Summerfield, 2002). Windeler & Sydow (2001) adds in this context that involving entertainment programs as a long-term strategy for the public broadcasters could erode their capability to maintain their competitive advantage in the German market. German public agencies question the legitimacy of this strategy (ibid.). Supporters of these developments argue that the public broadcasting organizations also have to assimilate to the global entertainment trend in the media. The fact is that in the future, the public broadcasting stations will need to establish *quality standards or criteria* for their entertainment formats, if they want to succeed with their strategy. Employing certain standards/criteria, can help them justify their activities in the entertainment field. Indeed, there can be strong differences in the quality of entertainment formats. TV makers from the public broadcasting stations maintained in this context that working together with sustainability experts to establish standards/criteria and using their research and/or advice about the portrayed sustainability themes from the research point of view (in E-E service collaborations) may support them to successfully go through changing processes and succeed with their strategy on the TV market.

6.2.1.3 Relation between Broadcasting Stations and Production Companies

To show why this relationship and its consequences play a decisive role in E-E practice, a short background of responsibilities of both the broadcasting stations and the production companies needs to be pointed out first. Media legislation must ensure the TV makers' independence (see section 6.1). The Interstate Broadcasting Treaty states in this context that broadcasting organizations need to take care of this issue (ASMABG, 2010). In fact, in practice, it has been the production companies and not the broadcasting stations that have created and implemented the programs. The broadcasting stations act as a kind of bank providing money for the television programs. They have to pass on the message of 'independent work' to the production companies, and they do that by fixing these issues in the production contract they sign with the production company.

The production company is a type of service provider for the broadcasting stations. Through the production contract, it should be – at least theoretically – assured that there are no other parties with steering power over the produced program.

At this point it is important to outline the following: in Germany, broadcasting stations have an oligopoly power, and this means that they decide what is broadcasted and which production company gets the assignment. They have the negotiating power in terms of rights and the production budget. Given this background, there are two crucial developments resulting from it which were pointed out by both the media legislation experts and TV makers: firstly, the broadcasting stations have used their power to slowly negotiate the production budgets down over the last years. Secondly, they have used their power in terms of setting up the production rights; producers are required to give up the rights to their produced format (i.e. the rights regarding the content of the format, the rights to repeat the format on TV, the rights to sell it overseas, the rights to use it on the internet or for merchandising). All of these rights belong to the broadcasting station, whereas in other countries, such as the United Kingdom, the majority of these rights stay with the producers and thus offers them additional means of income.

As a consequence of (1) having small production budgets and (2) signing away the TV production rights to the TV broadcasting stations, there is a general openness on the part of TV producers (as the 'people in charge', chapter 8.2.1.1) to let outside parties such as sustainability organizations finance parts of the TV production and, in return, offer them possibilities to be a part of the decision making process regarding the program content. In short, both the small budgets for producing quality productions and having few TV production rights (and thus less additional means of income) has led TV production companies to consider E-E co-productions and E-E inscript participations as an alternative way to finance their program. It is also a way for TV production companies to do something good, although, as pointed out in section 6.1, these partnership forms are not fully in line with the media legislation. Since the early 1990s both co-productions and inscript participations have become a ***practice in action nobody officially talks about***. It 'happens behind closed doors' as several of the television professionals (and also the sustainability experts) stated. When looking at the contracts between broadcasting organizations and production companies, nobody thinks that steering power on the program content has been handed out to external organizations in return of financial resources because these contracts forbid it. In practice, the data indicates that this can happen, although the contracts stipulate other things.

As will be outlined in chapter 7.2, there have been several well known cases which were 'scandals' because money was handed over in exchange for steering power on the program content. In the majority of these cases, the broadcasting stations distanced themselves from these issues, insisting that they did not know about the things taking place and that the issue was in the responsibility of the production company. As proof, the broadcasting stations referred to the contracts they made with the production companies. In the public debate, the broadcasters were criticized for being unable to control their production companies. However, this thesis will not further deal with the question whether the broadcasters were or were not informed about the issues taking place.

These developments play an important role as conditions for E-E collaborations: while co-productions and inscript participations are not officially allowed by media law (see section 6.1. esp. 6.1.5), they have become a routine practice for some of the players involved, though one which nobody wants to officially talk about.

6.2.2. Sustainability Field

In chapter 2.7.1, the health communication and the environmental communication field were described with respect to their developments and achievements in sustainability communication when trying to reach E-E target groups in so-called mainstream milieus. One main outcome in this context was that both research fields have experimented with an affective approach, but in fact, they usually concentrate their efforts on cognitively-orientated communication strategies (Lubjuhn & Pratt, 2009; Reinermann et al., 2012) in terms of 'if we provide facts, data and sophisticated elaborations, the people will be convinced'.

Affective communication approaches for lower socio-economic milieus are very much in an experimental stage in Germany. In chapter 2.7.1, one important reason was outlined in this context: the mainstream target groups are hard to reach and thus some stakeholders concluded that other target groups are more worthwhile addressing. In the following, additional reasons for why the E-E approach is still in a stage of first steps and experiments are given. The significant point made is that the sustainability research field and their stakeholders themselves first need to overcome barriers and preoccupations regarding the application of a more affective and entertaining communication approach, as the following results show.

6.2.2.1 The Bait must be Attractive to the Fish and not to the Fisherman

This metaphor mentioned by several study participants fits quite well in terms of explaining the ongoing situation in the sustainability field and prerequisites which play a role in E-E collaborations. According to the metaphor, the sustainability experts – as well as the TV makers – perceive themselves as the fishermen who want to catch the fish (the mainstream audience) with the help of the bait (entertainment TV programs and follow up communication activities). In this context 'catching the fish' means something different to each collaboration side. For the TV professionals, 'catching' means designing the TV format in an entertaining manner (drama, tension, conflict, etc.), so that viewing figures remain stable or even improve. TV makers know how to present their bait to catch the fish. For instance, they use a worm as bait and they would not switch to a piece of cheese or wood louse, because they understand that the fish expects a worm and nothing else. One environmental communication expert reinforces this issue by saying 'Al Bundy must stay Al Bundy and nothing else'.

In comparison, for the sustainability side 'catching' implies the need to address the audience members using the TV format and follow up activities (see section 6.6) with the aim to change their knowledge, attitude or behavior according to health, environmental or social themes. When the sustainability side teams up with television makers in E-E collaborations, they have discovered the necessity in presenting a bait in which the fish (the receiver) is interested and not the fisherman (themselves as senders of messages). Experimenting with Entertainment-Education instead of arguing facts and applying a cognitive communication strategy, as they usually do, means stepping outside the regular action radius. Sustainability experts participating in the study explained that while they wanted to experiment with affective communication approaches in order to reach the target group more effectively, they had difficulties with this completely new strategy: while applying this experiment, several sustainability experts had doubts that they could really influence or move the target group (see next section).

6.2.2.2 Doubts according to E-E Approach

Doubts and fears on the part of sustainability experts regarding the E-E approach derive from two central causes as the data show. Firstly, they are afraid of losing their respective reputation in their research or political community while dealing with popular media notions (see also Bouman, 1999). As sustainability experts stated, critics view popular entertainment as 'frivolous' or 'without standards', which is furthermore not a fully research-proven communication strategy for 'convincing' people. Only a few studies have testified so far as to how effective popular media culture can be when attempting to reach mainstream milieus in Germany (Gassmann et al., 2003; Schwender et al., 2008, Reusswig et al., 2004; also see chapter 2.6.2). Thus criticism and doubt will remain strong until new research studies prove the effectiveness of Entertainment-Education on a broader level.

Beside the fear of losing their respective reputation, the second reason for having doubts is that sustainability experts have to deal with the criticism that Entertainment-Education exerts *'latent influence'* on the audience members. As Entertainment-Education is a persuasive communication strategy, there is some truth to this argument (see chapter 3.4.2). The discussion about latent influence and the question of 'who is allowed to steer' goes with the debate described above (i.e. sharing a financial budget with sustainability experts who are taking part in the decision-making process regarding sustainability themes). These issues generally take on a great importance in Germany in comparison to other countries because of the aforementioned historical reasons.

Data shows, that sustainability experts generally belong to two distinct groups. The first group argues that they do not want to get involved in co-productions and inscript participations (i.e. sharing a financial production budget and being a part of decision making process). The second group thinks that both is okay.[141] The opposing group usually argues that they do not want to have steering power on the program content, because it is not their task to do so (referring to the independence of media makers and Germany's history). The group in favor argues that they are doing it for the common good and that the TV professionals also profit from it; they also mention the new product placement rule from 2010 as a kind of legitimization.

6.3. Field Logics and Motives

Field logics and motives can be considered as other prerequisites for E-E collaborations. They play a role during the whole collaboration process, but they are especially essential in the orientation phase of collaboration (chapter 2.4.2), when it comes to the initiation of a collaboration.

6.3.1 Field Logics and Characteristics

Both the entertainment and the sustainability professionals bring different 'field logics' into the collaboration.[142] Their motives for the collaboration are a *part of these field logics* (e.g. reaching the target group with sustainability messages or generating high audience ratings).[143]

Sustainability as well as entertainment professionals mention different field logics, and they refer to two 'languages' they speak and 'worlds' they act in. Interestingly, the differences in field logics are experienced in various ways, depending on which **E-E collaboration form** is implemented. In service and license collaborations (chapter 8.3 and 8.4) implementers hinted that field logics were not particularly disturbing during the collaboration. In fact, both professional sides stressed that these differences contributed to an enriching experience. In co-productions and inscript participations (chapter 8.1), the implementers perceived, on the one hand, the differences in the field logics as being exhausting and time-intensive. Bouman suggests (1999: 177-197) that they could use an E-E risk management to deal with it. On the other hand, there were other co-production and inscript participation implementers emphasizing that there had been no 'serious challenges' caused by the dif-

---

[141] The same differentiation applies to the TV side.

[142] Bouman (1999: 163-176) initially describes the characteristics and logics of both collaborations fields according to their different forms of economic, social and cultural capital (see chapter 7.2.3). E-E implementers also mentioned these different capital forms in a similar manner. As these issues were not the focus in the stories shared about the collaboration processes, this thesis will not elaborate them in detail.

[143] These motives can result in or become a gift, which is then given to and received by the counterpart in the collaboration process (see chapter 7.1).

ferences in the field logics.[144] As with Bouman (1999: 169-171), this study also collected data on how both collaboration parties perceived the field logics and their own characteristics as well as those of the collaborating partners (i.e. to characterize what is typical for their professional logics and the standards enacted in the partnering field). A portrayal can be summarized as follows:

Table 6.1: Perception matrix of the field logics of E-E implementers in Germany

Perception matrix of the field logics	Sustainability professionals	Television professionals
Sustainability professionals About >	• Head decision maker • In-depth investigations according to a topic • Criticize on other experts implementing 'content blank' collaborations	• Highly professional in the intervention of emotions • Reduce the complexity • Creative and spontaneous • They are 'one' with their stories • Stomach decision maker • Existence related to audience ratings/each second is money • Fishermen, who know which bait is needed to catch the fish
Television professionals About >	• Diplomatic and stiff • Theoretical and bureaucratic • Do not want to lose their face in front of their colleagues • Laymen cannot understand them (they do not want it) • Ponderous,but also can be flexible • Complicated • Cannot reduce complexity • Think they know everything better • Fishermen, who think the bait must be attractive to them and not to the fish	• Intuition for pictures • Extroverts • Occasionally self-aggrandizing and narcissistic • Search for actuality, tens and accuracy • Need stories, no theory • Time pressure worker, no time for detailed investigations • 'Sensitive nose' for themes and for what is possible in the story line

It is not easy to extract strategic values from these perceived statements, but what can be clearly pointed out is that the characteristics mirror their interdependency. Drawing on the work of Mauss (Caillé, 2008: 168; Mauss, 1990a: 33; Moebius & Papilloud, 2006: 97-101), the perceived characteristics and logics can be seen as symbols, developing in a reciprocal relation to each other in the context of collaboration. Thus, the characteristics create relations and, as a 'forerunner', may include the reciprocity of exchange processes within the partnership (chapter 7 and 8).

---

[144] One reason for that might be that both sustainability and entertainment professionals are aware that they cannot let the collaboration situation 'escalate' when problems arise, because it might then get very difficult or even risky for both collaborating parties (see chapter 8.2). Furthermore, German co-productions and inscript participations can regularly be characterized by deep, trustful and personal relationships between the partners (chapter 8.2.1.2). In most cases, the partners knew each other before through personal networks, and this might also create a sphere where potential conflicts were kept as small as possible.

6.3.2 Motives for Collaborating

Sustainability and entertainment professionals have different motives for collaborating which derive from their field logics and the characteristics of their professional context. Their motives influence which things they are willing to give, receive and reciprocate during the collaboration process (chapter 7 and 8). These motives also play a role in the decision making process about which form of E-E collaboration will finally be chosen. Entertainment and sustainability professionals described manifold motives for collaborating. These differences might lead to **antagonism** between the partners, as do differences in their collaboration aims.[145] **Television professionals** mentioned the following motives: they want to find (additional) financing for the program development, gain high viewership rates (economic capital), depict sustainability themes authentically, receive consultations on sustainability themes and contact details, tell compelling stories which polarize, create tension and emotion and thus have a high entertainment value, and make audience members think about sustainability topics through emotions. Several of them also stated that they want to take on social responsibility in the television programs and that they are personally interested or even voluntarily engaged in sustainability issues (and thus possess symbolic capital).[146]

The main motive mentioned by **sustainability experts** is to reach mainstream audience members with sustainability themes and thus change their knowledge or even attitude and behavior through the television program and/or the supportive follow up communication activities. Thus, their motive is to experiment with a new approach for reaching specific target group (milieus) which their regular cognitive approach cannot cover (Lubjuhn & Pratt, 2009). Like the television makers, they also want to reach a high number of viewers with the E-E collaboration program. According to the aim of the television program, different motives among sustainability experts became obvious, dependent on the collaboration form in which they worked. While sustainability experts implementing a co-production or an inscript participation wanted to affect the knowledge, attitude and behavior through the entertainment program (also see Bouman 1999: 156), sustainability experts collaborating in E-E service and license (chapter 8.3 and 8.4) did not mention that motive or did not explicitly say that they had this aim in mind. They were in particular interested in letting the television professionals do the work in the TV program and focusing on sensitizing the target group through follow up communication activities.

---

[145] Mauss (in chapter 7.1) identifies this antagonism between parties who have various motives and who want to exchange different things as *potlatch* (Mauss, 1990b: 5-7; Moebius, 2006a: 56-57 and 87; Moebius 2006b: 72-73).

[146] The majority of study participants from the television field are aware of the fact that their stories can have great influence on audience members in their everyday life and that the characters may serve as role models for them. Their motives for taking on a 'societal responsibility' goes with tendencies in the television sector to, by degrees, discover that their 'corporate social and sustainability performance' is an important element in their overall corporate image (Ries, 2004).

Interestingly, both entertainment and sustainability professionals mentioned 'doing something good' as a motive in terms of providing sustainability information to the public and making them think about these issues. This indeed can be characterized, in the words of Mauss (1990a: 75), as partly an anti-utilitaristic[147] motive.

6.4 Forms of E-E Collaborations in Germany

Beside co-productions, inscript participations and service collaborations, Germany's practice reveals a new E-E partnership arrangement form named E-E license collaboration. In chapter 2.4.1, E-E co-production was defined as "a formal transaction between a prosocial organization and either a broadcasting organization or a production company to design, produce and broadcast a new entertainment program for prosocial communication purposes". An E-E inscript participation was defined as "a formal transaction between a prosocial organization and either a broadcasting organization or a production company to use an existing entertainment program as a carrier of prosocial communication". Finally, an E-E service collaboration was defined as "a strategy of prosocial organizations to facilitate (through factual and timely information, contacts with experts, shooting locations, etc.) broadcasting organizations or production companies in dealing with prosocial communication in their entertainment programs".

An E-E license is defined here as "a strategy of prosocial organizations to have the right to use an existing entertainment program for educational purposes to create awareness about a prosocial issue after it has been broadcasted". In this collaboration form, sustainability professionals do not want to be a part of the decision making process for the program. They do not want to be related to that issue in any kind of way, thus claiming that every step of the program development and implementation is in the duty of the TV makers. Their main activity in license collaborations is to design and implement follow up communication measures relating to the TV program (e.g. an educational DVD or an event for the target group) in the implementation stage of collaboration (see chapter 8.4.2.2). Wherever possible, they also try to integrate the TV makers and celebrities of the TV program into these activities as ambassadors, so to speak, for the sustainability theme. In the produc-

---

[147] Utilitarianism can be defined as "the idea that the moral worth of an action is determined solely by its usefulness in maximizing utility and minimizing negative utility. When human beings are controlled by their own self-interest, it is good because there will be no other possible basis of ethical norms, but only the law of the happiness of individuals in a community of individuals" (Caillé, 1989: 17-18). Mauss argues that archaic societies can be characterized by exactly the opposite, non-egoistical behavior, which is not only broken down to logics of self-interest. Mauss wants to bring recent societies to more anti-utililtarianistic thoughts. Although we cannot deny that utilitarism of both E-E collaboration parties plays a crucial role within their motives (also see Papilloud, 2006: 251), there are several trends in the motives of E-E implementers which incorporate anti-utilitaristic tendencies. This goes with the results of the M.A.U.S.S. group and their concept that societal interaction takes place between the poles of interest and anti-utilitarism (see chapter 7.1 as well as Moebius & Papilloud, 2006: 137 and Caillé, 1991: 109-111).

tion stage, the entertainment and sustainability professionals can also come together and team up. This is mainly for two reasons: (1) the sustainability experts provide additional information material on the health, social or environmental theme which can be used as a basis for entertainment professionals who are doing their topic-related investigations and (2) both sides come together to negotiate the license fee. The license fee is the amount of money the sustainability organization needs to hand out to the television makers in order to receive the license for using the entertainment program for their educational purposes, for example integrating it in a media package and putting it on an educational DVD.

This means in consequence that a license collaboration is a partnership arrangement on the lowest level of collaboration. The sustainability experts are not a part of the decision making process on the program content (co-productions/inscript participations), nor do they advise the TV makers on the program content (service). Furthermore, they are not involved in the program development and implementation. Instead, they want to play off their prosocial concerns in the offline part, combining their educational purposes with the TV program.

In addition to the E-E license collaboration form, Germany's E-E implementers also apply the other original three collaboration forms. Chapter 7 and 8 will outline how these four forms are designed and implemented in Germany's E-E practice and how they work in detail.

6.5 Applying Theory and Research in E-E Collaborations

6.5.1 E-E Theory and Definition

Research activities and the application of theoretical notions according to Entertainment-Education are another important condition for fostering collaboration activities. Both can lead to conclusions about whether (1) the E-E intervention was effective in reaching audience members and (2) which lessons learned can be drawn for future projects. In chapter 2, theories and research implications were presented with the conclusion that Germany is experimenting in this field, but there is very little application so far. With respect to E-E theories mentioned, it can be said by looking at the German E-E collaboration examples that none of them involved a theoretical foundation. In chapter 2.1, the definition of Entertainment-Education was reformulated (according to Wang & Singhal, 2009: 272-273):

"Entertainment-Education is a theory-based communication strategy in which educational and entertainment professionals purposefully embed prosocial issues in the creation, production, processing, and dissemination process of an entertainment program in order to achieve different stages of change, either on individual, community, institutional or societal levels among the intended media user populations".

At this stage, a tentative conclusion should be given regarding this definition with respect to Germany. The outcomes of the analysis suggest that this definition is applicable to Dutch collaborations (Bouman, 1999) as well as to other E-E collaborations implemented in (non-western) countries worldwide. Nonetheless, in Germany the definition only partly fits the collaboration situation. Firstly, German collaborations do not apply theory-based notions yet and, secondly, the struggles specifically derived from Germany's Third Reich experience in the past and the media legislation affecting Entertainment-Education make it difficult for both parties to commonly and 'purposefully embed sustainability issues in the creation, production, processing and dissemination process of an entertainment TV program'. Purposefully embedding during the stages of creation, production, processing and dissemination can only be considered completely true for collaboration forms such as co-productions and inscript participations, where both partners are involved in the decision making process of the program. In Germany, several co-productions and inscript participations have taken place (see chapter 8.2) where the definition can be considered applicable.[148] However, there are other striking forms of collaboration (i.e. E-E service and E-E license collaborations, see chapter 8.3 and 8.4) for which the ideal definition mentioned above does not fully fit. In E-E service, the professionals collaborate on a lower level (i.e. the sustainability experts give advice and the TV professionals decide on the program content on their own). In E-E license, the level of collaboration is even lower. Here the sustainability experts do not even give advice on the program content. Rather, the TV makers develop and implement the program on their own and the collaborative aspects happen before and mostly after the design and implementation of the entertainment program. In this context other activities stand at the forefront, including the creation of *follow up communication activities* for the target group in order to get them actively involved rather than passively watching the TV program (see next paragraph).

Figure 6.2 below sums up the agreement between the ideal E-E definition and the different E-E collaboration forms in Germany:

---

[148] Beside the aspect of a theoretical basis for the E-E strategy.

Figure 6.2: Agreement of the ideal E-E definition with the E-E collaboration forms in Germany

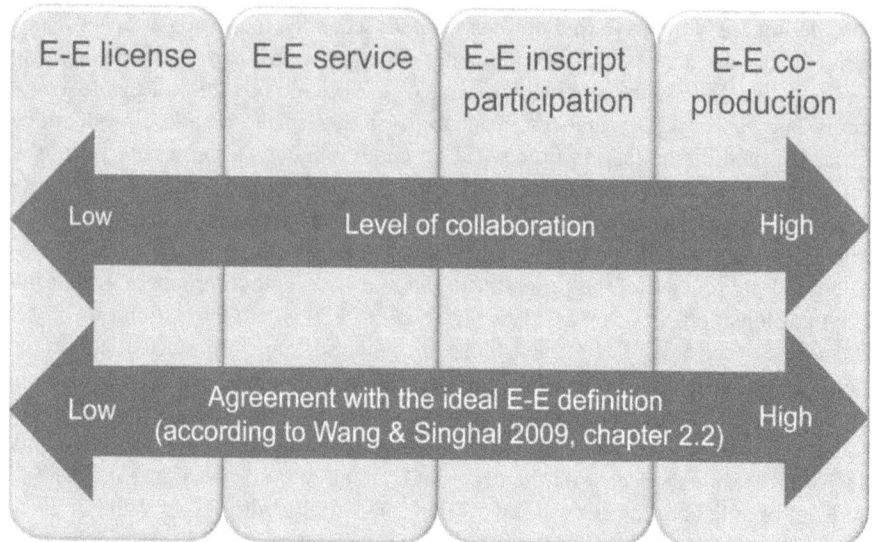

Source: Own illustration based on Bouman & Brown (2011: 10)

In summary, the ideal E-E definition does not fully fit within the collaboration picture that can be drawn for Germany. Germany's analysis will add some new, additional aspects to E-E collaborations which also must be taken into consideration.

6.5.2 Research Notions mentioned by the E-E Implementers

When focusing more detailed on the (formative, process and summative) research activities involved in the collaborations, several interesting issues can be pointed out. First and foremost, sustainability experts emphasize that one central reason for why E-E research is rare can be traced back to the difficult conditions regarding the *funding of the research*. Most of the potential funders, as perceived by sustainability experts, think that the 'entertainment bait' should not only fit to the mainstream audience members, but should also be attractive to the funders themselves. Thus it is often difficult to satisfy the funders' wishes. Moreover, the interviewed sustainability experts stressed that the funders are hesitant to invest in research in entertainment media in general and in E-E collaborations in particular, because usually entertainment studies and persuasion research is not highly valued (see section 6.2.2). Data indicates several options for E-E research. For example, research is implemented, but the results are not published. In such cases, the summative results 'only' serve as a legitimization for the sustainability organization that the effort and money they have invested has been worthwhile in terms of reaching audience members. This especially applies to co-productions and inscript participations, in which a financial budget is shared and where both partners are involved in the decision making process with regard to the program content. Some of the results were published in databases maintained by the sustainability organizations, but were not made available to a broader public (e.g. through publishing the results in journals or books) nor were they labeled as E-E research results.

The majority of sustainability experts and television professionals who *did not carry out research activities* often made *assumptions* (as a kind of legitimization) that their activities (1) reached audience members, probably changing their knowledge, attitude and behavior and (2) led to sensitization processes regarding sustainability themes among the actresses and actors. As *indicators* to strengthen their assumptions, they referred to letters written by audience members emphasizing that the sustainability depiction helped them in their everyday life. They additionally mentioned monitoring measurements, where audience members were questioned in general regarding how positively or negatively they perceived storylines. Moreover, they declared that high audience rates are an indicator for that their E-E project has been effective in terms of reaching audience members. Another indicator for measuring the success of the E-E project for sustainability experts are the high request rates for learning materials designed in conjunction with the TV program to be used by educational organizations such as schools or vocational training centers. Obviously, E-E implementers mentioned several indicators which point to the potential impact of their E-E project without involving research notions and thus without having distinct proofs. Future tasks will be to strengthen formative, process as well as summative research so that, for Germany's E-E formats, evident statements can be drawn and recommendations can be given.

6.6 Follow up activities

Follow up communication and participatory measures take place during and after the reception of the E-E program, and they try to spur the interpersonal communication processes (through talks, chats, blogs, hotlines, events, etc.) among the audience members. They aim to help them change their knowledge, attitude and behavior. Papa & Singhal (2008) point out that the interpersonal communication component can be considered one of the central influencing factors when it comes to facilitating changes among the audience members. The E-E program thus urgently needs to be supported by these measures in order to achieve changes among the intended media user populations (ibid. as well as Chatterjee et al., 2009; Valente et al., 1996; Valente & Saba, 2001).

The research data clearly indicates that the latter measures play a decisive role in Germany's collaborations along with the E-E program itself. The most striking activities are outlined in the following.

6.6.1 Media Package

In the case of a media package, the sustainability experts usually have full responsibility with regard to the design and implementation (including learning materials).

The media package is implemented to deepen the knowledge of audience members 'offline' and to draw an even closer link between the sustainability issue in TV format and their everyday life. Indeed, the TV format cannot achieve changes on its own. More background information, discussions and reflections are needed in addition to the brief presentation of sustainability issues during the TV program. The media package should ensure that audience members can deal with the sustainability issue as well as its potentials and problems more in depth. Furthermore, it should guarantee the long-term nature of the sustainability theme itself, because audience members can still access the media package several month or even years after the E-E format was broadcasted on TV.

The media package regularly contains background information pertaining to the E-E format and the sustainability theme. This content is exclusively produced for the media package. Furthermore, scenes taken from the E-E format itself are included in the media package (chapter 8.4.2.1). In several cases, additional background documentations on the sustainability issues are also incorporated.

Beside the film incentives, a booklet with supplementary information and didactical material is included in the package. Sustainability organizations distribute the media package within their networks, and they put it into the public domain so that every educational organization nation-wide has direct access to it. In recent years, sustainability experts have also made the media package available for download on their homepage.

6.6.2 Events and Other Side Activities

In addition to the activities around the creation of a media package, other essential participatory measures are public events (workshops, festivals, etc.) to promote the sustainability issues. Both collaboration sides regularly implement these measures. In one collaboration, for example, sustainability partners took the initiative and invited the actresses and actors as well as TV makers from the entertainment program to spend a day together and discuss the topic of drug use and its aftermaths with the target group, which, in this case, were teenagers. In another collaboration, television and sustainability experts arranged a festival providing both educational (e.g. through information booths and panel discussions with sustainability experts and TV makers) as well as entertaining elements (e.g. through live bands, booths where actresses and actors gave autographs as well as a cycling rally for climate protection). It is mostly the sustainability partners who are the main financier of these public-orientated activities.

In general, it is fair to say that these follow up activities serve to reach the audience members with sustainability messages. As a significant side effect, the collaboration partners get positive PR though these events.[149] Lubjuhn & Hoffhaus (2009) provide several recommendations for further follow up communication measures in Germany's E-E projects.

---

[149] This is a major issue when implementing a service collaboration (see chapters 2.4.1 and 8.3).

6.7 Summary

Chapter 6 elaborated crucial conditions and characteristics of E-E collaborations in Germany. As an *external condition*, the *media legislation* with regard to Entertainment-Education was introduced. In this context, five pieces of media legislation are relevant to E-E collaboration practice. The point was made that E-E implementers are confronted with a *complex and contradictionary media legislation portfolio*. There is one piece of legislation which indirectly forbids financial support for television makers (for being political advertising), while another states that payments are legislatively compliant when they are sponsorships. Furthermore, on the one hand, there is the most recent legislation, which liberalizes the television market and hence indirectly fosters developments that allow organizations and companies to have easier access to the decision making processes on the program content. On the other hand, two other legislations from the early 1960s clearly emphasize the liberality and freedom television professionals have in the decision making process. Obviously, this is an awkward 'grey zone' in which the E-E implementers need to act. The problems start when financial support is given and sustainability experts are involved in the decision making process of the program content. Then, the partners have to maintain a very fine balance.

Other important external conditions for E-E collaborations are *current developments in the television and the sustainability field*. According to the television field, the television professionals and media legislation experts described a trend where both commercial and public broadcasting stations are under increased economic pressure. Furthermore, they pointed to the trends towards more authentic and accurate portrayals in entertainment formats as well as an increase in 'entertainization' in general. These are two developments E-E research can profit from and contribute to. Lastly, television makers and media legislation experts stressed that only very small production budgets are available and that production companies have to give up their production rights. Both of these facts have led to a development in which producers are generally open-minded in terms of letting prosocial change organizations and other stakeholders finance the production of the television program and, in return, offer possibilities to have steering power (though this often happens 'behind closed doors'). The sustainability field was characterized as a field experimenting with affective communication strategies; however, there are several crucial barriers restricting the E-E strategy. Firstly, sustainability experts experienced that the mainstream milieus, who are a crucial target group of Entertainment-Education (see chapter 2.7), are unmanageable and hard to reach, so they prefer to focus on other groups. Secondly, the sustainability experts stressed that another barrier lies in their fears of losing their respective reputations in the political or research field. Third and last, it was pointed out that the educational experts also have to deal with the criticism that they are applying a latently influencing communication strategy. Being some kind of persuasive communication, it often generates references to the (mis)use of media during the Third Reich (see chapter 3.4.2).

With regard to essential internal conditions, this chapter dealt with the *field logics and motives* of E-E implementers, which are different ones for the television and the sustainability side. The motives affect what the implementers are willing to give, receive and reciprocate in the collaboration process, and thus they also affect the form of collaboration. It became clear that sustainability experts and television professionals have different motives, which can also overlap though.

According to *theoretical and research notions* involved in E-E collaborations, it was initially emphasized that no theoretical foundations for German E-E collaborations could be traced so far. Furthermore, it was outlined that the ideal E-E definition (see chapter 2.2) can be applied to several non-western countries as well as to the Netherlands (Bouman, 1999), although for Germany, the definition only partly fits and needs to be reviewed (chapter 9).

It was stressed that only a few of the analyzed collaborations included research methodologies (formative, summative and process) research in their collaboration projects. In case they did, the results were not published, or they were published without being made accessible to a broader audience (in journals, etc.). Reasons for conducting less research in the E-E field and the lack of enthusiasm for publishing it are, according to the sustainability experts, threefold: (1) the fear that they might be criticized when being a part of the decision making process, (2) the fact that the majority of potential E-E project funders still think that the bait has to fit to themselves rather than the audience members and (3) the challenge that entertainment is still perceived as something 'untrustworthy' among research and political stakeholders and thus might not yet be a worthwhile investment.

Follow up activities were described as a central characteristic for Germany's E-E collaborations. One reason for this is the fact that there are several tensions around the topic of steering power on the program content (see chapter 6.1), which however, do not arise in the field of follow up activities. In consequence the sustainability experts try to be fully engaged in this field. Typical German follow up activities, such as the implementation of a media package as well as public activities for reaching audience members with sustainability messages like events or discussion rounds were touched upon.

Finally, this chapter gave a short introduction to the *collaboration forms* as a vital prerequisite when transitioning into the next chapters. In this context, it was stressed that in Germany co-productions, inscript participations and service collaborations are designed and employed. In addition, there is also a new collaboration form named E-E license, which is typical for the German environment and has not been dealt with in academic literature so far.

7. Place of Gift Exchange and Correlations to Common Sense and Zeitgeist (According to the Third Reich Experience and the Media)

> "A central category (...) must be abstract; that is, all other major categories can be related to it and placed under it. It must appear frequently in the data. This means that within all, or almost all, cases there are indicators pointing to that concept. It must be logical and consistent with the data (...). It should be sufficiently abstract so that it can be used to do research in other substantive areas, leading to the development of a more general theory. It should grow in depth and explanatory power as each of the categories is related to it through statements of relationship".
>
> - Juliet Corbin & Anselm Strauss, 2008: 105

Whereas the last chapter dealt with conditions with regard to E-E collaborations, this chapter will focus on the introduction of the central category, the place of gift exchange, as well as two other significant categories and their central characteristics which the analysis revealed for the E-E collaboration topic in Germany.

E-E collaboration partners are very well aware of the different fields and levels they face in their collaborations. The most essential collaboration field is the *place of gift exchange*, which is where E-E collaborations take place in practice. Additionally, there are two other fields which have strong effects on E-E implementers in practice and which thus strongly influence the place of gift exchange. Firstly, this is the field of common sense (according to the Third Reich experience and the media) and the secondly field influencing E-E practice is zeitgeist (according to the Third Reich experience and the media).

The next section (7.1) will first argue why the theory of gift exchange according to Marcel Mauss and theoretical enhancements from Alain Caillé[150] were chosen for the analysis and not other theoretical concepts. In the second section, the basic principles concerning the place of gift exchange will be illustrated (7.2). Afterwards, those of common sense and zeitgeist will be outlined (sections 7.3 and 7.4). Moreover, recent circumstances (section 7.5) and the careful observation practices of the E-E implementers (section 7.6) will be described. Then the different components depicted before will be summarized in an integrative model (section 7.7). The last section of this chapter will then discuss the German research results of the

---

[150] When naming Alain Caillé here and in the following sections, he represents all of the other researchers who worked on the theoretical enhancements of Marcel Mauss' theory and investigated the reciprocity of gift exchange in postmodern societies (see below).

main categories in the context of international E-E collaboration literature (section 7.8) and afterwards a summary on the whole chapter will be given (section 7.9).

7.1 Theoretical Foundation of the Research Theme

First of all, it is important to clarify that there are different ways to look at the research field concerning E-E collaborations. It is possible to apply various theoretical perspectives such as sociological, anthropological or ethnological theories (e.g. those from Franz Boas, Emile Durkheim, Claude Lévi-Strauss, Bronislaw Malinowski, Marcel Mauss, George H. Mead, Alfred Schütz, Michael Tomasello, Max Weber), negotiation or bargaining theories (e.g. those from David Chruchman, Manie Spoelstra, Wynand Pienaar), theories from the perspective of business and economics (e.g. those from Martin Osborne, Ariel Rubinstein, John Nash), as well as conflict theories (e.g. those from Ralf Dahrendorf, Otomar Bartos, James Davis, Paul Wehr, Max Weber). These different perspectives and their epistemological principles[151] were taken into account during the reflection process of the theoretical foundation of the research data. For this research study, the sociological perspective of Marcel Mauss (Mauss, 1990a; Mauss, 1990b; Mauss, 2006; Moebius, 2006a; Moebius, 2006b; Moebius & Papilloud, 2006) and the postmodern enhancements of his theory which originated with the French research group around Alain Caillé (Adolff & Mau, 2005;) were chosen. This is because the main category developed out of the data showed clear evidence that both theories have a central role: all collaborations involved gift exchange structures and principles with attributes similar to those described by Mauss and Caillé.

Other theoretical perspectives are also suitable to a certain degree. However, they do not have as many intersections with the findings presented here as does the work of Mauss and Caillé. But of course, both theories also have their limitations as will be shown in the following sections and chapters. This is also why other theoretical concepts come in when necessary. For example, negotiation theories give additional fruitful hints in some sections, and they are integrated to describe the orientation stage of E-E collaboration in chapter 8.1.

7.2 Place of Gift Exchange

7.2.1 The 'Place of Gift Exchange' and the Theory of Marcel Mauss

The main category resulting from the analysis is the place of gift exchange. At this metaphorical place, the E-E implementers exchange their collaboration gifts. The

---

[151] The monistic principle argues that the spirit or thought develops through society (i.e. the human spirit can be understood as an inwardly turned outside) (see George H. Mead, Emile Durkheim or Marcel Mauss). The dualistic principle is based on the René Descartes mind-body dualism (of res extensa and res cognita). Followers argue that human spirit is there from birth on, or better yet, it is a precondition to develop culture and society (see Alfred Schütz, Peter L. Berger, Thomas Luckmann).

place of gift exchange is in its entirety reserved for the E-E implementers themselves and it is not easy to enter for outsiders. Gifts play a crucial role in this field.[152] They can be of a material (e.g. money, sustainability information, brochures, etc.) as well as of a non-material nature (providing networks, logistics, etc.). Following Mauss (2006: 357-358), they can be considered as symbols; through their exchange a symbolic interaction process takes place and the symbolic meaning of the gift has a specific value only in the exchange context itself (1990a: 33; Moebius 2006b: 72-73; Waltz 2006: 89).[153]

The central mechanism on the place of gift exchange is the *gift exchange procedure*. In this context the gift theory of Mauss (Mauss, 1990a; Moebius, 2006a; Moebius, 2009; Moebius & Papilloud, 2006) possesses a fundamental importance. According to Mauss (1990a: 3, 7, 29), although gifts are supposed to be given voluntarily, they include three main obligations: the obligation to give, to receive and to reciprocate. Mauss argues that the obligation to give the gift might be paradoxical on first sight (Mauss 1990a: 14), but that the inconsistency resolves when understanding that the gift exchange serves as an amalgamation of mental bonds between individuals and groups who exchange both material and non-material symbolic things. These things have a kind of 'soul'[154] which connect individuals and group members (Mauss, 1990a: 14, 20). The obligatory and the voluntary character combined in the gift emerge principally because of two reasons (Moebius, 2009: 66-67): the first reason is the *obsession*. Each gift has some kind of 'soul', and has been obsessed over by the giver; it has something from the giver – a certain symbolic reference (also see Moebius, 2006a: 86-87). This means that when gifts are exchanged, some kind of transsubstantiation of the participants take place: the receiver absorbs the gift along with the presenter himself; the giver in turn obsesses over the receiver then. Therefore, to give something always means giving something of oneself, something from one's person and from the power of the 'spirit of things'. Thus, presenter and receiver transcend themselves in the exchange process (Moebius, 2009: 66-67). Due to the obsessive character the gift includes, it 'must' be reciprocated (Mauss, 1990a: 5-8).

The second reason why a gift is obligatory and voluntary at the same time is the *hybridization of things and people* (Moebius, 2009: 67). As Därmann (2005: 102-104) points out, in Mauss' gift exchange theory things are personified, people are objectified and identification with oneself as well as with foreign things and people takes place. This mixture of people and things creates an obligatory character and builds social connectivity (Moebius, 2009: 67).

The gift mirrors the concept of the *total social phenomenon* (i.e. gifts simultan-

---

[152] They are embedded in the communication processes. For example one collaboration side gives a gift to the counterpart by announcing it (Reichertz, 2009).

[153] Mauss follows the tradition of his uncle Emile Durkheim (1981) in which each communicational act is symbolically transmitted. This is clearly reminiscent of the pragmatism of George Herbert Mead (also see Moebius, 2009: 64).

[154] Mauss names the 'soul' of exchange gifts 'hau' (Mauss, 1990a: 11-13).

eously include economical, juridical, moral, religious, mythological and esthetical dimensions) (Mauss, 1990a: viii, 7 and 79; Moebius, 2006b: 72). More generally speaking, Mauss argues that all social phenomena are connected with each other, and all kinds of institutions are expressed through them. Gifts are one part of this social whole. They are not to be considered as things, but as symbols (Caillé, 2008: 48).

Mauss in particular refers to the potlatch,[155] a specific form of gift exchange, which he defines as a total service of an agonistic type (Mauss, 1990a: 6-7). The central motive of the potlatch is (1) the antagonism and the rivalry of the gift exchange parties and (2) the destruction of gifts (compare chapter 8.3.1.2). The following sections and chapters will pick up on the potlatch as well as other characteristics of the gift exchange.

7.2.2 Postmodern Theoretical Enhancements for the 'Place of Gift Exchange' from the M.A.U.S.S. Group[156] around Alain Caillé

Mauss wrote his gift essay for archaic societies to specifically find out which legal principle stands behind the obligatory reciprocity of gift exchange. He also asked about the power in the gift that makes the recipient pay it back (1990a: 3). Besides looking deeply into the gift exchange phenomenon in archaic societies, Mauss tries to convey his thoughts on postmodern societies (Mauss, 1990a: 65-83). Mauss argues that postmodern societies should not go back to archaic ones, but he stresses that basic principles of the gift exchange may and should be applied instead of following pure market and utilitarianistic thoughts (Moebius, 2006b: 73). He sees the moral and the economy of the gift "subliminally, as it were, but also affecting our own societies" and it forms a foundation on which society can rest (Mauss, 1975: 14). When suggesting this, Mauss does not make his point clear in his essay how a translation in different postmodern societal areas may look like in detail (also see Papilloud, 2006: 248). Nonetheless, he provides fruitful remarks.

One central remark is that in postmodern societies hybrid forms of gift exchange can and should be practiced (Mauss, 1990a: 73). This thesis argues that E-E collaborations can be considered as a kind of *hybrid* or a mixture of what Mauss describes for archaic and our recent societies. Keeping this thought in mind, E-E collaborations have principles in common that are related to archaic gift exchanges as well as characteristics which are typical for postmodern societal forms. Mauss (1990a: 73) describes this hybrid as follows: "Yet this notion is neither that of the free, purely gratuitous rendering of total services, nor that of production and exchange purely interested in what is useful. It is a sort of hybrid that flourished".

To put this hybrid into practice, this thesis makes use of the enhancements of Caillé

---

[155] The name derives from the Chinook language and means 'gift' or 'feed' or 'use'.
[156] Alain Caillé founded the M.A.U.S.S. GROUP in 1981. The abbreviation M.A.U.S.S. stands for *Mouvement Anti-Utilitariste dans les Sciences Sociales*.

and the M.A.U.S.S. group on Mauss' theory. They give additional recommendations when aiming at the transmission of Mauss' theory in postmodern societies. They argue that the principle to give, receive and reciprocate is still a present one in postmodern societies and was not given up in favor of strict market rules and the cultural logic of strategic gift giving. They further claim that the implicit and explicit reciprocity norms are still active in postmodern societies (Caillé, 2008).

7.2.2.1 The Third Paradigm and the Four Poles of Action

Caillé discovered a *"third paradigm"* in Mauss' gift theory which overcomes normativistic holism (see Durkheim, Parsons) as well as utilitarian individualism (see Bourdieu or rational-choice theories). This third paradigm claims to be a universal principle and an open research program in social science which is applicable to modern societies (Caillé, 2008: 82), namely that of giving, receiving and reciprocating. Caillé states (2008: 63) about the other two paradigms that "the holism only knows traditional action and the individualism only the instrumental-rational action". His idea is that Mauss never had one of these two directions in mind. In fact, Mauss stresses the strong parallels with Georg Simmels' *Digression on Faithfulness and Thankfulness* in which he describes how the experience of social bonds develop and how they contribute to the tendency for social relations to outlast the original motive (Caillé, 2008: 17).

The M.A.U.S.S. group sums up its third paradigm in a concept, which makes the central point that exchanged gifts include four poles or aspects: ***voluntariness, obligation, interest and anti-utilitarianism*** (Caillé, 2008: 74; Caillé, 1991: 109-111; Moebius, 2009: 136-137). Gifts circulate among these four different poles of human action. Using this, Caillé argues that Mauss developed a multidimensional action theory (ibid.), though it did not include dimensions of individualism (interests of individuals) or holism (cultural and social forces). The four poles are included in the three acts of giving, receiving and reciprocating (Caillé, 2008: 76) and as a consequence a new typology arises.

Furthermore, he stresses that each postmodern institution is based on principles of a 'primary socialization' and includes gift exchange principles practiced primarily in archaic societies. According to Caillé this primary socialization is the basis for the 'secondary socialization', which include the market, the economy and the state in postmodern societies (Caillé, 2008: 94; Moebius, 2009: 137). Hence, Caillé's work (2008) as well as other recently published works from Adolff (2005) and Stegbauer (2010) argue that postmodern institutions are related to principles of gift exchange to some degree. The thesis follows this line of argumentation. As institutions or single individuals circulate gifts among the poles of voluntariness, obligation, interest and anti-utilitarianism, it becomes clear that some gifts are given more voluntarily and others less so.

Likewise, some gifts may be given, where anti-utlilitarianistic thoughts play a more essential role whereas in others the 'pure' interest stands in the foreground. So, for instance, this thesis does not argue that E-E collaborations proceed in a field of non-utilitarianistic action. This would in fact deny the reality of postmodern societies where utilitarianism, market thoughts and gaining attention play a role in the culture of societies (Franck, 2007: 84). In E-E collaborations, a sort of 'restricted utilitarianism' is predominant[157] on both sides or, in the words of Caillé, there is a "conditional unconditionality" (2008: 101) in the gift exchange and "the logic of benefits and conditionality can only spread if they can draw from anti-utilitarian and unconditional sense resources" (Caillé, 2008: 104). Caillé describes this principle of a "conditional unconditionality" or a partly utilitaristic behavior as follows: "There is no human alliance which could function without a certain unconditionality. It is the nutrient of sociality and trust. (...) In a primary unconditionality, everyone can according to their possibilities and needs enjoy the benefits that arise only in that there is this connection. Here and here only everyone begins to set conditions. This is possible because the connections are free and one is free to leave them. (...) As long as I remain trustful, I can assume that I am situated in a state of unconditionality. (...) And every hesitation to give something causes that trust to crumble. Then I am back in the area of conditionality and then behave conditionally, because the others do likewise" (2008: 111).

This quotation shows that Caillé's concept of the "conditional unconditionality" arises from the four poles of human action in which gifts are circulating: while obligation and interest have more conditional aspects, voluntariness and anti-utilitarianism comprise more non-conditional aspects and this mixture, or 'hybrid', is exactly what his theoretical concept is about (also see Caillé, 2008: 117) and what is also mirrored in the different gifts exchanged in E-E collaborations.

7.2.2.2 Critics

Mauss theory has generated its share of criticism. Caillé (2008: 166-170) explains that there are three groups critical of Mauss: the first group tends to interpret Mauss as unilateral reductionism. This means that the gift is reduced to a material resource or, introduced as only an intermediary. Within this group, there are several different dynamics which all describe the gift as a means to gain economic capital.[158] The second group has learned from the first, and their hypothesis ends with

---

[157] On the one hand, sustainability experts' aim is to reach audience members with sustainability messages by 'doing something good' for them. Moreover, they themselves as an organization also profit from an E-E project in terms of getting positive publicity. On the other hand, TV makers, especially those from public broadcasters, do not need to follow market principles and aim for high audience ratings as strictly as the private broadcasters do. They have more room to play, and they want to provide audience members with valuable, accurate and authentic sustainability content in terms of 'doing something good'. Moreover, of course, they are profiting from an E-E project (e.g. by receiving additional money for the production, gaining a positive image in the public, etc.). So, both utilitarianistic and altruistic components are involved in the E-E collaboration.

[158] Following Caillé (2008: 167, 2005: 161), Bourdieu also belongs to this group. He speaks of "investments, gain and capital as if prestige was a thing or a product which could be interpreted in terms of the market. Bourdieu explains that symbolic capital is only a modality and redirected funds to gain economic capital" (Caillé 2008: 167).

the non-existence of the gift. The third group argues that the gift theory is not closed and cannot carry itself. Thus, they declare the gift theory is incomplete.[159] Furthermore, Caillé and the M.A.U.S.S. group as well as other authors based on Mauss and following a 'restricted' utilitarianistic line of argumentation for postmodern societies have been criticized because they still have not described in detail how collective action can arise out of the four basic poles of human action (Moebius, 2009: 138).

The researcher is aware of these critics and limitations. She is also aware that the theory of Mauss (especially due to its primary reference to archaic societies), and the enhancements of Caillé and the M.A.U.S.S. group need to be advanced. Specifically, these enhancements still need to prove themselves and need to be reflected more in detail in terms of broader concepts such as democracy or globalization questions and their relation to the gift exchange (also see Caillé, 2008: 212). Nonetheless, this is not a reason for not applying this theory in the present study because, through the analysis, it has become obvious that the theoretical concept of Mauss and Caillé best fit (see introduction to the chapter).

7.2.3 E-E Exchange Gifts and Their Characteristics

E-E implementers exchange different gifts during the collaboration. This involves an interplay of giving, receiving and reciprocating. The following table 7.1 gives an outline of the various gifts involved in E-E collaborations and their characteristics.[160]

---

[159] In German sociology, Mauss' reception has failed to appear for a long time. This can also be considered a certain criticism, because sociologists did not recognize the importance of his theoretical suggestions. One reason might be that Mauss could be easily put into the category of ethnology because he studied with non-European cultures for a long time (Caillé, 2008: 8). Another reason might be that the theoretical level is difficult to comprehend. However, it is important to mention that Mauss (and the enhancements made by Caillé) nowadays are increasingly finding their way into the German sociological field.

[160] In chapter 8, the single gifts are portrayed more in detail according to the E-E collaboration forms in which they typically appear.

Table 7.1: Gifts and their characteristics in E-E collaborations

Gift itself \ Gift characteristics	Value	E-E collaboration forms (typical)	Sustainability or television gift (typical)	Endogenous/ exogenous gift	Determined gift in return	TV program/ follow up communication (typical)	Capital form	Total social phenomena (phenomena involved)
Financial support (for program development)	+++	Co-production, Inscript p.	Sustainability	Exogenous	Yes	TV program	Economic	Economical, juridical, moral
Involvement in (the decision making process on) the program content	+++	Co-production, Inscript p.	Television	Exogenous	Yes	TV program	Cultural	Juridical, moral
E-E research	++	Co-production, Inscript p.	Sustainability	Exogenous	No	TV program	Cultural	Not known
Sustainability (communication) consultation	++	Service	Sustainability	Mixed form	No	TV program	Cultural	Juridical, moral
Guest part	++	Service	Television	Exogenous	No	TV program	Cultural	Esthetical
Patronage	++	Service	Sustainability	Exogenous	No	Follow up communication	Cultural	Not known
Celebrity endorsement	++	Service	Television	Exogenous	No	TV program	Cultural	Esthetical
Reliability	++	Service	Sustainability	Endogenous	No	Both	Cultural	Not known
Networks/contacts	++	Service	Sustainability	Mixed form	No	Follow up communication measures	Social	Not known
Logistical support and organization know-how	++	Service	Sustainability	Mixed form	No	Follow up communication	Social	Not known
PR (for theme)	++	Service	Both	Exogenous	No	Follow up communication	Social	Moral
Give sustainability information	+	License	Sustainability	Mixed form	No	TV program	Cultural	Juridical, moral
License fee	+	License	Sustainability	Exogenous	Yes	Follow up communication	Economic	Economical, juridical, moral
License (for integrating the program in educational activities)	+	License	Television	Exogenous	Yes	Follow up communication	Cultural	Economical, juridical, moral

+++ = high value   ++ = medium value   + = low value

The figure illustrates eight different gift characteristics (see horizontal line of the table). In the following they will be described more in detail.

1. *Value*: The first gift characteristic is the value. A gift exchanged in an E-E collaboration context can have low (+), middle (++), or high (+++) value. For instance, finances or involvement in the program content can be considered as high value gifts, whereas offering a PR (for theme) or logistical support is less valuable.
2. *E-E collaboration forms (typical)*: Gifts can be typical for various collaboration forms. For example, the gift of finances or involvement in the program content is specific for co-productions and inscript participations, whereas the gift of networks/contacts is commonly provided in E-E service.
3. *Sustainability or television gift (typical)*: Some gifts are typically given and reciprocated by the sustainability (networks/contacts, reliability), others for the entertainment partners (celebrity endorsement, guest part), and still others are commonly given from both sides (PR for theme).
4. *Endogenous/exogenous gift*: The gifts can be differentiated in organizational

endogenous and exogenous ones. Endogenous gifts are visible from the outside (before the collaboration even starts) and the partners do not need to negotiate them, because they are organizationally inherent. This, for instance, includes a high level of reliability on the part of the sustainability organization from which the TV professionals might profit. In contrast, exogenous gifts must be negotiated and primarily through communication of both sides can these gifts be determined and thus become 'visible'. An example might be the guest part in the entertainment program. There are also some *mixed forms* (i.e. gifts which are 'visible' from the outside before starting the collaboration) such as networks/contacts, which need to be negotiated whether they will be given as a gift or not.

5. *Determined gift in return*: Some gifts include a directly linked or determined gift in return (after some time), such as in the case of finances (for the program development) and involvement in the program content. Other gifts are given and received *without a directly linked reciprocal gift in return* (e.g. give sustainability information or logistical support do not assume a specific gift in return).

6. *TV program/follow up communication (typical)*: E-E implementers exchange different gifts in the context of the *entertainment program* (e.g. sustainability consultation, guest part), whereas other gifts are primarily related to the *follow up communication measures* of the entertainment program (e.g. logistical support, networks/contacts etc.).

7. *Capital form*: Based on the classification of Bourdieu (Bourdieu, 1984, Bourdieu, 1991, Bourdieu, 1993), the various gifts can be characterized through the involvement of *economic, social and cultural capital* of the E-E implementing organizations (also see Bouman 1999: 126-127). Bourdieu draws on Mauss and he tries to establish a symbolic order out of his gift thinking (Moebius, 2009). He creates a habitus field concept, also described as "feel for the game", for analyzing societal structures. He therefore develops a specific sociological notion of capital. This notion does not revoke the notion of economical capital itself. It rather adds a social, a cultural and symbolic dimension. Bouman (1999) deploys Bourdieu's field concept in her analysis of Dutch E-E collaboration processes, and she differentiates between the economic, social and cultural capital forms, which are exchanged during the collaboration. In E-E collaboration practice, economic capital involves material wealth and economic goods (money, stocks and shares, property, etc.). Cultural capital comprises the competencies and qualifications, talents, knowledge and expertise as well as the level of mental and intellectual growth. Social capital involves the skills to socialize, interests in relationships and memberships to networks, image and goodwill.[161] These different forms of capital are also gift-inherent characteristics. So, for example, a license fee for receiving

---

[161] Bourdieu also calls the social and cultural capital 'symbolic capital' or 'symbolic power' (Bourdieu, 1991; Bouman 1999: 126-128).

the entertainment program license specifically affects the economic capital of the sustainability organization. Sustainability consultation involves the cultural capital, whereas networks/contacts particularly incorporate social capital aspects of the sustainability organization.

8. *Total social phenomena (phenomena involved)*: Coming to the last characteristic, gifts which are given, received and reciprocated in E-E collaborations also include different institutions of a more holistic nature or, as Mauss calls it, '*total social phenomenon*' (see above). For instance, finances for the entertainment program are economical, but they also include judicial as well as a moral institutions, because this gift is directly related to media legislation, the grey zone and the struggles of E-E implementers emerging in this context (chapter 6.1). However, not all gifts can directly be linked to 'total social phenomenon' institutions. As the figure also shows, this is indeed a limitation at this point.

7.2.4 Time Range in Gift Exchange

Within the context of the interviews and informal talks, the exchange of gifts was not necessarily brought up directly. On the one hand, several E-E implementers did so themselves. For instance, one TV maker stressed, "They get a good platform [for the topic] and in exchange we receive advice for the stories, for the scriptwriters". A sustainability expert stated, "And we said that if we take part in this issue, then we also want to be named in all publications". On the other hand, there were also study participants, who did not put the different gifts into a direct exchange context (also see chapter 8.2.1). The question arises of why the latter is the case or why several study participants did not explicitly mention the important phenomenon of gift exchange. Indeed, the gifts are given, received and reciprocated in time ranges, which can be quite long. Moebius (2006: 133) alludes in this context to the fact that usually the exchange is unconsciously concealed in that time range. Thereby the gifts seem to have no relation to each other. Bourdieu (1998: 133) adds that the time range functions as a shield, which makes the gifts appear to be unconnected single actions and thus something special.

7.3 Common Sense According to the Third Reich Experience and the Media

This section serves to introduce common sense with regard to the Third Reich experience and the media, its specific role in the E-E collaboration environment and its crucial impact on the main topic, the place of gift exchange. Before that, a brief general introduction of the term common sense in social science will be given.

7.3.1 Common Sense in Social Science

Since Aristotle, scholars have discussed what common sense is, what it consists of and what it involves. There are several debates in social science disciplines like *philosophy* (e.g. Aristotle (1975); Peirce (1940) Popper (1962) and Moore (1925) or *history* (see the analysis of Kant (1952); Reid (van Holthoon, 1987), as well as in specific historical concepts such as imperialism (Koebner), insanity (Foucault) and mind (Snell) (van Holthoon & Olson, 1987: 7). *Societal studies* of Luckmann (1987) or Lindenberg (Lindenberg, 1987) and *psychology* by de Gelder (1987) or Bowerman (1987) also touch upon the debate of what constitutes common sense. All of these scholars and others have presented common sense from different viewpoints and presuppositions, and they emphasized different aspects of it. Some scholars have paid more attention to the *judgment aspect* of common sense (van Holthoon, 1987), while others have focused on and analyzed the *body of common knowledge*[162] in common sense (Lindenberg, 1987; Luckmann, 1987). Van Holthoon & Olson (1987: 12) argue "At times common sense is used to refer to judgment and at times to the body of knowledge which individuals use to define normalcy of their social and natural surroundings". They add that "common sense consists of the knowledge, judgment, and taste which is more or less universal and which is held more or less without reflection or argument" (ibid.: 9). Characteristically, common sense has been discussed positively as well as negatively during different epochs. For instance, during the Reformation in the 16th century, it served as the basis for the growth of science. During the Enlightment, its meaning became problematic and it came to be referred to as "sound judgment" and at other times as prejudice and unreflective vulgarity (van Holthoon & Olson 1987: 8). Although at this point no detailed discussion can be provided, it should be obvious that common sense is a fundamental concept in science (and beyond). It refers to the body of knowledge about which people have agreed upon and which holds together the world of everyday life, as well as to judgments made on the basis of this knowledge. Needless to say, the given background focuses on discussions of a definition of common sense that can be made valid and adaptable to all societies around the world. Indeed, there are definitions of common sense that are specific to certain *cultures, societies or countries* (e.g. Germany), different *organizations* (e.g. broadcasting stations or sustainability organizations) or even in specific *fields* (e.g. the E-E collaboration field). The practice in the E-E collaboration field is immensely influenced by a specific common sense. As a result of the analysis carried out in the present research study, this type of common sense will be referred to as 'common sense according to the Third Reich experience and the media'. It applies to a specific societal system – the one of Germany. To understand the practices going on in the E-E collaboration field, it is first necessary to explain what common sense according to the Third Reich experience and the media exactly means. Furthermore, this common sense will be linked to the E-E collaboration field in order to illustrate the consequences for actions there.

---

[162] For example Lindenberg (1987: 202) defines common sense as "an operative body of knowledge, common to a group, pertaining to nature, human nature, and social situations and thought to be rooted in a uniformity of human experience".

7.3.2 Common Sense According to the Third Reich Experience and the Media and the E-E Collaboration Field

Germany has a unique position as public debates regularly focus on four different groups of people. Specifically, these groups are: immigrants, Hartz IV (social welfare) recipients, gay people and Jewish people. When it comes to public discussions, there are specific bodies of knowledge, values and norms that prescribe how these groups should be portrayed and how they should be treated (Hölscher, 2008; Wierlemann, 2002). Jewish people still have a specific status among those groups mentioned above. More generally speaking, the whole theme of Germany's Nazi history is still a sensitive one, and it draws on a specific public stock of knowledge, norms and values which are (more or less) shared by the German public.[163] Whenever it comes to the depiction of this theme in the *media* (i.e. depictions in documentaries, public speeches as well as the collaboration issue of media makers with external partners) these bodies of knowledge, norms and values become important. Thus, they also strongly affect the E-E collaboration field (in the following sections will describe in how far this is the case). Resulting from the analysis, the author calls these bodies of knowledge, norms and values "common sense according to the Third Reich experience and the media". It applies on German societal level, in public discussions all related to the media. Thus, it does not only affect the E-E collaboration field, but also several other fields (e.g. politics, business and even art) which come into contact – willingly or not – with these bodies of knowledge, norms and values.

Comparing the term common sense (section 7.2.1) as used in scholarly literature to common sense according to the Third Reich experience and the media, which derived from the analysis, there are two important extensions to make. (1) Common sense according to Third Reich experience and the media does not only represent a body of knowledge, it is extended here on a *moral level through norms and values*, which are integrated in this body and which strongly refer to the dos and don'ts connected to Germany's Nazi history and media exposure (Mittmann, 2008: 64-65). (2) Common sense resulting from the analysis does have a *content-related dimension*. That means, it does not include a general body of knowledge, norms and values but a *specific one* according to the Third Reich experience and the media in Germany. (3) It has a *stakeholder-related dimension*, which includes certain *stakeholders, individuals or institutions* who give the knowledge, norms and values a voice. For example, when study participants were asked what constitutes common sense or what gives it a voice, they regularly referred to journalists, intellectual people, media and also popular people.[164] On this basis it was decided to in-

---

[163] For instance, it belongs to the common stock of knowledge, norms and values for every German not to discriminate against Jewish people or to tell the 'Auschwitz lie'.

[164] The studies pertaining to the German context have not yet provided a clear answer to the question of who exactly belongs to this normative instance of common sense according to the Third Reich experience and the media. Nonetheless, clear is that the stakeholders can differ from one judgment to another (Bendikowski 2008: 115).

clude these "popular keepers" (Mittmann, 2008: 62; Bendikowski, 2008: 134, 166) in common sense according to the Third Reich experience and the media. Conclusively, when 'common sense' is mentioned in the following, it includes firstly, bodies of knowledge, norms and values which are shared by the German public and secondly, specific stakeholders who give a voice to this body by judging and sanctioning others when they apply them.

Common sense according to the Third Reich experience and the media[165] takes care of specific bodies of knowledge, norms and values. It serves as a ***moral arbitrator*** or as a (reflected) faculty of judgment which concludes whether the knowledge (e.g. not repeating the Auschwitz lie) and the norms and values are correctly applied by different members or fields in the society. Thus, it judges if actions are right or wrong, or in other words, whether borders are crossed or not.

Common sense can thus be considered as the supervising instance for an adequate or correct[166] association with the Nazi history. Hölscher makes the missing civil-religious foundation in the (political) community responsible for the gate keeping function that common sense took over in this field: "As a partial replacement for the civil-religious foundation of the German democracy, its rules and statements can be applied insofar as they stand for ethical, legal and not-enforceable basics of the community, which (…) must not be questioned" (Hölscher, 2008: 14-15).

There are specific borders, which common sense observes and controls and when it appears that they have been crossed, it negatively sanctions the institutions or individuals for crossing them. Although these borders exist, they are blurry and hard to see and nobody has fixed them anywhere (Bendikowski, 2008: 106). Furthermore, the borders where the norms and values were violated or knowledge was not treated adequately can change slightly through different circumstances (see section 7.5).

It is hard to say what a repertoire of common knowledge, norms and values according to the Third Reich experience and the media comprises.[167] There are hardly any studies available providing hints. Interestingly, Mittmann (2008: 64-65) and his colleagues did not focus on the bodies of knowledge, norms and values themselves, but they asked where the borders had been crossed with the consequence that those who overstepped them were negatively sanctioned (e.g. through bad publicity).

---

[165] To simplify, in the following the 'common sense according to the Third Reich experience and the media' will also be referred to as the only 'common sense' related to the E-E collaboration field.

[166] The debates around these 'invisible borders and rules of communication' have been present since after the Second World War and have recently been taken up and discussed under the term of political correctness (ibid.). Political correctness can be defined as an open and substantial field of political belief whose recognition serves as a condition for the participation in the political discourse in Germany (Hölscher, 2008: 14). The political correctness debate and its German phenomenon of historical correctness are not an objective matter of fact, but the expression of a controversial discussion.

[167] Through the analysis it was possible to outline which issues 'cross the lines' in the E-E collaboration field.

Mittmann found five main different groups of circumstances where this has been the case when presenting issues in media related contexts:
- when there is no clear distance between associated (stereotype) communication styles or behavior habits visible to the Nazis (and thus 'misunderstandings' can arise).[168]
- when somebody puts the Nazi history in a context that is closed.
- when actions have been undertaken that could be misunderstood and which create the impression of trivialization or relativization.
- when the singularity of the Nazi Regime is questioned and
- when national socialist terms are emotionalized.

Depending on the case common sense judged, sometimes critics from other stakeholder groups (e.g. journalists, politicians, business people, etc.) can be heard with regard to the judgment. This means that, depending on the case, there are also 'borderline' examples and this certifies that the knowledge, norms and values are floating and cannot be clearly outlined. However, the detractors also know that they need to be careful, because, as Mittmann (2008: 74) points out, not only can the institutions or people violating the knowledge, norms and values be negatively sanctioned, but those who define them can be sanctioned as well.

The negative sanctions that common sense permutes can be considered as quite harsh and drastic when taking into account that the violator who 'crossed the borders' had no objective standards to follow (Mittmann, 2008: 60-102). Several people serve as examples for cases where harsh sanctions occurred: the politicians Philipp Jenninger and Martin Hohmann or the writer Martin Walser. They all lost their political or societal position and/or saw their reputation suffer in public (ibid.). It would not have been sufficient to 'only' officially apologize for the things being said or done in relation to Germany's Nazi history.[169]

The drastic sanctions of common sense are also reflected in the following statement by a study participant of Bendikowski and his colleagues (Bendikowski, 2008: 120): "With one slip of the tongue, and although you do not mean to say it like that, you will be sanctioned and lose your office, your reputation and your income". Therefore, nobody really wants to consciously and purposefully cross the invisible borders and get into conflict with the 'gate keepers'. Far too much is at stake. This is why everybody behaves with a great amount of sensitivity and is being aware that her or his actions in public can cross the borders.

---

[168] This circumstance, especially the behavior habits, are important for the E-E collaboration field and will be discussed in detail in the next section.

[169] That an excuse is not enough when violating the knowledge, norms and values is very well documented by the case of Martin Hohmann, a Christian-Democrat politician who crossed the invisible borders of common sense with a speech he held about Nazi history in 2003. Later, he excused for his 'faux-pas'. However, this excuse was not enough of a sanction. As Hohmann still behaved unreasonably in the sense that he did not want to voluntarily step back from his position, the Christian-Democrats increased the pressure and blackballed him from the party with the argument that Hohmann is not acceptable any longer (Mittmann 2008: 96-97).

7.3.3 Common Sense and the E-E Collaboration Field

After the logics and mechanisms of common sense according to the Third Reich experience and the media have been depicted, in the following the consequences of common sense as it pertains to E-E implementers should become clearer.

E-E implementers collaborate in a sensitive environment. When entertainment TV makers and sustainability experts from governmental related authorities work together, it is possible to draw parallels to the closer relationship[170] of both parties during the Third Reich (also see chapter 3.5.2). This practice of (closely) 'working together' actually reminds common sense of former 'Nazi behavior' (also see above Mittmann 2008: 64-65). In other words, when both sides collaborate, common sense according to the Third Reich experience and the media *reacts critically anyway* because of the collaboration activity itself. When common sense is informed about collaboration activities, it asks for more details in order to get to know what exactly has happened during the collaboration process so as to make a judgment whether the borders have been crossed or not (see below).

Obviously, common sense can only react to and judge on how E-E implementers 'act' when they do and say something in public. This first 'action' step can arise in two ways. Firstly, *E-E partners themselves communicate* some issues concerning their collaboration to *external stakeholders* such as journalists, or these external stakeholders themselves *find out* about the collaboration practices through investigations. Or secondly, the 'action' to which common sense reacts is created through the *content presented in the broadcasted television program*, which suggests that sustainability experts have collaborated in with the TV makers. An example would be that the head of the sustainability organization plays a guest part in the entertainment program. Based on this indicator of collaboration action, common sense reflects and reacts through giving its judgments.

For judging the E-E implementers, common sense uses the so-called zeitgeist according to the Third Reich experience and the media (chapter 7.3) as an orientation background. The zeitgeist has stored former (re)action (cases) according to Germany's Nazi history and media issues (also see Hölscher, 2008: 16 and Mittmann, 2008: 60) that could be linked to the collaboration practice. These (re)actions are now harmonized with the current case. In short, common sense normatively judges using zeitgeist to determine which actions by the E-E implementers can be considered 'acceptable' or 'right' as well as which are 'not acceptable' or 'wrong' and which should be negatively sanctioned.

Indeed, E-E implementers are aware that each of their publicly 'visible' communication actions causes reactions in common sense. But the more interesting thing is that the E-E implementers are also conscious of the fact that they have to be very careful with their communication because *not every behavior they show and thus every gift they exchange is accepted by common sense*. In other words, they are aware that some of their gift exchange practices may cross the invisible borders. As

---

[170] To what degree this relationship was forced by the Nazis, shall not be debated at this point.

a result, this would mean being critically viewed and probably negatively sanctioned when common sense finds out about these practices. This exactly fosters a very *complex situation* for the E-E implementers. They cannot communicate anything straightforwardly. They need to reflect and, specifically, they need to know 'the rules of the communication game' and how to play it (see Goffman, 2000).

The *most important aim of the E-E implementers is to be in accordance* with *common sense* so that they are not negatively sanctioned nor blamed for failure (also see Bowerman, 1987). Consequently, orientation towards common sense plays a decisive role in all stages of collaboration. For instance, E-E implementers need to reflect in detail about what they want to communicate to common sense and how, especially if what they intend to communicate raises critical questions. If they decide to not communicate any collaboration action to common sense, the partners need to make sure that the practice performed on the place of gift exchange stays 'well protected'. This is regularly done in co-productions and inscript participations when financial resources are exchanged for the involvement in the program content (see chapter 8.2).

7.3.4 Common Sense (Proscenium) versus the Place of Gift Exchange (Backstage)

The two different fields or levels of common sense and the place of gift exchange create a sort of *two-fold standard* in terms of their relation to each other. This needs to be handled by the E-E implementers.[171] The role theorist Goffman (2000) provides a model that is applicable to the E-E practice and the differentiation of common sense and the place of gift exchange. Goffman describes social interaction in terms of the metaphor of the world as a stage. He uses this metaphor to explain human interaction and role behavior in detail. According to his theory, there is an ensemble of collaborating actors, which can be compared to the E-E implementers. Collaborating on stage, the ensemble performs a current situation to the societal

---

[171] This two-fold standard of common sense and the place of gift exchange also came up in the communication styles of the study participants during the data collection (interviews and informal E-E collaboration talks). Some E-E implementers mainly chose to communicate in the phrasing of common sense, and they explained in detail what common sense does accept or allow, but they did not want to talk about their exchange practice. Only at some points did the place of gift exchange come in (often times near the end of the interview). For instance, one TV maker communicated in a subordinate clause that the sustainability side financially supported the TV program, although earlier, he had denied this fact. Other study participants did not talk in the wording of common sense and fully revealed the 'place of gift exchange' taking place in their collaboration, though only after anonymity had been guaranteed to them. The following quotation of a health expert may strengthen the E-E implementers' awareness of both common sense and the place of gift exchange, as well as the decision making process regarding the field they chose for the interview: "It is of course very difficult, because you [the interviewer] told us in our discussion before that many of your interview partners emphasized that no money was handed out to television makers for the entertainment production. Thus, I really do not know what I should tell you right now (...). This means that there is a big protection attitude".

audience which, in the object of research, represents common sense. The prerequisite of this performance is an ethos (ethical consciousness, conventions, usages, norms, etc.), which is sustained by integrity and rules of politeness. Given this background, Goffman (2000: 100-106) makes the crucial separation between *proscenium and backstage* as an essential and inevitable issue of human concept. On the proscenium, the actors perform their roles. On the backstage, the impression of the performance is challenged. Transferred to the object of research, the E-E implementers perform their role on the proscenium of common sense. However, on the backstage – the place of gift exchange – other issues can be practiced and communicated. Furthermore, Goffman notes that the ensemble of actors consciously controls the entrance to the backstage to hold the societal audience and others off. This necessitates a lot of trust (see chapter 8.2.1.2), solidarity and secrets, all of which hold the ensemble of actors together. Goffman also stresses that the actors develop a specific repertoire of techniques and measures to keep outsiders away from the backstage.[172] In addition, Goffman emphasizes that keeping outsiders away also comprises permanent work on their 'masks' (i.e. their behavior types). There are three different types of such work: (1) idealization (take action according to accepted norms and values), (2) repetition and stabilization of the identity and (3) the mystification (partly fading out the character). This all serves the aim to save face and to be accepted.[173]

After pointing out that the E-E implementers want to be accepted by common sense and not negatively sanctioned (see Bowerman, 1987) and that they therefore have to follow the 'invisible' knowledge, norms and values of common sense, the situation gets difficult, because there are specific rules which are not compatible with all of the practices permuted on the place of gift exchange.[174] Thus, it now may be interesting to explore this tense situation more in depth: how do E-E implementers handle this challenge in practice? For communicating accepted issues, the E-E implementers indeed need to have a deeper knowledge and understanding of which gifts they can communicate to common sense and which ones they cannot. But what are these gifts and which information and context knowledge do E-E im-

---

[172] This is (1) the dramaturgical care (plans, what they will communicate on the proscenium and what not), (2) dramaturgical discipline (self-control or covering up something) and (3) dramaturgical loyalty (keeping secrets) (2000: 193-207).

[173] Similarly to Mauss, Goffman argues in favor of monism, because he also assumes that the ensemble actors internalize the outer world into themselves (habitualized rules of face work, actions accepted, etc.), and thus intersubjectivity is possible.

[174] For E-E collaborations it is important that both the proscenium and the backstage are taken seriously, because in both fields, there are different codes and behavior rules. In the beginning of data collection, several study participants told the researcher about the codes and standards they practice on the proscenium. The researcher later realized through analyzing this data, that there is another stage or field which is only accessible for members of this field. Only through building up trust and a personal relationship to the study participants, it was possible to receive a more integral picture about reported codings and standards for the place of gift exchange, which are regularly available for the E-E field members themselves only.

plementers need to take into consideration for a 'good performance' on the proscenium?

The following three sections (7.3.5-7.3.7) describe which gifts exchanged in E-E collaboration practice are not accepted by common sense of the Third Reich experience and the media as well as which are. They will also clarify which strategies the E-E implementers employ to communicate their gifts. These sections further aim to make short statements about how the E-E implementers frame their collaboration gifts for common sense on the proscenium.[175]

7.3.5 Gifts Not being Accepted

There are three different gifts that are not accepted by common sense with regard to Germany's Third Reich experience. Thus E-E implementers cannot give, receive and reciprocate these gifts without creating challenges through the exchange procedure. They have to follow specific rules in the gift exchange and they have to be aware of how (far) they communicate the gifts to common sense. These gifts are the high value ones of 'involvement in (the decision making process on) the program content', 'finances (for program development)'. Moreover, the medium value PR gift is only accepted under specific circumstances. The following paragraphs will shortly summarize the three gifts according to common sense rules and logics.

7.3.5.1 The Gifts 'Involvement in (the Decision Making Process on) the Program Content' and 'Finances (for Program Development)'[176]

The analysis of the interviews and informal talks clearly reveals that common sense does not accept any kind of involvement in the program content from the sustainability professionals on the entertainment program. This is the case although, speaking with the words of Caillé, there are not only aspects of interest and obligation involved, but furthermore aspects of anti- utilitarianism and voluntariness (i.e. 'promote a good or prosocial issue'; 'personal engagement for the theme' or 'support target group members'): common sense simply does not accept the gifts themselves because of the history and cultural background in Germany. The involvement in the program content is an awkward topic in common sense and in former years, several so-called 'scandals' came to light in which companies, NGOs or governmental authorities paid television makers money in order to be involved in the program content (Treffer & Baden, 2006; FAZ, 2005; Spiegel 1996; Spiegel, 1997; FAZ, 2005a; FAZ, 2005b). Many sustainability and entertainment profes-

---

[175] In this context shall not be illustrated what they exactly do in practice on the place of gift exchange (section 7.2). Moreover, the following results show the status quo of common sense reactions in the data collection period from June 2009 to January 2010. Thus, it is a snapshot; more recent developments could not be taken into consideration.

[176] These gifts are exchanged in co-productions and inscript participations. In the following description, as well as in chapter 8.2 (which is also related to these collaboration forms), there are no or very few voices recorded from the participants, because they did not want to talk about these two gifts while being taped. This is a pity, as this would have made the analysis results more vivid. However, original recordings are used whenever possible.

sionals refer to nearly the same incidents or precedents perceived as 'scandals' in the 1990s and early 2000. These 'scandals' or 'negative cases' include *Klinik unter Palmen* (which will be elaborated upon in the following), the *Bavaria Scandal*[177], which includes *Marienhof,* as well as the case of *Jürgen Emig*.[178]
The study participants implementing E-E collaborations have the opinion that there could be fine nuances in terms of differentiating between being involved in the content of 'bad theme promotion' (e.g. for pharmaceutical products) or the content of 'good or sustainability theme promotion'. In the latter situation, the negative sanctions may be, generally speaking, not as drastic as in the case of 'bad theme promotion'. However, the principle stays the same for common sense according to the Third Reich experience and the media, and the study participants strongly assume being negatively sanctioned, if they communicated the gift of involvement in the program content to the public. Specifically, they fear getting a bad reputation or that they may have to step back from their position. For them, it does not matter if they want to do something with good intentions and thus also including the aspects of voluntariness and anti-utilitarianism; common sense sanctions each gift of 'involvement in the program content' negatively, and it does not matter from which organization or for which topic this gift is given, received or reciprocated.
The study participants indicated that common sense differentiates between two sorts of violations against the rule to not exchange the gift of involvement in the program content (for finances). The first type of violation can be considered an *'apparent violation'*. This is the case when 'outsiders' such as journalists find out and publicize to common sense that an organization participated in the development of the program content and that they also gave away financial resources. In this violation case, both the ***involvement in the program content*** as well as the ***financial support*** clearly become visible and this exchange structure as a whole is negatively sanctioned, even though financial support itself complies with media legislation (see chapter 6.1). This was the case in the *Klinik unter Palmen* (Spiegel, 1996; Spiegel, 1997) where it was revealed that a governmental organization financially supported the program and in return participated in decision making processes on the program content (for more information see next section). One social

---

[177] Bavaria is a production company producing TV formats for German public broadcasting stations. In 2005, it was made public that they received financial resources from several (non) governmental organizations to include products or themes into their productions, such as in the case of the daily soap *Marienhof* (which was referred to by most of the study participants in the context of this big 'scandal' as an example) or the program *In aller Feundschaft*. There are details on *Marienhof* in section 7.3.8. Section 7.6 provides descriptions on the Bavaria case more in general.

[178] In the case of public broadcasting moderator Jürgen Emig, it was revealed to the public that he invested the money in his private consulting company which was given by external stakeholders to introduce a topic placement (FAZ (2008); Hanfeld, 2008; Schwan, 2008). So the financial resources he received were not used to support the television program itself (which would already have been negatively sanctioned) but even worse, he used the money for his personal financial gain. This personal advantage seeking case resulted in Emig having to go to court and his eventual conviction.

expert commented on this case: "Klinik unter Palmen received very bad criticism. It has also never been repeated. But the money was gone. But here is... people still talk about it today".

The second type of violation can be considered as a *'presumed violation'*. Here, only the gift of *financial support* becomes visible to common sense, though there is no information about whether involvement in the television program content has been reciprocated in return. In this case the financial support can also be negatively sanctioned. This is especially noteworthy because, as discussed in chapter 6.1, there is already media legislation allowing for the transfer of money. Why then is this financial support a problem for common sense? The answer is that if the involvement of financial resources becomes visible, common sense according to the Third Reich experience and the media assumes that some actors were involved in the development of the program content, because who would give something away without expecting a gift in return (see chapter 6.1)?

In consequence, the two types of violation make apparent that the ***involvement in the decision making process with regard to the program content*** is in any case negatively sanctioned. Furthermore, although the media legislations (see chapter 6.1) stand in contrast to it, the ***financial resources from the sustainability side*** supporting the program content can also lead to negative sanctions when they are the only visible gift.[179] Thus E-E implementers try ***to avoid being connected to both gifts***. The E-E implementers are even prepared to stop the gift exchange in practice at any time they think that the situation is getting too dangerous for them. One example to illustrate this context very well is a collaboration which, in the orientation stage (see chapter 2.4.1), was originally designed to be an inscript participation (see chapter 8.2), but was then 'reduced' to a license collaboration (see chapter 8.4).

The social expert who was involved in this partnership stated: "And then we said, if the film is produced, then it should also be authentic, and then we take over the overhead costs for the shooting... So... and then of course it is very dangerous for a broadcasting station, if it takes public funds, right ... because the independency of the broadcasting station must be ensured and the influence of the government or politics need to be vigilantly watched. The discussion, which started years afterwards began with product placement (...). Back then, there was a great amount of sensitivity there". Originally, the sustainability partners wrote a script for the program episode and handed it over to the TV makers, and they suggested financially supporting the production, as described above. At that time several cases of external involvement on program content and financial resource payments had 'become official' and were negatively sanctioned in common sense. Therefore, the partners

---

[179] How far the gift of financial resources will be negatively sanctioned in the future, especially when only the gift itself (but not the gift of involvement on the program content) becomes visible to common sense, remains unclear. It is possible that the new product placement legislation of April 2010 might change something in this context, as several study participants reflected.

decided that an inscript participation may be 'too risky' and they stopped designing and implementing their gift exchange and switched to a license collaboration.

The social expert commented on this, saying: "The broadcasting station reacted very fast and said we do not want one cent from you (…) we will take over the costs, but leave us alone now (…). Hence, there was a correspondence, in which the [collaboration] contract was formulated as a non-contract. And so the contract, which never existed, or which existed had never really existed (laughs)… it had been taken back. Well, not taken back, but it was never paid attention to". This example clearly indicates how sensitive the theme of involvement in the program content and financial support is handled, and that the collaborators will do anything to be not connected with these two gifts. They erase them, change the collaboration form or even quit the whole collaboration process when they think it is getting too risky.

7.3.5.2 Public Relation Gift

Data analysis furthermore shows that PR measures are accepted by common sense but only in terms of doing PR for the sustainability theme itself as well as addressing the target group members in this context. In contrast, when the organizational PR promotion of the broadcasting station, the production company or the sustainability organization (e.g. banners or leaflets promoting the organization) has a stronger emphasis than the PR for the sustainability theme, the collaboration also receives negative sanctions in form of bad publicity.

Klinik unter Palmen may also serve as a concrete example in this context. In this case, rather than promote the sustainability theme, the sustainability organization itself was first and foremost emphasized. Clearly, the involved stakeholders were not aware of the fact that this emphasis would lead to trouble with common sense. Otherwise they obviously would have implemented the collaboration with a stronger focus on promoting the sustainability theme. The organization specifically promoted itself by showing PR banners in the storyline. Furthermore, the former head of the organization played a guest part. He showed up in the program to say 'hello' instead of addressing a sustainability theme or promoting sustainable lifestyles. Indeed, the pitfall in *Klinik unter Palmen* was that the PR promotion of the organization itself was too strong in comparison to the promotion of the sustainability part, which, in this particular case, was nonexistent. Moreover, no educational media package (see chapter 6.6.1) or other follow up communication measures were implemented by the organization, which would have assured a long-term access for the target group members to the sustainability theme. One social expert commented on this try from *Klinik unter Palmen* (the gist of which is taken from a field memo) that this first attempt in this field really failed because of the fact that it focused on organizational PR.

Several other collaborations learned from this example. First of all, they learned to strongly emphasize the sustainability theme itself in public and then to integrate a bit of organizational PR, but to keep it more in the background. This is especially true for E-E service collaborations (chapter 8.3) in which the PR issue plays a more important role. The norm of 'first sustainability PR' is exemplified through the statement of one entertainment professional who implemented a climate protection action day together with environmental and health experts in the frame of a service collaboration: "the worst thing that could have happened would have been if we had done a climate protection day with 80% of the program advertising our show and 20% of the program advertising the environment. This would have been devastating".

Interestingly, the study participants also applied common sense rule of 'sustainability PR first' during the interviews and informal talks. They mostly talked about the sustainability theme and the PR measurements in this context. Only later, near the end of the interview/informal talk, they mentioned the PR benefits for the collaborating partner organizations.

7.3.6 Gifts Being Accepted

The data analysis shows, and this is an easy rule for E-E implementers to comply with, that all gifts except for **high value gifts and PR measures** for **organizational purposes** are **accepted by common sense**. This encompasses all medium – except for PR – and low value gifts (e.g. logistical support and organizational know-how or license fee). These gifts are mainly exchanged in E-E service and license collaborations (also see figure 7.1). How these gift exchange processes work in practice will be described in chapter 8.3 and 8.4. Medium and low value gifts can regularly be communicated straightforward to common sense without expecting any kind of struggles. No specific behavior rules need to be followed according to common sense, which is also why this section is a short one compared to the precedent one.

7.3.7 Border Case Gifts 'Sustainability Consultation' and 'Guest Part'

These two medium value gifts are not easy to handle for E-E implementers in common sense similarly to the above-mentioned gifts that are not accepted. They cannot easily be communicated in terms of 'we have consulted the television professionals' as would be the case with 'we have given logistical support'. The difference between the accepted gifts and these two is that they are not self-explanatory. For common sense, these gifts need to have an additional justifiable component. As a strategy for E-E implementers, this means that when they communicate these gifts to common sense, they have to clearly delineate them from the gift of 'involvement in (the decision-making process on) the program content'. They need to justify themselves to prevent the call that they took part in the decision making process of the program content. Therefore, when the gifts of sustainability consultation or guest part were exchanged in a collaboration, the partners have to explain to the common sense what the content and the actions of these gifts included. For instance, one entertainment professional from a broadcasting station stated: "I said afterwards to the press that, yes, the ministry drew our attention to the topic and they gave us ideas which we picked up and we thought, it would be important to deal with it, but as I said, this [the program] was implemented without any kind of influence from the ministry". And an entertainment professional from a production company involved in another collaboration added that: "[For] officially announcing the whole story [of the collaboration]... there were also critical questions from the journalists, like: 'Are you now letting the ministry tell you how to write your stories? Isn't that pointing the finger and doesn't that come across to the young people?' But this wasn't the case. We wrote quite independently and, as stated above, using only the ministry's advice".

The same applies to the guest part. When a high-ranking person from the sustainability side plays a guest part in the entertainment program, collaboration partners often point out how it was initiated and which exact tasks both collaboration sides took over. One entertainment professional stated in this context: "This ended up as a guest part for Mrs. Schader in the series. This was not originally planned, but it turned out that way through the collaboration process. In this case Mrs. Schader got a text, or rather she wrote a speech, which the scriptwriters agreed with, and then she gave this – so to say – fiery speech against drug abuse". This case shows that even the guest part is downplayed to some degree so that common sense does not get the impression that sustainability experts were involved in the program development to some degree.

7.3.8 General Fear Related to the Sanctions of Common Sense

The possible negative sanctions of common sense are perceived with fear and uncertainty among E-E implementers. For instance, one environmental expert noted that, "This [the collaboration] was during the time of the *Marienhof*[180] scandal, and there was a great fear that one is brought into disrepute to buy the television. As well with sustainability themes. Hence, this would have been illegal". Especially co-production, inscript participation implementers and also service implementers mentioned this fear. The latter ones have to justify the border case gifts, whereas partners from the first two collaboration forms need to take care that the high value gifts do not become visible for common sense. The fear related to common sense is there, because orientation standards are missing, and this makes it very difficult to judge for the implementers. To orient themselves, they can only use test cases (section 7.3.2), which were reflected and sanctioned by common sense in former times. Furthermore, the contradictory media legislation causes additional uncertainties (chapter 6.1). A media legislative expert summed up this fuzzy situation with the following: "There are no pieces of media legislation in this context and there will never be clear rules with regard to them".

Furthermore, a health expert told the researcher in an informal talk that her request

---

[180] *Marienhof* is a daily soap, which is broadcasted by the ARD since 1st October 1992 and which is produced by the production company Bavaria. In September 2005, it was made public that several organizations such as the initiative *Neue Soziale Marktwirtschaft* integrated topics of their interest through financial resource payments (Holzapfel, 2007).

for an interview on a collaboration project caused troubles in the health organization. Nobody wanted to react to the request. They later let the researcher know through the PR department that no interview was possible. However, the health expert was willing to help and thus contacted the researcher on a private initiative. He stressed that all of the information given was to be made anonymous and should not become identifiable to his organization. This example clearly shows that access to the backstage is supervised by collaboration parties and that there is a big fear in telling outsiders too much about what is going on there (although it is for research purposes).

In contrast to the uncertainties, the 'standard knowledge' described above with regard to the acceptance (or non acceptance) of the different gifts may provide useful hints for collaboration framing in the public. Nonetheless, the explanatory power of this standard knowledge needs to be limited or relativized in so far that this knowledge (1) is composed of snapshots and may change after some time, and that it is thus only preliminarily valid and (2) in each single case the specific context, the circumstances and the actual happenings in which the case is embedded also need to be integrated. Therefore, it is not necessarily true that just following the above-mentioned gift rules will result in everything turning out fine. The situation is more complex, as the next sections 7.4 and 7.5 will outline.

7.4 Zeitgeist According to the Third Reich Experience and the Media

Before zeitgeist according the Third Reich experience and the media is described as well as its influence on the E-E collaboration field (section 7.4.2), a short general introduction of the usage of the term zeitgeist in social science is necessary as a foundation (section 7.4.1).

7.4.1 Zeitgeist in Social Science

Zeitgeist displays thoughts and feelings of an age and refers to a character of a specific era and the attempt to make it conscious to its contemporaries. In 1769, it was Johann Gottfried Herder introduced the term zeitgeist during a discussion of the piece *Genius Saeculi* (published in 1760) by Christian Adolph Klotz.[181]

The term zeitgeist originates in the German Romantic movement. The Romantics applied the term as a characteristic of their age (Safranski, 2007). Zeitgeist suggests to contemporaries a specific view, as was the case with the Romantic Movement as well as in other ages such as in Vormärz or during the French Revolution. Moreover Goethe refers to zeitgeist in his Storm and Stress work Faust I as "basically the own spirit of men, mirroring the times" (see Würtenberger, 1987). In short,

---

[181] In the context of the "zeitgeist" (Herder) or the earlier word "genius saeculi" (Klotz), the word genuis loci (spirit of place) has also been in use since antiquity to describe the spirituality of specific places. Later, it was also used to describe the atmosphere in places such as abbeys or churches.

zeitgeist contains the characteristics of an epoch.

The ***place-related dimension*** of zeitgeist (i.e. a place in which zeitgeist is applied or is typical for) can comprise different levels. For example, a cultural environment (e.g. Europe or Asia) or even smaller, specific societies or countries (e.g. Germany) are characterized through it. The ***time-related dimension*** of zeitgeist refers to a whole epoch or age, and it can imply incidents, actions and reactions in the present, but also those, which happened decades ago.

7.4.2 Zeitgeist According to the Third Reich Experience and the Media and the E-E Collaboration Field

Zeitgeist according to the Third Reich experience and the media, which results from the analysis, is a zeitgeist which is, from the viewpoint of the ***place-related dimension***, specific for Germany. Moreover, from the ***time-related*** point of view, it is a zeitgeist which comprises the characteristics as well as incidents, actions and reactions of the German society including nearly a whole century of Germany's development, which pertains to the 'German Reich' including the Weimar Republic as well as the Third Reich (1933-1945), and beyond.

In addition to the place and the time dimension of zeitgeist, the analysis adds a third dimension, which is the ***content-related dimension***. This refers to the exposure of media in the Third Reich and happenings after the Second World War until nowadays, which are connected to the Third Reich experiences. A component of this content-related dimension of zeitgeist that plays a significant role for the E-E collaboration field is the ***influence on the media program content from external organizations***.

Zeitgeist makes its contemporaries reminiscent of the influence of the Third Reich on the media stakeholders, though it happened several decades ago. There is a 'collective memory'[182] (Halbwachs, 1991; Welzer, 2002) which connects German people in this context and which remains present.

This zeitgeist is ubiquitous in German society and it demands a previous knowledge of the society's history in the Third Reich, the exposure through media at that time and the consequences that arouse out of it. Thus, it has a content strongly re-

---

[182] The 'collective memory' has been discussed in several theoretical settings, but the main representative in the field is Maurice Halbwachs who, like Mauss, is in the tradition of the French sociological Durkheim school (Moebius, 2009). The crucial notions of the Halbwachs theory of collective memory include five principles (Echterhoff & Saar, 2002: 17-19; Moebius, 2009: 71-72): (1) the ***context of memories***. Thus, to remember means to orientate on social and intersubjective frames of reference, (2) the ***situatedness of memories in groups***. Remembering is related to groups, and these groups form a remembering community, (3) remembering is related to communication processes and ***contexts of transformation*** (life story, norms, usages, etc.), (4) the ***reconstruction of memories***: memories are not a representation of the past, but they represent specific versions of the past, (5) memories are a part of the process of ***identity formation***. To remember thus always means for Halbwachs that society members reconstruct happenings of the past, which is only possible through a common frame of ideas, thoughts, conceptions, terms and actions.

lating not only to the past, but also to the present. Much like common sense, it plays a crucial role for E-E implementers as the following demonstrates.

In zeitgeist, all events and developments in terms of the influence of the Nazi regime on the media are stored, as is the German way of dealing with the influence of outsiders on the media after the Third Reich until the present.

In contrast to common sense, *zeitgeist does neither 'judge' nor 'sanction'* actions of the E-E implementers; it exists without sanctioning positively or negatively. The main effort of the medium is to *store* the judgments that common sense made on E-E related incidents, and use it *as a basis* for future judgments. Common sense, at a later point of time, also takes this into consideration when judging a new case. As the analysis indicates, zeitgeist and common sense are interdependent, much like a helix running continuously onwards.

7.5 Recent Circumstances

Interestingly, in addition to common sense and zeitgeist, *recent circumstances* in society also play a striking role for E-E implementers. Each collaboration case is embedded in the specific societal climate that each time period belongs to (e.g. the implemented political and societal debates on relevant collaboration issues, actual incidents that took place and other time-related happenings such as elections or legislations[183]). These and other recent circumstances may crucially affect the different E-E collaboration stages (see section 7.6).

Moreover, the *topicality of sustainability themes* itself plays a role in this field of recent circumstances; some themes may be more en vogue than others. This also may be important to take into account for E-E collaborations, as Bouman (1999) outlines. When a sustainability theme is en vogue in zeitgeist (e.g. the case of healthy lifestyle issues, or climate change, or, more recently, the topics of biodiversity)[184], implementing a collaboration around this theme becomes much more probable than with a sustainability theme nobody is currently interested in or which is controversial. The reason for that is clear: the television industry deals with themes which are currently top issues on the societal agenda, and thus a collaboration with sustainability professionals relating to these themes has a greater appeal.

Sustainability themes which are en vogue and which have proven to be a constant companion to public discussion usually achieve a higher level of acceptance in general. One health expert mentioned in this context "Health is a highly valued moral theme, and all those who are against health or health activities which serve the population or, more specifically, the health of the population... Well, this high

---

[183] For instance, the product placement law from April 2010 (see chapter 6.1.5) may also influence future debates, actions and reaction, but how and to which extent cannot be foreseen for so far.

[184] These themes were introduced by the study participants. A systematic and comprehended overview according sustainability themes in media (e.g. tendencies how often certain sustainability themes are illustrated in different German media channels) is not yet available for the German context.

moral value makes [this theme] hard to criticize". She adds that the topic of development cooperation is obviously "not so highly value that it shuts the critics up completely". This shows that it is much easier to collaborate on healthy lifestyle themes instead of themes relating to development cooperation, because development collaboration is, in general, less accepted and more controversial when discussed in public.[185] As a consequence, this would probably lead to a tendency for common sense to more negatively judge a partnership dealing with the topic of development cooperation than one focusing on health issues. Another example comes from a scriptwriter, who told about a storyline he wrote involving issues of Islam and the empowerment of female role models. This is certainly one of the more controversial current topics discussed in public. He had the idea to initiate a collaboration with an organization from the sustainability field on the theme. However, the head producers (see chapter 8.2.1.1) ultimately decided to delete the social theme in the script mainly because some weeks before broadcasting there had been a blighted bomb attack at the Cologne main station by a radical Muslim. Thus, the producer thought it would have been a bad idea to raise this issue at that time.

Lubjuhn & Pratt (2009) also strengthen this context by pointing out that sustainability themes implemented in entertainment programs refer to different levels of societal acceptance and that this needs to be taken into consideration in an E-E collaboration. Data indicates that when the sustainability theme applied in the collaboration is not up to date, the sustainability professionals have to offer higher qualitative and quantitative gifts than for current themes. In a co-production, this could mean that the sustainability professionals have to invest a higher amount of money to be part of the decision making process regarding the program content.

7.6 E-E Implementers Carefully Observing Common Sense, Zeitgeist, and Recent Circumstances

In section 7.3.3, it was argued that E-E implementers can make their collaboration actions visible to common sense on two levels. The first level is through direct public communication and the second level is indirectly via the broadcasted entertainment program (e.g. when a minister or another high-ranking sustainability expert plays a guest part in the television episode). For both levels, E-E implementers need to *observe the public field (i.e. common sense, zeitgeist and recent circumstances)* very carefully and act on both levels in order to 'control' what becomes visible. One legislative media expert also calls this behavior a "question of a strategic approach" if, in his words the E-E implementers "prefer to be open rather than silent with what they're doing". This quote shows that the E-E implementers take conscious decisions on what they can communicate and what not referring to the current collaboration environment they are in.

Many sustainability and entertainment professionals mention nearly the same in-

---

[185] This context was mentioned by the study participants. There is no systematic description available of differences in the effects of themes with a 'positive' and 'negative' connotation.

cidents or precedents perceived as 'scandals' in the 1990s and early 2000 including *Klinik unter Palmen,* the *Bavaria Scandal* and the case of *Jürgen Emig* (see above). E-E implementers are well aware of these incidents, which were negatively judged by common sense and adapted by zeitgeist as critical examples. In fact, their strategy is not to be one of the bad future examples (also see Bowerman, 1987), and thus they observe a lot and act carefully. Furthermore, when 'negative cases' show up, common sense is very sensitized and questions the activities of other collaboration projects even more than before. This may lead to an even more careful approach taken by E-E implementers. As one scriptwriter indicates, "what was okay two years ago is now not possible to show under any kind of circumstances". Another scriptwriter adds "And then I wrote a dialogue where the character donates money to Wild Life [changed name of an environmental organization] and I eventually had to remove it. Ten years before, nobody would have said anything about it. Only this was after the scandal. Even though I have not received any money from Wild Life and have not had any contact to them. However, it was concrete and obvious enough for me, and therefore I incorporated it [the dialogue] into the script. This is too risky now. One could have imputed something to us or to the broadcasting station and that could have meant trouble and for that reason it is not possible anymore (…) because we can always be suspected of doing, in the broadest sense, an advertisement for a product or something".

Through the careful observation of the public field, the E-E implementers have discovered changes in judgments made over time. They grasp in which situation their own collaboration case is embedded and, furthermore, how they could (or could not) best perform and communicate their partnership.

But as everything moves or is in a ***constant flow*** with respect to common sense decisions, the stored cases in zeitgeist and the recent circumstances in society, there are consequently ***no definite rules*** or orientation lines that can be drawn for E-E implementers on how to behave or react when they want to start a collaboration at a specific point of time. The gift rules described above regarding which gifts are or are not accepted by common sense (sections 7.3.5-7.3.7) rather serve as a kind of orientation frame for the E-E implementers. However, the role of the ***recent circumstances*** is also important in this context, because a gift might be accepted by common sense at one time, but the next time it might not be like that. For instance, E-E implementers who know how to play the game and consider common sense, zeitgeist as well as recent circumstances may delete a guest part – which is usually an accepted gift – as a precaution when they think that there is a recent circumstance which might cause a negative judgment by common sense and thus get the E-E implementers into trouble. This context is well documented by the example of an entertainment professional, who invited a minister of a federal public authority to have a guest part in an entertainment episode. He offered the gift, because he assumed it would be a good gift being in line with the gift exchange process going on in the partnership and not causing any problems. He based this assumption on the fact that in the same collaboration, several weeks before there had been another sustainability authority from the local governmental level playing a guest part in the TV program. The federal public authority also received the gift, scriptwriters had already written the guest part itself and it had been agreed. However, the head producer and the person in charge from broadcasting station then stopped the exchange of the guest part at this point. The TV professional stressed that the head producer and the broadcaster said: "Have you gone crazy? You can't have a federal minister as a patronage of this event, in August, when it's only one month left until elections. You can do it, but later in the series. Doing it now would amount to a quasi product placement for a political party, which of course we must not do". This is an interesting point, because the head producer and the head of the broadcasting station, as the people in charge of the collaboration (see chapter 8.2.1.1), assumed that common sense would have reacted negatively to their case due to the elections (recent circumstances). This is despite the fact that the minister would have 'only' got people involved with climate protection issues in the guest part without sending politically related messages. They furthermore brought forward the argument that the broadcast time of his performance could be interpreted as an advertisement itself for electing his political party because, while the minister was promoting a sustainability theme, he was also promoting a political party and attitude.

This example makes clear how complex the collaboration situation is for E-E implementers when paying respect to common sense, zeitgeist and recent circumstances as well as their constant changes. They have to observe them very carefully and, based on this, they can take action in their collaboration context (e.g. deciding on which gifts to exchange and which not).

7.7 Integrative Model of the Place of Gift Exchange, Common Sense, Zeitgeist and Recent Circumstances

The figure 7.1 brings the place of gift exchange, common sense, zeitgeist as well as recent circumstances together in an integrative model. This model works for every collaboration case which becomes visible in the public sphere regardless of whether it is negatively or positively judged and sanctioned by common sense. In the following, the Bavaria case will serve as an exemplified collaboration case to elaborate the single steps of the model more in detail.[186]

---

[186] The six steps depicted in the figure can be considered as ideal steps and might slightly vary in different collaboration cases.

Figure 7.1: Integrative model of the fields related to E-E collaboration practice in Germany

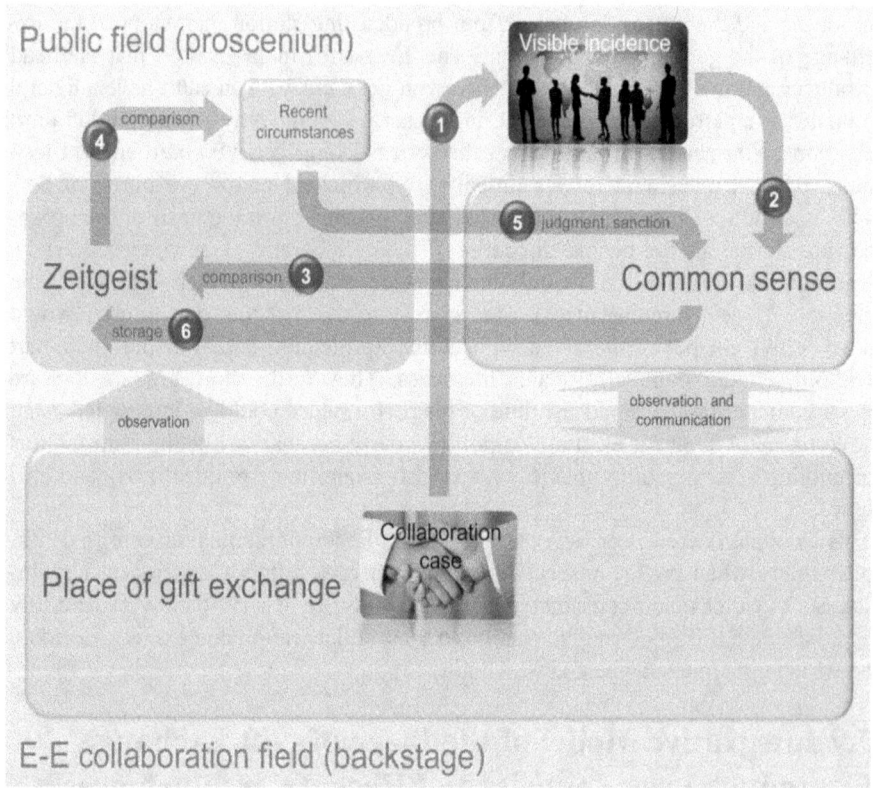

In 2003, the journalist and scholar Volker Lilienthal revealed the Bavaria scandal (Spiegel, 2005, FAZ, 2005c). In this collaboration case, the implementers decided not to communicate anything to the public field, because they anticipated bad sanctions by common sense. But then Lilienthal made obvious to the public that the production company Bavaria had received money from different companies as well as political organizations and associations in exchange for 'integrating' products as well as topics into the storylines of many entertainment programs or involving those outsiders in the decision-making process on the program content (step 1). As this incident became public, it was picked up by common sense of the Third Reich experience and the media (step 2) who compared the Bavaria case to former incidences (i.e. similar incidences appearing in the past) accumulated in zeitgeist (step 3). Afterwards, common sense also compared the Bavaria case with recent circumstances in society (step 4), before making a judgment on the case and sanctioning the involved stakeholders (step 5). In this case the judgment was negative, and the involved stakeholders received negative media coverage; several involved persons left office. As a last step, the Bavaria judgment, reactions and opinions were stored in zeitgeist (step 6). The Bavaria case then serves as the basis for the next collaboration case and the six different steps restart for the next incident.

As common sense, zeitgeist and recent circumstances have a close reciprocal relationship to each other, it can be difficult to clearly distinguish in all the interviews and informal talks which one of the three the E-E implementers exactly referred to. Indeed, the boarders *can fluently merge*, because the reactions and opinions to E-E practice by common sense arise from zeitgeist (step 3) and recent circumstances (step 4), and the judgments based on both are incorporated in zeitgeist afterwards (step 6) and taken into consideration for future judgments. In short, again, it becomes obvious that everything is in a continuous process and the E-E implementers have to be updated and observe carefully the developments, as figure 7.1 also outlines.

7.8 Putting Germany and International E-E Collaborations into a Context

For the international E-E experienced reader, the research results described in this chapter – specifically common sense and zeitgeist according to the Third Reich experience and the media – may be more comprehensible when having learned about Germany's historical background, the media system, media legislation and cultural practices.[187] However, they could justifiably argue that these results on first sight devalue the *ideal E-E definition* (chapter 2.1). According to this definition, both prosocial and entertainment professionals are *jointly involved in the decision making process on the program content* in all stages of the design and implementation process of an E-E program, as is specifically the case in *co-productions and inscript participations*. The author must agree with this argument, though this is not the aim of the depictions of Germany's E-E collaborations to devalue the ideal E-E definition. The quality of the prosocial program is indeed highest when both sides are jointly working on the program development and going through a mutual decision making process (both accept each other as mutual partners). This should not be questioned. Consequently, it is important to draw a clear line between the results from non-western countries and from the Netherlands on the one hand and the results from Germany on the other hand. Germany finds itself in a specific cultural situation in which *external influence on the TV program content, whatever it is or might be, is not allowed and also not accepted by others*.

However, this does not mean that co-productions and inscript participations, which represent the ideal design and implementation of an E-E intervention, are not practiced in Germany's TV field (see chapter 8.2). But, and this is a challenging point, because it is not allowed by German law in public and commercial TV ('influence from external organizations') and because it is a taboo in the societal discussions, the findings of this thesis might throw a bad light on these activities, not only in

---

[187] This thesis, e.g. chapter 6, can only provide some single insights in these topics.

Germany, but also with regard to the E-E collaboration activities of this type in general.

Regarding the first point – the critical aura surrounding these collaborations in Germany – the author wants to make clear that this is a pity because, through these kind of collaborations, sustainability themes can effectively be presented (proven through research results) and thus have the ability to generally enhance the prosocial performance of Germany's societal members. And, without the past and the history that Germany has, the only suitable reaction in the eyes of the author would be to perform this ideal type of collaboration and use it as a support for a more sustainable societal development, as it is the case in many other countries around the world. But Germany does have its specific history and therefore it is understandable that there are opposing voices and fear as well as such strict rules, and that there is the tendency to reject ideal E-E collaboration forms for public and commercial TV formats in Germany.

With regard to the second point, which concerns the devaluating effect that the results might have on E-E co-productions and inscript participations in general, the author wants to argue that this is not the intention. To compare and then devaluate them would be, in the eyes of the author, tantamount to comparing apples to oranges. Germany finds itself in a very specific historical and cultural situation and cannot be compared to other countries. This specific situation for E-E implementers turns everything upside down and it is unique. For instance, in Europe only the United Kindom finds itself (for several various reasons) in a comparable situation with regard to media law and the media system, but for this country there are no studies available providing useful hints on E-E collaboration practices so far. In the majority of European countries such as Poland or the Netherlands (and quite apart from non-western countries) the situation is another one and governmental or other agencies can jointly work with TV makers on sustainability TV program content. The reader should keep this difference in mind when reading the next chapters.

For Germany, the situation could mean in consequence (1) a switch to more alleviated collaboration activities (e.g. E-E service) where there is collaboration in the public or commercial TV field, and/or (2) using other media channels, such as the web 2.0, where E-E co-productions and inscript participations are allowed and where, ultimately, implementers could develop and implement the ideal form of an E-E intervention, as described in chapter 2.

The author has the opinion that it is worthwhile and enlightening to explore German E-E collaboration forms that are allowed (E-E service), but also those which have a challenging status when designing and implementing them in Germany's public and commercial television. Both sides belong to the research question posed in chapter 1 (conditions and forms of E-E collaborations in Germany) and having covered both might (along with other work on this topic) contribute to a more multilayer debate in different societal fields in Germany.

7.9 Summary

E-E implementers face three different fields when they collaborate. The essential field in which E-E collaborations proceed in practice is the place of gift exchange. Furthermore, strongly interrelating to this field is common sense and zeitgeist according to the Third Reich experience and the media.

The central mechanism of the *place of gift exchange* are the gift exchange procedures and due to many intersections and parallels, Mauss' theory of gift exchange was chosen to analyze and explain in depth the processes going on in E-E collaborations. Mauss considers a gift exchange process as free and simultaneously obligatory. The obligatory part is to give, to receive and to reciprocate the gift. The *obligation* mainly develops for two reasons: firstly, because of the obsession the gift has on the receiver and secondly, because of the hybridization of things and people, which creates an obligatory character and a social connectivity.

According to Mauss' theory, E-E collaborations are regarded as a kind of *hybrid form* between the principles of archaic societies (e.g. the hybridization of people and things, anti-utilitarianism, etc.) and characteristics of postmodern societies (market share, competition, interest driven behavior, etc.). In the words of the M.A.U.S.S. group, the gift exchange procedures in E-E collaborations circulate between the poles of voluntariness, obligation, interest and anti-utilitarianism. This thesis understands and analyzes the collaboration processes from this standpoint. Indeed, some gifts and actions are more interest-driven while others are more anti-utilitaristic. Some gifts incorporate more voluntary notions while others have more obligatory ones. Hence, all four principles will be constant attendants in the further descriptions. Moreover, 14 different gifts were identified in context with the place of gift exchange. These gifts incorporate various characteristics, and they are applied in diverse collaboration forms, stages and contexts.

Common sense according to the Third Reich experience and the media is a field that has a strong impact on the place of gift exchange and its implementers. It represents a critical populace, one which sanctions the E-E partners positively and negatively. The main aim of E-E implementers is to be in accordance with common sense, because they do no not want the collaboration to serve as a negative future example. Common sense and the place of gift exchange create a *two-fold standard* in connection with each other in which (1) common sense displays the proscenium on which the E-E implementers 'perform' compliant actions and (2) the place of gift exchange mirrors the backstage where the gift exchange procedures take place in practice. This backstage is not (fully) accessible to outsiders. Furthermore, it was pointed out that common sense does not accept some of the gifts while others are accepted and, in addition to that, a third group of gifts, the border case gifts, need a specific demarcation from the unaccepted gifts.

The second field having an essential influence on the E-E implementers and the place of gift exchange is *zeitgeist* according to the Third Reich experience and the media. It stands in close relation to common sense. This zeitgeist displays the feelings and thoughts of a society over the course of a whole century. In contrast to common sense, it does not sanction or judge, but is a medium of storage for incidences, judgments and sanctions and it also serves as a basis for common sense. When an E-E collaboration incident becomes visible, common sense first *compares* the newly visible case to the stored incidences and reactions in zeitgeist. It does so as well with the *recent circumstances* the collaboration case is involved in. Afterwards, common sense makes *new judgments and sanctions* on this specific recent case and lastly these are *stored* in zeitgeist and serve as a part of the zeitgeist portfolio for new future incidences and decision making processes. Thus, in their interplay with each other, common sense, zeitgeist and recent circumstances create a continuous change process. Because everything is in a constant flow, there are no definite guidelines available on how to behave in specific collaboration situations. The E-E implementers need to observe very carefully and act upon this basis.

8. Entertainment-Education Collaboration Forms and Stages on the Place of Gift Exchange

> "Basically it is a question of mixtures. One intermixes the souls with things, one intermixes things with the souls. One intermixes people's lives and, behold: each of the intermixed persons and things steps out of their sphere and they intermix again: this is exactly what constitutes the contract and the exchange".
>
> - Marcel Mauss 1950: 173 cited by Stephan Moebius 2009: 67

After depicting the three fields of E-E collaboration practice, the field of gift exchange is analyzed in detail in the following, as it is the most striking field in which E-E implementers work together. For describing the place of gift exchange, four collaboration forms – co-production, inscript participation, service and license – are presented in this chapter. While co-production, inscript participation and service partnership arrangements were depicted in chapter 2.4.1, the latter one, license, is a new type that arose from the German analysis (chapter 6.4).

For outlining the partnership arrangements with regard to the place of gift exchange as well as how common sense, zeitgeist and recent circumstances in society (see chapter 7.3-7.5) influence them, the stages of collaboration – orientation, crystallization, production, implementation – described by Bouman (chapter 2.4.1) are used as a theoretical orientation framework, because the data indicates strong parallels to the stages. This framework needs to be extended and adapted to the specific context of Germany, questioning how the stages of collaboration look in co-production and inscript participation contexts and, furthermore, how they can be described in German service and license partnerships.

Therefore, this thesis uses the following approach: in the first section (8.1), the first (and follow up) face-to-face meeting(s) are described in detail for all four collaboration forms. These meetings take place in the orientation and crystallization stage[188] of collaboration, which applies to every partnership arrangement as Bouman also suggests (see 1999: 127). Afterwards, the different characteristics and stages of co-productions/inscript participations (section 8.2), service (section 8.3) and license (section 8.4) arrangements are illustrated separately.

In section 8.5 an integrative model summarizes the characteristics and stages of each collaboration form and section 8.6 critically reflects on the E-E collaboration

---

[188] Although there are mostly common elements in the crystallization stage for all partnership arrangements, however, there are some specific aspects of this stage relevant for E-E co-productions/inscript participations (see 8.2.2.1) and E-E service (see 8.3.2.1).

forms in Germany. At the end, section 8.7 gives a summary of the chapter.

8.1 First (and Follow up) Face-to-Face Meeting(s)

The first face-to-face meeting takes place during the orientation stage of collaboration. The orientation stage has two main characteristics: firstly, in this stage the initial choices for an E-E partnership and the forms of collaboration arrangements are made. Secondly, the first face-to-face meeting is common in all collaboration forms. The initial decisions for the initiation and the willingness to engage in the E-E collaboration are based on external (media law, current developments in the television and the sustainability field, common sense, zeitgeist, recent circumstances in society) as well as internal conditions (field logics, motives) and characteristics described in chapters 6 and 7.

The initiative and willingness for collaboration does by no means indicate that it will actually and finally be implemented. In Germany, the situation is very complex during the orientation stage of collaboration. Stakeholders, who are willing to collaborate need to be very careful and thoughtful in the first (and follow up) face-to-face meeting(s) until it is definitively decided that a collaboration will take place and which form of collaboration the partners will choose. The first meeting(s), especially during the orientation stage, are in a risky phase in the sense that the collaboration plans made by each potential partner side can be easily destroyed and the potential partnership can fall apart (section 8.1.1 and 8.1.2). When the potential partners see that they match, they proceed with their activities in the crystallization stage and agree on certain gifts to be exchanged (section 8.1.3).

8.1.1 Contact Initiation - Orientation Stage

Based on external and internal conditions, one of the collaboration partners initiates the first contact either via e-mail, telephone or by letter. In this present study, sustainability as well as entertainment professionals both initiated the contact, whereas by tendency it were more often the sustainability experts than the TV makers.[189] The initiator introduces himself[190] and points out the wish to collaborate, though at this point, the details about a collaboration are generally vague. For all collaborations investigated, it was characteristic that the initiator first of all asks 'what might generally be possible'. One PR expert from a broadcasting station said "And initiated it was, really, [when] I wrote a normal e-mail to them. (...) They called me back immediately and said, let us sit together and generally talk". One sustainability expert, for instance, added in the context of another collaboration that: "The show and the producers came to us and asked if we were interested in working together with them in some form on a show addressing climate change themes". This question of 'what might generally be possible' is used for reasons of

---

[189]Particularly in E-E service data showed that both parties in similar parts initiated the contact.
[190]For reasons of simplification, roles such as the 'initiator' are used in their male forms.

uncertainty. The initiator regularly has no idea about the potential partners he is facing or what the counterpart thinks about such an 'unusual' E-E experiment. He furthermore does not know whether the potential partner is willing to exchange gifts and, if so, which ones. Indeed, there are many uncertain factors, so the initiator prefers to only give a small amount of information about what he and his colleagues could imagine implementing in a collaboration. The initiator hints at the possibility of gift exchange, but does not refer directly to the sort of gifts he can imagine exchanging. Frequently, the initiating contact goes with an offer for a face-to-face meeting to negotiate more details. If the counterpart also thinks that it might be worthwhile (according to external and internal conditions) discussing collaboration possibilities, they signal their interest and by accepting the invitation for a face-to-face talk, they moreover show their general willingness for a gift exchange. The *first face-to-face meeting(s)* are the main characteristic of the *orientation stage* of collaboration. They are very important because both the potential partners from the sustainability and the entertainment field try to find out whether they fit to each other in the sense that both sides are trying to discover if they are willing to work together on the same form of collaboration (co-production, inscript participation, service or license).

8.1.2 First Meeting(s): 'Feeling Out' and 'Putting Gifts on the Table' - Orientation Stage

In the first face-to-face meeting, the people in charge – usually the heads of both the sustainability organization (project leaders or president) and the entertainment organization (head producers, head of broadcasting station) (also see chapter 8.2.1.1)[191] – meet each other to signal right from the start that a potential collaboration might be beneficial. But what exactly happens in this first meeting? The primary phase implemented in the first face-to-face meeting is to feel out the potential partner side, as well as to put, little by little, some of the *gifts* which might be exchanged *'on the table'*. This is quite an interesting stage because, through the gifts which are 'put on the table', the potential partners show in which form they are willing to collaborate. One health expert stated in this context: "And then we met for the first talk in Aachen for the purpose of getting to know each other a bit better". Another professional from a broadcasting station described the first face-to-face meeting as follows: "There sat three (...) men and three (...) women and they talked about what they want from each other".

At this point, Mauss might give helpful hints about what exactly is happening in this phase. Mauss distinguishes between three forms of exchange which have developed on the way from archaic to recent societal systems: "In the initial phase it found that certain things, almost all magic and precious, were not destroyed by use, and to these was given purchasing power (...). At that time we had only discovered

---

[191] Data analysis also brought up several cases where people from the middle management met in the first meeting(s). However, these have been exceptions in the data and they were limited to E-E service and E-E license collaboration.

the early origin of money. Then, in a second phase, after having succeeded in putting these objects into circulation, within the tribe and in a wide area outside it, humanity found that these instruments of purchase could serve as a means of setting a figure on riches, and for putting these riches into circulation. (...) In a third phase (...) the means of separating these precious objects from groups and people, in order to turn them into permanent instruments for the measure of value, and even a universal measure, although not a rational one – whilst waiting for something better to come along" (Mauss 1990a: 101-102) was discovered. Interestingly enough, the gifts, which are, little by little, 'put on the table' by the two parties do not follow typical 'trade or market place' rules of western societies (see third phase in Mauss' citation). The potential gifts do not obey the principle of separating objects from people and groups as a universal and permanent instrument for the measure of values. Indeed, the gifts exchanged in E-E collaborations belong to the second phase Mauss points to where the gifts are still related to groups and individuals and do not have an 'overall, permanent value. As the gift values are not omnipresent and thus are very much associated with the E-E implementers themselves, each collaboration decides uniquely which gifts are given, received and reciprocated, and they determine their exact exchange values (Mauss 1990a: 101). This could mean, for instance, that from collaboration to collaboration it differs what the sustainability partners reciprocate after receiving a guest part from the entertainment makers. Or it also varies in how far the sustainability experts are involved in the decision making process on the TV program's content when the entertainment makers receive the financial gift.

In short, the gift exchange in E-E collaborations can be considered, according to Mauss (Mauss 1990a: 101-102, see also chapter 7.2), as being some kind of hybrid exchange between archaic and recent societies: gifts and their values are very much related to the *unique exchange structure of each E-E collaboration and their implementers* and are not a universal and enduring instrument for measuring the value of the gift.

The specific value of a gift is determined during the collaboration process itself by receiving and reciprocating other, new gifts. However, all stakeholders are very much aware of the difference between *high value gifts* (financial support for program development and involvement in the program content) and *medium/low value gifts* (logistical support, PR, networks/contacts, etc.) (see gift overview in chapter 7.2.3). This specific awareness is related to the media legislation, common sense and zeitgeist the E-E implementers are confronted with. Now, the processes of *feeling out* and *putting a few gifts 'on the table'* serves as a fundamental mechanism for finding out from the counterpart which *gift type* he *represents* (i.e. which gifts he is willing to give, receive and reciprocate).

The differentiation in the gift types is easy to explain. There are two gift types which can be distinguished – one each on the sustainability side and the entertainment side. On the one hand, there are those who are willing to (and thus do) exchange high value gifts. For example, one producer referred to the high value gift exchange practice: "I cannot convince somebody to pay me money without offering something of equal value". On the other hand, there are those who are unwilling to exchange high value gifts to the point of being strictly against it and being appalled when hearing that high value gifts are exchanged in other collaborations. One sustainability expert stated: "No, me, personally, I would reject this. Again, if an audience member (…) switches on his TV set, he does not want to be influenced by anyone and in any particular direction".

However, for identifying these gift types (i.e. the acceptance or non-acceptance of high value gifts as well as the (un-)willingness to exchange them), E-E implementers apply different communication strategies[192], namely the latent and the apparent gift presenter. These different strategies require more reflection and detailed description, as given in the next two sections 8.1.2.1 and 8.1.2.2, through an introduction of the two different gift presenters. Which one is applied depends on personal characteristics of each collaboration partner, as well as on their motives and the gifts they want to exchange.

8.1.2.1 The Latent Gift Presenter

The latent gift presenter puts some of his potential gifts on the table, but only after a long conversation about sustainability contents. He is very much interested in talking about ideas related to the sustainability theme (sustainability professionals) and the issue of how to deal with sustainability themes in the storyline (entertainment professionals). So, *time needs to pass* until he talks about gifts. When he finally broaches the latter issue, the *exchange process* of gifts is *concealed,* mainly because he wants to keep the trade or market place logic, which he thinks is not appropriate to introduce though being well aware of it, away from the 'good cause' collaboration. To do so, this presenter type needs to apply some kind of 'pseudo-communication'. If he mentions certain gifts, they are framed independently and not in an exchange context. This is reminiscent of an indirect, tacit type of communication. Spoelstra & Pienaar find this type also in negotiation theory where people conceal passing messages using hints or signs. It "is typically used whenever communication is incomplete or impossible, whenever either party will not negotiate directly and whenever neither will trust his counterpart in a direct confrontation. Sometimes norms exist that prohibit direct negotiation, so the only way is through indirect means" (Spoelstra & Pienaar, 2008: 12). A specifically prohibited norm for this gift presenter type that is morally objectionable is talking about finances in the context of sustainability issues (see chapter 7.3.5). This means in consequence, that

---

[192]These strategies need to be considered as ideal types and, needless to say, in practice mixtures of both types are possible. Furthermore, it should be pointed out that an E-E implementer may not always follow only one of the two communication strategies. It is probable that, with regard to the external and internal conditions, the media legislations, former experiences, the situative context and the counterpart, he changes this communication strategy during a collaboration process or from one collaboration to another. Both strategies come into play during the whole collaboration process. However, in the orientation stage, they have their strongest impact, and this is why they are depicted in this paragraph.

the latent gift presenter communicates **medium and low value gifts** freely after some time has passed. But with regard to *high value gifts*, he only talks about them when the situation requires it. Normally, the presenter tends to hint at issues rather than speaking clearly about them. He generally avoids and regularly does not come across with the theme of high value gifts by his own initiative. So when two latent gift presenters are both interested in exchanging high value gifts, it can take hours or even several long and intensive meetings over weeks or even months until they get to the point.

As hinted above, the latent presenter is facing a double moral standard: he encounters the collaboration context knowing that it works according to the mechanisms of market or trade exchange, though he does not want to explicitly bring these thoughts into the collaboration. This is why he, on the one hand, at least behaves according to the exchange standards (give, receive and reciprocate), but on the other hand, he tries to conceal them, consciously or not, as far as possible. A central mechanism for his concealing strategy is the large time range in which gifts are mentioned and exchanged to camouflage their connection to each other. Bourdieu (1998: 133) stresses that putting a big time range through exchange procedures functions to shield the given, received and the reciprocated gifts against each other and makes them appear as unconnected single actions (also see chapter 7.2.4). The time range between the three obligations lets each single gift appear as an act of *generosity* (also see Moebius, 2006a: 133). And this is one of the main aims of the latent gift presenter: showing generosity to the counterpart as if simply doing something for a 'good cause'.

When gifts are put on the table, they are often framed as a 'means to an end' for acting in a 'good cause'. One TV producer for example said that they did the collaboration and thus exchanged (high value) gifts with the aim to "bundle the strengths [through the collaboration] for the children [target group] so that they profit". Some latent gift presenters in the study also call their activities an "honorable credit". Within this presenter type, there are several parallels with the traders of the intertribal *kula potlatch* exchange on the Trobriand Islands (Mauss 1990a: 21-22; Hetzel 2006: 272). The *kula*[193] is a noble kind of trade involving dignity of soul, pride, generosity and moral standards (Mauss 1990a: 22). The traders act decently and also seem to be disinterested in the exchange of the gift itself (ibid).

Moreover, when it comes to the gift of *vaygu'a*, a kind of money (Mauss 1990a: 23), Mauss indicates that regularly, the trade is not implemented by the tribal chief himself, as is usually the case when other gifts are exchanged, but by his supporters. Interestingly, the latent gift presenters as being the persons in charge in both the sustainability and the television organizations also tend to let their deputies or representatives discuss more the details of the high value gift exchange after having set the course and strengthened the importance of the sustainability theme dur-

---

[193] *Kula* means 'circle' and refers to a whole gift exchange system of the Trobriands Islands where all tribes and their exchanged gifts are caught up in a circle and following this circle means a regular movement in time and space (Mauss 1990a: 22).

ing the first meeting(s) themselves. One TV chief producer noted: "In this context, there were many talks with Mr. Hölsch [from the sustainability organization], (...) the producers and Mr. Berwart [from the sustainability organization], which I did not follow in detail". One reason for that behavior might be that by negotiating high value gifts in detail, he might loose his 'dignity' which may be perceived as very important. Thus, he would come closer to the trade details as the high value gifts are in close connection to each other, which would make it difficult for him to conceal the exchange logic.

More generally, by applying his latent communication strategy, this gift presenter wants to find out which gift type he is facing in his counterpart. However, it is not crucial *when* he identifies the gift type, but the *way of detecting* it plays a decisive role, because this needs to happen in a dignified and upright manner.

In short, the latent gift presenter might be perceived as 'beating about the bush', putting emphasis on the content discussion in terms of 'doing something good' while trying to camouflage the exchange logic in the collaboration. This helps him frame his gifts as generosity and act with dignity, morality and pride. This presenter goes with the remarks of Mauss (1990a: 68-70) that also in postmodern societies moral actions and 'humanization' of professional groups is a striking issue to consider beside pure interest and market principles (also see chapter 7.2.2).

8.1.2.2 The Apparent Gift Presenter

The apparent gift presenter does not think much of the concealing strategy of the latent gift presenter. He speaks 'plain text' right from the start. He communicates his intentions, aims, the gifts he can offer and the gifts he hopes to receive from his counterpart. This goes with a direct or explicit strategy, as Spoelstra & Pienaar (2008: 12) describe in for the field of negotiation theory: the apparent gift presenters "do not necessarily act rationally or know their own and the other's preferences or values, but they do communicate openly, making demands, stating preferences, asking for information, offering proposals and making concessions. In doing so they manoeuvre, use tactics and follow strategies that are observable by an onlooker".

In contrast to the latent presenter, he thus communicates *the gift exchange procedure straightforwardly,* and thus reveals the full trade details right from the beginning. One latent gift presenter characterized this apparent one as having neither normative attitude nor dignity. Another emphasized that the apparent gift presenter has "the calculation in his pocket at the first meeting". An apparent gift presenter said of his approach in the first face-to-face meeting: "We said this and that are our topics and that we would offer this and that, and what we would like to have accordingly". This quote shows the straightforward approach of the apparent gift presenter. Furthermore, he is less interested in talking very much about sustainability contents than the latent gift presenter; he wants to come into action and change something fast. However, this does not mean that he is less interested in the sustainability theme itself. Rather, he has come to the insight that he can achieve his goals and motives (e.g. changing the audience knowledge, attitude and behavior) more easily when clearly revealing the trade principles, gifts and intentions.

The behavior of the apparent gift presenter becomes more obvious with the help of Mauss (1990a: 22). He describes the *gimwali*, or trade, which can be considered as unworthy when comparing it to the *kula*: "Of an individual who does not proceed in the *kula* with the necessary greatness of soul, it is said that he is 'conducting it like a *gimwali*'" (ibid.). The *gimwali* is characterized by hard bargaining, a method which is typical for trades and embodied by the apparent gift presenter, who is willing to intensively bargain about what is at stake for both potential partners.

When the first face-to-face meeting starts, this presenter gets to the point very fast. He puts **medium and low value gifts** as well as **high value gifts** straight ahead on the table, and he is willing to negotiate more in detail about what should be given, received and reciprocated in an open manner. So he wants to have a clear line regarding what both potential partners may want to achieve, how and in which time period. Sustainability as well as entertainment professionals following this communication strategy act according to their belief that thus they can best achieve their organizational aims. The apparent presenter furthermore focuses on detecting in quite a short period of time, which gift type he faces in the counterpart. Thus, for him the **way of detecting** the gift type does not play a decisive role; to him the issues of talking plainly, 'coming into action' shortly afterwards and moving something are more important.

In short, the apparent gift presenter might be perceived as 'going like a bull at the gate', operating straightforwardly and completely revealing his trade thoughts, potential gifts and interests.

8.1.2.3 Fitting

The previous sections made clear the difference in **gift types** (supporting versus refusing high value gift exchange) and **gift presenters** (latent and apparent). The gift presenters serve to find out which gift type the potential E-E implementer is facing in his counterpart.

It is self-evident that in the first face-to-face meeting various combinations of both the gift types and gift presenter are possible. For instance, the parties can be equally for or against a high value gift exchange, or one is pro and the other con and thus they differ in their gift types. The same goes for the gift presenter; both could be latent or apparent, or one is the latent and the other the apparent presenter. Clearly, when two equally latent or apparent communicating partners come together and are of the same gift type (i.e. when the **highest possible accordance** in the combination between the partners is achieved), it is very probable that the collaboration will be implemented in terms of moving forward to the next collaboration stage, which is the crystallization stage (section 8.1.3). However, what happens when the potential partners differ in their gift types? Or even more importantly, what happens when they additionally disagree in their communication strategies (gift presenter)? Indeed, the more differences there are, the more unlikely it becomes for them to work together in collaboration. Imagine, for instance, that two latent presenters come together, and one is pro high value gift exchange and the other is against it. It might be easy for them to communicate, because they have the same communication style. However, problems may arise regarding the gifts, because the partner who is willing to exchange high value gifts must scale down his expectations and make compromises if he wants to collaborate with the partner he is facing. Or, if he is not willing to do so, he falls apart and tries to find a new partner. Even more challenges arise when not only the one variable of gift type differs as previously described, but when both potential partners differ in terms of gift type and gift presenter. One example might be that a latent and an apparent presenter come together, and the apparent presenter indicates quite fast that he wants to exchange high value gifts. The latent presenter might first feel taken aback by the counterpart's way of communicating the issues, and second it might be against his principles to exchange high value gifts. In consequence, what could happen is that the latent presenter "flees in horror" as one TV producer stated, and that he ends the meeting because, as he said, "this has nothing to do with our ethos, which we bring in our storylines on our own".

In summary, the more the gift types as well as the gift presenter strategies are equivalent to each other, the more likely it becomes for a collaboration to take place. As it is not easy to find a fully compatible partner, potential implementers tend to make compromises. However, what is very important and the one issue where no compromises are made is with regard to the gift type: to be willing to exchange high value gifts or not is more a question of principles, and this is where opinions can strongly differ.

By now it should have become clear that the first phase of 'feeling out' and 'putting gifts on the table' is a decisive stage in which potential implementers are facing the fact that everything and nothing is possible. One entertainment professional summarizes this issue by saying: "You never know who is sitting in front of you at the table".

8.1.3 Follow Up Meeting(s): 'Bundling Gift Packages' – Crystallization Stage

When E-E implementers pass the first phase and decide that they want to collaborate, *follow up face-to-face meeting(s)* are needed (1) to further substantiate the gifts and (2) if applicable and possible to add new ones which might fit in the context of the collaboration agreed upon during the first meeting(s). With this step they move onward into the ***crystallization stage*** of collaboration. At this point, it is very likely that the collaboration will take place, because the partners saw in the first meeting(s) of the orientation stage that they match. For example, one TV professional stated: "After the first meeting it was clear that we fit to each other".

The follow up meetings aim to ***bundle a gift package*** for each side containing the significant gifts that might be exchanged in the collaboration. These bundled packages for each side regularly incorporate more or less an equivalent perceived value of given and reciprocated gifts (e.g. the partners agree that each partner side gives, receives and reciprocates one high value and three medium value gifts).

Depending on the respective gift presenter strategy, as mentioned above, the gifts in the bundled gift packages are put into a stronger or weaker reciprocity and obligatory context with each other. An example for strong reciprocity would be like 'we give networks/contacts and you receive and reciprocate a guest part from us'. In the opposite case, both gift packages are bundled without communicating any kind of connectivity to each other. Frequently, when some of the important gifts are mentioned, discussed and thus 'bundled into packages' the E-E implementers leave further specification to collaboration practice itself (e.g. the time range in which gifts are given, received and reciprocated against each other).

The packages bundled in the crystallization stage can change during later stages of collaboration, i.e. in the production and implementation phase; for reasons correlating with the developments in common sense and zeitgeist, a gift can be added or another can fall apart. For example, gifts can be scaled down (section 8.3.1.2) when one partner side feels that the counterpart does not 'fulfill the promise' he made with regard to a gift. Or, one partner side adds another gift (section 8.3.1.2) because they are satisfied with the gift exchange process so far and hope to receive another gift in return. In consequence, the gift package bundled in the crystallization stage needs to *prove itself in gift exchange practice*.

When changes are made to one of the gift packages, i.e. one gift falls apart or another one is added, the gift packages to be exchanged do not have an equivalent value anymore; they are in a stage of inequality. Mauss stresses that with each gift ownership is given, received and reciprocated. "It is ownership and possession, a pledge and something hired out, a thing sold and bought" (Mauss 1990a: 24). This also means that when gifts are scaled down or new ones are added, the ownership structure changes and one partner side perceives less or more ownership with regard to the gifts (in both their values and numbers). Clearly, a system of property ownership may develop in a gift exchange process which cannot be foreseen by the partners in the orientation and crystallization stage. The partners can only 'estimate' the gift values by looking at previous trends. They cannot foresee what will happen in practice when changes occur and a gift, which was included in the gift package, needs to be dropped or perhaps added. Indeed, then an awareness of inequality arises and other steps need to be undertaken to recreate a kind of perceived equality (and ownership) in the gifts, as was in the crystallization stage when the gift packages were originally bound (see Caillé, 2008: 102-103; Mauss 1990a: 26; Waltz, 2006: 88).

Obviously, when one party scales down gift(s), the other party has to react to it in the sense that they also have to scale down gift(s) (Hetzel, 2006: 272). The same goes with adding gift(s); when this happens, the counterpart also perceives an obligation to follow and thus to recreate equality in the gift values (see Caillé, 2008: 102-103) (see section 8.3.1.2).

8.2 E-E Co-production and Inscript Participation

After E-E implementers have decided in the orientation stage to implement a co-production or inscript participation,[194] and have bundled the gift packages in the crystallization stage, the analysis reveals that they follow the same stages of collaboration that Bouman (1999: 151-162) illustrates in her dissertation: now the production and the implementation stage can take place, as the figures 2.4 and 2.5 also outlined in chapter 2.4.1. Thus, this approach is not only applicable for co-productions and inscript participations in non-western countries and the Netherlands, but also for Germany. However, there are several differences in the German context.

The next section (8.2.1) shows crucial *characteristics* of co-productions and inscript participations taking place in Germany. Afterwards, *the stages of collaboration* are described (8.2.2): firstly, the specific aspects of the crystallization stage in co-productions and inscript participations are outlined (section 8.2.2.1); secondly, the production and the implementation stage (section 8.2.2.2-8.2.2.3) are illustrated.

8.2.1 Characteristics
8.2.1.1 People in Charge and Middle Management Staff Members

The people in charge from the entertainment and the sustainability fields connect with each other for the first time in the initial face-to-face meeting(s) in the orientation phase (section 8.1.2). From the television side, this usually includes the head producers and the manager responsible for the television format at the broadcasting station. On the sustainability side, the people in charge are commonly the project leader in the field of sustainability communication or even the president or head of the sustainability organization. These people have in common that they are able to **initiate and implement central processes around the high value gift exchange** of involvement in the decision making process on the program content and finances for the program development. They play a crucial role, specifically in co-productions and inscript participations.

These people in charge often possess a high degree of information and experience of what exactly is going on in common sense, zeitgeist and recent circumstances in society, and they are very familiar with the media legislations relating to E-E collaboration activities. Without this expertise it could, for example, happen that 'sensitive' information from the place of gift exchange becomes visible in common sense or that they underestimate their collaboration situation which can lead to negative sanctions by common sense. How experienced the people in charge need to be is also documented in the following quote from an environmental expert in charge: "it [collaboration] needs to be reflected in a certain context. But, you [the interviewer] are right that this is a juristically difficult story and you need very ex-

---
[194]The reader might note in the following that not many quotations are used in the text. This is because the majority information given about E-E co-productions and inscript participation were described in informal talks and not in tape-recorded interviews.

perienced implementers".

Half of the ten interviews implemented with sustainability experts and the 13 interviews conducted with television professionals were conducted with people in charge and the rest with the middle organizational management, who were centrally involved in the collaboration, though not in charge of it (e.g. researchers, production assistants, scriptwriters or responsible PR people).

In comparison to the people in charge, the people from the ***middle management field*** were generally less informed about media legislations with regard to E-E collaborations as well as about happenings in common sense and zeitgeist which might effect the collaboration. During the data collection, they were asked about which media legislations they think could have an influence on their collaboration. They were also questioned about which incidents (in common sense and zeitgeist) they are aware happened in former or recent times which might affect their own collaboration and which incidents were instructive. With regard to ***media legislation,*** the middle management staff members found it very hard to comprehend what is allowed and what is not. Some gave inconsistent answers, which showed their difficulties in looking through the integral situation. For instance, one PR expert working with a production company said, "we can do it [collaborate] with political organizations, there is no problem with product placement anyway". Or one scriptwriter said, "the ministry was also involved, and this is okay. (...) [because] we do not advertise for anybody. It gets difficult with parties. This is another topic". Furthermore, several other professionals from middle management admitted that they do not know details about the legislative background when collaborating. One health expert stressed, "(...) this is indeed very interesting. I also do not know at which point this would be okay". Others admitted the same, and in addition they also (in-between the lines) expressed that they do not have to know, because it is not their responsibility and they referred to their bosses (people in charge of the collaboration). Here is another example from a PR expert working in a production company: "I do not know, if there is a law in this context. I am not well schooled in this (...) this is a story that Mr. Adrem should answer".

Only a few of them mentioned important incidents[195] which had been negatively sanctioned by common sense in the past and which their current collaboration might find instructive in terms of 'being sensitive'.

In short, it became obvious that middle management staff members are less ***informed about the holistic and complex field their E-E collaboration*** is involved in when compared to their bosses who are in charge of the E-E project. Hence, the differentiation between people in charge and middle management staff members might be an important point to make for co-productions and inscript participations in Germany's collaboration environment.

---

[195] The case of *Klinik unter Palmen* as well as the 'Bavaria scandal' was named in the context.

Single Case Decisions of the People in Charge regarding Common Sense
In comparison to middle management staff members of E-E implementers, the ***people in charge*** know exactly (1) what they can broadcast in the E-E episode without being negatively sanctioned by common sense and (2) they know what they have to communicate to common sense in order to successfully employ their ideas (see chapter 7.3). Their decision regarding what is broadcasted or not and what is communicated and how is very much related to the situational context the collaboration finds itself in. The people in charge take '*single case decisions*' as they themselves emphasize. These decisions are based on common sense, zeitgeist and recent circumstances in society. One producer said, "I would say one always has to decide according to the single case". A media legislation expert adds in this context that because it is a question "of the single case, how should the law establish rules? How should the law do this?"

The people in charge, for example, must take into consideration the last product or topic placement incident, when it became visible and how common sense reacted on this. Furthermore, recent circumstances (elections, changes in filling of political positions, etc.) also need to be taken into account as a basis for their decisions. Therefore, it is very important in a co-production and inscript participation that the people in charge have the ability to generally judge the situation the collaboration is confronted with (see chapter 7.7). Practicing these single case decisions could also mean that the people in charge might have to ***revise the decisions*** which have formally been made by their middle organizational management.

Moreover, and this is obvious, the single case decisions are ***person-dependent*** decisions. As one TV producer stressed, "one could also say, okay, this is very person-dependent. There are different preferences. The producer makes the decision about who is in charge of the whole production process". For instance, a producer may have decided to broadcast a guest part in which a politician promotes a sustainability theme shortly before an election takes place while another producer in the same situation would maybe have decided against it. As a rule, these decisions result out of former personal experience made by the people in charge and through observing common sense, zeitgeist and recent circumstances, all of which are taken into account for the decision making process. Another example of these person-dependent decisions is, as informal E-E talks have indicated, that several people in charge of public broadcasting stations have enforced an internal order since 2006, that stipulates their stations should not implement co-productions using external financial resources anymore. This decision is a result of 'bad experiences' they have made in the past, and the fear that further co-productions could cause trouble when they become visible to common sense.

Consequently, because single case decisions are, as illustrated above, very much related to the decision makers themselves as well as to the context in which they are embedded, these decisions seem to be made ***arbitrarily*** for middle management as well as for outsiders. They cannot be made transparent to them in detail. This is well documented through the following example from a middle management staff members, explaining the decision of a person in charge and complaining that he and his colleagues had to take back the gift of a guest part without really understanding what the problem was about it: "Then, we had to say (...) realize, it does not work (...). And then, unfortunately, we had to disinvite Mr. Maibrand".

8.2.1.2 Trust Among the Partners

Servet (1994) writes about Mauss' theory that trust plays a decisive role in the gift exchange process and cannot be separated from the gift procedure itself. Caillé (2006: 186), in discussing the trust component in the gift exchange process, adds that people establish "a network (which) is an ensemble of people who allow through the maintenance of their personal relations, friendship and fellowship to build up trust and hope".

Trust plays a role in each E-E collaboration. However, both sustainability and entertainment professionals (respectively the people in charge) stressed the importance of the trust component when exchanging high value gifts. They underlined that in general, a *deep level of trust* is a central prerequisite for the gift exchange. One sustainability expert stated "the reciprocal trust, the calculability. Each problem can be discussed, but one has to talk". And a TV producer from another collaboration added that a "very intense trust was created between Mr. Dregger and us". These quotes also indicate that the collaboration is very much focused on the personal ties the partners have to each other and much less on the organizational context they are embedded in. While collaborating, the implementers communicate only with a few selected people in the counterparts' organization with whom they have a deep level of trust.

However, what does deep trust exactly mean? How is trust created? And why is it crucial to the E-E implementers? These questions can be answered when facing the differences between the field of gift exchange and common sense. E-E implementers have to trust (or, even more, hope) that the counterpart is at least as well experienced as oneself (i.e. that the counterpart is aware of the sensitivities in the public, the common sense judgments and sanctions, zeitgeist and recent circumstances). They need to know how to behave so that only those things which the partners are willing to share 'become visible' and nothing else (such as the high value gifts). This is the reason why only co-production and inscript participation with a high level of trust can take place. Implementers trust each other to be careful because, when the high value gift becomes visible, both might get into trouble. One example which stresses this context comes from a social organization involved in a 'visible incident' which was negatively sanctioned. One expert from this organization stated: "Specifically because of the experience with the former project [the visible incidence], I learned a great deal about mistrust then".

The entertainment makers as well as the sustainability experts furthermore indicate that it creates trust among them when they demonstrate to the counterparts an understanding of their logics, challenges, fears, preferences and interests: one producer claimed that the contact with the social expert "has been exceedingly comfortable, very informative and not in any case strayed from his ostensible interests, which he could have stated crudely. But without exception he has provided pertinent information to us. This is a very seldom case when you talk to people from this kind of organization, and it had created a great amount of trust between us".

When the partners do not know each other before the collaboration starts, which can but does not have to be the case, both partners have to give each other a bit of blind faith at the beginning and over time, as the partners prove to each other that they are trustworthy, the amount of trust may grow and the partners become much more familiar with each other. On both collaboration sides, the partners even emphasized that they had built up a personal relationship to the other side. One health expert stressed that personal ties were the central key for implementing co-productions and inscript participations, though this could only be documented by field memos and not through a quote.[196] Several partners also repeated a high value gift exchange collaboration with the same counterpart, because the partner has proven to be personally 'very trustworthy' (documented through personal talks). Referring to Caillé (2006: 201) only the fact of deeper trust in the gift allocation enhances the situation of all participants objectively and subjectively.

Furthermore, the E-E implementers also mentioned another vital component which is **trust on the intra-organizational level**. Several sustainability experts who were project managers in charge of the E-E collaboration mentioned that the president or head of their own organization trusted them and that they had a mandate to act freely 'in their own responsibility'. One of them said "they gave me the freedom, and hence I enjoyed their confidence and nothing would have worked out if I had been dependant and, well, it is necessary to be able to make decisions".

One health expert indicated moreover that the heads of the organization did not exactly want to know what he was doing in the partnership. The first reason for that was that, in his opinion, they trusted in his skills as well as in his ability to choose a sufficient partner (i.e. both sides knew how to behave so that only those things become visible that should become visible). The second reason he thought of was 'self-protection' in the sense that they could distance themselves from his activities if something went 'wrong' or caused troubles. This context is documented through a field memo of several informal talks, though not through a quote.

Clearly, E-E implementers exchanging high value gifts need to cope with a **risky collaboration situation,** and several interview partners from both sides reiterated that only a few people they know in their own organizations are fit to work in this constantly high-risk context.

As indicated above, **trust grows over time** after first giving each other a bit of blind

---

[196] Interestingly, this central trust issue also played a role in the study context itself. To several study participants the researcher had to build up a level of trust (through meeting them once or twice and telling them something about her background, her study aims and the organizational contexts and interests) before the study participants were prepared to give her more information about their co-production or inscript participation activities in which they also referred to the deep level of trust required in their field.

faith at the beginning. However, what happens when the counterpart does not prove to be trustworthy and makes crucial mistakes? One collaboration example is relevant in this context: it was first planned as an exchange of high value gifts, but later was scaled down to a low value gift exchange, because the sustainability partners were found to be untrustworthy. In this collaboration, a formal contract was made about the gift exchange (section 8.2.2.1). Unfortunately, at that time the high value gift exchange of another collaboration became visible to common sense, which involved the same sustainability organization but with other people in charge. Since the case was strongly criticized, this was reason enough for the entertainment makers to, in a way, 'mistrust' the person from the sustainability organization, though they had just made a formal contract. Although the sustainability expert urgently stressed that he had nothing to do with the other case and that it had been a completely different context, in the end, it did not matter. Undoubtedly, it got too 'hot' for the entertainment makers, and they declared the contract made for the high value gift exchange null and void (also see chapter 7.3.5).

In summary, E-E implementers exchanging high value gifts give each other a certain amount of blind faith at the beginning of the collaboration. If something goes wrong in their eyes, this leads to scaling down the trust level as well as the gifts so that, for example, instead of exchanging high value gifts, medium/low value gifts are exchanged or the collaboration is even cancelled.

8.2.1.3 No Action Routine

Having no action routine is specifically a characteristic of co-productions and inscript participations. The contradictions in media legislation and the resulting grey zone specifically related to high value gift exchange (chapter 6.1) lead to a tendency for practical knowledge about action routines in collaborations to not be passed onward to other stakeholders interested in a collaboration (e.g. through talks, experience or lessons learned summarized in a leaflet, etc.). This knowledge stays with the E-E implementers who have had the experience themselves. One sustainability expert stated here that, "as a public authority you have to protect yourself on all sides. It was virgin territory for me. Who should tell me something? In contrast, most people [in his organization] were very skeptical". The quote shows that the expert initiated the collaboration on his own and faced resistance on the part of his colleagues. To ask other organizations regarding their experience for advice is something out of the question. After depicting the status quo in media legislation (chapter 6.1), common sense (chapter 7.3) and giving a first introduction to co-production and inscript participation (chapter 2.4 and 8.2.1.1 and 8.2.1.2), it becomes clear why this is the case: E-E implementers 'stay on their own' because they are not sure how far they can go, and furthermore they are afraid that their actions might be misinterpreted and thus negatively sanctioned.

Indeed, in general terms, legislations can be paradoxical and orientation standards are also missing in other societal fields. They normally need to be interpreted and 'translated' by practitioners who have made experiences with the application of the legislations. When this translation into practice takes place, the implementers start to introduce communication mediums such as books, 'frequently asked questions' on webpages, leaflets, etc. to tell *people how legislations can be interpreted and enacted in practice*. Most importantly, this has not happened with regard to E-E practice so far in Germany. Stakeholders interested in E-E collaborations thus do not find any kind of practical interpretation about how to get involved with potential partners from the other collaboration side or, even more, about how to plan and implement the collaboration process.

Evidently, this means that, in addition to the paradoxical media legislation and the resulting grey zone practice, E-E implementers commonly cannot consult external people or resources about the knowledge and experience gained in an E-E collaboration practice. As hinted at above, experiences accrued during former collaborations stay with the involved stakeholders and do not find their way to other organizations. Data also indicates that even passing knowledge and E-E collaboration experience onward to other departments of the same organization is regularly not an option because of the 'high risk' reasons mentioned above.

Thus, the only orientation sustainability and TV professionals have in all stages of collaboration is their personal knowledge and practice experience, their knowledge about the media legislation, the (re)actions and feedbacks from their counterparts and, most importantly, how common sense deals with E-E incidences in practice and what might be important to consider when observing zeitgeist (chapter 7.4) and other recent circumstances (chapter 7.5).

8.2.2 Stages of Collaboration in E-E Co-production and Inscript Participation

The previous sections 8.2.1 showed significant characteristics of E-E co-productions and inscript participations. In the following, the stages of collaboration are described in detail.

In the orientation stage both the entertainment and the sustainability side have identified the gift type (section 8.1.2) of the counterpart, which – with special regard to co-productions and inscript participations – implies that both have found out that the other party is willing to exchange high value gifts (i.e. to exchange involvement in the program content for financial support). In the crystallization stage, the specific gift packages are bundled (section 8.1.3). In co-productions and inscript participations this means to negotiate the details of the high value gift exchange.

The next section adds further specific aspects of the crystallization stage (section 8.2.2.1) in co-productions and inscript participations. Afterwards, the production stage (section 8.2.2.2) and the implementation stage (section 8.2.2.3) are introduced for these collaboration forms.

8.2.2.1 Crystallization Stage

Subsequent to the bundling of the gift packages as described in section 8.1.3, the E-E implementers design cooperation contracts on the TV program and develop and implement E-E briefings. Both the contract and the E-E briefings will be described in the following as a central characteristic of the crystallization stage in co-productions and inscript participations.

Cooperation Contracts

When co-productions and inscript participations reach crystallization phase, the partners set up formal contracts on the TV program, as Bouman also indicates (1999: 156-157). However, the situation in Germany differs to some extent from the Dutch one as the following paragraph outlines.

Contracts are regularly made **between the broadcasting organization and the sustainability organization**. Thus, in all co-productions and inscript participations analyzed, the broadcasting station was involved right from the start (e.g. being either the initiator of the collaboration or being contacted by the sustainability side). Data did not show any indications for multi-client collaboration (Bouman 1999: 158) contracts (e.g. in which the sustainability organization also made a separate contract with the production company). Frequently, when a contract is made between the sustainability and the broadcasting organization, the broadcasting organization at least informs the production company involved about the issues already discussed and it enforces an additional contract with them – one in which the sustainability side commonly does not participate. One reason may be that the sustainability partners may not have any interest in or see a use for being involved in additional contracts with a production company. They regularly rely on the agreement with the broadcasting organization.[197] Furthermore, the broadcasting organization may feel that it is 'their business' to figure out issues with the production company (chapter 6.2.1.3).

The signed contract is based on standard contracts of the broadcasting organization. The sustainability organizations have less experience in this context and have to get used to the procedure. One sustainability expert in charge stressed: "We did all the legal negotiations together with the broadcaster Gamma and the broadcaster Beta. And, really, there were so many details to clarify. This was completely new to us, that is when it came to the question of collaboration. This was a completely new field".

Both the entertainment and the sustainability side regularly hire media lawyers to

---

[197] Some television professionals, sustainability experts and also media experts talked about possible co-productions or inscript participations where the broadcasting organization denies any involvement in money payments and then the production company takes over the negotiation with the sustainability makers regarding the high value gift exchange. However, in all the analyzed collaboration examples the main communication and the contract were made between the broadcasting organization and the sustainability experts. If there had also been a contract or other written agreements between the production company and the sustainability side, it was not mentioned at all by the study participants.

screen the standard contract and make suggestions for modifications. This of course means investing extra time and financial resources; however, it is worthwhile at the end (also see Bouman 1999: 156-157). The contract springs out of several agreements, mainly retaining three issues: (1) the kinds of gifts and responsibilities of the partners, (2) issues related to the television program, for example exploitation rights, broadcasting rights, transmission rights, etc. (3) specific agreements on the high value gift exchange (e.g. the conditions of payment or the amount of money).

According to the latter, a differentiation needs to be made: whereas some E-E implementers **agreed on details on both the high value gifts**, other collaboration partners preferred to agree only on the **details of one gift, namely finances on the program development**. Thus, they did not agree on the detailed conditions and the kind of participation in the decision making process on the program content on the side of the sustainability makers.[198] Why is this the case? Interestingly, this action can be explained though the motive of being 'on the safe side' in the collaboration contract; indeed, when both gifts are agreed upon in the contract and the contract accidentally comes into the 'wrong hands', a potentially 'illegal' action may be traced by 'outsiders' (see chapter 6.1), thus causing many troubles. In contrast, when only the financial support is fixed in the contract and it gets into the 'wrong hands', the partners can argue that the sustainability side 'sponsored' the program (see chapter 6.1), which is a legal action and thus the expected negative sanctions might be smaller. In the case of choosing the contract solution where only the financial gift is integrated, the sustainability side specifically needs to rely on the 'gentlemen's agreement' (Bouman, 1999) verbally made with the television makers regarding the involvement in the program. As both partners are aware of the high-risk context in which they are collaborating, they try very hard to stick to their contract and the gentlemen's agreements they made. This also goes with the deep level of trust and the personal ties the collaboration partners need to have (chapter 8.2.1.2). In a case where the contract (and the verbal gentlemen's agreements) would not have been honored, one solution would be to end the partnership, but a 'legal sanction' in the sense of going to court (see Bouman 1999: 158) would not be a way out of the situation. This would make the partnership visible to common sense, and this is an issue which both sides try to avoid as well as they can. However, such a case was not detected in the investigated collaborations.

Generally, the content mentioned above is agreed upon in the contracts. However, the contract might not cover all details and in practice, several issues may arise and need to be dealt with separately. One environmental expert emphasized in this context: "We had the contract, but the contract of course does not regulate everything. Both sides were always prudent about not breaking the contract, because nobody knows what would happen then".

---

[198]There was only one sustainability expert who was willing to give full details about his contracts. The majority of partners moreover only referred to their contracts in informal talks.

Signing a contract helped in a way to stabilize the 'blind faith' given to the counterpart. However, it does not guarantee that problems do not arise. As one of the environmental experts stated: "It was difficult in the collaboration, but not in the sense that it did not work at all, but more in the sense that both sides had to and did learn something new and got closer to each other every day".

Entertainment-Education Briefings
The E-E briefing regularly takes place between the people in charge and without staff members from the middle management or the creative artists (scriptwriters, actors, actresses, PR team members, etc.). After finishing the briefing, the people in charge pass the information onwards to them, in a way 'translating' what has been discussed in the briefing.
As Bouman also says (1999: 156), both the briefing and the briefing document are essential for becoming more *aware of the partners' aims and objectives*. Starting with the objectives of the sustainability experts, the E-E television program was considered and explained as a part of a larger campaign involving a media package and several other follow up communication measures for the target group. Sustainability experts strengthened these educational components a lot during the interviews/informal talks, and they stressed the importance of those when conveying their aims to the television makers. Clearly, the sustainability experts did not want to be put in the same category as those backing pure product or topic placement and wanted more than 'just incorporating' a sustainability theme in a television program. For them, the *issue of holistically educating* the target group members is of paramount importance in helping the audience members to accurately deal with a sustainability topic and to change their knowledge, attitude and behavior. Several sustainability experts even got a bit upset when explaining that many people are not aware that their approach differs strongly from pure 'product placement' or even 'sponsoring'. They indicated that the core reason for this is that product/topic placements, PR and sponsoring have become an everyday practice even among political (and on their behalf working) agencies as well as several NGOs who are trying to promote social or sustainable topics.[199] Furthermore, some sustainability experts also criticized the media legislation (chapter 6.1) their work is mixed up with as well as the kind of approaches they are forced to take and which they strongly bemoan.
Consequently, during the E-E briefings, sustainability experts stressed the holistic education approach they wanted to implement, and they strongly maintained boundaries between their approach and pure 'product/topic placement'. In this context they tried to make their point clear to the television makers by providing the

---

[199] One example that might serve here is the case of the Federal Employment Agency, which paid around 2.3 Million euros to the youth journal *Bravo* with the goal in mind that youths read more about employment and career topics. The German Press Council and the German Federal Court of Auditors (Die Zeit, 2010) strongly criticized this topic placement. For further examples, see Lehr (2007) and Volpers et al. (2008).

objectives of their holistic campaign approach. As one environmental expert explained, in the briefing they made clear to the television makers what they wanted to see implemented in the program according to campaign and policy goals – nothing more and nothing less.

Furthermore, sustainability experts did not bring behavior change, social learning or other theories (see chapter 2.3) into the briefings and did not ask, for instance, that a character be designed with the help of these theories. This might be explained by the fact that none of the sustainability experts had a classical health or an environmental communication background.[200]

In comparison to the sustainability experts, the entertainment professionals emphasized in the briefings that for them it was important to tell compelling and entertaining stories. They also made clear that they wanted to follow this path and make their decisions on how they thought the audience members could be sustainably caught by providing more entertaining than educating elements. Clearly this addresses issues of professional freedom, and this is a point where problems can arise.

Whereas some described no problems arising as the partners had different aims and objectives – this can be related back to the fact that they were aware that they are obliged to stick together (see section 8.2.1) – other implementers described tensions in the briefings.

One collaboration, for instance, realized a script competition for the television productions they wanted to implement together, and each partner side had to choose their ten favorite scripts. The environmental expert explained in this context: "And this was the interesting thing. Looking at this example, one realizes how different our approaches were. We met each other and presented our favorites. None of our favorites and none of the favorites from the TV makers overlapped. We had selected completely different products. The scripts that we had chosen were too content-loaded for the TV makers (…) the drama and the action were missing. The favorites of the TV makers were very much focused on action and entertainment, and we could not really identify the content, and we had the feeling that the messages were not conveyed". Consequently, it became a challenge for the partners to agree upon three winning scripts. Finally they found a compromise by pointing out which scripts chosen by the counterpart they could imagine producing, and then telling them what specifically should be changed. This situation was very much comparable to the one depicted by Bouman (Bouman, 1999, also see chapter 4.3) for the Netherlands.

---

[200] Specifically in environmental communication, the E-E strategy is not widespread and many theoretical discussions focus on conveying messages in a fact-based, cognitive manner. In health communication the E-E strategy is more strongly embedded. However, health communication especially is quite a new apprenticeship field in Germany (Pundt, 2006). There is only a small range of professionals working in this field, and they have not penetrated the field very deeply so far.

8.2.2.2 Production Stage

In the production stage, the entertainment and the sustainability side go through the script phase, the shooting and editing together, as Bouman also describes (1999: 159-162).

In this collaboration stage, the high value gifts are exchanged, i.e. finances for the program development and involvement in the program content. This indicates that talking with E-E implementers about this stage was the most awkward point in the interview/informal talk. Because of the challenging status this gift exchange has (as outlined before), both the sustainability and entertainment side were not willing to openly share many details of the exchange process (e.g. how much money has been handed out exactly? How high were the production costs for the program in total? How exactly did the sustainability experts participate in the decision making process in the scripting, shooting and editing?). Only one environmental expert was an exception, and he freely talked about all the details of the collaboration process. Generally, there were many more sustainability experts willing to talk about this context than TV makers. Certainly, this *tendency of closeness* among the E-E implementers can also be considered an essential outcome, because it shows how sensitive this exchange is perceived to be in terms of dealing with the information very carefully and not sharing it with outsiders (even though the information had been for research purposes only and the researcher had guaranteed anonymity). Therefore, the majority of the analytical outcomes in the following section results from informal talks.

The high value gifts, as a central mechanism, have immense impacts on the stages of scripting, shooting and editing. Hence, it does not make sense to differentiate between single stages and depict them separately. Rather, it makes more sense to put the gift exchange in the foreground and use examples from the three stages to outline what happens in the production phase.

In the following sections, the two gifts of finances (for the entertainment program) and involvement (in the entertainment program content) are depicted in more detail.

The High Value Gift Exchange 'Finance' and 'Involvement in the Program Content'

The gift of financial support from the sustainability side is very crucial in the production phase because the **amount of money determines to what extent** the sustainability experts are involved in the decision making process regarding the content. With regard to the financial gift, Mauss (1990a: 101) stresses the term *vaygu'a*, or a kind of money, that not only serves as a means of exchange but also as a **standard to measure values**. It has purchasing power and this power has a figure attached to it. For instance, for a copper object, a payment of so many blankets is due consisting of such and such *vaygu'a* which corresponds to so many baskets of yams. This means the **idea of a number is present** even if that number is not fixed by the authority of state and **varies during different tribal exchanges** (ibid.). In pursuance of Mauss, "The first gift of *vaygu'a* bears the name of *vaga*, 'opening gift'. It is the starting point, one that irrevocably commits the recipient to make a reciprocating gift, the *yotile*, which Malinowski felicitously translates as the 'clinching gift': the gift that seals the transaction. (...) It is obligatory; it is expected, and it must be equivalent to the first gift" (ibid.: 26). This **equivalence**, according to the gift of *vaygu'a*, plays an essential role. In E-E collaborations, it is the same with the high value gifts; the idea of a number is present, and in exchange, the sustainability side can have a certain degree of involvement in the program content. Only when they give a **high amount of money**, in other words, when they are the **main financier** of the new program (co-production) or of specific episodes of an existing program (inscript participation) do they receive an **equivalent gift consisting of a high level of involvement in the program content**. In contrast, if the amount is not as high (e.g. 15% of the program development costs), the equivalent gift is lesser involvement in the decision making process on the program content. Both low(er) and high financial support and involvement in the program were traced in the collaborations and, as the following paragraph outlines, this difference between 'high' and 'low' financial gifts has an impact on how the collaboration proceeds and how the game of power is played.

Low(er) Finances and Low(er) Involvement Gift
When a low(er) financial gift is given by the sustainability side, the analysis indicates that the entertainment makers hold the **upper hand** in the three stages of production. As one entertainment maker stated, in that case the theme is always subordinated to the story and the drama. Sustainability experts **cautiously** try to get in their aims and (campaign) agenda. They feel insecure in the new field they are experimenting with. Moreover, they behave cautiously in 'pushing an agenda' because they know that when they get to assertive in pushing their points, they get the short end of the stick. One environmental researcher working in an inscript participation said: "We tried to rouse a sensitivity. We knew, in any case, if we try to force something, the opposite is likely to result".
Sustainability makers emphasized that everything is very fine as long as their remarks fit or add something to the thoughts and pretensions the television makers have in mind. One environmental expert mentioned: "The TV makers collaborated largely in an uncoordinated manner with us. They did participate in joint workshops, but it was very clear at the end that they did what they wanted". So the strategy carried out by the sustainability side in the **script phase** then was to initiate meetings, to do workshops and to make suggestions on the script about what they think is more authentic and accurate and, through that, '**indirectly**' get the TV makers to change contents. In another inscript participation, the sustainability side applied formative research during the first broadcasted episodes and the results were used to strengthen their goals. This convinced the television makers to follow these goals when they scripted, shot and edited the next episodes. An environmental expert described the situation as follows: "And, there [in the episodes] they im-

plemented what we had initiated in the workshops before. The implementation was completely independent, but at least they considered (…) fewer talking heads, sympathetic protagonists, different settings like living rooms and everything, which belongs to that. There [in the episodes] were all the things inside which (…) our hypothesis argued is well received, and this was indeed the case". This *latent strategy in approaching the television makers* is not only typical for the script phase, but also for the *shooting and editing phase*. However, in the latter stages the sustainability side experienced even fewer chances to get their goals in because the script moved to a next stage, and this meant that the chances for changing issues were less probable. As one environmental expert stressed: "And thus they [the television makers] did the test shoots on their own, let me say. And we all found this interesting and exciting, or also dangerous, as it was a risk for us. Would they also manage it without our guidance?"

There were also collaborations in which the sustainability experts *raised their voices*, thus clearly indicating that they have a *differing* opinion about what should stand in the script, how it should be shot or how it should be edited. At this point the entertainment makers regularly *took control over the process* and made clear that they had the last word. They said this was because they had the feeling they were 'heteronymous'. Furthermore they stated that they could not do the collaboration in good conscience anymore. They would have decided against their own will and opinion by giving control to the sustainability side which had only supported the program development with a small amount of money. Moreover, giving any decisive power to the sustainability experts would not have been in accordance with the role they are attributed by media legislation, namely to have the *program sovereignty*. They discussed this issue with sustainability experts and in that context an interesting phenomenon occurred: sustainability experts were indeed understanding of the situation the entertainment makers were in, and they at least tried to be less pushy on the content side. One social expert said: "We tried to raise our sensitivity (…). The program sovereignty must be with *Bena* [name of the TV show]". Other sustainability experts stressed in this context that there were still the follow up communication measures and the research, which was beholden as their main terrain, where they felt 'at home'. How can this behavior be explained? At this point the external conditions of collaboration must be considered: media legislation (chapter 6.1) clearly forbids undermining the program autonomy of the television makers, as both sides are well aware. As a central consequence in the production process, sustainability experts do not want to *clearly cross this border*. Thus, they prefer to stay on the safe and legal side. A good example which demonstrates this context comes from an environmental expert, who explained why he stepped back and behaved less pushily: "At that time there was the scandal in the series *Marienhof*, and we didn't want the bad reputation of buying the television side. This also counts for sustainability themes and would have been illegal". This quote indicates that sustainability experts not only respect that certain behavior is illegal, but they also fear becoming visible in common sense if they 'play with the fire' and cross the border.

Consequently, the entertainment side has the upper hand and decides about how to do the scripting, shooting and editing when a low(er) financial gift is given by the sustainability side. Sustainability experts only have a chance to latently impact the three production phases. When they behave too pushy in trying to accomplish their goals, it commonly results in a counterproductive situation, and the entertainment side completely takes over, which is reminiscent of a 'Hobson's choice mentality'.

High Finances and High Involvement Gift

The situation is different when the television side receives a high financial gift, or, in other terms, when the sustainability side is the **main financier** of the new program (co-production) or of specific episodes of an existing program (inscript participations). Both E-E collaboration sides talked about several million euros in this context. This circumstance turns the situation upside down. Through a high financial gift, the collaboration becomes more **tensional**, as Bouman (1999) characterizes E-E collaborations in her dissertation. The high financial gift is, in the words of Mauss, some kind of prototype for the **potlatch**, which stands for rivalry and antagonism in the gift exchange (Mauss 1990a: 6-7, see also Moebius, 2006a: 87-88). Different institutions are expressed in the potlatch gift exchange itself. It is a **total societal phenomenon** (see chapter 7.2.3), whereby the gift of high finances warrants a high level of involvement in the decision making process on the program content. Exchanging these gifts is **economic** (i.e. the values of both gifts, their meanings, cause and effects in the exchange process need to be estimated), it is **moral**, because the behavior of E-E implementers can be seen critically and they are pushed under great pressure and enragement through the exchange, and it is **juristical** in the sense that with this gift exchange the border of legality and illegality is regularly crossed (Mauss 1990a: 38).

The high financial gift legitimates the sustainability side to ask for **equivalence in the values of exchanged gifts** and, with receiving the gift, it obligates (Mauss, 1990a: 38-39; Hetzel, 2006: 273) the television side to **reciprocate and hand over power in the production process**. One environmental expert mentioned his thoughts about the equivalence in the gift values as follows: "We thought that since we invested a lot of money, we should also have much more design options and influence. After all, the television side had put in very little money only".

At this point an interesting issue comes in. Specifically, the informal talks showed that several of the study participants from the entertainment field were not fully aware how 'high value' their reciprocated gift of involvement in the program content had to be in order to establish an equivalence to their received high financial gift. One entertainment maker for example mentioned that he had no experience with the situation, and he was surprised when the sustainability side got so demanding and tried very hard to put their goals through. He thought that he had the sovereign program power enforced by media law. However, his experience during the collaboration process was that, because of the high financial gift, the power level immediately changed in the sense that he had to reciprocate something, making the gift exchange equivalent. This only was possible through 'handing over' at least a high level of participation in the program content to the sustainability partners. This is also the reason why several television makers mentioned in informal talks that the lesson learned out of their collaboration was to never receive a high financial gift again, because this amounts to both partners (consciously or not) crossing the line into 'illegality' (see chapter 6.1. and chapter 7.3). Once this happens, the television professionals are no longer the only ones having the sovereign power over the program content. One of the environmental experts described this issue as follows: "But, one needs to say, today [it] would have gone another way. We had a talk with the TV makers and here it became very obvious that they do not collaborate with partners (...) anymore. And if somebody wants to give money, then he can do this in the context of follow up activities (...) but not for the production. Maybe this is due to the experience (laughs). I do not know (...). They do not want to discuss it with just anyone. It is a one-in-only thing for them that they can say 'we do the production. This is our business'".

Hence, the essential difference between a low(er) and the high financial gift is that the sustainability experts *expect in the latter case an equivalent power level* in the script phase, the shooting and editing.[201]

When exchanging gifts of high finances and a high level of involvement in the program content, the incidences happening between the partners in the scripting phase, shooting and editing draw on the procedures described by Bouman (1999: 159-162). With receiving the mutual level of involvement through the gift exchange, sustainability experts fully try to get their goals and agenda through in the program development. In the *script phase,* sustainability experts acted as "delegated producers" (Bouman 1999: 159). They frequently met the television professionals face-to-face in editorial meetings to work on the script and they had additional long telephone conversations. In the eyes of the sustainability experts, the television professionals often did not show the sustainability issue accurately and authentically. As one environmental professional said: "For them, it does not matter at all how the animal dies in the television format, but for us, it was of huge importance to get the environmental message through. (...) The television makers were freer in this context, because they said 'it is just a fictional story'. But for us it was essential that it is authentic and that it fits into the content. And such problems we had to solve all the time".

For their part television professionals often criticized the experts from the sustainability field claiming they only had their agenda in mind and that they had less sense for drama, storytelling and televised pictures. Another critique was that they only wanted to have 'the good things' about the sustainability theme depicted. One entertainment professional stated: "We have to initiate emotions. The motivation to do something good is *per se* nothing I would look at as an audience member and

---

[201] The high finance and high involvement gift exchange is not a typical phenomenon for Germany. The variety of stakeholders who implemented this gift exchange is very rare.

say, 'oh yes, great, he has done something good'. We need tension and drama".

Although several challenges and problems arose during the script phase, E-E implementers managed to find compromises and finally agreed upon the script. Then, the next stage, the *shooting* could start. Generally, the experts from the sustainability field stressed in informal talks that at this point, they had fewer possibilities to intervene than in the script phase. However, one strategy to still gain power in this phase is to hold back parts of the high finance gift until the shooting or even the editing is finished. By handing out the whole finance gift right from the start, sustainability experts feared of losing an essential power mechanism in the process of the production. In the majority of collaborations analyzed, the sustainability side agreed to give a part of the high finances gift only after the partners had finished both the scripting phase and the shooting. So, for example, when the sustainability side financed 60% of the program development, it was agreed to give 40% in the beginning of collaboration and 20% after 'successfully' finishing the shooting or even editing.

In the *editing phase*, the sustainability experts were not very interested anymore in gaining control of the process. As Bouman also indicates (1999: 161), a lot of sustainability experts were absent then, although several of them had agreed upon a presence in their contract. For those who were present in the editing room, this was their last chance to intervene in the program, though this was not done in the collaborations analyzed. In sum, when a high financial gift is exchanged for a gift of a high involvement in the program content, tensions arise through in all three production phases. However, the tension is highest in the scripting phase, because then the sustainability experts can best involve their aims; this is more difficult in the shooting and editing phase. When several tensions and challenges arise in the production process, because of the gifts of high finances and the high level of involvement in the program content, it is appropriate to raise the question of how to overcome these challenges and to arrive at better collaboration solutions. In the words of Bouman (1999: 177-194), it is a matter of asking how to do 'risk management'. At this point it must be reiterated that the aim of this thesis is not to analyze and portray management strategies for handling and minimizing these kinds of tensions. Bouman (1999) has already described them extensively. Furthermore, the gift exchange of high finances and high level of involvement in the program content is something which is relatively rare in E-E collaborations designed and implemented in Germany's TV landscape and thus not worthwhile to intensively focus on. This thesis aims more to illustrate the conditions (chapter 6) and the variety of E-E collaboration forms in the German context (chapter 7 and 8) and, based on this, give recommendations for fruitful future developments (chapter 9).

8.2.2.3 Implementation Stage

The implementation stage starts at the point where the program is broadcasted. Both the entertainment and the sustainability professionals carefully look at the viewing rates, which are an essential factor for measuring their success. At this stage, entertainment makers regard their job as finished (Bouman 1999: 162). However, for the sustainability side, work continues. In the implementation stage, sustainability experts implement the follow up communication measurements (see chapter 6.6) for the target group without the help of the television professionals. The environmental experts from one collaboration, for instance, initiated a media package including learning materials as well as periodical exchange forums and learning trips. Furthermore, all co-productions and inscript participations investigated did summative research[202] (chapter 2.4.3.3). However, a pre-post control group design had not been implemented. The sustainability experts did not conduct a basline measurement before the broadcasting of the TV format, but started afterwards. Some did this measurement more substantially than others. The striking issue is that none of these results were made available to a broader public (e.g. through publishing them in a journal). They were only made available on organizational databases or made accessible to the public on demand. Another strategy of the sustainability experts was to do summative research and to use the positive results to convince their funders that the money was worth investing. However, the results are internal documents. As mentioned above, one collaboration also implemented formative research, and the results were used to improve the depiction of the sustainability content in the program. The following figure sums up the different collaboration characteristics and stages in German co-productions and inscript participations.

Figure 8.1: Characteristics and stages of E-E co-productions and inscript participations in Germany

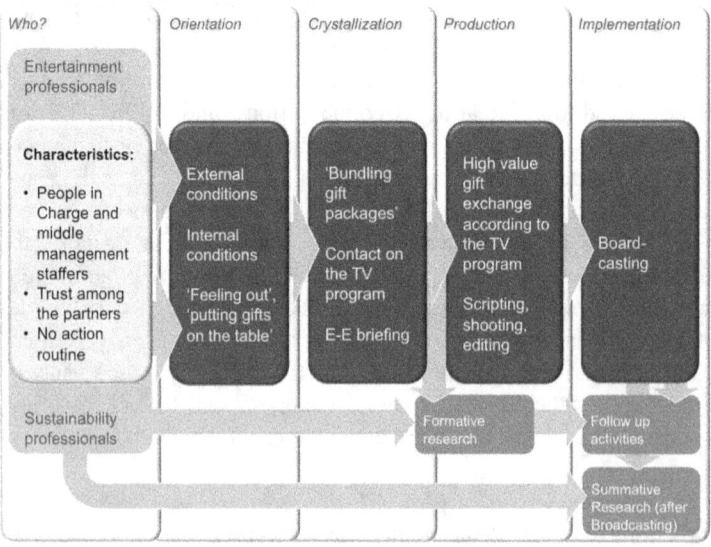

---

[202] Characteristically, this summative research was a mixture of qualitative and quantitative methods.

8.3 E-E Service

E-E service is designed and implemented in existing TV programs. It seems to be a good alternative when German stakeholders try to find more *media legislation conforming* ways (comparing it with co-productions and inscript participations) of implementing an E-E collaboration. In this collaboration form, the sustainability experts have little or no influence on the program content but in return, they are on the 'safe and legal side'. Later in the collaboration process, they try to play out their abilities in the follow up activities which they regularly implement together with the television makers (section 8.3.2.3). In recent years the service approach has become a more common procedure, though ongoing activities are still very much in the experimentation stage.

The next section (8.3.1) shows crucial *characteristics* of E-E service collaborations taking place in Germany. Subsequently, *the stages of collaboration* are described (section 8.3.2): these descriptions not only include further specific aspects of the crystallization stage in E-E service (section 8.3.2.1), but moreover they include details on the production stage (section 8.3.2.2) and the implementation stage (section 8.3.2.3).

8.3.1 Characteristics

8.3.1.1 Different Approaches to E-E Service

In the following, the processes and developments of experimenting with E-E service will be depicted more in detail. In this context, *two different approaches of E-E service* are examined (Reinermann & Lubjuhn 2011):

- The first approach is a *constant E-E service approach* of sustainability organization(s); by this approach the sustainability side holistically addresses (over a constant time frame) a variety of entertainment professionals working in different broadcasting organizations as well as production companies through service activities (consultations, workshops, award ceremonies, etc.). In return, they hope to 'gain something back' through accurate and authentic sustainability themes portrayed in the program. In this approach, it is rarely only one specific theme that is dealt with, but the sustainability organization(s) have a broad portfolio of themes for which they can offer service support. Hollywood, Health & Society can be considered as a specific practice example of a constant E-E service approach from the USA.
- The second approach is the *occasional E-E service approach.* In this collaboration setting, one sustainability organization works exclusively together with one entertainment partner[203] for a specific time frame in order to address a specific sustainability theme in particular episodes of a program as well as in the follow up activities they implement together. Sever-

---

[203] Regularly there is one organization involved on each partner side. However, in the analysis there were also cases in which two organizations teamed up on each partner side.

al examples of the occasional E-E service approach are depicted by Lubjuhn & Reinermann (2010).

The aim of this section is to briefly illuminate some starting-points for the *constant E-E service approach* perspective. However in Germany, there are only some activities regarding the constant E-E service approach and it is too early to point to first results.

Therefore, the main focus will be on the *occasional E-E service approach* (see next section as well as sections 8.3.1.2 and 8.3.2), for which the research study offers transparent results. Next, further general characteristics of E-E service are portrayed with regard to the occasional E-E service approach (sections 8.3.1.1 - 8.3.1.2). Finally the stages of collaboration are illustrated (sections 8.3.2).

During the last decade, there were several isolated activities from different sustainability as well as other research organizations, which have experimented with a service approach through, for example, implementing briefings, discussion rounds and award ceremonies with television professionals. This is similar to the approach of Hollywood, Health & Society (chapter 4.2). However, these activities take place insularly, and they are not standardized, nor harmonized, and they do not yet involve research activities (e.g. summative research), which have been made available to a scientific community. Moreover, these activities are in the majority of cases not developed with a specific focus on the needs of *entertainment* professionals. Sustainability organizations primarily try to reach television professionals who implement *information* programs such as documentaries, news reports, etc. (Lubjuhn & Hoffhaus, 2009).[204]

The *MINTIFF* program located at the Technical University of Berlin is the only stakeholder visible so far who has started implementing a constant service approach specialized on collaboration processes specifically with *entertainment professionals*. They are trying to find out how to approach entertainment professionals in terms of depicting natural scientific and gender issues in fictional formats. They are willing to experiment with the E-E strategy and they are trying to discover how the strategy may support collaboration processes on the entertainment side. Recently, they have focused on face-to-face briefings, consultations, discussion rounds and a fellowship program. With the latter one, the program financially supports scriptwriters in the development of their plot. Through these additional financial resources (fellowships) the scriptwriters have the possibility to do in-depth investigations on the natural scientific and gender issues they want to portray in the program. Furthermore, in September of 2010, the *MINTIFF* program implemented an international conference, where many entertainment professionals, different re-

---

[204] An example in this regard might be the activities of the *Adolf Grimme Institute* which, in former years, had specialized on networking with journalists and other media professionals in implementing information formats. In recent years the institute has taken more entertainment media professionals into consideration. Another example is the *Deutsche Umweltstiftung*, which bestows environmental awards to journalists, television and other media makers, most of them coming from the information field.

searchers and the *MINTIFF* program funders from the government had been invited to discuss E-E topics together with international E-E experts. In this context, the first timid discussions about the German situation took place and the first bridges were built between the sustainability and the entertainment professionals for further collaboration processes. However, these activities are very much in the experimental stage and not even close to a nation-wide approach such as that in the USA or the Netherlands.

This is also the reason why this thesis cannot provide insights in the gift exchange processes nor answers to questions such as: is there a gift exchange at all in a German constant E-E service approach? If so, which services would be given as gifts by the sustainability side and are there gifts, which are reciprocated by the entertainment side? For sure, further research and practical pilot projects need to be implemented in this context to find the answers.

In the occasional E-E service approach one sustainability organization teams up with one partner from the entertainment field. This is Germany's increasingly common approach in recent years, so this approach will be depicted as an E-E service approach 'par excellence' in the following sections of this chapter.

The E-E implementers exchange ***medium value gifts*** (chapter 7.2.3). These medium value gifts have the characteristic that (1) they do not ask for a ***specific determined gift in return*** and (2) all together (both given and reciprocated by each partner side) they need to have an ***equivalent perceived gift value by the end of the E-E collaboration*** (i.e. after the implementation stage (section 8.3.2.3) all the gifts exchanged need to have the same value to be considered as a 'success' for both sides).

Due to the above-mentioned reasons, i.e. the early stage of developments in context with the constant approach, the following sections of 'Scaling Down Gifts and Adding New Ones' (8.3.1.2) as well as the 'Stages of Collaboration' (section 8.3.2) relate to the occasional E-E service approach only.

8.3.1.2 Scaling Down Gifts and Adding New Ones

As also described in the orientation stage, several gifts are 'put on the table' from each partner side (section 8.1.1 and 8.1.2), and if they fit to each other, they move onward to the crystallization stage to concretize and bundle their gift packages (section 8.1.3). However, in a later stage, i.e. in the production and implementation phase, it is possible for new gifts to be incorporated into the gift exchange process. For example, one PR expert at a broadcasting station said: "After the press conference [when the collaboration was announced] a journalist called (…) and said, 'Will Mrs. Waller also receive a guest part in your show?' And I said 'This I cannot tell you now, but it is not impossible, of course.' And I think it was a bit like the birth hour when we said, okay Mrs. Waller indeed plays a guest part". Thus, the broadcasting station brought the new, additional gift of a guest part into the collaboration. Also, gifts can be scrapped from the gift exchange agenda. A short quote for this context comes from a scriptwriter who stated: "And they [the sustainability organization] said, 'If you do this [for us], [we can promote and support you in return] in our sheets.' But this [the promotion and support on the sheets] has never happened. That is the joke of the story".

The phenomenon of scaling down gifts and adding new ones is not a regular procedure in E-E collaborations, but it can happen, and then it is most common in E-E service. One essential reason may go back to the issue that, in this collaboration form, no formal agreements are made on the gifts and implementers have to rely on their gentlemen's agreement. Hence, there are no formalized or potential legal consequences when a gift is scaled down, and this makes it even easier for the partners to scrap (or add new) gifts.

Scaling down means that medium value gifts included in the bundled gift package fall apart during the production or implementation stage (sections 8.3.2.2 - 8.3.2.3). Initial reasons for that can be twofold (also see section 8.1.3). Firstly, one partner side scraps a gift, because they fear sanctions by common sense if it becomes public that the partners exchanged this specific gift in the collaboration. Or, secondly, another plausible reason would be that they think the counterpart does not fulfill the promises made with regard to the gift in the beginning. But latter-mentioned was not the case in any of the examined E-E service collaborations. The only reason why gifts were scrapped was because, through observing common sense, zeitgeist and recent developments, the implementers drew the conclusion that gifts could be negatively sanctioned. For instance, in one E-E collaboration the partners agreed during the orientation and crystallization stage that the television professionals should give a guest part and celebrity endorsement for the sustainability theme. The sustainability experts decided to give networks/contacts, a patronage and logistical support for the follow up activities. Then, in the production stage, the television partners cancelled the guest part, because they were afraid that common sense would perceive it negatively at that specific point in time. The TV professional explained: "This caused annoyance [on the sustainability side]. Then we tried to rescue the situation and said to come around for a guest part later. But this Mr. Miller [guest part owner] did not like. Well then". As a result, the sustainability experts decided to scrap the logistical support and the network/contacts they had agreed upon before.

As the latter example indicates, one scrapped gift leads to another and ***the perceived equality of gifts has been recreated*** (Caillé 2008: 102-103). Mauss (Mauss 1990a: 16 and Hetzel 2006: 272) also describes this procedure of scaling down gifts in the context of the potlatch. Both exchange parties destroy their potential gifts and the partner side reciprocates the destroying procedure. In Mauss' delineation of archaic societies, the potlatch is characterized as a procedure in which gifts are destroyed to demonstrate the counterpart power and anti-utilitarianism (1990a: 16) as well as to play off prestige and show that one does not attach importance to a reciprocated gift (also see Hetzel 2006: 272). In an E-E collaboration, the scaling down process primarily demonstrates power as well. However, the trigger to scaling down is, as just mentioned above, out of concern about common sense and zeitgeist. But clearly, when one side scraps a gift, the counterpart perceives this as a power demonstration, and demonstrates power in return by scaling down some of the gifts to be reciprocated. However, this description of Mauss seems to have some limitations and Caillé (2008: 204-205) is useful to apply in this context. He extends the views of Mauss by saying that, when gifts are scaled down, the processes are turned around. It is a negation of the gift itself. He states (2008: 204) "the negation of the cycle to give, receive and reciprocate is to take, reject and to retain". And this is exactly what is taking place when the E-E implementers scale down their gifts. Furthermore, there have been collaboration cases where the partners *added medium value gifts* during the production and implementation stage. This procedure is quite common for E-E service where partners collaborate on a long-term basis (e.g. several months or a year). During the collaboration process they find out that it may be fruitful for both partners to add several new gifts. For instance, during the implementation stage, television professionals of one collaboration gave the additional gift of celebrity endorsement for a health campaign. The endorsement originally had nothing to do with the health topic the collaboration was related to. The sustainability expert explained: "I had the idea, at that point the collaboration had actually already ended, but we had an idea for a health campaign which had to do with walking. Then I said this would be a good end to the collaboration (...). We did that in the park named Mainer and took some actresses and actors with us to advertise for the health issue".

In return, the television makers reciprocated positive PR and they benefited from the high credibility of this campaign. So in a way, the actual collaboration context was extended by both partners through additional gifts, and they both profited from it.

8.3.2 Stages of Collaboration in E-E Service

After the description of the general characteristics in German E-E service, the collaboration stages (crystallization, production and implementation stage) are depicted with regard to their process and gift exchange structures.

In the orientation stage (section 8.1.1 - 8.1.2), both the entertainment and the sustainability side have identified the gift type of the counterpart, which – with special regard to E-E service – implies that both have found out that the other party wants to exchange medium value gifts (e.g. logistical support, guest part, celebrity endorsement). In the crystallization stage, the specific gift packages are bundled (section 8.1.3), which contains the negotiation details regarding the medium value gift exchange. The next section adds further specific aspects of the crystallization stage (section 8.3.2.1) in E-E service and then the production stage (section 8.3.2.2) and implementation stage (section 8.3.2.3) are introduced for this collaboration form.

8.3.2.1 Crystallization Stage Contracts on Follow up Activities

In some cases, E-E service partners like to do a contract which deals with the gift exchange procedures regarding the *follow up activities* they want to design and implement together with the counterpart. However, such contracts do not include issues on the program development itself, as the sustainability side does not play a crucial role in the program development anyway. One E-E service collaboration, for instance, made a contract in connection with a huge climate protection event, which was implemented in relation to the broadcasted climate protection episode on television. One partner from an environmental organization described these contracts: "They govern that the TV organizations have access to these official places. That is, that we make this place available (...). One has to stick to the public rules. When implementing a big event, many departments have to work together. Questions need to be dealt with, for example, with regard to the noise, the traffic, the garbage collection. These things need to be organized (...). That one partner side does not do something without the other side – these are also things which are fixed there [in the contract]. And that, for example, the agency [for the organization of the event] is only paid by the TV makers and not by us (...). And for us as public authorities, we would like to fix these issues so that it is transparent and so that nobody can say afterwards, 'why did you give this to them and not to the others?' And that the topic of climate protection should also play a very important role and that we don't suddenly talk about something else. And through the event, there are city rules, which need to be adhered to. It starts with that we, for example, say 'we do not want to have one-time tableware, because we are an environmental department'". This quote indicates that if contracts are made in E-E service, they serve to substantiate **medium value gift exchange**, but not high value gift exchanges regarding the program development, as is the case in co-productions and inscript participations. However, there was only one E-E service collaboration located in the data in which a contract had been agreed upon for designing and implementing follow up activities. It seems that for E-E service collaborations informal 'gentlemen's agreements' are often sufficient when medium value gifts are exchanged (see section 8.1.1 and 8.1.2 and as well as Bouman 1999: 122).

8.3.2.2 Production Stage

Having made first agreements about the gifts in the orientation and crystallization stage, the partners move onward to the production stage and start the gift exchange procedures. In this stage of E-E service, it is characteristic for the *television professionals to be fully responsible for the scripting, shooting and editing* (i.e. sustainability professionals take no part in the decision making process of the program content at all). In the production stage, there are typical gifts to be exchanged; they are specified as follows.[205]

---

[205]These gifts can also be given, received or reciprocated in other E-E forms and stages of collaboration, but they are illustrated here, because they are very common gifts in the production stage of E-E service.

Sustainability Communication Consultation
The gift of sustainability communication consultation is given by the sustainability partners (see chapter 7.2.3). A consultation gift comprises two different parts. The first part is given shortly *before the scriptwriter* start to work on the script. In this context the sustainability side passes on information such as fact-sheets, web links, leaflets, etc. over to the television makers (see also section 8.4.2.1 and the gift of giving sustainability information). One health expert described this step as follows: "We can provide our expert opinion. We have a lot of materials, information, links to information pages, etc. which are provided by different public authorities about the drug topic". If required, additional brainstorm sessions or workshops may be implemented together, and the sustainability experts tell more about the sustainability theme while at the same time involving interesting stories from which the television makers can draw their information and lessons learned. One environmental expert stated: "And then we made the suggestion to do a workshop series".[206] A sustainability research expert, while talking about this type of workshop, stated: "That means to say 'what is interesting for you [TV professionals], also in a broader context of sustainability? And thus for your future planning, does this play a role for you? (...) Which questions are you daring to ask?' And we tried to communicate the sustainability theme subliminally". The counterpart experienced another workshop as follows: "The sustainability organization contacted us (...) and they invited us to the research center (...). And, such a visit is of course excellent (...). You are sitting there with these people and listening to stories you have never heard of before. And of course, I think that this is conceivable on every [sustainability] area". This quote shows that if these workshops are effectively done and in a way that reaches the TV makers, then it is likely that they learn something out of it and mirror these issues in their storylines.

The second part of the gift comes in *after* the scriptwriters have *finished the first drafts of the script*. The sustainability side then critically looks at the first ideas of the sustainability storyline and judges whether the theme is authentically and accurately depicted.[207]

A scriptwriter commented: "These are the [story] cases which we have invented, like this and that, and then they can say, 'oh, this is outrageous' or they say, 'yes this is brilliant, but couldn't it also be like this and that?'" Another TV professional mentioned: "Thus, there had been an exchange between the story department, the authors and the advisors, which employ the theme of drug misuse very well. They

---

[206] Such workshop activities were also implemented by the *MINTIFF* program as a constant E-E service approach.

[207] Differences between the first and the second part of the consultation gift can be mirrored in different consultations types at Hollywood, Health & Society (see chapter 4.2). On the one hand, there are consultations to provide main ideas about the sustainability content before the script is developed. On the other hand, they also offer consultations, which advise on an existing script in an advanced stage of development.

always asked 'Is that right? Can you become addicted that fast? Can you also come back from therapy that fast and does this all fit into the content frame?'" A third scriptwriter added that "They [sustainability experts] said, 'you should depict this as well, so that it makes sense'. (…) This was great and they fairly helped us". This last quote indicates that most TV makers really could use support through focused advice, which is targeted to their needs.

On a more general level, it becomes clear that the sustainability side gives recommendations through their consultations, which does not mean that the television side should or will definitively realize them. In an E-E service partnership, the television side receives the consultation gift, and they are free to do and to portray whatever they want; they can follow the advices or leave it. Clearly, an essential prerequisite for creating this kind of exchange situation is that there is no financial gift involved in the program development because if this is the case, the collaboration situation can strongly differ (section 8.2).

When E-E service implementers communicate the consultation activities to common sense, they are carefully distinguishing their consultation gift from the gifts of involvement in the program content exchanged in co-productions and inscript participations (chapter 7.3.7). As one television professional indicated after a press conference on the collaboration activities, journalists asked critical questions about whether the sustainability partner was now writing the stories for the scriptwriters. The television maker then had to repeat and emphasize what she had already pointed out several times before: "This was not the case, of course. We wrote the story ourselves, and we have had the consultation of the sustainability partner – nothing more". Conclusively, the line of communication to common sense is very important for both partner sides when a consultation gift is given and received. Moreover, both sides clearly emphasized that they refrained from exchanging the high value gift of financial support. Most of the E-E service partners clearly expressed that financial resources had not been involved, in fact, their tendency was to over-emphasize it. One TV professional stated: "Money has never been involved at all. This has never, never been the guiding idea because I think we are very much biased in this context. This issue did not enter the picture, and I don't think we would have done this because then we would have had the feeling that, if there is money involved, then we also need to let more influence happen, and this we did not want to in any case. For us, the story is very important and therefore the production works very independent".

Another health expert implementing an E-E service collaboration also made a clear statement about the involvement of financial resources: "Giving money for the collaboration: we did state right from the beginning that we cannot offer financial support. We can give our know-how, our materials (…), but not material goods. This has always been clear. We did not want to do this".

The question of how far financial support for program development really was (or was not) involved backstage in the place of gift exchange cannot be answered through the data collection. Furthermore, this was not the aim of this research.

With the research question and the methodological approach, the researcher decided to look at the field more from the 'proscenium' than from the 'backstage' (see chapter 5.3.3). The even more important result is that, independent of whether any financial resources were involved or not, the E-E implementers needed to strictly separate the medium value gift of consultation from the high value gift exchange in order to lower the risk of being negatively sanctioned.

Guest Part

The television professionals give the gift of guest part. It can either be raised right from the start in the orientation phase, where first gifts are 'put on the table', or it is brought up later during the production phase itself. In the latter case, the E-E service collaboration and thus the broadcasted sustainability storyline runs over several months or a year. In this situation E-E implementers have time to rethink their gifts and also to add new ones (section 8.3.1.2).

A characteristic for this gift is that the guest part owner not only comes in to say 'hello', but he should convey sustainability content to the audience members. On the one hand, cases were mentioned where the television side wrote the first script for the guest part, and then the sustainability side had the chance to look on it afterwards. As one TV maker stated: "Elena [one character in the storyline] had the idea of an environmental day in the series. Now this needs to be realized. What did the woman do? The authors thought it would be a good idea to let her wander around in the [environmental] department and by incidence meet Mr. Schroder there [the guest part owner]. Then she explains her idea and he says 'yes, we will do this event together'". After the authors had scripted the story and the dialogue of the guest part owner, Mr. Schroder could inspect and say if it was okay for him. On the other hand, entertainment and sustainability partners also described a procedure, where the sustainability organization had the possibility to make a first guest part suggestion for the script and then the television professionals edited it. As one TV maker said "she [the guest part owner] wrote a speech and then it was agreed to by the authors". The health expert involved in this collaboration case stated in an informal talk that the TV makers had made crucial changes in the script.

In both cases, however, sustainability experts do not participate in the decision making process on the program content. Television professionals decide what is included in the guest part and which content is transmitted and how. They are most of the time not willing to make compromises. Several sustainability experts perceive this non-intervening situation as a risk because, when the television professionals take over and, to give an example, decide that the person playing the guest part should do his speech in a very emotional manner, sustainability experts are to some degree afraid of damaging their reputation in the political and/or research field. One health expert stated on a guest part speech, which was written by the health organization first and then edited through the scriptwriters: "For us, it seemed so altered, apart from the fact that they removed a lot of facts... they added a lot more emotion. That was for me, how should I explain... it [the speech after the

TV professionals did editing] was like 'how awful this all is and how terrible that one has to get out of this stuff and call for support – Schacka!' (...) this [edited] speech was not one of the most representative ones given by Mrs. Kahler [the guest part owner from the heath organization]".

Hence, sustainability experts are sometimes confronted with that risk and need to act against their better judgment and take on the guest part. If they at least decide to receive a guest part gift, they stressed that they were aware of this risk and a bit afraid of how it is portrayed, but that at the same time the aim of reaching specific target group members with messages outweighed these concerns, and they made a positive decision to experiment. One health expert from an organization which was willing to take that risk, described the process of receiving a guest part as follows: "Just to try if this is something useful for us (...). Thus, one should not have blinders on and say 'uwa, this is such a cheap' ... – cheap is not allowed – ... (laughs) 'an entertainment program and we do not want to get involved with this. We want to inform the youth'. But this... one should not separate both from each other. One should be open... to experimenting with other things and trying them. That can be difficult for an institutional organization such as our health department. That people think, hmm, this is probably not that serious. We do not want to look bad. These concerns, according to the motto 'it has never been like that. Why then should we start now?' I think one should be open for such things".

Another quote from a sustainability expert shows the same interesting phenomenon as was described in section 8.2.2.2 with regard to the low(er) finances and low(er) involvement gift exchange: "We worked hard and at least we produced a lot of text [in the first script draft], dates, facts and figures (...). You cannot expect that too much from a normal daily soap audience. Hence, I completely understand that this was getting too much for them [the television professionals]". The quotation indicates that, with regard to the gift of guest part, the sustainability side demonstrates their acceptance that the television professionals take over in the guest part discussion and that they cannot get too 'pushy' in wanting to be involved in the decision making process on program content. Indeed, in E-E service collaborations, this behavior can be understood, because sustainability experts have no gift which they can reciprocate to warrant involvement on the program content (as was indicated in section 8.2.2.2, this can only be another high value gift, i.e. financial support). They can try, but in the end the TV professionals make the decision. One health expert stated: "Maybe for us it would have been nice if it [the hotline number] would have been shown again at the end of the episode or what, but that was too much for them. Well, I do not want to fight. They showed it [once during the guest part] and this was also great".

Generally speaking, sustainability experts are not so much interested in getting too pushy, as they said in informal talks, because they want to avoid crossing the line into illegality with regard to media legislation. Furthermore, they mentioned the possibility of 'playing off' their agenda in the follow up activities during the implementation stage (see next paragraph).

Moreover, some of the television makers also offered their partners from the sustainability field the chance to present their *materials* (leaflets, banners, or a hotline number) in the program itself in relation to the guest part performance. As a health expert said, "We also provided the leaflets and poster for the shooting which stood or hung around on the set". A central prerequisite for such material is that this depiction serves a 'greater good' through supporting the audience members (e.g. they can call a nation wide hotline to talk about problems they have). Whether sustainability materials are also included in the program content or not depends very much on the producers and the broadcasting station in charge. Data clearly shows that commercial broadcasters and the production companies working on their behalf have a greater affinity for integrating sustainability materials. One main reason for this may be that they feel that they have less to fear than public broadcasting stations, which need to guarantee a balanced depiction of content. In contrast, the private broadcasters are more commercially orientated and common sense may be more likely to 'turn a blind eye', specifically when considering this in light of the new product placement legislations (chapter 6.1).

8.3.2.3 Implementation Stage

While in the implementation stage of co-production and inscript participation the television professionals consider their job as 'done' and the sustainability partners move on to conduct follow up and also research activities (see section 8.2.2.3), the implementation stage of E-E service can be characterized through further *profound medium value gift exchange procedures* between the partners. This means that in this stage of collaboration *both sides are equally responsible* for the design and the implementation of the follow up activities.

The *broadcasting* of the consulted sustainability storylines as well as the guest part performance serve as a starting point for jointly implementing several follow up activities for the audience members.[208]

In the following, the implementation stage of E-E service is illustrated according to the different gifts which are typically exchanged, in order to get a clear picture of what is happening there.

Gifts from the Sustainability Side: Networks/Contacts, Logistical Support/Organization Know-How, Patronage and Reliability

The *networks/contacts gift* is brought in by the sustainability side and is regularly given by them in the context of follow up activities.[209]

Television makers know even before getting in contact with the sustainability side

---

[208] These activities can take place in the frame of a bigger health or environmental campaign by the sustainability organization, but this was frequently not the case in the analyzed collaboration examples.

[209] Moreover, sustainability experts also may give this gift in relation to their consultation work during the production phase (e.g. referring to other organizations for specific details, etc.).

that this may be a gift to receive because obviously all sustainability organizations have a good network in their field of expertise. However, although this gift is visible for the television partners before engaging in a collaboration, both sides have to negotiate and agree on the conditions and the kind of networks and contacts which should be provided.

Data indicates that the networks/contacts gift plays an important role, firstly to *border* and secondly to *specify sustainability expertise*. In the first case, the sustainability organization hands out several contact details from other organizations to extend the field of expertise on a sustainability theme for TV makers. Here, the sustainability side plays off their networks/contacts gift in the sense that they bring in the contacts which may be integrated in the follow up activities (e.g. a sustainability event, workshops, discussion rounds). For example, one TV professional explained the networks/contacts gift for a follow up activity, which the TV makers were in charge of, as follows: "Well, the environmental and health department, they named all the organizations, [including] which ones we could contact, which ones they also know and which ones may also have an interest. I think we contacted or we let others [an agency which was in charge of organizing the event] contact 30. From those, 10 or 12 came [to the environmental event] because at the end, we didn't have so much space". He added that he and his colleagues appreciated these fast-made and high-quality contacts through their collaborating sustainability partner. Another entertainment professional emphasized: "They strongly supported us. Without their input or their saying which organizations to contact or their telling us where to find the contact people or their giving us the telephone numbers, the whole thing [the environmental event] would not have taken place". Thus, the networks/contacts gift in this case serves to enlarge and deepen the expertise about a sustainability theme in the follow up activities. The overall aim was to reach target group members through a diverse information approach, provided by various sustainability partner organizations involved in the follow up activities.

In the second case, the gift is applied to *specify expertise on the sustainability theme*. In this case, the sustainability experts handed out one specific contact of a partner organization because the partnering organization had an expertise, which the sustainability organization itself could not provide. In the collaborations analyzed, the sustainability organizations handed out this gift, because the television professionals asked to get in contact with real people who dealt with the sustainability theme in their daily routine, or the sustainability experts themselves made the suggestion to get connected with these 'real incidences'. However, because the TV professionals had no direct link to these people, they used the sustainability organization's networks to connect to their partner institutions. In one collaboration, the sustainability side provided a contact to a drug information center. As one health expert explained: "Yes, and during the talk the idea developed that one could visit an advice center together with the actress playing the main character who then comes in contact with… relevant people. She can find out how they experienced their drug addiction. In the city of Leipzig, there is such a center and we organized a meeting there". The actress playing the main character used this experience to more authentically play her character in the daily soap. Hence, the networks/contacts gift here served to specify the expertise from the sustainability side by providing a contact partner who additionally helped to foster an accurate and authentic depiction of sustainability content through a real case incidence.

The second gift that can be handed out by the sustainability side is *logistical support and organizational know-how* (i.e. the sustainability experts support the joint follow up activities with logistics and organizational efforts). For example, they organize the agenda of a sustainability event, they write the invitation for guest speakers and they organize how the people and the equipments are transported in a sustainable manner. In a way, this gift offers some kind of event management skills. For instance, one climate expert stated: "And then I had to make sure that everything worked out and that everything was really there (…). We were here, 11 or 12 people, and we also had to take over the management of the event". The television professionals commonly have very little experience in organizing a sustainability event related to a sustainability program or episode, so they are very happy that the sustainability experts help with their gift in this context.

The third gift which can be given by the sustainability side during the implementation stage is *patronage*. In this case, a very high-ranking person (e.g. a federal minister from the sustainability field) serves as the patron of a follow up activity. The sustainability side gives this gift in order to underline the importance of the follow up activity, to promote the theme, to raise attention and to create a credible and reliable notion of it. The entertainment professionals profit very much from it because the patron also transmits her or his credible and reliable notions to them (see the following gift).

The last gift, *reliability*, is an endogenous gift, in the sense that it is inherent to the sustainability organization (chapter 7.2.3); it is a gift the partners do not need to discuss. It resonates in all gifts that the sustainability experts hand out in different forms and during different stages of collaboration. Certainly it plays an essential role particularly in the implementation stage of E-E service, and this is why it is depicted in this context. The collaboration partners communicate through their follow up activities with a huge amount of target group members. In addition through PR measures their collaboration becomes very much visible in the public field. One health expert illustrated why she thinks that the reputation of her organization plays an important role in the collaboration: "This [the department] is a good seal of quality which you can put on your products, right? And this is a very important point. And for many producers who are interested in this field, I think that collaborating with such an organization generates a high amount of corporate political significance". And a TV professional from another collaboration adds that: "We profit immensely from the reliability of the whole. Well, it is a different thing when you just stand there and tell your story and then nothing happens (…). Here we do awareness training [together]. The actress playing a drug addict in the series visits schools and participates in health activities (…). Well, everybody gets something from that". The quotation indicates to some degree that through the gift exchange, the joint activities and the presentations in public, the reliability seems to transfer from the sustainability organization to their collaborating partners also. This 'transfer' fits very well with the Mauss hybridization of people and things and can be considered as a central prerequisite for a free and, at the same time, obligatory gift exchange: "Basically it is a question of mixtures. One intermixes the souls with things, one intermixes things with the souls. One intermixes people's lives and, behold: each of the intermixed persons and things steps out of their sphere and they intermix again: this is exactly what constitutes the contract and the exchange" (Mauss 1950: 173 cited by Moebius 2009: 67).

E-E research activities are also a *potential gift* from the sustainability partners. It should be mentioned that there was no collaboration in which the E-E service implementers involved research activities (e.g. through measuring the impact of the sustainability messages broadcasted by the program or during follow up activities). However, when asking them to reflect on the research issue, sustainability experts mentioned that they had not implemented research activities so far due to the lack of further financial resources. A health expert stated here that there "has not been an evaluation. If we had had the money, we would have invested it. I am sure that at that time, there were also no financial resources left for it". Many partners from both collaboration fields additionally added things like this comment made by a sustainability expert: "I can imagine that this [doing research] would be very interesting. I really can imagine" or this statement made by a TV professional: "If a governmental organization, ministry or research organization conducts research, let's say on their own resources, that would be wise, I mean, where's the fault in that?" The quotations indicate that the study participants from both sides are by trend interested but that there is also no real awareness about investing in research. A typical reaction when talking about 'research' has been for the TV makers to mention their monitoring activities, which regularly do not take Germany's television sustainability themes into account. Both sides also mentioned the audience ratings as an indicator of having reached the target group.

Certainly, both explanations do not directly contribute to scientific results about the depiction of sustainability content, nor about the knowledge, attitude or behavior changes of audience members.

However, they noted that it is not necessarily enough to only use high audience ratings as an indicator for success. They are well aware that the issue of to what extent specific messages reached the audience members in their daily life and at least changed their knowledge, attitude or even behavior through the program and the follow up activities needs to be investigated.

Gifts from the Entertainment Side: Celebrity Endorsement
Celebrity endorsement (see chapter 2.3.5 for its advantages and disadvantages) is used as a gift given by the television professionals to strengthen the outreach of the broadcasted sustainability messages in the follow up activities. In one example, the

actresses and actors who were involved in a long-term health storyline visited schools and other educational institutions together with the sustainability partners to strengthen the messages in participative communication measures. Or the actresses and actors showed up at the open house of the sustainability organization. One sustainability expert, while discussing this visit, stressed, "they said they would come around and support the theme" and another added that "they signed autographs, they talked about the drug issue and they told stories from their perspectives. This caught the attention of the target group members very well".

In addition, the gift of celebrity endorsement was used to involve target group members to reflect on sustainability themes and thus make them change their knowledge, attitude and behavior accordingly. This included having sustainability experts create a health quiz, and the participants who sent in the right answers entered a raffle with the prize being a meet and greet with an actress who had played the main character in the sustainability storyline.

Also, the actresses and actors themselves got more sensitized to the sustainability theme, especially through their celebrity endorsement during the follow up activities. A TV professional stated: "Changes were visible in the ensemble, because the actors had to deal with the issue (…). I think this was worthwhile because, in addition, it strengthened the interest regarding the environmental theme and has allowed us to increasingly integrate environmental themes into our show".

Television professionals showed their respect for the actresses and actors, because they constantly and continuously emphasized to the target group members how important the sustainability issue is, and thus they strongly supported, in the eyes of the target group members, a role-model (see Bandura, 1977, Bandura, 2004). One TV professional said: "They had a lot to do with this [sustainability theme] in one year. And there were also times when they said they were exhausted and couldn't talk about it 300 times. But I admired how they did it and with enthusiasm, especially Britta, who always stood there saying again and again how important it is to do something about it". This quotation hints at the importance of celebrities' credibility when promoting sustainability issues (see chapter 2.3.5).

Gifts given from Both Entertainment-Education Partner Sides: PR (for Theme)
The **PR gift** can be given and reciprocated by both the sustainability and the entertainment side. Specifically in E-E service, this gift is crucial. Both partner sides **advertise the sustainability theme** which was broadcasted in the program and which was deepened through follow up communication activities. The advertisements for example take place through press releases or press conferences and are mainly implemented by the PR departments of both partner sides. As mentioned in chapter 7.3.7 about common sense, the PR gift is first and foremost related to the sustainability theme itself. Furthermore, the E-E collaboration partners are also mentioned, but they are not in the main PR focus. This could lead to the conclusion that the E-E implementers have the primary aim to promote the sustainability theme and not so much their institutions. However, this is not the case, specifically

in terms of the entertainment professionals. They behave like that because both parties are aware that their E-E service collaboration is only accepted by common sense when putting the sustainability theme into the foreground and slightly introducing the partnering organizations involved.

The following figure sums up the crucial characteristics and different collaboration stages in German E-E service.

Figure 8.2: Characteristics and stages of E-E service in Germany

Who?	Orientation	Crystallization	Production	Implementation
Entertainment professionals			Scripting, shooting, editing	
Characteristics: • Different approaches to E-E Service • Scaling down gifts and adding new ones	External conditions Internal conditions 'Feeling out', 'putting gifts on the table'	'Bundling gift packages' Contact on the follow up activities	Medium value gift exchange according to the TV program	Broadcasting Medium value gift exchange according to the follow up activities
Sustainability professionals				

8.4 E-E License

License arrangements were defined in chapter 6.4 as 'a strategy of prosocial organizations to have the right to use an existing entertainment program for educational purposes to create awareness about a prosocial issue after it has been broadcasted'. E-E license is a typical collaboration form for Germany. The two potential partner sides exchange in this collaboration type *low value gifts*, i.e. a license fee is paid by the sustainability professionals to receive a license from the TV professionals for integrating the TV program in educational. Moreover, in some cases the gift of sustainability information is also provided.

The next section (8.4.1) portrays significant *characteristics* of E-E license collaborations taking place in Germany. Afterwards, the *stages of collaboration*, that is the production stage (section 8.4.2.1) and implementation stage (section 8.4.2.2) are described with regard to their gift exchange processes and logics.

8.4.1 Characteristics
8.4.1.1 No Strong Partnership Ties
E-E license collaborations have the lowest level of collaboration and that means the activities of the collaboration partners are even further away from the ideal definition of Entertainment-Education (see chapter 2.1) than service collaborations. They only have a few collaboration interfaces. This loose collaboration is due to the fact that they only exchange two low value gifts (and sometimes in addition the sustainability information gift). In the words of one social expert implementing an E-E license, "What was our collaboration? Actually, not that much". This is in contrast to the service collaborations and even more so to the co-productions and inscript participations, where a deep trust level is an essential prerequisite and constant attendant (section 8.2 and 8.3). One social expert explained that he only met the television makers during the orientation stage, and their only contact was through the issues of the license gift exchange. He added that "through the reception of the licenses of the program product, we could develop our media package. You have to read it in that kind of way. It is not like a typical partnership at all, but it is more like when you go into a shopping store and you buy a desk there". This citation makes even clearer how loose the ties in the E-E license collaboration are.

Thus, in a way a legitimate question is whether license can be considered as a collaboration form at all. However, analysis clearly indicates it is, since gifts are exchanged, even though only a few and with low value. Moreover, license arrangements have an essential meaning for Germany's collaboration environment, and the next section will explain why this is the case.

8.4.1.2 Total Compliance with Common Sense
License agreements enable stakeholders to collaborate and thereby avoid any kind of pitfalls which may arise in the other collaboration forms. To successfully handle a service or even a co-production or inscript participation, the collaboration partners need to be careful; they need to be sensitized and furthermore they have to personally contribute to a large extent when interpreting the media legislations and dealing with common sense, zeitgeist and recent circumstances in society (see chapter 7). By applying an E-E license collaboration, the implementers *bypass* dealing with these issues. They have nothing to fear from critical voices coming from common sense, and there is no need to be careful, overly sensitive or reflective in terms of how issues could be interpreted by others. But why is this specifically the case? This is due to the fact that in an E-E license, the implementers can play the game of gift exchange while remaining fully *compatible* with both the media legislations and common sense (i.e. no high value or border-case medium value gifts (chapter 7.3) are exchanged). As one social expert put it, "we never acted as a sponsor. We didn't have any influence on the program content". Through the low value gift exchange, their professional fields do not overlap during the collaboration and only come together when it is necessary to team up and exchange gifts. Thus, they 'leave each other alone while also collaborating'.

Both the implementers from the sustainability and the television side do unequivocally belong to the gift type (section 8.1.2) that is *strictly unwilling to exchange high value gifts* and some are even disapproving of the fact that these gift exchanges take place at all. One social expert stated: "This is the danger: when we want to deliver messages [in the TV program], then we influence the medium. The question is always if the messages we want to bring to the people, if they are always right then. In consequence, I would keep my hand off it. My personal opinion is that one should protect the public from any kind of bad messages, however".

In the interviews and informal talks, the study participants clearly differentiated between 'the others' and their license collaboration form. One sustainability expert indicated that it had never been their interest to participate in the decision making process on the program content in any kind of way, even not to consult the television professionals (section 8.3.2.2). He claimed: "If the audience members switch on their television sets (...), they do not want to be influenced by anybody. Not in any kind of direction whatsoever".

In addition, it is interesting to take into consideration that some of the sustainability organizations practicing an E-E license nowadays had been involved in co-production or inscript participations in the past. In those collaborations, the sustainability organizations got into risky situations with regard to common sense (see chapter 7.3). Furthermore, a PR collaboration where the sustainability side used a partnership with entertainment professionals to make organizational advertising in the program became visible and was negatively sanctioned. In this context, one expert on social themes noted "I think in the past one tried it, but crashed and burned... and... since then one has never done it again". Hence, the main lesson learned out of the risky environment in which co-productions and inscript participations take place was to *orientate oneself into another collaboration direction* by 'being completely on the safe side' with an E-E license form. In contrast to the implementers of E-E co-productions and inscript participations, these stakeholders have no interest in playing with fire and behaving in a *risky* manner. When sustainability experts choose a license collaboration, they indeed do not participate in the decision making process on the program content in any kind of way (which is similar to E-E service). Furthermore, they do not even consult on storylines in the sense that they do proof-read scripts for accuracy or authenticity. Both implementing sides want to *clearly separate* their field of expertise and responsibilities as far as possible in the collaboration, and this means that the sustainability experts do not get involved to any extent in the scripting, shooting or editing, and the television makers do not participate in the follow up activities for engaging target group members in sustainability themes.

8.4.2 Stages of Collaboration in E-E License

After the description of the general characteristics in German E-E licenses, the collaboration stages (production and implementation stage) are depicted with regard to their process and gift exchange structures.

In the orientation stage (section 8.1.1-8.1.2), the two sides have identified that they are the same gift type and (moreover) both interested in a low value gift exchange (which are the license fee, the license for integrating the TV program in educational activities, as well as giving sustainability information). So when the decision has been made to jointly design and implement a license collaboration, both partners normally know what they can expect from each other and what will happen in the single collaboration stages. This gives both partner sides a strong feeling of security. In the crystallization stage, the specific gift packages are bundled (section 8.1.3), which contains the negotiation details regarding the low value gift exchange.

The next sections describe the production stage (section 8.4.2.1) and implementation stage (section 8.4.2.2), whereas – in contrast to co-productions/inscript participations and service – there are no further specific aspects regarding the crystallization stage in an E-E license.

8.4.2.1 Production Stage

In the production stage, the main gift exchange procedure takes place. It is then that the partners exchange the gifts of the *license fee* and the *license* and sometimes the *sustainability information gift*. All three gifts are illustrated as follows.

License Fee and License

These two gifts have two principles in common with the high value gifts of financial support (for the program development) and involvement on the entertainment program, although they follow completely different logics and have different aims. Firstly, both are *determined gift exchanges*. This means that when one of the gifts is given, the other gift (and not another one) must be reciprocated within a specific timeframe.[210] Secondly, both gifts share the fact that the *sustainability experts give financial resources* to the television professionals, and in return the TV professionals reciprocate another gift. However, whereas in the high value gift exchange a high amount of money from the sustainability experts obligates the TV professionals to reciprocate involvement on the program development, a lesser amount of money is given in a license collaboration, because a license fee serves to reciprocate the license and hence the rights for using the produced program for educational purposes. A health expert described the exchange as follows: "What is interesting for us is to offer it to the schools and other pedagogical institutions so that they can use it in their lessons. This means we buy a license, copy it – in former times as a VHS and now as DVD (…) – and then we disseminate it through our distribution system. That is the jargon here. This means that we load federal state, city and local educational media institutions, protestant and catholic media centers, the German film center and so on with such exemplars and with that there goes a license for lending".

---

[210] In other gift exchange procedures the kind of gift is not stipulated – only the obligation to reciprocate.

Receiving the license for the payment of a license fee means for the sustainability organization that they are allowed to use the produced program in a specific time frame (e.g. for two years or forever), in a specific region (e.g. Germany-wide or European-wide) and in a specific mode (e.g. DVD, television) for their educational follow up activities. The longer the time frame of usage, the wider the region for usage and the more modes for which the program can be used by the sustainability organization, the higher the license fee they have to pay the television professionals. According to the course of this gift exchange, some collaborations prefer to do a short contract before implementing the exchange itself, while others carry out the exchange without drawing up a formalized agreement. If a short contract was signed on the gift exchange, this took place in the production phase while the TV program was scripted, shot and edited through the TV makers.

At first, it is the sustainability experts handing out their license fee gift (this can range from 1000 to 3000 euros or even more). The television makers usually receive this gift when the program is being shot or edited. Frequently, sustainability experts *reciprocate their license gift* shortly before the broadcast of the program. However, there was one collaboration where the license was reciprocated several months after the broadcast. This special case was largely due to a delaying tactic by the television professionals and happened for the two following reasons: firstly, the sustainability experts presented the license fee and hoped to soon receive the license gift for their media package (chapter 6.6) in return. What they did not expect or forgot to take into consideration was that they had implemented an E-E production which was involved in the same media package, and this production also contained 60 seconds of the original TV program for which they had purchased the license. The sustainability experts had failed to inform the television makers about this use and to consider this in the context of their license fee gift (which would have been a higher amount of money than they handed out originally). Thus, the television makers got a bit upset and delayed their gift in return. The sustainability expert from this collaboration said: "There were several media people shaking their fingers and saying 'You are not allowed to do this' and they threw a monkey wrench into our plans (...). This caused a delay of more than eight months (...). Well, we reminded them over and over again about the situation and asked them which decision they had made (...). This got on our nerves, because we took money for producing that thing and then it comes up to 60 seconds of moved material for introducing it to the market. That was... difficult I must say". The second reason why the television professionals took their time was that they also had had an interest in implementing the commissioned E-E production of the sustainability organization for the media package, but at the last minute the sustainability experts had decided against them and engaged another production company. Mauss (Mauss, 1990a: 26) also considers the case of a *delayed gift in return*. He found that the recipient often times hands out a standby gift, as a kind of delay interest, which does not complete the exchange case, but serves to temporarily appease the presenter. In the collaboration case, the television professionals did not hand over a real standby gift. Rather they verbally appeased the sustainability experts by saying that they were working on this case and asked for a bit more patience. Nevertheless, undoubtedly they consciously put off reciprocating their gift in order to 'pay them back'.

Television professionals, who were engaged in a license collaboration, furthermore noted that in their eyes, there is no real equality in the gift exchange (of license and license fee) at all, because they give away the license for a small amount of money (see above) which cannot be considered an additional support for the program development at all. One TV producer stated that, "The important condition for that [media package] has been that we give up our rights. This can mean a lot of money, if it is repeated so and so often (…). The broadcasting station also gives up its broadcasting rights (…) it is a limitation if the DVD is everywhere available for free in schools". However, the television professionals added in this context that they found it important to nevertheless engage in this gift transaction, because they believed in the 'greater good' that the media package could achieve by reaching additional target group members with sustainability messages. It is this ideal additional value that makes the gift exchange more or less equivalent for them at all. One TV professional said, "What they wanted right from the start, was to [go] into the schools, and this was why I found the idea very good, to do something together with Mr. Dander, using a kind of education platform". Clearly, the anti-utilitarianistic motive of 'acting for a good cause' comes into play here (see chapter 7.2).

Giving Sustainability Information
Besides the exchange of license fees and licenses, another gift can be handed out by the sustainability experts: the **gift of giving sustainability information**. Interestingly, this gift has a relation to the communication consultation gift in E-E service, but it can also be separated from it. The consultation gift includes two parts, as described in chapter 8.3.2.2. The first part contains a consultation before the scriptwriter starts to work on the scripts (passing on information and doing brainstorming sessions) and then a second part which consists of a consultation at an advanced stage, where the first draft of the script is written and the sustainability experts then make suggestions on the authenticity and accuracy of the depiction. The sustainability information gift in a way mirrors a fragment of the first part of the consultation gift and primarily aims at informing the television side about the sustainability subject through fact-sheets, web links, leaflets, etc. before they start writing the scripts. However, brainstorming sessions or workshops on the sustainability content, such as in the service collaboration form, are regularly not implemented between both sides.

Beyond that it became clear that the sustainability experts as well as the television professionals are willing to share a sustainable information gift, but only a few could imagine receiving or giving advice. Others saw a line being crossed when they were asked whether they could also imagine implementing a consultation on the accuracy and authenticity of the portrayal of the script content. For instance, one TV producer stated in this regard "I find this critical". A social expert expressed in an informal talk that involvement in the program content is a 'no go' and for him personally also a consultation gift itself. When they were asked about their reasons, several implementers mentioned that they wanted to be 'on the complete safe side' with their actions. Some sustainability experts also noted that involvement in the program could start with a kind of 'editing consultation' and that they wanted to avoid it[211] because of the bad experiences some of the others had made in the past. These principles of thinking are very interesting and show how strongly common sense and zeitgeist impact the E-E implementers. They are aware of the fact that they have to justify and legitimize their actions with regard to common sense when talking about a consultation instead of only saying, 'We gave them some information (e.g. leaflets) and that was it'. Obviously, to 'only' give sustainability information defines an even clearer line between the two professional fields and their activities in contrast to a consultation, which needs to have the justification of a practice included about what exactly has taken place during the script consultation (chapter 7.3.7 and section 8.3.2.2).

The gift of giving sustainability information can (but must not) be included in the gift exchange process, such as the license fee and the license. It is an optional gift. A crucial reason for this also may be that in several of the license collaborations analyzed, the television professionals did not need sustainability information anymore, because they were about to script the program or they were even a step further in the shooting when the collaboration was initiated.

8.4.2.2 Implementation Stage

In the implementation stage the television program is broadcasted and the broadcasting is used as a starting point for the follow up activities. The sustainability experts implement their follow up activities for promoting sustainability themes on their own. This is due to the strict separation of their professional fields and expertise, both of which play an essential role in the E-E license.

These follow up activities are akin to those in E-E co-productions and inscript participations. The difference is that in license collaborations, the activities are regularly focused on creating a media package (see chapter 6.6) and providing it to the public for rental for educational institutions national-wide, whereas in co-productions and inscript participations, other educational activities can be traced besides the media packages itself (section 8.2.2.3).

When it comes to the follow up activities of E-E service, they clearly differ from those of E-E license. The service activities are more measures affecting the public through events, discussion rounds, etc. and aim to catch the public with the theme while also stimulating their affective notions. Thus, in a way, the license activities are more educationally focused and have fewer entertaining components. This res-

---

[211] This point strongly picks up on the discussions on media legislation in chapter 6.1 and the question of where involvement or influence on the program content starts. Indeed, this cannot be objectively answered.

ults from the fact that in an E-E license the television makers regularly play no role (comparable to E-E co-productions and inscript participations) in the follow up activities, whereas in E-E service, balance between education and entertainment is more overt due to the participation of the television professionals who may also be in charge of some activities. There may also be follow up activities in an E-E license, which both sides jointly implement. However, they are commonly not framed like that in order to strengthen each side's own approaches, expertise and independence. For example, during one license collaboration the premiere of the television program took place in a movie theater before the regular broadcasting date. The program was shown to a selected audience. At this premiere, the production (for the media package) implemented by the sustainability experts was also introduced as a supporting movie. So in a way it was a joint follow up event, though the partners did not like the idea to be framed as such. One expert on social themes mentioned: "Well, we [TV and sustainability side] did... actually it wasn't us, but rather the television makers, who were behind the premiere event at the movie theater. Addressed were the general public, well... I would not say the general public, but more regional people instead were addressed, and they watched the program". After more in-depth questioning he added as a side note: "And at the premiere, the making-off which we had commissioned was shown as well".

Lastly, it is important to stress that in this collaboration form no summative and formative research is applied with regard to the program or with regard to the follow up communication measures. However, the sustainability experts stressed that they found the perspective interesting in the context of the program content but even more the impact studies with regard to their follow up activities.

The following figure gives an overview of how the E-E license collaboration proceeds.

Figure 8.3: Characteristics and stages of E-E license collaborations in Germany

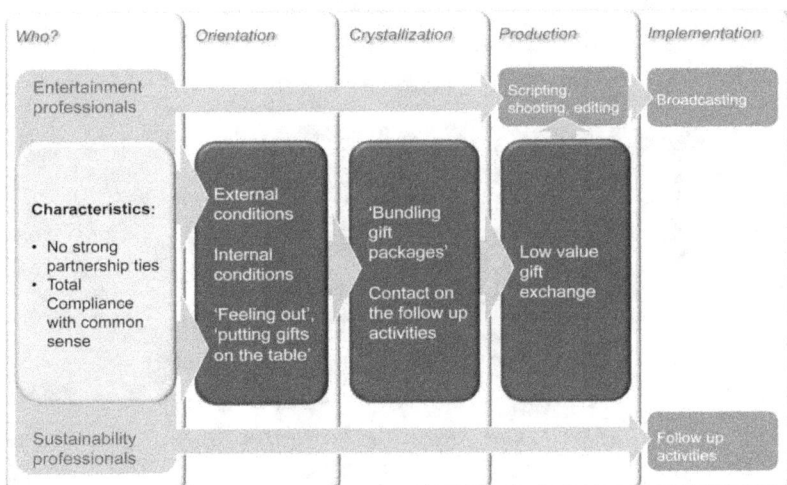

8.5 Integrative Model: Condition and Forms of E-E Collaborations in Germany

In chapter 6 central conditions and characteristics of E-E were depicted, whereas chapter 7 focused on the place of gift exchange (E-E collaboration field), common sense according to the Third Reich experience and the media and zeitgeist according to the Third Reich experience and the media. It was shown that the place of gift exchange has a multilayer relationship with common sense and zeitgeist. Chapter 8 focuses in depth on the activities at the place of gift exchange in E-E co-production/inscript participation, E-E service and E-E license collaborations in Germany.

The following integrative model of conditions and forms of E-E collaborations in Germany refers to the central outcomes of the study and sums up the results of the chapters 6 to 8.

Figure 8.4: Integrative model of conditions and forms of E-E in Germany

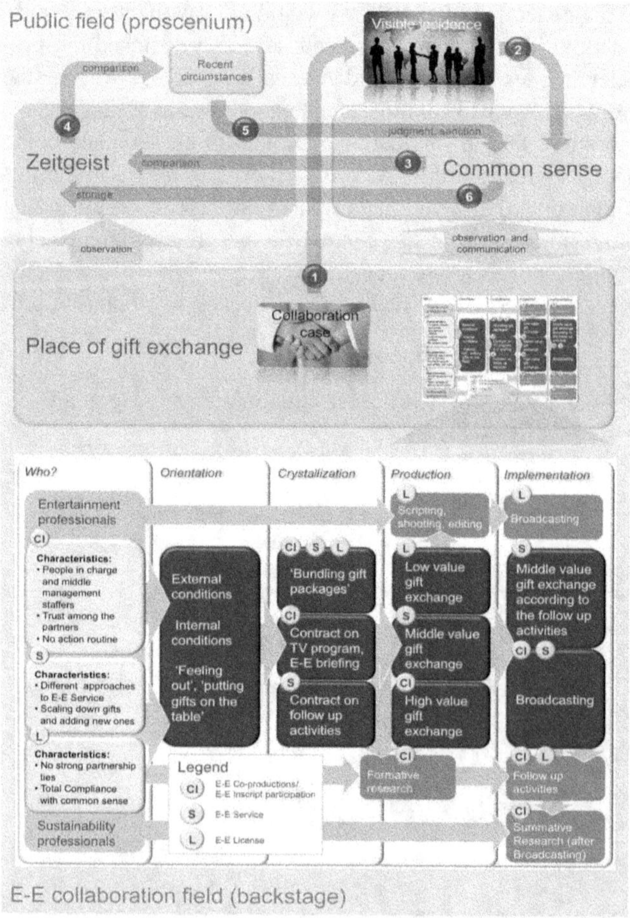

8.6 Critical Reflection on the E-E Collaboration Forms in Germany

Each of the four E-E collaboration forms illustrated for the German environment of course has its advantages and disadvantages. From a prosocial change perspective, the chance is best to effectively reach media users with sustainability messages when E-E co-productions or inscript participations can be designed and implemented. In these collaboration forms, E-E theory and research can be comprehensively applied to ensure the highest sustainability impact possible. Thus, it may be very desirable to increasingly apply these collaboration forms. But for this to happen, several restrictions need to be considered: for the research theme examined in this thesis – a theme which covers collaborations in public and commercial television – their implementation is critically viewed in public. Furthermore, these collaboration forms are in a legislative grey zone where nobody can be sure when exactly the legal borders are crossed. Nonetheless, this does not change the issue of the potential for the great amount of change which can be achieved through these collaboration forms. For Germany, the questions to be asked are: (1) in which media formats might it be effective to design and implement co-productions and inscript participations? And (2) how can German experts from sustainability organizations gain (more) expertise in how to set up an E-E intervention and guide it with research measurements? Both questions will be dealt with in chapter 9.

The advantage of E-E service collaborations in the German environment is that they can be designed and implemented in compliance with the media legislation. The public completely accepts this collaboration form, especially when it is well separated from the high value gift exchange of financial resources for involvement in the program content. From a prosocial change point of view, a disadvantage of E-E service is that, unlike in co-productions and inscript participations, it is challenging to comprehensively apply the theoretical foundation and research activities to it. As a result, there is less of a chance to effectively reach audience members with sustainability messages. In the German collaboration environment, the challenge is to bring the recent practice activities up to more of a research-based level, such as it is the case in the USA, where collaboration activities are strategically created and research activities comprehensively guide the collaboration activities. Germany also needs to develop more capacities and expertise here (chapter 9).

The German-specific E-E license collaborations conform completely with media legislation and since the implementers are completely on the safe side, this is perhaps why this form is used in television collaborations. From a prosocial change perspective, less impact can be exerted on the audience members, because the sustainability organization is not involved in any way in the TV format. Still, they can try to reach their target group through the follow up activities they are implementing. The formation of a research-based foundation would enhance the recent practice. That would mean examining how the TV makers 'did their job' to reach the audience members with a sustainability theme and looking at how far the follow up activities from the sustainability organization managed to increase the impact on the audience members (chapter 9). As the expected impact is higher in service and even higher in co-productions and inscript participations than in the E-E license collaboration, funders might primarily be interested in gaining research results in these collaboration forms rather than in an E-E license.

8.7 Summary

In Germany, four different forms of E-E collaborations can be composed at the place of gift exchange: co-productions, inscript participations, services and licenses. All of these forms have been applied in recent times, whereas co-productions and inscript participation more often took place in the 1990s and early 2000s and are nowadays less implemented due to developments in common sense and zeitgeist – developments which entail pointing at incidents which are considered to be 'critical examples'. Hence, if at present times, co-productions and inscript participations are designed and implemented, it is even harder to detect them, because the collaborations are taking place even more on the 'backstage' (Goffman, 2000).

All collaboration forms share three qualities: (1) they go through the same sharpened *orientation stage*, (2) they concretize their gifts (i.e. bundle them into gift packages) in the *crystallization stage* and (3) they implement **high, medium or low value gift exchange procedures** in the production and the implementation stage, depending on the collaboration form.

Regarding the *orientation phase*, it was pointed out that *internal* as well as *external conditions* strongly influence the willingness to exchange different gifts of a certain value, and thus they play a decisive role in the *first (and follow up) face-to-face meeting(s)*. In the *first meeting*, the potential partners go through the phase of 'feeling out' their counterparts and 'putting the gifts on the table'. This is an essential and critical phase, because then they have to find out if they *fit with each other*. Thus, everything and nothing is possible depending on whether their ideas are in line to each other or not. Both parties have to 'play with all of their cards on the table' and communicate which *gift type* they are (i.e. they have to reveal which gifts – high, medium or low value – they are willing to exchange), and furthermore they need to find this out from the counterpart. Therefore, they play a strategic game and apply different communication strategies to presenting and framing their potential gifts. Two different strategies, that of *the latent gift presenter and that of the apparent gift presenter,* were outlined. If the potential partners overcome this critical phase and find out that they are interested in similar gift exchanges, they move onward to the next phase: the *crystallization stage*. In this stage the *follow up face-to-face meetings* take place and the gifts are more clearly articulated. In this phase, the gifts which, up to this point, have been lying on the table, are summarized and thus 'bundled into packages' so that each side clearly knows which gifts they can expect from the counterpart and what is expected from them. These bundled gift packages regularly amount to approximately the same value for each side.

In *co-productions and inscript participations*, high value gifts (financial support for the program development and participation in the decision making process on the program and its content) are exchanged. These two gifts are predetermined gifts (i.e. when one of the gifts is given and received, the other gift – and no other – must be reciprocated in return). Another characteristic of both collaboration types is that they are crucially influenced by *single case decisions* of the *people in charge* from both the television as well as the sustainability side. In addition, these two forms are marked by a *deep level of trust* between the collaborating parties. They have to trust that the counterpart is at least as well versed as themselves and that they are well informed and know the 'internal rules of the game', because otherwise, the high value gift exchange can become visible in common sense, which might cause troubles for both. Thus, a *risky and illegal* (in terms of influence on the program content) *collaboration environment* is characteristic for these collaboration forms.

In the *crystallization stage* an *E-E contract* is made regarding the *high value gift exchange*. In this contract, the responsibilities of the partners are laid out, the issues related to the television program itself (e.g. the rights) are identified and the specific agreements on the gift exchange procedure (e.g. conditions of payment, etc.) are clarified. In addition, the partners do *E-E briefings* in this stage in order to become more aware of the other side's aims and objectives. In the *production stage,* the high value gift exchange itself proceeds so that a differentiation can be made between gifts of a low(er) financial contribution and involvement on the program content or gifts of a higher financial value and involvement on the program content. In the latter case, the sustainability experts are the main financiers of the television program. This leads to the same level of participation in the decision-making process on the program development as the television professionals, and this can create a tense collaborative situation, according to Bouman (1999). When a low(er) financial gift is handed out by the sustainability experts (i.e. they are not the main financiers), they have a lower level of involvement in the program development and the television professionals clearly have more decision making power. In the final *implementation stage*, both partners commonly broadcast the program. However, afterwards the sustainability experts move forward alone to realize follow up activities for the target groups. They focus on educational measures such as media packages, and they implement additional activities such as periodical discussion forums, learning trips, etc. Besides the educational follow up activities, the sustainability experts conduct *summative research*. Strangely enough they are usually not published. If they are, the results may be accessible on an organizational platform, but they are generally not freely available for a broader scientific community (e.g. in journals or books) or for the wider public. Therefore, it is difficult to say something about the design of these studies or reports.

E-E service is a collaboration form which has been specifically applied in recent years. It is a good alternative to co-productions and inscript participations, because it conforms completely with media legislation. In E-E service *medium value gifts* are bartered, but none of the gifts require a preset gift in return (such as in the high value gift exchange).

The anticipated value of the gifts discussed and included in the gift packages in the ***crystallization stage*** can also change a bit in an advanced collaboration stage (i.e. gifts can be scrapped or added). Finally, the ***value of the gifts needs to stay approximately the same*** during the whole collaboration process. In this stage, E-E implementers make, if required, contracts on the follow up activities.

Afterwards, they move onward to the ***production stage***, in which the television professionals are completely responsible for the scripting, shooting and editing of the program. Normally, there are mainly two gifts, which are exchanged: the sustainability communication gift and the guest part gift. Both gifts can (but do not have to) be coercively exchanged.

In the ***implementation stage***, further profound exchanges of medium value gifts take place with regard to the follow up activities in order to reach audience members with the sustainability theme (in addition to the television program). Therefore, both the sustainability experts and the television professionals work together and implement public-orientated activities such as events, discussion rounds, meet-and-greets with the actresses and actors. In this stage, further gifts can be exchanged: whereas the sustainability experts can hand out the gift of networks/contacts, logistical support and organizational know-how as well as patronage and reliability, the entertainment professionals can give celebrity endorsements as a gift. Furthermore, both sides may exchange a PR gift to advertise the sustainability theme and thereby at least profit along with their organizations from the positive public feedback they regularly receive. Since both parties implement the follow up activities together, the mixture of entertaining and educational elements can be described as more balanced than the follow up activities of co-productions and inscript participations. Finally, neither formative nor summative research has been included so far in service collaborations.

In ***E-E license,*** the exchange includes only a few gifts with a low value. The collaboration form stands in complete contrast to the co-productions and inscript participations, as the implementers' professional fields and expertise only have a few interfaces. In a way, they leave each other alone whenever possible and collaborate in terms of gift exchange, whenever they think it is necessary. Both the television professionals and the sustainability experts want to avoid risk and they aim to be on the safe side with their collaboration. That is to say, they want to bypass pitfalls and troubles which might arise in the other collaboration forms.

In the ***production stage*** of E-E license collaborations, the gifts of license fees and license as well as the gift of sustainability information are exchanged. Whereas the latter gift given by the sustainability experts is optional in this collaboration form, the other two gifts are predetermined gifts as was the case in the high value gift exchange.

During the ***implementation stage,*** the sustainability experts also try to reach their target groups without the help of the television makers, which is similar to co-productions and inscript participations. Their follow up approach usually includes a media package, which can be accessed via public educational media institutions. As in E-E service, there are no research activities involved in this collaboration form.

Epilogue II
Conclusions and Lessons Learned

This section provides an overview regarding the practice, experience and the lessons learned from the E-E collaboration processes in Germany as analyzed in part II of this thesis (chapter 5-8), and thus seeks to answer the main research question *'What are the conditions and forms for Entertainment-Education collaborations between entertainment television professionals and sustainability experts from governmental (related) authorities?'* through answering the following two sub-questions:

B1 *Researching conditional collaboration factors*: What are significant conditions (i.e. external and internal conditions as well as crucial characteristics) of present E-E collaborations in Germany which influence the collaboration process?

B2 *Investigating collaboration practices and their forms in depth*: Based on the conditions and characteristics, how can the present collaboration process between sustainability experts and television professionals in Germany be described in different forms and stages with regard to the development and implementation of collaborations?

Conditional Collaboration Factors and Characteristics (Sub-question B1)

E-E collaborations are implemented in a very complex system or environment of conditions and characteristics. An important – perhaps the most important – *external condition* influencing E-E practice behavior is the relevant media legislation. This has a crucial influence on how the collaboration practice proceeds. The main characteristic of *media legislation rules* has been described as both contradictory and multilayer. E-E implementers could not clearly infer whether payments for supporting the program content are allowed and it is not clear to what extent the sustainability experts can participate in the decision making process on the program development without overstepping the border line into 'illegality'. This fosters a complicated starting point for stakeholders interested in an E-E partnership. Another external condition, which the analysis has revealed to be important for the E-E collaboration practice activities are *current developments in the television and sustainability field*. In the television field several conditions were found which are beneficial to fostering E-E collaborations in Germany. These conditions include an increased focus on 'entertainization' on the market as well as the demand for increased accuracy and an authentic entertainment television depiction, both of which may be supported and satisfied through the expertise of sustainability professionals. Nevertheless, within the sustainability field there are still many barriers. Those barriers include the difficulty of reaching the E-E main target groups, the fear of losing one's respective reputation when working with the entertainment field and the persuasive character of the E-E strategy causing divergent opinions due to Germany's bad experience during the Third Reich with entertainment propaganda. All of these factors currently contribute to a conservative application of the E-E approach.

With regard to *internal conditions* for E-E practice, it became obvious that the *field logics and motives* of the television professionals and sustainability experts play a decisive role as a collaboration prerequisite. Indeed, because of their different professional working standards television professionals and sustainability experts often encounter difficulties while working together. Moreover, in part II of the thesis, applying theory and research in E-E collaborations as well as follow up activities were depicted as also having a crucial impact in partnership processes.

E-E Collaboration in Practice (Sub-question B2)

Based on the conditions and characteristics, it was argued that E-E practice proceeds on the *place of gift exchange*. This can be considered the heart of E-E collaboration processes in practice. For illustrating the actions in this field, the *gift theory of Mauss* strongly guided and supported the research subject in gaining more insight into the 'hows and whys' of E-E collaborations. At the heart of Mauss' theory is the gift exchange process, which is voluntary and at the same time obligatory. Given this background, this thesis regards E-E implementers as stakeholders who voluntarily and obligatorily exchange gifts in their collaborations. By the end of the collaboration, both sides need to perceive the gifts as amounting to equivalent values. E-E implementers give, receive and reciprocate 14 different gifts which have various characteristics and thus are, for example, specifically given by only one partner side or only exchanged in certain collaboration forms. Through the theoretical enhancement carried out by the M.A.U.S.S. group, which centered around Caillé, it became more obvious that E-E collaborations are a kind of hybrid form between the principles of archaic societies, which Mauss preliminary portrayed, and postmodern society forms in the sense that: (1) arguing from the archaic perspective, in E-E collaborations persons and things are still hybrid and anti-utilitarianistic and both are characteristic of archaic societal forms and (2) arguing from the perspective of postmodern societies, trade and market thoughts rule societal behavior, and indeed this is also predominant in E-E partnerships. Based on this *hybrid argument* and following the M.A.U.S.S. group argument line, E-E collaborations are considered to be vacuums in which gift exchanges circulate between the poles of *voluntariness, obligation, interest and anti-utilitarianism.* The stipulated task of this thesis has been to describe this circulation processes in practice on the place of gift exchange for each collaboration form, which was the focus of chapter 8.

Furthermore, it was pointed out that the place of gift exchange is crucially influenced by two other fields, *common sense* as well as *zeitgeist according to the Third Reich experience and the media.* Common sense represents a critical populace which sanctions E-E implementers positively and negatively when a collaboration becomes visible or is communicated according to the different gifts exchanged in the collaboration – some are accepted, while others are not. Zeitgeist represents feelings and thoughts of a society; it is a collective memory in which happenings and incidents related to Germany's media experience and 'external influences' are stored. Zeitgeist refers to a time frame of a whole century. Common sense makes its decisions on the basis of zeitgeist and the E-E implementers' main aim is to behave in accordance with the judgments of common sense.

E-E Collaboration Forms and Stages (Sub-question B2)

In Germany's E-E collaboration practice, four different collaboration forms can be traced: co-productions, inscript participations, services and licenses, although the last one seems to be a specific form implemented in Germany since it has not been referred to by international E-E literature so far. In all four collaboration forms, the implementers go through the same *orientation and crystallization stage* of collaboration in which *first (and follow up) face-to-face meeting(s)* take place in order to find out from the counterpart which gift type she or he fits into (i.e. finding out if the counterpart is willing to exchange high, medium or low value gifts), because this determines the form of collaboration. There are two communication strategies for finding this out. The main difference between these two strategies is the way the gifts and aims are put on the table, i.e. whether the objectives are presented more *latent* or *apparent*. As the gift type and the gift presenter can differ between the potential partners, it is not easy to find a fitting partner for E-E collaborations and compromises need to be made. Otherwise potential partnerships may also fall apart.

In *co-productions and inscript participations,* high value gifts are exchanged. For both collaborations forms, the role of the E-E professionals as the people in charge and as the ones who implement single case decisions in accordance to the happenings in common sense and zeitgeist is of paramount importance. Furthermore, these collaboration forms are characterized through a risky collaboration environment, because finances are handed out and, in return, involvement in the decision making process on the program content is reciprocated as a gift. This arrangement is not accepted by common sense. Indeed, in these collaboration forms the partners need to rely on and trust each other deeply. In the crystallization stage, the E-E contract, the E-E briefings are implemented and in the production stage, the high value gift exchange takes place. At that point, a distinction between high finance and influence and low(er) finances and influence gifts needs to be made. In the implementation stage, the sustainability experts permute follow up activities with an educational focus and they also establish summative research activities.

E-E services can be applied through a constant approach in which one sustainability organization uses a service strategy to reach several television broadcasting stations and productions companies with sustainability messages with a variety of themes over an indefinite time frame (similar to Hollywood, Health & Society, chapter 4.2). An E-E service can also be applied as an occasional approach in which one sustainability organization teams up with one partner regularly on an existing program for a specific time frame and a specific theme. In the latter approach, the partner sides exchange medium value gifts and, after finishing the orientation stage, they move onward to the crystallization stage and to the production stage. During the scripting, shooting and editing in the production stage, the sustainability experts are not involved content-wise. Nonetheless, in this phase the gift exchange process, which consists of the sustainability consultation gift and the guest part, is played out. The implementation phase is then denoted through further comprehensive gift exchange procedures with regard to public-orientated follow up activities, which the sustainability and the television partners commonly implement. In E-E services, no research activities have been conducted so far.

In *E-E licenses* there are only a few exchange activities, which exclusively include low value gifts. This is due to the fact that the implementers want to strictly separate their professional fields as much as possible. Thus, both sides act conform to the media legislation and common sense, as low value gifts are tolerated. While partners of other collaboration forms need to be careful and reflective, the license implementers have nothing to fear. After finishing the orientation and crystallization stage, the partners move forward to the production stage where the gift of the license fee and the license for integrating program content in educational activities are exchanged as is the optional gift of sustainability information. The implementation stage of license is similar to the one of co-productions and inscript participations in the sense that only the sustainability experts get active in the context of promoting follow up activities with a strong educational focus. In E-E licenses, no research activities have been implemented yet.

9. Theoretical Concept on Entertainment-Education Collaborations in Germany, Discussion and Recommendations

> "Serendipitous discoveries are always made by people in a particular frame of mind, people who are focused and alert because they are searching for something. They just happen to find something else".
>
> - Steven Strogatz, Sync, cited by Arvind Singhal and Karen Greiner 2010: 47

Part I of this thesis analyzed theoretical debates and good practice center approaches in Entertainment-Education and with that information established sensitizing concepts for the German collaboration field. Part II portrayed the conditions, characteristics and forms of E-E collaborations. For each of these parts, epilogues I and II summed up the most crucial outcomes. Nonetheless, to holistically answer the main research question regarding conditions, characteristics and forms of E-E collaborations, this thesis will deal in this final chapter with the following remaining sub-question:

B3 Developing a theoretical concept and making recommendations for the future: Based on the conditions, characteristics and forms, how can the theoretical concept of E-E collaborations in Germany be summarized and what are the best recommendations for the German collaboration context when managing E-E collaborations in the future?

9.1 The Research Subject Paradigm and Theoretical Concept

In order to present a theoretical concept as a summary of part II of this thesis, which might also serve as a basis when providing recommendations for future E-E developments, the paradigm mentioned in the context of the conditional/consequential matrix in chapter 5.4.5 will be applied:

Action motives and aims resulting from the field logics of the sustainability and television professionals as well as media legislations and the current developments in the sustainability and television field (conditions) lead to circumstances that connect both sides, so that they may negotiate collaboration options in which high, medium or low value gifts are exchanged. By choosing the type of gift exchange as being of high, medium or low value, they decide on one of the four collaboration forms – co-production, inscript participation, service or license – which in the end lead to specific rules and logics that they apply in the gift exchange practice (consequence).

Given this background, the ***theoretical concept of E-E collaborations in Germany*** can be described as follows:

(1) Implementing ***E-E co-productions and E-E inscript participations*** on the place of gift exchange means performing a high value gift exchange of finances in return for involvement in the decision making process on the program content. This gift exchange should not become visible to common sense according to the Third Reich experience and the media. Consequently, this means collaborating in a high-risk context in order to purposely and jointly design and implement an entertainment program. The sustainability experts design the follow up activities on their own and apply research activities. As the research activities often serve as internal organizational studies, they are not made accessible to a broader scientific community (through journals, etc.), and thus no clear statement can be made about the research design and implementation.

(2) Realizing an ***E-E service*** means first deciding whether to implement a constant or occasional approach. For the ***constant approach***, further research needs to be done in order to infer clear results as well as cause and effect statements. Implementing an ***occasional approach*** on the place of gift exchange means carrying out a medium value gift exchange in which the sustainability partners consult on the development of the program content. This must be strongly separated from the high value gift exchange, so as to not be sanctioned negatively by common sense according to the Third Reich experience and the media. Moreover, both parties develop and implement public-orientated follow up measurements. Research activities have not been yet included in this collaboration form.

(3) Implementing an ***E-E license*** on the place of gift exchange means performing a low value gift exchange in which the license fee and, in return, the license are bartered. This exchange is completely compatible with common sense according to the Third Reich experience and the media. The implementers separate their professional fields as much as possible from each other during the collaboration, and the sustainability experts design and implement follow up activities on their own behalf. Research activities have not been realized so far in this collaboration form.

9.2 Consequences for E-E Definition

In chapter 2.1, a reformulated definition of Entertainment-Education was established: "Entertainment-Education is a theory-based communication strategy in which educational and entertainment professionals purposefully embed prosocial issues in the creation, production, processing, and dissemination process of an entertainment program in order to achieve different stages of change either on individual, community, institutional or societal level among the intended media user populations" (based on Wang & Singhal 2009: 272-273). In chapter 6.5.1 it was stressed that this definition is an ideal one. Especially E-E co-productions and in-script participations in non-western countries as well as in the Netherlands are designed and implemented according to the described content. However, as became clear through the results of the German analysis, Germany's E-E practice is by contrast further away from this ideal type. Thus, this definition only fits to some extent and only for the **minority of collaboration cases** taking place in Germany, i.e. for co-productions and inscript participations – and if these forms are practiced, the theory-based elements of the definition (see chapter 2) are not yet applied (according to the study results).

The analysis in part II of the thesis indicated that service as well as license collaboration activities play a crucial role in Germany's TV collaboration environment, more than co-productions and inscript participations. However, in Germany, E-E service has a low, and E-E license (see chapter 6.5.1) an even lower level of agreement with the ideal E-E definition mentioned above.

Following this unique situation, two lines of argument are possible (in the eyes of the author) when dealing with these conflicting elements. The first argument is that service and license collaborations cannot be considered as Entertainment-Education, specifically because the ideal E-E definition mentioned above as well as other internationally established ones (Brown & Singhal, 1999; Singhal, 2004) exclude Germany's E-E service and license activities from the field of Entertainment-Education.

Or, the second possible argument is that it is useful to expand the ideal E-E definition and to establish other E-E definitions in order to encounter a more holistic picture of collaboration activities as well as the collaboration approaches which have recently been established in practice.

Through having the results of the analysis in Germany, this thesis argues that it might be recommendable to expand the scope of an E-E definition to other collaboration activities. It needs to be taken into consideration that the established ideal E-E definition as well as other prominent ones (Brown & Singhal, 1999; Singhal & Rogers 1999) are specifically applicable for non-western countries. Furthermore, as has become clear, these definitions are also well-suited for the Netherlands, where collaboration activities are mainly applied in the forms of co-productions and inscript participations. But what about collaboration activities in other western countries? What about the service collaborations in the USA?[212] And, what about the results for Germany? These collaboration activity results have not yet been integrated into the discourse of academic E-E definitions. Conclusively, these developments and outcomes should be integrated into more recent E-E definitions. Also,

---

[212] In recent years, Hollywood, Health & Society has started to frame their activities increasingly as 'Entertainment-Education'. For example, its new logo, which was launched in 2009, now explicitly incorporates the term Entertainment-Education. However, the integration of their E-E service approach into a new, broader scientific definition of the term Entertainment-Education has not taken place so far.

an E-E definition should take the results of this thesis into account. These results contribute to the German context by examining the question of how sustainability experts proceed when they want to collaborate with entertainment television professionals in order to bring their sustainability theme more into the forefront and to engage regularly 'unreachable' (Schwender et al., 2008) media users with it. Here, in the final chapter of this thesis, are different ways of how Entertainment-Education can be practiced are summarized, based on the results of the German analysis:
"Entertainment-Education is, in the best collaboration circumstances, a theory-driven communication strategy in which sustainability professionals from the educational field and entertainment TV professionals team up to:
1. *exchange financial resources for involvement in the decision making process on the program content. This means purposefully and jointly embedding sustainability issues in the creation, production, processing and dissemination of an entertainment program through the collaboration forms of* **co-production and inscript participation**.
2. *exchange services (e.g. consultations, networks/contacts) (a) to depict a sustainability theme in the TV program more accurately and authentically and (b) to jointly foster the sustainability theme in follow up activities through the collaboration form of* **service**.
3. *exchange the license of a program with sustainability content for a license fee and then use this program for educational purposes through the collaboration form of* **license**".

In all forms of collaborations, the sustainability side wants to achieve desired stages of individual, community, institutional or societal changes among the intended media user populations. The television professionals' main aim is to achieve high audience ratings; they also want to transmit authentic and accurate sustainability information from which the audience can learn something.

This German related E-E summary may serve as a discussion basis and should be advanced using results on the collaboration processes and activities from other western countries.

9.3 Discussion and Recommendations for Future E-E Developments

Based on the analysis results from part II, the following section will serve to discuss and provide recommendations for future E-E developments in Germany. How could the process be designed and implemented to effectively foster E-E collaborations in Germany? Which forms should preferably be applied? Which strategies should be used? For answering these and other questions, the next sections' task will be to point at some piloting options, which must be explored and guided through research. Clearly, final responses are not possible yet and need to be developed through the process, but one can at least come closer to answering these questions through experimenting with Entertainment-Education, such as it has also been done in the American and the Dutch cases.

The discussion and the recommendations regarding E-E future partnership developments will focus on the fields of (1) the collaborative environment (including ethical discussion), (2) the agenda setting process, presenting ideas of how Entertainment-Education can be made more assessable (expertise and trainings; positive deviance approach) and (3) collaboration activities, all three of which had been focused in chapter 4. The approach of depicting Germany's discussion results using the same three themes will serve to create a framework for Germany, which is more comparable to the portrayals of the US and Dutch good practice approaches.

9.3.1 Collaborative Environment
9.3.1.1 Entertainment-Education Collaboration Forms and relating Media Channels

Although striving to have the highest level of collaboration possible on the development of a sustainability program, the current collaboration environment indicates that it is not an option to explore possibilities for ***co-productions and inscript participations*** in broadcasted TV programs in Germany. These collaborations may be considered 'too risky' for potential implementers. The challenges rest on the contradictory media legislation and the questions of how far sustainability organizations may be allowed to (a) financially support the production of the program and (b) be a part of the decision making process on the program content. The situation is complicated, because these collaboration forms are not accepted by common sense according to the Third Reich experience and the media (see chapter 7.3).

Thus, one crucial and interesting question to bring up may be to ask about the circumstances under which Germany would accept the design and implementation of E-E co-productions and inscript participations. One circumstance may be using *other media channels* for the collaboration and then implementing partnerships not in broadcasted TV programs (the research focus in this thesis) but, for example, in web 2.0 formats such as the *Sound* project from the Center for Media & Health (see chapter 4.3.5). In this way, partnerships could be implemented and the jointly designed program for sustainability communication purposes could be aired without the above-mentioned restrictions. Obviously, when developing and implementing E-E co-productions or inscript participations on web 2.0, other challenges occur, such as the question of how to effectively address the media users for visiting the webpage on which the program for sustainability purposes is aired. Furthermore, via internet, fewer media users are reached than with a broadcasted TV program. These and other observations also need to be taken into account. In summary, co-productions and inscript participations are not a feasible collaboration form for broadcasted TV programs in Germany. Nonetheless, other circumstances need to be explored through piloting research projects and guiding research activities (also see section 9.3.2) which answer the question in how far it may become possible to apply co-productions and inscript participations in a legal media legislation framework while, at the same time, being culturally accepted.

In contrast to the co-productions and inscript participations, *service and license collaborations* are not in conflict with the media legislations and they are culturally accepted. Thus, recommendations can be given to team up in both collaboration forms designed and implemented in broadcasted TV programs.

It depends on the implementers themselves and the gifts, they are willing to exchange in a partnership, whether they decide for either an E-E service or an E-E license. The medium value gifts exchanged in a service collaboration include the small risk of the potential implementers being negatively sanctioned when they do not clearly separate the consultation gift from the gift of involvement in the program development. By being aware of this separation issue and by acting in accordance to it, the implementers can minimize this risk. If they are not willing to take this risk and prefer to be completely on the safe side, then they team up in a license collaboration.

A recommendable approach in E-E service is to *implement occasional approaches*, where one sustainability organization works together with one production or broadcasting team in one or several program episodes that depict a sustainability theme for a definite time frame. Another recommended option is to explore further service collaboration activities through a *constant approach*, which is in its infancy in Germany. However, it has great potential. One advantage of the constant approach is that it can reach many entertainment television professionals from different broadcasting organizations and production companies at the same time with various sustainability topics. Thus, E-E measurements may be developed and implemented on a broader basis. It is recommended to implement research projects with different nuances in this kind of approach (i.e. for example asking which circumstances and strategies are important to consider when a constant approach should be effective and successful) so that it reaches many TV makers with accurate and authentic sustainability content. In the USA, the constant approach is well established (chapter 4.2). Giving this background, it is recommendable to ask, in how far Germany can learn from the single activities of the US program.

As a result of dealing with recommendations for the collaborative environment and specific forms of collaborations, it can be stressed that one or several sustainability research institutions should take the lead in establishing an *E-E media center* or maybe several ones

1. to do research on circumstances accepted by Germany's collective consciousness which support and lead to an increased design and implementation of *co-productions and inscript participations* in Germany's practice and which are guided by E-E theory as well as formative, process and summative research.
2. to do research on the effective and successful circumstances which support and lead to the design and the implementation of a *service program having a constant approach* to E-E collaborations. This program should also be guided through research.
3. to increasingly foster and/or facilitate the design and implementation of *service collaborations having an occasional service approach*. These activities

should also be guided through research.
4. to increasingly foster and/or facilitate the design and implementation of *E-E license collaborations* which should also be accomplished through research.

Which priorities are set to follow the above-mentioned recommendations is obviously related to the aims and objectives of the involved institutions that are part of these developments.

9.3.1.2 Ethics in E-E collaborations

When it comes to the discussion about recommendable collaboration forms in Germany's E-E environment, ethical aspects should centrally be addressed, because they play a crucial role in this context. A good example is when sustainability experts take part in the decision making process on the program content in co-productions and inscript participations. Ethical issues also arise in service and license collaborations, since the implementers are also confronted with the same ethical sensitizations. For instance, in service collaborations, the implementers have to separate themselves from the issue that the sustainability professionals took part in the decision making process on the program content, because this behavior is to be considered as 'unethical' in Germany. This paragraph in consequence deals with the question of how Germany can handle the ethical issues in future debates.

As developments in other countries indicate, the sustainability experts are in demand, and they should take on the role as initiators and facilitators of an ethical discourse surrounding Entertainment-Education. In chapter 3, a structure of ethical approaches was presented based on Coady and Bloch (2002) as well as Bouman & Brown (2008b) in which the levels of *meta ethics* (or theoretical principals), *normative ethics* (or policies such as charters, guidelines, procedures), and *micro ethics* (or ethical questions in practice), are discerned. This differentiation can also work for Germany, and it is recommended for the sustainability field that they invest in ethical research and discussions based on the latter-mentioned three levels. For example, according to meta ethics, research on the communitarian ethics of sustainability campaigns and collaboration work could be implemented and serve as a theoretical model for E-E implementers. On the normative level, guidelines and other papers established by the sustainability side may also support the ethical foundation process of the practical E-E work. Finally, on the micro ethics level, sustainability experts should comprehensively deal with ethical questions that arise in the process of designing and implementing an E-E intervention, and they should discuss these issues in a dialogue with TV professionals (e.g. pose questions such as 'what are border situations for them in which the line of unethical behavior is crossed?'[213]). However, there is one thing to consider on all levels and to compromise at any time in Germany's ethical discussions: sustainability experts need to understand and accept that the television professionals have the authority over the

---

[213] These examples go with the suggestions of Bettinghaus & Cody (1994) and Coady & Bloch (1996) to deal with ethical aspects in Entertainment-Education, which were presented in chapter 3.5.1.

program content that is broadcasted on television, and that they should affirm not to harm this authority. The offensive articulation of the strict separation and affirmation is a crucial strategy the author sees. She therefore recommends it for dealing with the ethical aspects and for building trust among the partner sides as a solid and fruitful precondition for establishing different collaboration forms.

9.3.2 Agenda Setting Process

Whereas the last section gave short reflections on the recommendations for collaboration forms in developing an environment that fosters Entertainment-Education in Germany, this part will concentrate on the 'hows' of establishing Entertainment-Education. Specifically, it is necessary to address the question of whether there are practices available which can be diffused and which support the initiation of an agenda-setting process for Entertainment-Education. From the international cases, we learned that discovering these practices and picking them up in order to diffuse them takes plenty of time. Using Bouman (1999) one, for example, learned that for entertainment television professionals Entertainment-Education should not be framed with the term 'Entertainment-Education' but with other terms such as 'social themes'. Or from the USA, one learned that it is fruitful to communicate with the E-E implementers in different communication frames. These and other results (see chapter 4) have helped both countries establish a developing agenda-setting process. Nonetheless, the question of how to come to solutions for framings that may work for Germany's E-E activities remains.

The analysis in part II of this thesis showed that ***E-E service partnerships with an occasional approach*** as well as ***license*** collaborations are very well suited to the German TV context; furthermore circumstances or framings were identified from the past to make them work effectively (also see chapter 8). In contrast to that, there is still high potential in the collaboration forms of **co-productions, inscript participations** and ***E-E service with a constant approach***, because for those three forms, circumstances and framings that effectively work in Germany's media system, legislation context and cultural environment have not been discovered yet.

Thus, the next section will raise the question of how far framings, which attract entertainment (TV) makers and which are not criticized by the public, can be discovered and made accessible for exactly those latter-mentioned collaboration forms. Two recommendations are presented here, which in the eyes of the author have much potential to initiate agenda setting processes: firstly fostering expertise and training and secondly, doing research with the help of the positive deviance approach.

9.3.2.1 Expertise and Training

The study showed that in Germany there is a big gap of expertise with regard to Entertainment-Education. For instance, awareness must be sharpened about the issue of addressing different target group members with different media strategies that are more cognitive or affective-orientated. There is also no expertise about which collaboration forms can be effectively designed and implemented or in which media channels (e.g. TV, radio, web 2.0).[214] When designing and implementing, for example, E-E co-productions or E-E inscript participations, there is no vision for how to use theoretical notions (chapter 2.3). This and other E-E expertise first needs to be established through (1) university training programs. For example, at German universities E-E teaching modules (chapter 4.3.5) could be integrated into different studies in the field of media, journalism and sustainability communication (i.e. as a part of the studies in environmental and health communication as well as in studies which are related to communication for social change in non-western countries). Importantly, through these training programs, both future entertainment media and sustainability professionals may be reached. Such studies or programs are very rare in Germany and should be developed to promote Entertainment-Education. Moreover, (2) communication experts working in sustainability organization should have the possibility of educating themselves in the E-E field through training and workshops. Here, Germany can profit from the expertise in other countries and could develop and implement training measures in cooperation with them.

These educational measurements and 'ideas through an international exchange' have a high potential to foster E-E expertise and resulting from it, culturally accepted ways of developing co-productions and inscript participations as well as service activities with a constant approach.[215]

9.3.2.2 The Positive Deviance Approach

Without a doubt, there might be several ways to proceed in finding and diffusing framings for Entertainment-Education in Germany (especially for co-productions, inscript participations and service collaborations with a constant approach). In the following, one specific inquiry is presented – the ***positive deviance*** (PD) approach – because it appears to be a successful one for fostering agenda setting process in the sense that the approach enables institutions or individuals to discover their inherent wisdom with regard to sustainable issues and to change their behavior (Singhal et al., 2010, Singhal & Dura, 2009).[216]

---

[214] As the thesis shows, for public and commercial television, it may be the most effective strategy to design and implement E-E service or E-E license collaborations and thus be on the ‚safe side'.

[215] For example, in the field of E-E service activities with a constant approach, the *MINTIFF* program at the Technical University of Berlin (see chapter 8.3.2) started in 2010 an international E-E expertise exchange initiative.

[216] The PD practices have been utilized in over 40 countries over the past two decades and have led to significant results. For example, earlier PD projects worldwide have led to significant reductions in hospital-acquired infections in the USA, a decrease in child malnutrition in Vietnam, an increase in primary school retention rates in Argentina and a reduction of HIV transmission among those at high-risk in Myanmar and Indonesia (Dura & Sinbghal 2009; Singhal, 2010a; Wollinka et al., 1997). Furthermore, in 2010 the Center for Media & Health also started to apply this approach in their research portfolio to a mental resilience

The PD approach identifies individuals or institutions whose uncommon behaviors or practices enable them to find better solutions to problems than their peers who have access to the same resources. These individuals or institutions are 'positive', because they are doing things 'right'. They are also 'deviant', because they engage in behavior and practices that most others do not. Instead of focusing on 'What is the problem?' the PD approach asks: 'What is working against all the odds?' In PD projects, researchers act as facilitators, and they identify uncommon but effective institutional and individual practices and make them visible and accessible to other peers. An important element in this context is to design activities (e.g. creative workshops or using social media) that enable the others to practice the behavior and strategies identified during the PD inquiry and verified by the 'deviants' themselves.

The PD approach can be used as an innovative paradigm for discovering the circumstances and framings under which E-E co-productions, E-E inscript participations and the constant approach to E-E service might work in the German collaborative environment. For these collaboration forms, it is necessary to reveal institutional or individual 'deviants' that team up in the latter-mentioned collaboration forms or in similarly functioning collaborative settings[217] which have been culturally accepted and in which (entertainment) media professionals have successfully and effectively been engaged. In this context, the researchers implementing a PD approach as a first step do in-depth research on the E-E practice of people, networks and institutions and ask what has worked very well. As a second step, when finding these successful practices, they make them available to other peer institutions and individuals via 'learning by doing' or enabling them. This process cannot only be facilitated through the researchers, but also through the positive deviance institutions or individuals themselves. So unlike the good practice approaches in deviance, the PD interventions are designed in a way so that institutions and individuals can 'act their way into a new way of thinking rather than think their way into a new way of acting'.

In the tradition of the PD approach, the research activities focus on finding positive deviant stakeholders and then asking how these stakeholders (e.g. universities) managed under the existing circumstances to find ways of implementing the collaboration forms. What did they do to reach the entertainment TV makers? How did they frame it? Which mechanisms made that possible? And how could they 'get away' with it? Further research needs to be done on these and other questions, and this thesis can be considered as a first step among others to contribute answering these questions. The question of how to enhance E-E activities needs to be answered through in-depth research projects which collect data, design suitable re-

---

project among youngsters.

[217] Other collaboration settings, which have parallels, may be collaborations in the corporate environment or in academics (Singhal, 2010b). However, standards for drawing parallels and finding similarities in collaborative settings that can be integrated in a PD project also need to be discovered through research.

search programs and training modules.

The PD approach can be a new paradigm for both experiments and exploration. However, the point should also be made that the PD approach asks 'what is it that is working against all odds?' In the case of E-E collaborations, it might be very challenging and is currently not very realistic to apply the approach, because there are only a few E-E projects in western countries, and thus it might be hard to find projects or cases that work against 'all odds'. So, the PD approach might be interesting to apply in the future when there are more E-E projects which have been successfully designed and implemented.

In sum and based on the study outcomes, the author considers international expertise exchange, trainings and research activities, such as the PD approach, as having a significant role to foster agenda setting in the E-E collaboration field.

9.3.3 Collaboration Activities

Unlike the above sections, this section sums up useful hints for designing and implementing E-E collaboration activities in the future. Obviously, these activities will also take a longer period of time to develop and they should involve research activities in order to raise their quality standards.

Both the USA and the Netherlands offer their activities in a flexible mix, combining elements which evoke dialogue between the partner sides and, at the same time, distribute information to deepen the dialogue processes before or/and after the conversations. This mix is also recommended for future collaboration activities in Germany.

There are differences between the centers from abroad. Hollywood, Health & Society, for example, runs their activities mainly side by side as a part of an E-E service strategy and the activities are not limited to the specific time periods of projects (see chapter 4.2.5). The Dutch approach is project-related; the team members from the Center for Media & Health run their activities in specific project contexts and periods, e.g. one activity is implemented in one project which runs for a specific time frame (see chapter 4.3.5). For Germany, it is not clear which approach might fit better, or even if there is another approach which has not been invented yet, when running collaboration activities in the context of an E-E media center. Both strategies mentioned above are theoretically possible, and a next step could be to design and implement pilot projects in both contexts and draw conclusions for further approaches based on these evaluations.

Nonetheless, HH&S and the CMH have similar activity structures. One activity group focuses on the *research, methods and evaluation* aspects of the E-E interventions while a second concentrates on the *outreach* to TV makers and to sustainability experts (e.g. through providing advice and consultations) and a third is centered on *educational matters* to educate and sensitize students in the context of the E-E strategy. Obviously, establishing a similarly suitable activity structure in Germany is recommended. At least the group of research, methods and evaluation is one which is very important: it is urgently needed to guide the other activity groups and must be combined with them.

The thesis has been written at an intersection of different developments. It maintains the status quo in an ongoing process; take for example:
- the increasing interest by German sustainability experts in communicational aspects for promoting their sustainability topics through the help of entertainment media
- the increased tendencies of competition not only among German commercial but also among public broadcasting stations or
- the liberalization of media legislation which goes with a less strict separation of what is considered 'program content' and what is considered 'advertising'.

Several fast changes are currently being experienced, and the situation for E-E collaborations (in the public/commercial TV sphere but in other media channels as well) may be quite different in the coming years. This can be regarded as positive, and with each additional research and practice experience in the E-E field, the possible structures and action patterns become more visible and may also give way to effective future activities for Germany. In other words, the ongoing activities may form the basis for future ones. As previously described, several African-American people had to refuse to sit in a segregated bus area, until Rosa Parks' refusal ultimately contributed to large scale changes and the civil rights movement. It is to be hoped that, in analogy, German research programs and practical activities recently raised and implemented in the field of Entertainment-Education will ultimately contribute to future large-scale changes, or, in the words of Roger Housden: "The pattern (…) is there from the start. Your task in life is to discern that pattern, listen for it, and give room for it to emerge".

References

Abraham, C.; Sheeran, P.; Johnston, M. (1998): From health belief to self-regulation: theoretical advances in the psychology of action control, *Psychology and Health*, 13, 569-591.
Adams-Price, C.; Greene, A. L. (1990): Secondary attachments and adolescent self-concept, *Sex Roles*, 22, 187-198.
Adolff, F.; Mau, S. (2005): Vom Geben und Nehmen: Zur Soziologie der Reziprozität (Theorie und Gesellschaft), Frankfurt am Main: campus.
Adorno, T. (1957): Television and the pattern of mass culture. In: B. Rosen and D. White (Eds.): *Mass culture: the popular arts in America*, Glencoe, IL: Free press.
Adorno, T.; Horkheimer, M. (1973): Dialectics of enlightment, London: Allen Lane.
Ajzen, I. (1980): Understanding the attitudes and predicting social behavior, Englewood Cliffs, NJ: Prentice-Hall.
Albeda College, aldeling ETV.nl (2009): Eindrapportage Echt Elly: een realitysoap die aanzet to duurzaam consumeren, Rotterdam.
Alexander, A. (1985): Adolescents' soap opera viewing and relational perceptions, *Journal of Broadcasting and Electronic Media*, 29/3, 295-308.
Alexander, A.; Owers, J.; Carveth, R. A.; Hollifield, C. A.; Greco A.N. (2003): Media economics: theory and practice, Mahwah, NJ: Lawrence Erlbaum Associates.
Ali, T. (2002): Mit Fernsehserien nachhaltig wirken. Ein praktisches Handbuch für Drehbuchautoren, Hannover: Deutsche Stiftung Weltbevölkerung.
Altendorfer, O. (2004): Das Mediensystem der Bundesrepublik Deutschland, Wiesbaden: VS Verlag für Sozialwissenschaften.
Altgeld, T.; Hofrichter, P. (2000): Reiches Land - Kranke Kinder? Gesundheitliche Folgen von Armut bei Kindern und Jugendlichen, Frankfurt am Main: Mabuse-Verlag.
Anderson, R.; Baxter, L. A.; Cissna, K. N. (2004): Dialogue: theorizing difference in communication studies, Thousand Oaks, CA: Sage.
Andreasen, A. R. (2001): Ethics in social marketing, Washington DC: Georgetown University Press.
Andrejevic, M. (2004): Reality TV: the work of being watched, Lanham, MD: Rowman & Littlefield Publishers.
Arango, T.; Stelter, B. (2009): Messages with a mission: embedded in TV shows, New York Times, retrieved from http://www.nytimes.com/2009/04/02/arts/television/02gates.html (1st April 2009).
ARD (2008): Medienbasisdaten. Zeitbudget für audiovisuellen Medien, *Medien Basisdaten*.
ARD (2009): Medienbasisdaten. Mediennutzung und Freizeitbeschäftigung 2009, *Medienbasisdaten*.
Arendt, K. (2008): Adolescents and politics - a match made in the media? On the role of Entertainment-Education for political education, *Journal of Social Science Education*, 7/8, 56-73.
Aristotle (1975): On the soul, parva naturalia, on breath (Greek with English translation), transl. W.S. Hett: Harvard University Press, W. Heinemann.
Association of State Media Authorities for Broadcasting in Germany (ASMABG) (2010): Interstate Treaty on Broadcasting and Telemedia (Interstate Broadcasting Treaty) in the version of the 13th Amendment of the Interstate Broadcasting Treaties, retrieved from www.kjm-online.de/files/pdf1/RStV_13_english.pdf (18th November 2010).
Aufenanger, S. (2004): Edutainment. In: J. Hüther und B. Schorb (Eds.): *Grundbegriffe der Medienpädagogik*, München: KoPäd.
Babrow, A. S. (1987): Students motives for watching soap operas, *Journal of Broadcasting & Electronic Media*, 31, 309-321.

Bae, H. S. (2008): Entertainment-Education and recruitment of cornea donors: the role of emotion and issue involvement, *Journal of Health Communication*, 13/1, 20-36.

Bandura, A. (1977): Social learning theory, Englewood Cliffs, NJ: Prentice-Hall.

Bandura, A. (1979): Sozial-kognitive Lerntheorie, Stuttgart: Klett-Cotta.

Bandura, A. (1986): Social foundation of thought and action: a social cognitive theory, Englewood Cliffs, NJ: Prentice-Hall.

Bandura, A. (1995): Exercise of personal and collective efficacy in changing societies. In: A. Bandura (Eds.): *Self-efficacy in changing societies*, New York: Cambridge University Press, 1-45.

Bandura, A. (1997): Self-efficacy: the exercise of control, New York: Freeman.

Bandura, A. (2004): Social cognitive theory for personal and social change by enabling media. In: A. Singhal, M. J. Cody, E. M. Rogers and M. Sabido (Eds.): *Entertainment-Education and social change: history, research and practice*, Mahwah, NY: Lawrence Erlbaum Associates, 75-96.

Barker, J. R. (1999): The discipline of teamwork: participation and concertive control, Thousand Oaks, London, New Delhi: Sage.

Barker, J. R.; Tompkins, P. K. (1994): Identification in the self-managing organization: characteristics of target and tenure, *Human Communication Research*, 21, 223-240.

Barthelmes, J. (2001): Funktionen von Medien im Prozess des Heranwachsens. Ergebnisse einer Längsschnittuntersuchung bei 13- bis 20-Jährigen, *Media Perspektiven*, 2/2001, 84-89.

Bartholomew, L. K.; Parcel, G. S.; Kok, G.; Gottlieb, N. H. (2006): Planning health promotion programs: an intervention mapping approach, San Francisco, CA: Jossey-Bass.

Bauer, R. A.; Bauer, A. (1960): America, mass society and mass media, *Journal of Social Issues*, 10/3, 366.

Bayer, R.; Gostin, L. O.; Jennings, B.; Steinbock, B. (2003): Public health ethics: theory, policy, and practice, Oxford: Oxford University Press.

BBC World Service Trust (2008): Annual review 2006/2007, London, BBC World Service Trust, retrieved from http://downloads.bbc.co.uk/worldservice/trust/pdf/annual_review/annual_review_0708.pdf (26th September 2009).

Beck, V. (2000): Entertainment-Education at CDC, paper presented to the CDC research conference: setting a research agenda for Entertainment-Education, Atlanta, May 2000.

Beck, V. (2004): Working with daytime and prime-time television shows in the United States to promote health. In: A. Singhal, M. J. Cody, E. M. Rogers and M. Sabido (Eds.): *Entertainment-Education and social change: history, research, and practice*, Mahwah, NJ: Erlbaum Associates, 207-224.

Beck, V. (2009): Working with Hollywood to encourage timely, accurate health storylines...and drama too!, unpublished paper.

Beck, V.; Pollard, W. E. (2001): How do regular viewers of prime-time entertainment television shows respond to health information in the shows? Paper presented to the American Public Health Association, Atlanta, October 2001.

Becker, M. H. (1974): The health belief model and personal health behavior, *Health Education Monographs*, 2/4, 324-473.

Behrens, G. et al. (2001): Gabler-Lexikon Werbung, Wiesbaden: Schweizerische Stiftung der Gesundheitsförderung - Glossar.

Bellah, R. N.; Madsen, R.; Sullivan, W. M.; Swidler, A.; Tipton, S. M. (1985): Habits of the heart, Berkeley, CA: University of California Press.

Bendikowski, T. (2008): Erfahrungen und Einschätzungen in Interviews. In: L. Hölscher (Eds.): *Political Correctness. Der sprachpolitische Streit um die nationalsozialistischen*

Verbrechen, Göttingen: Wallstein, 106-205.
Bentley, E. (1967): The life of drama, New York: Atheneum.
Berg, C.; Milmeister, M. (2008): Im Dialog mit den Daten das eigene Erzählen der Geschichte finden. Über Kodierverfahren der Grounded-Theory Methodologie, *Forum Qualitative Sozialforschung*, 9/2, Art. 13.
Berger, P. L.; Luckmann, T. (2000): Die gesellschaftliche Konstruktion der Wirklichkeit. Eine Theorie der Wissenssoziologie, Frankfurt am Main: Fischer Verlag.
Berkowitz, J. M.; Huhman, M.; Heitzler, C. D.; Potter, L. D.; Nolin, M. J.; Banspach, S.W. (2008): Overview of formative, process and outcome evaluation methods used in the VERB campaign, *American Journal of Preventive Medicine*, 34/6S, 222-229.
Bettinghaus, E. P.; Cody, M. J. (1994): Persuasive communication, Fort Worth, TX: Harcourt Brace.
Bilandzic, H.; Busselle, R. W. (2008): Transportation and transportability in the cultivation of genre-consistent attitudes and estimates, *Journal of Communication*, 58, 508-529.
Bittencourt, I.; Borner, J.; Heiser, A. (2003): Nachhaltigkeit in 50 Sekunden. Kommunikation für die Zukunft, München: oekom.
Bogdan, R.; Bilken Knopp, S. (1992): Qualitative research for education: an introduction to theory and methods, Boston: Allyn and Bacon.
Bonfadelli, H.; Friemel, T. (2006): Kommunikationskampagnen im Gesundheitsbereich: Grundlagen und Anwendungen, Konstanz: UVK Verlagsgesellschaft.
Bordwell, D. (1989): Making meaning: inference and rhetoric in the interpretation of cinema, Cambridge, MA: Harvard University Press.
Bouman E&E Development (2005): Gezondheid en Beeld, EE-referentiekader, Eindnotitie. Belemmerende en bevorderende factoren bij samenwerking ten behoeve van EE-soap/dramaseries, Gouda: Bouman E&E Development.
Bouman, M.P.A. (1999): Collaboration for prosoial change. The turtle and the peacock. The Entertainment-Education strategy on television, published thesis, University of Wageningen.
Bouman, M.P.A. (2002): Televisieamusement en overheidscommunicatie, *Tijdschrift voor Communicatiewetenschap*, 30/4, 331-346.
Bouman, M.P.A. (2004): Entertainment-Education television drama in the Netherlands. In: A. Singhal, M. J. Cody, E. M. Rogers and M. Sabido (Eds.): *Entertainment Education and social change: history, research and practice*, Mahwah, NJ: Lawrence Erlbaum Associates, 225-242.
Bouman, M.P.A. (2005): Sex und Soaps. Entertainment-Education in niederländischen TV-Serien, *TELEVIZION*, 18/1, 47-54.
Bouman, M.P.A. (2006): Verslag van de Dag van de Soap 2006 met als thema Tijd voor een Nederlandse EastEnders?!, Gouda: Bouman E&E Development.
Bouman, M.P.A. (2009): Personal communication with Martine Bouman at the Center for Media & Health, 17th February 2009.
Bouman, M.P.A. (2010): Personal communication with Martine Bouman during the MINTIFF-Conference "Don't think it is only entertainment, MINT und Chancengleichheit in fiktionalen Fernsehformaten", Berlin, 08th September 2010.
Bouman, M.P.A. (2011a): SOUND, the design and implementation of a websoap about love, ambitions and decibels, paper in process.
Bouman, M.P.A. (2011b): The Sound Effects hearing loss prevention campaign: an entertainment-education approach, paper in process.
Bouman, M.P.A.; Houten, M. v. (1993): Cooperation between national and regional health education: fiction between ideals and reality, *Health Education Special, Mid-section of GGD-News*, May 1993, 8-11.

Bouman, M.P.A.; Wieberdink, E.A.M. (1993): Villa Borghese: a soapseries on heart health, *Canadian Journal of Cardiology*, Vol 9 (Suppl.D), 145D-146D.

Bouman, M.P.A. (1995): Health Education in drama series; Medisch Centrum West: a Dutch Experience. In: Hideyasu Aoyama: *Proceedings XVth IUHE World Conference 'Health Promotion & Education'*, Tokyo, Japan, August 1995.

Bouman, M.P.A.; Maas, L.; Kok, G. J. (1998): Health education in television entertainment: a Dutch drama serial, *Health Education Research*, 13/4, 503-518.

Bouman, M.P.A. & Hutten, A. (2001): The international EE2000 event, the third international Entertainment-Education conference for social change, Evaluatierapport, Gouda: Stichting E-E Nederland.

Bouman, M.P.A.; Draaisma, E. (2006): Find Out: een televisie-interventie volgens de user-as-designerbenadering, *Tijdschrift voor Communicatiewetenschap*, 34/3, 307-318.

Bouman, M.P.A.; Brown, W. J. (2008a): Creative processes for health communication: Entertainment-Education collaboration, submitted paper.

Bouman, M.P.A.; Brown, W. J. (2008b): Ethical approaches to lifestyle campaigns, *Journal of Mass Media Ethics*, 25/1, 34-52.

Bouman, M.P.A.; Hollemans, H. (2008): Deelrapport pretest synopsis Sound Soap: pre-test Script: een 10-delige internet-soap over liefde, ambitie en decibellen, Gouda: Centrum Media & Gezondheid.

Bouman, M.P.A.; Hollemans, H.; Fokkens, P.M. (2009): Media Strategie Sound Effects, Daalrapport 5, Gouda: Centrum Media & Gezondheid.

Bouman, M.P.A.; Brown, W. J. (2011): Facilitating a transcultural approach to Entertainment-Education and health promotion: a model of collaboration, paper presented to the International Communication Association, Boston, 26th-31st May 2011.

Bouman, M.P.A.; Hollemans, H. (2012): SndBites. Formatieve onderzoek, Gouda: Centrum Media & Gezondheid.

Bouman, M.P.A.; Drossaert, C.H.C.; Pieterse, M.E. (2012): Mark My Words: The Design of an Innovative Methodology to Detect and Analyse Interpersonal Health Conversations in Web and Social Media, Journal of Technology in Human Services, 30:3-4, 312-326.

Bourdieu, P. (1984): Distinction: a social critique of the judgement of taste, Cambridge, MA: Harvard University Press.

Bourdieu, P. (1991): Language and symbolic power, Cambridge: Polity Press.

Bourdieu, P. (1993): The field of cultural production: essays on art and literature, Cambridge: Policy Press.

Bourdieu, P. (1998): Über das Fernsehen, Suhrkamp: Frankfurt am Main.

Bowerman, W. R. (1987): The structure of commonsense reasoning about personal causality: the case of avoiding blame. In: F. van Holthoon and D. R. Olson (Eds.): *Common sense. The foundation for social science*, Lanham, MD: University Press of America, 297-318.

Bramsted, E. K. (1956): Goebbels and national socialist propaganda, 1925-1945, East Lansing, MI: Michigan State University Press.

Breuer, F. (1996): Qualitative Psychologie. Grundlagen, Methoden und Anwendungen eines Forschungsstils, Opladen: Westdeutscher Verlag.

Breuer, F. (2000): Qualitative Methoden zur Untersuchung von Biographien, Interaktionen und lebensweltlichen Kontexten. Die Entwicklung eines Forschungsstils, *Forum Qualitative Sozialforschung*, 1/2, Art. 3.

Breuer, F. (2009): Reflexive Grounded Theory. Eine Einführung für die Forschungspraxis, Wiesbaden: VS Verlag für Sozialwissenschaften.

Brown, B. (1958): Words and things, New York: Free Press.

Brown, W. J. (2008a): Untangling processes of involvement with media personas, in press.

Brown, W. J. (2008b): Turning celebrity capital into political influence: lessons learned from Arnold Schwarzenegger, Regent University, VA, USA.

Brown, W. J. (2009): Mediated influence of Pope John Paul II., *Journal of Communication and Religion*, 32/2, 33-62.

Brown, W. J. (2010): Steve Irwin's Influence on Wildlife Conservation, *Journal of Communication*, 60, 73-93.

Brown, W. J.; Singhal, A. (1990): Ethical dilemmas of prosocial development, *Communication Quarterly*, 38/3, 268-280.

Brown, W. J.; Cody, M. J. (1991): Effects of prosocial television soap operas in promoting women's status, *Human Communication Research*, 18/1, 114-142.

Brown, W. J.; Singhal, A. (1993): Ethical considerations of promoting prosocial messages through the popular media, *Journal of Popular Film and Television*, 31/3, 92-99.

Brown, W. J.; Brasil, M. D. (1995): Media celebrities and public health. Responses to "Magic" Johnson's HIV disclosure and its impact on AIDS risk and high-risk behaviors, *Health Communication*, 7, 345-371.

Brown, W. J.; Singhal, A. (1997): Ethical guidelines for promoting prosocial messages through the popular media. In: G. Edgerton, M. T. Marsden and J. Nachbar (Eds.): *In the eye of the beholder. Critical perspectives in popular film and television*, Bowing Green, OH: Bowling Green State University Popular Press.

Brown, W. J.; Singhal, A. (1999): Entertainment-Education media strategies for social change: promises and problems. In: D. Demers and K. Vishwanath (Eds.): *Mass media, social control and social change*, Ames, IA: Iowa State Univenity Press.

Brown, W. J.; Fraser, B. P. (2004): Celebrity identification in Entertainment-Education. In: A. Singhal, M. J. Cody, E. M. Rogers and M. Sabido (Eds.): *Entertainment-Education and social change: history, practice, and research*, Mahwah, NJ: Lawrence Erlbaum Associates, 97-116.

Brown, W. J.; Fraser, B. P. (2007): Global identification with celebrity heroes. In: S. Drucker and G. Gumpert (Eds.): *Heroes in a global world*, Cresskill, NJ: Hampton Press.

Brown, W. J.; Barker, G.; Presnell, K. K. (2008): The social influence of mediated sports celebrities: cognitive and emotional responses to the death of Dale Earnhardt, paper presented to the Mass Communication Division of the National Communication Association's 94th Annual Convention, San Diego, CA, 21st-24th November 2008.

Brown, W. J.; Basil, M. D. (2010): Parasocial interaction and identification: social change processes for effective health interventions, *Health Communication*, 25, 601-602.

Brown, W. J.; deMatviuk, M.A.C. (2010): Sports celebrities and public health: Diego Maradona's influence on drug use prevention, *Journal of Health Communication*, 15, 358-373.

Bruhn, M. (2006): Non-Profit-Marketing. Zukunftsperspektive für Non-Profit-Organisationen? *Soziale Arbeit*, 2006/3, 95-100.

Bruhn, M.; Tilmes, J. (1993): Social Marketing. Einsatz des Marketings für nichtkommerzielle Organisationen, Stuttgart, Berlin, Köln: Kohlhammer.

Brunsdon, C. (1998): Structure of anxiety: recent British television crime fiction, *Screen*, 39/3, 223-243.

Buba, H.; Globisch, S. (2008): Ökologische Sozialcharaktere: von Weltveränderern, Egoisten und Resignierten. Persönlichkeitstyp und Lebenswelt als Basis von Umweltverhalten, München: oekom.

Bundesministerium für Arbeit und Soziales (BMAS) (2005): Lebenslagen in Deutschland. 2. Armuts- und Reichtumsbericht, Berlin: BMAS.

Bundesministerium für Arbeit und Soziales (BMAS) (2008): Lebenslagen in Deutschland. 3. Armuts- und Reichtumsbericht, Berlin: BMAS.

Bundesministerium für Gesundheit (BMG) (2007): Aktionsplan zur Umsetzung der HIV/AIDS-Bekämpfungsstrategie der Bundesregierung 2007-2010, Berlin: BMG.
Bundesministerium für Gesundheit (BMG) (2008): Drogen- und Suchtbericht 2008, Berlin: BMG.
Bundesregierung (2004): Perspektiven für Deutschland. Unsere Strategie für eine nachhaltige Entwicklung, Fortschrittsbericht 2004, Berlin: Bundesregierung.
Bundesverfassungsgericht (1961): 1. Rundfunk-Urteil, Bundesverfassungsgericht, Bundesverfassungsgericht, retrieved from http://www.bundesverfassungsgericht.de (25th May 2009)
Buxton, D. (1990): From the Avengers to Miami Vice: form and ideology in television series, Manchester: Manchester University Press.
Castro Buffington, S. de (2011): Personal e-mail communication with Sandra de Castro Buffington, 27th February 2011.
Caillé, A. (1989): Critique de la raison utilitaire. Manifeste du MAUSS, Paris: La Découverte.
Caillé, A. (1991): Une soirée á 'l'Ambroisie'. Rudiments d'une analyse structural du don, *La Revue du M.A.U.S.S.*, 11, 106-112.
Caillé, A. (2005): Die doppelte Unbegreiflichkeit der Gabe. In: F. Adolff and S. Mau (Eds.): *Vom Geben und Nehmen. Zur Soziologie der Reziprozität*, Frankfurt, New York: campus, 157-184.
Caillé, A. (2006): Weder methodologischer Holismus noch methodologischer Individualismus. Marcel Mauss und das Paradigma der Gabe. In: S. Moebius and C. Papilloud (Eds.): *Gift – Marcel Mauss' Kulturtheorie der Gabe*, Wiesbaden: VS Verlag für Sozialwissenschaften.
Caillé, A. (2008): Anthropologie der Gabe, Frankfurt am Main: campus.
Callahan, D. (2003): What price better health? Hazards of the research imperative, Berkeley, CA: University of California Press.
Callahan, D.; Jennings, B. (2002): Ethics and public health: forging a strong relationship, *American Journal of Public Health*, 92/2, 169-176.
Casey, B.; Casey, N.; Calvert, B.; French, L.; Lewis, J. (2008): Television studies: the key concepts, London, New York: Routledge, Taylor & Francis Group.
Chaiken, S.; Liberman, A.; Eagly, A. H. (1989): Heuristic and systematic information processing within and beyond the persuasion context. In: J. S. Uleman and J. A. Bargh (Eds.): *Unintended Thought*, New York: Guilford Press, 212-252.
Charmaz, K. (2006): Constructing Grounded Theory. A practical guide through qualitative analysis, Thousand Oaks, CA: Sage.
Chatterjee, J. S.; Bhanot, A.; Frank, L. B.; Murphy, S. T.; Powers, G. (2009): The importance of interpersonal discussion and self-efficacy in knowledge, attitude, and practice models, *International Journal for Communication*, 3, 607-634.
Cooke, L. (2001): The police series. In: G. Creeber (Eds.): *The television genre book*, London: bfi.
Cheng, H.; Kotler, P.; Lee, N. (2011): Social Marketing for public health: global trends and success stories, Sudbury, MA: Jones and Bartlett Publishers.
Christians, C. (2006): The case for communitarian ethics. In: M. Land and B. Hornaday (Eds.): *Contemporary media ethics,* Spokane, WA: Marquette, 57-69.
Cialdini, R. B. (1985): Influence: science and practice, Glenview, IL: Scott, Foresman.
Soul City (2000): The evaluation of Soul City 4. Methology and top-line results, Johannesburg: Soul City, September 2000.
Clobes, H. G.; Hagedorn, F. (2008): Nicht nur das Klima ändert sich. Fernseh-Programme auf dem Weg zur Nachhaltigkeit? In: C. Schwender, F. S. Schulz and M. Kreeb (Eds.):

Medialisierung von Nachhaltigkeit. Das Forschungsprojekt balance[f]: Emotionen und Ecotainment in den Massenmedien, Marburg: Metropolis Verlag, 221-234.

Coady, M.; Bloch, S. (2002): Codes of ethics and the professions, Carlton: MUP.

Cooper, A. F. (2008): Celebrity diplomacy, Boulder, CO: Paradigm Publishers.

Cooper-Chen, A. (1994): Games in the global village: a 50-nation study of entertainment television, Bowling Green, OH: Bowling Green University Popular Press.

Corbin, J.; Strauss, A. (1990): Grounded Theory method: procedures, canons, and evaluative criteria, *Qualitative Sociology*, 13/1, 3-21.

Corbin, J.; Strauss, A. (2008): Basics of qualitative research. Techniques and procedures for developing Grounded Theory, Los Angeles: Sage.

Corcoran, N. (2007): Communicating health: strategies for health promotion, Thousand Oaks, CA: Sage.

Cox, R. (2010): Environmental communication and the public sphere, Thousand Oaks, CA: Sage.

Creeber, G. (2001): The television genre book, London: British Film Institute.

Därmann, I. (2005): Fremde Monde der Vernunft. Die ethnologische Provokation der Philosophie, München: Fink.

DeJong, W.; Winsten, J. A. (1990): The Harvard alcohol project: a demonstration project to promote the use of the "designated driver", Chicago: National Safety Council.

Denzin, N. K. (1994): The art and politics of interpretation. In: N. K. Denzin and Y. S. Linclon (Eds.): *Handbook of qualitative research*, Thousand Oaks, CA: Sage, 500-515.

Dervin, B. (1974): 'The urban information needs projects', *Interim Report*, Seattle: University of Washington.

Dervin, B. (1976): Strategies for dealing with human information needs: information or communication? *Journal of Broadcasting*, 20, 324-333.

Deutsche Bundesstiftung Umwelt (DBU); Kinderkanal (KI.KA) (2003): Die Graslöwen. Grundschulmaterialien zur Umweltserie, retrieved from http://www.grasloewe.de/files/die_graslowen.pdf (18th May 2009).

Deutscher Bundestag (2010): Basic law for the Federal Republic of Germany, Berlin: Deutscher Bundestag, retrieved from https://www.btg-bestellservice.de/pdf/80201000.pdf (11th May 2009).

Deutsches Kinderhilfswerk (2007): Kinder-Report 2007, Daten, Fakten, Hintergründe, Freiburg: Velber Verlag.

Dickson, T. (2000): Mass media education in transition. Preparing for the 21st century, Mahwah, NJ, London: Lawrence Erlbaum Associates.

Die Zeit (2010): Bundesagentur für Arbeit: Medienservice, Nr. 17, 33, 22. April 2010.

Dillard, J. P.; Pfau, M. (2002): The persuasion handbook: developments in theory and practice, Thousand Oaks, London, New Delhi: Sage.

Doyle, P. (2008): Value-based marketing: marketing strategies for corporate growth and stakeholder value, Chichester: John Wiley & Sons.

Draaisma E.; Bouman, M. P. A. (2005): Pre-test pilot Find Out, Gouda: Bouman E&E Development.

Draaisma E.; Bouman, M. P. A. (2006): Find Out: Procesevaluatie designers, Gouda: Bouman E&E Development.

Dunlap, J. W. (2005): VeggieTales: moral education through the media using entertainment-Edcuation strategy, thesis, Regent University.

Dura, L.; Singhal, A. (2009): Will Roman finish sixth grade? Positive deviance for student retention in rural Argentina, *Positive Deviance Wisdom Series*, 2, (Boston, Tufts University: Positive Deviance Initiative): 1-8.

Dura, L.; Singhal, A.; Elías, E. (2008): Listener as producer Minga Peru's intercultural radio educative project in the Peruvian Amazon, Social Justice Dialogue and Publication Series, El Paso, TX: Sam Donaldson Center for Communication Studies.

Dutta-Bergmann, M. J. (2005): Theory and practice in health communication campaigns: a critical interrogation, *Health Communication*, 18/2, 103-122.

Dutta, M. J. (2006): Theoretical approaches to Entertainment Education campaigns: a subaltern critique, *Health Communication*, 20/3, 221-231.

Dutta-Bergman, M. J. (2004): An alternative approach to entertainment education, *Journal of International Communication*, 10/1, 93-107.

Dyer, R. (1991): A 'star is born' and the construction of authenticity In: C. Glendale (Eds.): *Stardom: industry of desire*, London: Routledge, 132-140.

Echterhoff, G.; Saar, M. (2002): Kontexte und Kulturen des Erinnerns. Maurice Halbwachs und das Paradigma des kollektiven Gedächtnisses, Konstanz: UVK Verlagsgesellschaft.

Eiling, E.; Goebbels, A.; De Vries, N. K. (2006): Effectevaluatie Find Out, Maastricht: University of Maastricht.

Elkeles, T.; Mielck, A. (1997): Entwicklung eines Modells zur Erklärung gesundheitlicher Ungleichheit, *Gesundheitswesen*, 59, 137-143.

Empelen, P. van (2009): Evaluatie van de pilotcampagne Sound Effects ter preventie van gehoorschade onder uitgaande jongeren, Gouda: Center Media & Health.

Empelen, P. van; Bouman, M. P. A.; Jurg, M. E. (2010): Effect evaluation of Sound Effects: a Dutch hearing loss prevention campaign, paper in progress.

Epstein, E. J. (2005): The big picture: money and power in Hollywood, New York: Random House.

Etheridge, E. W. (1992): Sentinel for Health: a history of the Centers for Disease Control, Berkeley, CA: University of California Press.

Etzioni, A. (1998): Introduction, In: A. Etzioni (Eds.): *The essential communication reader*, Lanham, MD: Rowan & Littlefield, ix-xxxix.

European Parliament; Council of the European Union (2007): Amending Council Directive 89/552/EEC on the coordination of certain provisions laid down by law, regulation or administrative action in Member States concerning the pursuit of television broadcasting activities, European Parliament, Official Journal of the European Union. In: *Council of the Europen Union*, L 332/27.

Falkenroth, C. (2010): Gestaltungsspielräume in der Stoffauswahl. Ausgewählte Ergebnisse aus der Befragung von deutschen Film- und Fernsehschaffenden MINT und Chanchengleichheit in fiktionalen Fernsehnformaten, Vortrag auf der Konferenz "Don't think it is only entertainment, MINT und Chancengleichheit in fiktionalen Fernsehformaten", Berlin, 06.-08. September 2010.

Fasel, C. (2001): Die Nase ist die Nachricht. Wie Menschen Medienereignisse machen. In: J. Häussermann (Eds.): *Persönlichkeit und Medien. Inszeniertes Charisma*, Tübingen: Max Niemeyer-Verlag.

Feinberg, J. (1980): Rights, justice, and the bounds of liberty: essays in social philosophy, Princeton, NJ: Princeton University Press.

Festinger, L. (1954): A theory of social comparison processes, *Human Relations*, 7, 117-140.

Festinger, L. (1957): A theory of cognitive dissonance, Stanford, CA: Stanford University Press.

Feuer, J. (1992): Genre study and television. In: A.C. Robert (Eds.): *Channel of discources. Reassembled: television and contemporary critisism*, London: Routledge, 138-159.

Figueroa, M. E.; Kincaid, D. L.; Rani, M.; Lewis, G. (2002): Communication for social change: an integrated model for measuring the process and its outcomes, *Communication for social change working paper series*, 2002/1, New York: New York Rockefeller Foundation.

Fishbein, M.; Ajzen, I. (1975): Belief, attitude, intention, and behavior: an introduction to theory and research, Reading, MA: Addison-Wesley.
Fiske, J. (1987): Television culture, London, New York: Routledge.
Flick, U. (1995): Handbuch qualitativer Sozialforschung: Grundlagen, Konzepte, Anwendungen, 2nd edition, Weinheim: Beltz.
Flueren, H. J.; Klein, M.; Redetzki-Rodermann, H. (2004): Das Altersbild der deutschen Daily Soaps, *medien praktisch*, 26/2004/101, 23-27.
Forster, K.; Knieper, T. (2005): Germany. In: A. Cooper-Chen (Eds.): *Global entertainment media: content, audience, issues*, Mahwah, NY: Lawrence Erlbaum Associates, 59-80.
Frankfurter Allgemeine Zeitung (FAZ) (2005a): Den WDR kommt Schleichwerbung teuer zu stehen, Frankfurter Allgemeine Zeitung (online), retrieved from http://www.faz.net/s/Rub8A25A66CA9514B9892E0074EDE4E5AFA/Doc~EF3A77FE7F51B4825B6B6BF9FFAB57E41~ATpl~Ecommon~Scontent.html (23rd May 2008).
Frankfurter Allgemeine Zeitung (FAZ) (2005b): Schleichwerbung auch bei Schimanski, Frankfurter Allgemeine Zeitung (online), retrieved from http://www.faz.net/s/Rub8A25A66CA9514B9892E0074EDE4E5AFA/Doc~E243DDCB1663F4546B5551DA376AF2734~ATpl~Ecommon~Scontent.html (23rd May 2008).
Frankfurter Allgemeine Zeitung (FAZ) (2005c): Schleichwerbung. Der öffentlich-rechtliche Zuschauerverrat, Frankfurter Allgemeine Zeitung (online), retrieved from http://www.faz.net/s/Rub8A25A66CA9514B9892E0074EDE4E5AFA/Doc~EF52851B42C684025B91CE3592F488729~ATpl~Ecommon~Scontent.html (23rd May 2008).
Frankfurter Allgemeine Zeitung (FAZ) (2008): Mitangeklagter belastet Emig schwer, Frankfurter Allgemeine Zeitung (online), retrieved from http://www.faz.net/s/Rub9CD731D06F17450CB39BE001000DD173/Doc~EC05623F2E7684A5BBECBDD433F3775C7~ATpl~Ecommon~Scontent.html (11th March 2009).
Freire, P. (2006): Pedagogy of the oppressed, 30th anniversary edition, New York: Continuum.
Franck, G. (2007): Die Ökonomie der Aufmerksamkeit. Ein Entwurf, München: Deutscher Taschenbuch Verlag.
Gassmann, C.; Vorderer, P.; Wirth, W. (2003): Ein Herz für die Schwarzwaldklinik? Zur Persuasionswirkung fiktionaler Fernsehunterhaltung am Beispiel Organispende-Bereitschaft, *Medien und Kommuniaktionswissenschaft*, 51/3-4, 478-496.
Gecas, V. (1989): The social psychology of self-efficacy, *Annual Review of Sociology*, 15, 291-316.
Geene, R.; Hans, C.; Gold, C. (2001): Armut macht krank! Berlin: Verlag b_books.
Gehlen, A. (1972): Der Mensch. Seine Natur und seine Stellung in der Welt, Wiesbaden: Athenaion.
Gelder, B. de (1987): Commonsense metalism and psychological theory. In: F. van Holthoon and D. R. Olson (Eds.): *Common sense. The foundation for the social science*, Lanham, MD: University Press of America, 277-296.
Gergen, K. J.; Gergen, M. M.; Barrett, F. J. (2004): Dialogue: Life and death of the organizations. In: D. Grant, C. Hardy, C. Oswick and L. Putnam (Eds.): *The Sage handbook of organisational discourse*, Thousand Oaks, CA: Sage, 39-60.
Glaser, B; Strauss, A. (1967): The discovery of grounded theory, Chicago: Aldine.
Glathe, C. (2010): Kommunikation von Nachhaltigkeit in Fernsehen und Web 2.0, Wiesbaden: VS Verlag für Sozialwissenschaften.
Gledhill, C. (1985): 'Genre'. In: P. Cook (Eds.): *The cinema book*, London: bfi, 58-109.
Glik, D.; Berkanovic, E.; Stone, K.; Ibarra, L.; Jones, M. C.; Rosen, B.; Schreibman, M.; Gordon, L.; Minassian, L.; Richards, D. (1998): Health education goes Hollywood:

working with prime-time and daytime entertainment television for immunization promotion, *Journal of Health Communication*, 3/3, 263-282.

Goffman, E. (2000): Wir alle spielen Theater. Die Selbstdarstellung im Alltag, München: Piper Verlag.

Gomery, D. (2008): A history of broadcasting in the United States, Malden: Blackwell.

Gottberg, J. v. (2007): Verlorene Werte? Orientierungsangebote der Medien und gesellschaftlichen Ethik, *TV-Diskurs*, 39, 1/2007, 34-37.

Grant, A. E.; Guthrie, K. K.; Ball-Rokeach, S. J. (1991): Television shopping: a media system dependency perspective, *Communication Research*, 18, 773-798.

Gray, J. (2008): Television entertainment, New York, London: Routledge.

Greenberg, B. S.; Salmon, C. T.; Patel, D.; Beck, V.; Cole, G. (2004): Evolution of an E-E research agenda. In: A. Singhal, M. J. Cody, E. M. Rogers and M. Sabido (Eds.): *Entertainment-Education and social change: history, research and practice*, 191-206.

Griffin, J. (2005): The United Kingdom. In: A. Cooper-Chen (Eds.): *Global entertainment media: content, audience, issues*, Mahwah, NY: Lawrence Erlbaum Associates, 39-58.

Gripsrud, J. (1998): Television, broadcasting, flow: key metaphors in TV theory. In: C. Geraghty and D. Lusted (Eds.): *The television studies book*, London: Arnold.

Grossberg, L.; Wartella, E.; Whitney, C. D.; MacGregor Wise, J. (2006): Media making: mass media in a popular culture, Thousand Oaks, London, New Delhi: Sage.

Grunwald, A.; Kopfmüller, J. (2006): Nachhaltigkeit, Frankfurt am Main, New York: campus.

Gudykunst, W. B.; Kim, Y. Y. (1984): Communication with strangers: an approach to intercultural communication, New York: Random House.

Guttman, N. (2000): Public health communication interventions: values and ethical dilemmas, Thousand Oaks, CA: Sage.

Haas, A. (2007): Medienmenüs. Der Zusammenhang zwischen Mediennutzung, SINUS-Milieus und Soziodemographie, München: Verlag Reinhard Fischer.

Halbwachs, M. (1991): Das kollektive Gedächtnis, Frankfurt am Main: Fischer.

Hall, S. (1973): Encoding and decoding in the television discourse. In: Centre for Contemporary Cultural Studies, Birmingham: *Occasional Papers* 7, 1-12.

Hallenberger, G. (2008): „Das ganze Leben ist ein Quiz." Spiele im Fernsehen im alltagskulturellen Kontext. In: T. Thomas (Eds.): *Medienkultur und soziales Handeln*, Wiesbaden: VS-Verlag, 259-276.

Hallenberger, G.; Foltin, H.-F. (1990): Unterhaltung durch Spiel. Die Quizsendungen und Game Shows des deutschen Fernsehens, Berlin: Spiess.

Hammond, S. C.; Anderson, R.; Cissna, K. N. (2003): The problematics of dialogue and power. In: P. J. Kabfleisch (Eds.): *Communication Yearbook 27*, Mahwah, NJ: Lawrence Erlbaum Associates, 125-158.

Hanfeld, M. (2008): Der Fall Jürgen Emig. Der HR und das Prinzip Verantwortung, Frankfurter Allgemeine Zeitung, retrieved from http://www.faz.net/s/Rub475F682E3FC24868A8A5276D4FB916D7/Doc~E48974782D 28B430E84081FEEE3D142F8~ATpl~Ecommon~Sspezial.html (19th July 2010).

Hardt, H. (1992): Critical communication studies: communication, history, and theory in America, London, New York: Routledge.

Hartley, J. (2001): Situation comedy, part I. In: G. Creeber (Eds.): *The television genre book*, London: bfi, 65-67.

Hauff, V. (1987): Unsere gemeinsame Zukunft. Der Brundtland-Bericht der Weltkommission für Umwelt und Entwicklung, Greven: Eggenkamp Verlag.

Heider, F. (1958): The psychology of interpersonal relations, New York: Wiley.

Helmert, U.; Bammann, K.; Voges, W.; Müller, R. (2000): Müssen Arme früher sterben?

Soziale Ungleichheit und Gesundheit in Deutschland, Weinheim: Juventa.

Hether, H. J.; Huang, G.; Beck, V.; Murphy, S. T.; Valente, T. W. (2008): Entertainment-Education in a media-saturated environment: examining the impacts of single and multiple exposure to breast cancer storylines on two popular medical dramas, *Journal of Health Communication*, 13/8, 808-823.

Hether, H. J.; Murphy, S. T. (2009): A content analysis of sex roles in health storylines on primetime television, *Sex Roles*, DOI 10.1007/s11199-009-9654-0.

Hetzel, A. (2006): Interventionen im Ausgang von Mauss: Derridas Ethik der Gabe und Marions Phänomenologie der Gebung. In: S. Moebius and C. Papilloud (Eds.): *Gift – Marcel Mauss' Kulturtheorie der Gabe*, Wiesbaden: VS Verlag für Sozialwissenschaften.

Hill, A. (2005): Reality TV: audience and popular factual television, New York: Routledge.

Hill, L. (2004): Social marketing: evidence of (in)effectiveness and when it might be useful, paper presented to the Asia-Pacific Meeting on Alcohol Policy, Auckland, 23th September 2004, retrieved from: http://apapaonline.org/APAPAnetwork/Meeting_Reports/files/Auckland_Sept04/Hill_Social_Marketing.pdf (11th January 2011).

Hilmes, M. (2003): The television history book, London: bfi.

Hochmuth, T. (2008): Weltfernsehen - die internationale Vermarktung der Quizshow "Wer wird Millionär?" München, Ravensburg: Grin.

Hollywood, Health & Society (2007): Hollywood, Health and Society. 5-Year summary table, Los Angeles: Hollywood, Health & Society.

Hölscher, L. (2008): Political Correctness. Der sprachpolitische Streit um die nationalsozialistischen Verbrechen, Göttingen: Wallstein.

Holthoon, F. van (1987): Common sense and natural law: from Thomas Aquinas to Thomas Reid. In: F. van Holthoon and D. R. Olson (Eds.): *Common sense. The foundation for the social science*, Lanham, MD: University Press of America, 99-114.

Holthoon, F. van; Olson, D. R. (1987): Common sense. The foundation for the social science, Lanham, MD: University Press of America.

Holzapfel, A. (2007): Liberalisierung von Product Placement, Saarbrücken: VDM Verlag Dr. Müller.

Horton, D.; Wohl, R. R. (1956): Mass Communication and para-social interaction: observation on intimacy at a distance, *Psychiatry*, 19, 215-229.

Houlberg, R. (1984): Local television news audience and the para-social interaction, *Journal of Broadcasting*, 28/4, 423-429.

Hovland, C. I.; Lumsdaine, I. L.; Sheffield, F. D. (1949): Experiments on mass communication, Princeton, NJ: Princeton University Press.

Hovland, C. I.; Janis, I. L.; Kelley, H. H. (1953): Communication and persuasion: psychology studies of opinion change, New Haven, CT: Yale University Press.

Hübner, G. (2005): Soziales Marketing. In: G. Michelsen and J. Godemann (Eds.): *Handbuch zur Nachhaltigkeitskommunikation. Grundlagen und Praxis*, München: oekom, 287-296.

IPC Media Impact (2010): My Island - My Community. A public awareness and behavior change program for climate change in Anguilla, Antigua and Barbuda, British Virgin Island, Dominica, Grenada, Montserrat. St. Kitts and Nevis, St. Lucia, St. Vincent and Grenadines, New York, St. Lucia: PCI Media Impact.

Jankowski, P. J.; Clark, W. M.; Ivey, D. C. (2000): Fusing horizons: exploring qualitative research and psychotherapeutic applications of social constructionism, *Contemporary Family Therapy*, 22/2, 241-250.

Janz, N.; Becker, M. (1984): The health belief model: a decade later, *Health Education*

Quarterly, 11, 1-47.
Janz, N. K.; Champion, V. L.; Strecher, V. J. (2002): The health belief model. In: B. Glantz, B. K. Rimer and F. M. Lewis (Eds.): *Health behavior and health education: theory, research and practice*, San Francisco, CA: Jossey-Bass, 510-529.
Johansson, A. (2001): Product Placement in Film und Fernsehen. Ein Vergleich der rundfunk- und wettbewerbsrechtlichen Zulässigkeit der Einblendung von Markenprodukten in Kinofilm und Fersehen unter besonderer Berücksichtigung der Kunstfreiheit nach Art. 5 III GG, Dissertation, Berlin: Mensch & Buch Verlag.
Johnson, B. T.; Eagly, A. H. (1989): Effects of involvement on persuasion: a meta-analysis, *Pychological Bulletin*, 106, 290-314.
Jordan, A. B.; Kunkel, D.; Manganello, J. (2009): Media messages and public health: a decisions approach to content analysis, New York, NY: Routledge.
Joseph, J. (2010): The experience effect: engage your customers with a consistent and memorable brand experience, New York: AMACOM.
Jugend, Information (Multi-) Media (JIM) (2006): Basisstudie zum Medienumgang 12- bis 19-Jähriger in Deutschland, Baden-Baden: Medienpädagogischer Forschungsverbund Südwest.
Jung, C.G. (1958): Psychology and religion, New York: Panthon.
Jung, C.G. (1970): Archetypes and the collective unconscious, Buenos Aires: Editorial Paidos.
Jurg, M. E.; Bouman, M. P. A. (2009): Procesevaluatie Sound Effects: een pilotcampagne ter preventie van gehoorschade tijdens het uitgaan, Deelrapport 6, Centrum Media & Gezondheid en GGD-Amsterdam.
Jurin, R. R.; Roush, D.; Danter, J. (2010): Environmental Communication: skills and principles for nature resource managers, scientists, and engineers, Dordrecht, Heidelberg, London, New York: Springer.
Kahle, L. R.; Homer, P. M. (1985): Physical attractiveness of the celebrity endorser: asocial adaptation perspective, *Journal of Consumer Research*, 11, 954-961.
Kaiser Family Foundation (2004): Entertainment Education and health in the United States, Washington DC, Kaiser Family Foundation.
Kaiser Family Foundation (2008): Television as a health educator: a case study of Grey's Anatomy, Menlo Park, CA: Kaiser Family Foundation.
Kamins, M. A.; Brand, M. J.; Hoeke, S. A.; Moe, J. C. (1989): Two-sided versus one-sided celebrity endorsement: the impact on advertising effectiveness and credibility, *Journal of Advertising*, 18/2, 4-10.
Kant, I. (1952): The critique of judgement, Oxford: The Clarendon Press (1790).
Kauschke, A.; Klugius, U. (2000): Zwischen Meterware und Massarbeit. Markt und Betriebsstrukturen der TV-Produktionen in Deutschland, Gerlingen: Bleicher.
Kawachi, I.; Kennedy, B. P.; Bruce, P.; Lochner, K. (1997): Social capital, income inequality and mortality, *American Journal of Public Health*, 87, 1491-1498.
Kawachi, I.; Kennedy, B. P.; Lochner, K. (1997): Long live community: social capital as public health, *The American Prospect*, 8/35, 56-59.
Kelle, U.; Kluge, S. (1999): Vom Einzelfall zum Typus. Fallvergleich und Fallkontrastierung in der qualitativen Sozialforschung, Opladen: Leske + Budrich.
Kelley, H. H. (1973): The process of causal attribution, *American Psychologist*, 28, 107-126.
Kelman, H. (1958): Compliance, identification and internalization: three processes of attitude change, *Journal of Conflict Resolution*, 2/1, 51-60.
Kelman, H. (1961): Process of opinion change, *Public Opinion Quarterly*, 25, 57-58.
Kennedy, M. G.; O'Leary, A.; Beck, V.; Pollard, W. E.; Simpson, P. (2004): Increase in calls to the CDC National STD and AIDS hotline following AIDS-related episodes in a soap

opera, *Journal of Communication*, 54/2, 287-301.
Kenway, J.; Bullen, E. (2001): Consuming children: education entertainment advertising, Maidenhead: Open University Press.
Kiefer, M. L. (2007): Medienökonomik - Einführung in eine ökonomische Theorie der Medien, München, Wien: R. Oldenbourg Verlag.
Kincaid, D. L.; Coleman, P. L.; Rimon II, J. G.; Silayan-Go, A. (1991): The Philippines multimedia campaign for young people project: summary of evaluation results, paper presented to the American Public Health Association.
Kiruswa, S. L. (2004): Evaluating effects of an Entertainment-Education film on self-efficacy towards HIV/AIDS prevention in the Kenyan military, published thesis, Regent University, Virginia.
Klapper, J. T. (1960): Effects of mass communications, New York: The Free Press.
Kline, S. (1993). Out of the garden: toys and children's culture in the age of TV marketing, London: verso.
Klein, P. (2008): ARD-Tatort in Zahlen. Retrieved from: http://satundkabel.magnus.de/medien/artikel/hintergrund-tatort-die-hoechsten-einschaltquoten-der-ard-krimireihe.html (05th October 2009).
Klimmt, C.; Vorderer, P. (2003): Media psychology "is not yet there". Introducing theories on media entertainment to the presence debate, *Presence*, 12/4, 346-359.
Kolandai-Matchett, K. (2008): Improving news media communication of sustainability and the environment: an exploration of approaches, published thesis, Christchurch: University of Canterbury retrieved from http://ir.canterbury.ac.nz/bitstream/10092/2109/1/thesis_fulltext.pdf (21st January 2011).
Konrad-Adenauer-Stiftung (2001): Seifenopern für sozialen Wandel – Entwicklungspolitische Möglichkeiten der Unterhaltungsmedien, Internationale Fachtagung 30. März 2001, Bornheim: Konrad-Adenauer-Stiftung.
Kornblum, J. (2008): First-episode controversy: the vaccine-autism link, USA TODAY, Los Angeles, retrieved from http://www.usatoday.com/news/health/2008-01-28-eli-stoneside_N.htm (21st March 2009).
Kotler, P. (2006): Social marketing and the broadening of marketing movement. In: A. Singhal and J. Dearing (Eds.): *Communication of innovation. A journey with Ev Rogers*, Thousand Oaks: Sage, 136-146.
Kotler, P. & Zaltman, G. (1971): Social marketing: an approach to planned social change, *Journal of Marketing*, 35, 3-12.
Kotler, P.; Armstrong, G.; Saunders, J.; Wong, V. (2011): Grundlagen des Marketing, 5th edition, München: Pearson.
Kremers, S.P.J.; Bouman, M.P.A. (2004): Nederland in Beweging!-televisie: Onderzoek naar de gebruikswaarde, *Tijdschrift voor Gezondheidswetenschappen*, 82/5, 332-333.
Krüger, U. M.; Zapf-Schramm, T. (2007): Sparten, Sendungsformen und Inhalte im deutschen Fernsehangebot 2006. Programmanalyse von ARD/Das Erste, ZDF, RTL, SAT.1 und ProSieben, *Media Perspektiven*, 04/2007, 166-186.
Krüger, U. M.; Zapf-Schramm, T. (2008): Sparten, Sendungsformen und Inhalte im deutschen Fernsehangebot 2007, *Media Perspektiven* 04/2008, 166-189.
Kuchenbuch, K. (2003): Die Fernsehnutzung von Kindern aus verschiedenen Herkunftsmilieus. Eine Analyse anhand des Sinus-Milieu-Modells, *Media Perspektiven*, 01/2003, 2-11.
Kuckartz, U. (1997): Qualitative Daten computerunterstützt auswerten. Methoden, Techniken, Software, In: B. Friebertshäuser and A. Prengel: *Handbuch qualitative Forschungsmethoden in der Erziehungswissenschaft*, Weinheim, München: Juventa, 584-595.
Kuckartz, U.; Schack, K.; Bruhn, H. (2002): Umweltkommunikation gestalten, Leverkusen:

Leske + Budrich.
Kurian, G. T. (1984): The new book of world ratings, New York: Facts on File.
Lacayo, V.; Singhal, A. (2008): Popular culture with a purpose! Using edutainment media for social change, Den Haag: Oxfam Novib.
Lalonde, M. (1974): A new perspective on the health of Canadians, Ottawa: Ministry of Supply and Services, Canadian Federal Government.
Lampert, C. (2007): Gesundheitsförderung im Unterhaltungsformat. Wie Jugendliche gesundheitsbezogene Botschaften in fiktionalen Fernsehangeboten wahrnehmen und bewerten, Dissertation, Baden-Baden: nomos Verlag.
Landesmedienanstalten Deutschland (2000): Gemeinsame Richtlinien der Landesmedienanstalten für die Werbung, zur Durchführung der Trennung von Werbung und Programm und für das Sponsoring im Fernsehen, Berlin: Landesmedienanstalten Deutschland.
Lasswell, H. (1927): Propaganda techniques in the first world war, New York: Alfred Knopf.
Lazarsfeld, P. F., Berelson, B.; Gaudet, H. (1944): The people's choice: how the voter makes up his mind in a presidential campaign, New York: Columbia University Press.
Le, K.; Cantu, M.; Brandon, V.; Miller, M.; Hardison Wang, B.; Miller, M.; Huang, G. (2009): Internet information seeking behavior of television medical drama viewers, paper presented to the American Public Health Association Meeting, Philadelphia, PE: 07-11th November, 2009, also compare http://apha.confex.com/apha/137am/webprogram/Paper208630.html (26th April 2011).
Legewie, H. (1993): Buchbesprechung zu Anselm Strauss. Grundlagen qualitativer Sozialforschung, *Journal für Psychologie*, 1, 86-88.
Lehmann, M.; Sabo, P. (2003): Zielgruppe. In: Bundeszentrale für gesundheitliche Aufklärung (BZgA): *Leitbegriffe der Gesundheitsförderung. Glossar zu Konzepten, Strategien und Methoden in der Gesundheitsförderung*, Schwabenheim an der Selz: Peter Sabo, 242-243.
Lehr, G. (2007): Auf dem Grat zwischen religiöser/weltanschaulicher Programmveranstaltung und Ideenwerbung. *Gedanken zu den Medien und ihrer Ordnung. Festschrift für Dr. Victor Henle*, Baden-Baden: Nomos, 175-177.
Leeuwen, G.B. van; Renes, R.J.; Leeuwis, C. (2013): Televised Entertainment-Education to Prevent Adolescent Alcohol Use: Perceived Realism, Enjoyment, and Impact. *Health Education and Behavior*, 40(2013)2, 193-205.
Lesser, G. S. (1975): Children and television: lessons from Sesame street, New York: Vintage Books, Random House.
Levy, M. R. (1979): Watching TV news as para-social interaction, *Journal of Broadcasting* 23, 69-80.
Li, Y. (2008): Towards a conceptual framework for participation and empowerment in digital storytelling and participatory video, paper presented to the International Communication Association Conference 2008, Montréal, Canada, 22nd-26th May 2008.
Lichtl, M. (1999): Ecotainment. Der neue Weg im Umweltmarketing, München: Redline.
Lichtl, M. (2007): Markenwerbung und nachhaltiger Konsum. Faszination Nachhaltigkeit oder Bedrohung Nachhaltigkeit? Dissertation, Berlin: dissertation.de.
Liedtke, C.; Welfens, J.; Stengel, O. (2007): Ressourcenschonung durch lebensstilorientierte Bildung. In: G. Altner, H. Leitschuh and G. Michelsen (Eds.): *Jahrbuch Ökologie 2008*, München: C.H. Beck, 142-153.
Lindenberg, S. (1987): Common sense and social structures: a sociological view. In: F. van Holthoon and D. R. Olson (Eds.): *Common sense. The foundation for the social science*, Lanham, MD: University Press of America, 199-216.
Linnan, L; Steckler, A. (2002): Process evaluation for public health interventions and research: an overview. In: L. Linnan and A. Steckler: *Process evaluation for public health*

interventions and research, Jossey-Bass: San Franscisco, CA: 1-24.
Linssen, M. (2008): Interview with the entertainment professional Mark Linssen on Entertainment-Education collaborations, Amsterdam, 26th June 2008.
Lopez-Pumarejo, T. (2006): The Influence of the developing world's television practices on U.S. health education efforts: entertainment-education and the Centers for Disease Control, *Journal of International Marketing and Marketing Research*, 31/3, 111-126.
Lubjuhn, S.; Bouman, M. (2009): Wie funktioniert Entertainment-Education in den Niederlanden und den USA und was können wir in Deutschland daraus lernen? *merz, medien+erziehung, Zeitschrift für Medienpädagogik*, 4/2009, 44-49.
Lubjuhn, S; Hoffhaus, M. (2009): Integrating sustainability themes into media: tools for the public sector. Report implemented by the UNEP/Wuppertal Institute Collaborating Centre on Sustainable Consumption and Production on behalf on the Ministry of the Environment and Conservation, Agriculture and Consumer Protection of the German State of NRW.
Lubjuhn, S.; Pratt, N. (2009): Media communication strategies for climate-friendly lifestyles: addressing middle and lower class consumers for social-cultural change via Entertainment-Education, *IOP Conf. Series: Earth and Environmental Science*, 8/2009, doi: 10.1088/1755-1315/8/1/011001.
Lubjuhn, S.; Reinermann, J. L. (2010): Entertainment-Education in Deutschland. Beispiele aus der Praxis und Weiterentwicklungsmöglichkeiten, *merz, medien+erziehung, Zeitschrift für Medienpädagogik*, 04/2010, 63-69.
Lubjuhn, S; Liedtke, C. (2008): Elterliche Normäußerungen im Themenfeld des nachhaltigen Konsums. Qualitative Ergebnisse aus der Praxis, paper presented to the Wuppertal Institute Research Meeting, Research Group "Sustainable Production and Consumption", 15th January 2008.
Luckmann, T. (1987): Some thoughts on common sense and science. In: F. van Holthoon and D. R. Olson (Eds.): *Common sense. The foundation for the social science*, Lanham, MD: University Press of America, 179-198.
Lüders, C.; Reichertz, J. (1986): Wissenschaftliche Praxis ist, wenn alles funktioniert und keiner weiß warum. Bemerkungen zur Entwicklung qualitativer Sozialforschung, *Sozialwissenschaftliche Literaturschau*, 12, 90-102.
Marcuse, H. (1964): One-dimensional man: studies in the ideology of advanced industrial society, Boston: Beacon.
Mauss, M. (1975): Soziologie und Anthropologie, München: Hanser.
Mauss, M. (1990a): The gift: the form and reason for exchange in archaic societies, New York, London: W.W. Norton.
Mauss, M. (1990b): Die Gabe. Form und Funkion des Austauschs in archaischen Gesellschaften, Frankfurt am Main: Suhrkamp.
Mauss, M. (2006): Mauss' Werk von ihm selbst dargestellt (~1930). In: S. Moebius and C. Papilloud (Eds.): *Gift. Marcel Mauss' Kulturtheorie der Gabe*, Wiesbaden: VS Verlag Für Sozialwissenschaften, 345-359.
MacLean, P. D. (1973): A triune concept of the brain and behavior, Toronto: University of Toronto Press.
Marshall, J.; Werndly, A. (2002): The language of television, London, New York: Routledge.
McChesney, R. W. (2008): The political economy of media: enduring issues, emerging Dilemmas, New York: Monthly Review Press.
McDaniel, A. M.; Casper, G. R.; Hutchinson, S. K.; Stratton, R. M. (2005): Designing and testing of an interactive smoking cessation intervention for inner-city woman, *Health Education Research*, 20/3, 379-384.
McCarthy, A. (2001): Realism and soap operas. In: G. Creeber (Eds.): *The television genre*

book, London: bfi, 49-54.

McGuire, W. (1989): Theoretical foundations of campaigns. In: R. E. Rice and C.K. Atkin (Eds.): *Public communication campaigns*, 2nd edition, Newbury Park, CA: Sage, 43-65.

McMillan, S. J. (2002): A four-part model of cyber-interactivity: some cyber-places are more interactive than others, *New Media and Society*, 4/2, 271-291.

McQuail, D. (2000): McQuail's mass communication theory, 4th edition, London: Sage.

McQuail, D. (2005): McQuail's mass communication theory, 5th edition, London: Sage.

McQuail, D.; Blumer, J.; Brown, R. (1972): The television audience: a revised perspective. In: D. McQuail (Eds.): *Sociology of mass communication*, Middlesex, England: Penguin, 135-165.

Merton, R. K.; Fiske, M.; Kendall, P. L. (1956): The focused interview: a manual of problems and procedures, New York: Free Press.

Merton, R. K.; Kendall, P. L. (1979): Das fokussierte Interview. In: C. Hopf and E. Weingarten (Eds.): *Qualitative Sozialforschung*, Stuttgart: Klett, 171-204.

Messenger-Davis, M. (2001): Studying children's television. In: G. Creeber (Eds.): *The television genre book*: bfi, 96-97.

Mey, G. (1999): Adoleszenz, Identität, Erzählung. Theoretische, methodologische und empirische Erkundungen, Berlin: Köster.

Meyen, M.; Riesmeyer, C. (2009): Diktatur des Publikums: Journalisten in Deutschland Konstanz: UVK Verlagsgesellschaft.

Michelsen, G. (2007): Nachhaltigkeitskommunikation: Verständnis – Entwicklung –Perspektiven. In: G. Michelsen und J. Godemann, J. (2007): *Handbuch zur Nachhaltigkeitskommunikation. Grundlagen und Praxis*, München: oekom, 25-41.

Michelsen, G.; Godemann, J. (2007): Handbuch zur Nachhaltigkeitskommunikation. Grundlagen und Praxis, München: oekom.

Mielck, A. (2002): Soziale Ungleicheit und Gesundheit, Bern: Huber.

Mielck, A. (2003): Soziale Ungleicheit und Gesundheit/Krankheit. In: Bundeszentrale für gesundheitliche Aufklärung (BZgA): *Leitbegriffe der Gesundheitsförderung. Glossar zu Konzepten, Strategien und Methoden in der Gesundheitsförderung*, Schwabenheim an der Selz: Peter Sabo, 213-216.

Mittmann, T. (2008): Vom "Historikerstreit" zum "Fall Hohmann": Kontroverse Diskussionen um Political Correctness seit Ende der 1980 Jahre. In: L. Hölscher (Eds.): *Political Correctness. Der sprachpolitische Streit um die nationalsozialistischen Verbrechen*, Göttingen: Wallstein, 60-102.

Moebius, S. (2006a): Marcel Mauss, Konstanz: UVK Verlagsgesellschaft.

Moebius, S. (2006b): Die sozialen Funktionen des Sakralen. Marcel Mauss und das Collège de Sociologie. In: S. Moebius and C. Papilloud (Eds.): *Gift – Marcel Mauss' Kulturtheorie der Gabe*, Wiesbaden: VS Verlag für Sozialwissenschaften, 57-80.

Moebius, S. (2009): Kultur, Bielefeld: transcript Verlag.

Moebius, S.; Papilloud, C. (2006): Gift - Marcel Mauss' Kulturtheorie der Gabe, Wiesbaden: VS Verlag für Sozialwissenschaften.

Montgomery, K. C. (1993): The Harvard Alcohol Project: Promoting the designated driver on television. In: T. Backer and E. Rogers (Eds.): *Organizational aspects of health communication Campaigns: what works?* Thousand Oaks: Sage, 178-213.

Moore, G. E. (1925): A defense of common sense. In: G. E. Moore: *Philosophical Papers*, London and New York: The Macmillan Company, 1959, 32-59.

Morrell, P. (2001): Social factors affecting communication. In: R. B. Ellis, R. J. Gates and N. Kenworthy: *Interpersonal communication in nursing*, London: Churchill, Livingstone, 33-44.

Morgan, S.; Movius, L.; Cody, M. J. (2009): The power of narratives: the effect of entertainment television organ donation storylines on the attitudes, knowledge, and behaviors of donors and non-donors, *Journal of Communication*, 59/1, 135-151.

Morse, J. M. (1994): Emerging from data: the cognitive processes of analysis in qualitative inquiry. In: J. M. Morse (Eds.): *Critical issues in qualitative research methods*, Thousand Oaks: Sage, 23-43.

Movius, L.; Cody, M. J.; Huang, G.; Berkowitz, M. (2007): Motivating television viewers to become organ donors, *Cases in Public Health Communication & Marketing*, 2007 June, retrieved from http://www.casesjournal.org/volume1/peer-reviewed/cases_1_08.cfm (17th November 2010).

Movius, L.; Lapsansky, C.; Schuh, J.; Cody, M. J.; Woodley, P. (2009): The impact of transportation, identification, and motivational appeal on viewers' knowledge and planned actions regarding bone marrow donation, paper presented to the International Communication Association, Chicago, IL, 21st-25th May 2009.

Moyer-Gusé, E. (2008): Towards a theory of entertainment persuasion: explaining the persuasive effects of entertainment-education messages, *Communication Theory*, 18/3, 407-425.

Murphy, S. T.; Frank, L. B.; Moran, M. B.; Patnoe-Woodley, P. (2011): Involved, transported, or emotional? Exploring the determinants of change in knowledge, attitudes, and behavior in Entertainment-Education, *Journal of Communication*, 61 (2011), 407-431.

Mruck, K. unter Mitarbeit von Mey, G. (2000): Qualitative Sozialforschung in Deutschland, *Forum qualitative Sozialforschung* 1/1, Art. 4.

Müller, O. (1997): Product-Placement im öffentlich-rechtlichen Fernsehen: In der Grauzone zwischen unlauterem Wettbewerb und wichtiger Finanzierungsquelle, Frankfurt am Main, Berlin, Bern, New York, Paris, Wien: Peter Lang.

Murphy, S. T.; Frank, L. B.; Moran, M. B.; Patnoe-Woodley, P. (2011): Involved, transported, or emotional? Exploring the determinants of change in knowledge, attitudes, and behavior in Entertainment-Education, *Journal of Communication*, 61 (2011), 407-431.

Murphy, S. T.; Hether, H. J.; Rideout, V. (2008): How healthy is primetime? An analysis of health content in popular primetime television programs, A Kaiser Family Foundation report.

Murphy, S. T.; Wilkin, H. A.; Cody, M. J.; Huang, G. (2008): Health messages in primetime television: a longitudinal content analysis. In: D. Kunkel, J. Jordan, J. Manganello and M. Fishbein (Eds.): *Media messages and public health: a decision approach to content analysis*, Mahwah, NJ: Lawrence Erlbaum Associates, 173-191.

Jack Myers Media (2002): Cable nets lay out upfront strategies, Jack Myers Report.

National Social Marketing Center (NSMC) (2006): It's our health, London: NSMC.

Nariman, H. N. (1993): Soap operas for social change: towards a methodology for Entertainment-Education television, media and society series, Westport: Praeger Publishers.

Neale, S. (1980): Genre, London: bfi.

Neale, S. (2001): Sketch comedy. In: G. Creeber (Eds.): *The television genre book*, London: British Film Institute.

Nelson, R. (1997): Television drama in transition: forms, values and cultural change, London: Macmillan.

Nielsen Media Research (NMR) (2007): Television trends, Nielsen Media Research.

Nielsen Media Research (NMR) (2008): Television trends, Nielsen Media Research.

Norman Lear Center (NLC) (2008): USC Annenberg school announces the 9th annual sentinel for health awards call for entries, Los Angeles: Norman Lear Center, Hollywood, Health & Society.

O'Brien, M. E. (2004): Nazi cinema as enchantment: the politics of entertainment in the Third Reich, Woodbridge, Suffolk, UK: Camden House.

O'Leary, A.; Kennedy, M.; Pappas-DeLuca, K. A.; Nkete, M.; Beck, V.; Galavotti, C. (2007): Association between exposure to an HIV story line in The Bold and the Beautiful and HIV-related stigma in Botswana, *Aids Education and Prevention*, 19/3, 209-217.

O'Sullivan, E. L.; Spangler, K. J. (1998): Experience marketing: strategies for the new millennium, State College, PA: Venture.

Ouellette, L. (2002): Viewers like you? How public TV failed the people, New York: Columbia University Press.

Panyr, S.; Kiel, E.; Meyer, S.; Grabowski, J. (2004): Quizshow-Wissen vor dem Hintergrund empirischer Bildungsforschung, Bildungsforschung, 2/1, retrieved from www.bildungsforschung.org/Archiv/2005-01/quiz/ (15th January 2010).

Papa, M. J.; Auwal, M. A.; Singhal, A. (1995): Dialectic of control and emancipation in organizing for social change: a multitheoretic study of the Grameen Bank in Bangladesh, *Communication Theory*, 5/3, 189-223.

Papa, M. J.; Singhal, A. (2008): How entertainment-education programs promote dialogue in support for social, paper presented to the International Communication Association Conference 2008, Montréal, Canada, 22nd-26th May 2008.

Papa, M. J.; Singhal, A.; Law, S.; Pant, S.; Sood, S.; Rogers, E. M.; Shefner-Rogers, C. (2000): Entertainment-Education and social change: an analysis of parasocial interaction, social learning, collective efficacy and paradoxical communication, *Journal of Communication*, 50/4, 31-55.

Papa, M. J.; Singhal, A.; Papa, W. H. (2006): Organizing for social change: a dialectic journey of theory and praxis, Thousand Oaks, CA, London, New Delhi: Sage.

Papilloud, C. (2006): Hegemonie der Gabe. In: S. Moebius and C. Papilloud (Eds.): *Gift. Marcel Mauss' Kulturtheorie der Gabe*, Wiesbaden: VS Verlag für Sozialwissenschaften, 245-267.

Parrot, R.; Egbert, N.; Anderton, J.; Sefcovic, E. (2002): Enlarging the role of environment as a social influence construct in health campaigns. In: J. P. Dillard and M. Pfau (Eds.): The persuasion handbook: developments in theory and practice, Thousand Oaks, CA: Sage, 289-308.

Parvanta, C. F.; Freimuth, V. (2000): Health Communication at the Centers for Disease Control and Prevention, *American Journal of Health Behavior*, 24/1, 18-25.

Paus-Haase, I.; Hasebrink, U.; Mattusch, U.; Keuneke, S.; Krotz, F (1999): Talkshows im Alltag von Jugendlichen. Der tägliche Balanceakt zwischen Orientierung, Amüsement und Ablehnung, Opladen: Leske + Budrich.

Paus-Haase, I.; Wagner, U. (2001): Soaps und Talks auf der Basis der Talkshow-Interviews. In: U. Göttlich, F. Krotz and I. Paus-Haase (Eds.): Daily Soaps und Daily Talks im Alltag von Jugendlichen. Eine Studie im Auftrag der Landesanstalt für private Rundfunkveranstalter Rheinland-Pfalz, Schriftenreihe Medienforschung der Landesanstalt für Rundfunk Nordrhein-Westfalen (LfR), Band 38, Opladen: Budrich + Leske, 171-212.

Paus-Hasebrink, I.; Bichler, M.; Wijnen, C. W. (2007): Kinderfernsehen bei sozial benachteiligten Kindern, *MedienPädagogik - Zeitschrift für Theorie und Praxis der Medienbildung*, 13, 1-15.

Peirce, P. S. (1940): Critical common-sensism. In: J. Buchler (Eds.): *The philosophy of Peirce. Selected writings*, New York: Dover, 290-301.

Perry, D. K. (2002): Theory and research in mass media: contexts and consequences, Mahwah, NJ: Lawrence Erlbaum Associates.

Petty, R. E.; Cacioppo, J. T. (1981): Attitudes and persuasion: classic and contemporary approaches, Dubuque, IA: W.C. Brown.

Petty, R. E.; Cacioppo, J. T. (1986a): Communication and persuasion: central and peripheral routes to attitude change, New York: Springer.

Petty, R. E.; Cacioppo, J. T. (1986b): The elaboration likelihood model of persuasion. In: L. Berkowitz (Eds.): *Advances in Experimental Social Psychology*, 19, 123-205, San Diego, CA: Academic Press.

Pine, J; Gilmore J. (1999): The experience economy, Boston: Harvard Business School Press.

Piotrow, P. T.; de Fossard, E. (2004): Entertainment-Education as a public health intervention. In: A. Singhal, M. J. Cody, E. M. Rogers and M. Sabido (Eds.): *Entertainment-Education and social change. History, research and practice* Mahwah, NJ: Lawrence Erlbaum Associates, 39-60.

Plake, K. (2004): Handbuch Fernsehforschung: Befunde und Perspektiven, Wiesbaden: VS Verlag für Sozialwissenschaften.

Poindexter, D. L. (2004): A history of Entertainment-Education, 1958-2000. In: A. Singhal, M. J. Cody, E. M. Rogers and M. Sabido (Eds.): *Entertainment-Education and social change. History, research and practice* Mahwah, NJ: Lawrence Erlbaum Associates, 21-37.

Poindexter, D. L. (2008): Speech at the Everett M. Rogers award for achievements in Entertainment-Education, 2nd October 2008, Los Angeles, Annenberg School for Communication.

Pollard, W. E.; Beck, V. (2000): Audience analysis research for developing Entertainment-Education outreach. Soap opera audience and health information, Paper presented to the American Public Health Association, Boston.

Popper, K. (1962): Conjectures and refutations: the growth of scientific knowledge, New York: Basic Books.

Porter Novelli; Centers for Disease Control and Prevention (CDC); Hollywood, Health & Society (HH&S) (2000): TV Drama/Comedy Viewers and Health Information, 2000 Porter Novelli HealthStyles Survey.

Porter Novelli; Centers for Disease Control and Prevention (CDC); Hollywood, Health & Society (HH&S) (2005): TV Drama/Comedy Viewers and Health Information, 2005 Porter Novelli HealthStyles Survey.

Portes, A. (1998): Social capital: its origins and applications in modern sociology, *Annual Review of Sociology*, 24, 1-24.

Postman, N. (1986) Amusing Ourselves to Death; Public Discourse in the Age of Showbusiness, New York: Viking Pinguin.

Pratt, N.; Lubjuhn, S.; Hoffhaus, M. (2010): Klimawandel in der Daily Soap? Nachhaltigkeitskommunikation in den Massenmedien, *Forum Nachhaltig Wirtschaften*, 03, 19-21.

Preece, J. (2002): Supporting community and building social capital, *Communications of the ACM*, 45/4, 37-39.

Prochaska, J. O.; DiClemente, C. C.; Norcross, J. C. (1992): In search of how people change. Applications to addictive behaviors, *American Psychologist*, 47/9, 1102-1114.

Pundt, J. (2006): Public Health Absolventen mit Doktorhut. In: J. Pundt: *Professionalisierung im Gesundheitswesen*, Bern: Huber, 234-245.

Puppis, M. (2007): Einführung in die Medienpolitik, Konstanz: UVK Verlagsgesellschaft.

Putnam, L. L. (1986): Contradictions and paradoxes in organizations. In: L. Thayer (Eds.): *Organization and communication. Emerging perspectives I*, Norwood, NJ: Ablex, 151-167.

Rat für Nachhaltige Entwicklung (2006): Nachhaltigkeit als Programm. Ein Kreativ-Workshop für Fernsehschaffende, Berlin: Rat für Nachhaltige Entwicklung, 26.-27. September 2006.

Ratner, C. (2005): Epistemological, social, and political conundrums in social constructionism, *Forum Qualitative Sozialforschung*, 7/1, Art. 4.

Rawls, J. (1999): A theory of justice, Cambridge, MA: Harvard University Press.

Reardon, K.K. (1991): Persuasion in practice, Newbury Park, CA: Sage.

Reichertz, J. (2000): Die Frohe Botschaft des Fernsehens. Kultursoziologische Untersuchung medialer Diesseitsreligion, Konstanz: UVK Verlagsgesellschaft.

Reichertz, J. (2007a): Qualitative Sozialforschung – Ansprüche, Prämissen, Probleme, *Erwägen – Wissen – Ethik* 18/2, 1-14.

Reichertz, J. (2007b): Nach den Kirchen jetzt das Fernsehen? Kann das Fernsehen Werte vermitteln? In: D. Hoffmann and L. Mikos (Eds.): *Mediensozialisationstheorien*, Wiesbaden: VS Verlag für Sozialwissenschaften, 147-167.

Reichertz, J. (2008): Wer nur einen Hammer hat, dem gerät die Welt leicht zum Nagel. Eine Polemik – nicht gegen Udo Kelle, sondern gegen die, die sich zu Unrecht auf ihn berufen, Symposium: Zur Integration qualitativer und quantitativer Sozialforschung, 4. Berliner Methodentreffen Qualitative Forschung, 4.-5. Juli 2008.

Reichertz, J. (2009): Kommunikationsmacht. Was ist Kommunikation und was vermag sie? Und weshalb vermag sie das? Wiesbaden: VS Verlag für Sozialwissenschaften.

Reichertz, J. (2010): Die Macht der Worte und Medien, Wiesbaden: VS Verlag für Sozialwissenschaften.

Reichertz, J.; Iványi, N. (2002): Liebe (wie) im Fernsehen. Eine wissenssoziologische Analyse, Opladen: Leske+Budrich.

Reinermann, J. L.; Lubjuhn, S.; Bouman, M.P.A.; Singhal, A. (2013, accepted for publication): Entertainment-Education for Sustainable Lifestyles: Storytelling for the Greater, Greener Good, *International Journal for Sustainable Development*.

Reinermann, J. L.; Lubjuhn, S. (2011): "Let me sustain you". Die Entertainment-Education Strategie als Werkzeug der Nachhaltigkeitskommunikation, *Medien Journal - Zeitschrift für Kommunikationskultur*, 01/11, 43-56.

Reinermann, J. L.; Lubjuhn, S.; Reichertz, J. (2012): *Nachhaltigkeit in Unterhaltungsmedien – (k)ein Widerspruch*. In: H. Leitschuh, G. Michelsen, U. E. Simonis, J. Sommer and E.U. Von Weizäcker (Eds.) Jahrbuch Ökologie 2013, S. Hirzel Verlag: Stuttgart, 101-107

Reisch, L. A.; Bietz, S. (2006): Sustainment für die Massen? Einige Erkenntnisse aus dem Projekt „balance", *Forum Ware*, 34/1-4, 68-72.

Reisch, L. A.; Bietz, S.; Kreeb, M. (2006): How to communicate sustainable lifestyles to hard-to-reach consumers? A report on the large scale experiment „balance-f". Competitive paper at the SCORE! Launch Conference, November 2006, Wuppertal, Institute for Climate, Energy, and Environment, in cooperation with the UNEP Centre for Sustainable Consumption and Production (CSCP), Wuppertal, 23rd - 25th November 2006,

Reisch, L. A.; Kreeb, M. (2007): Kommunikation des nachhaltigen Konsums: Forschung und Praxis. In: G. Michelsen & J. Godemann: *Handbuch Nachhaltigkeitskommunikation, Grundlagen und Praxis*, München: oekom, 463-473.

Reusswig, F.; Schwarzkopf, J.; Pohlenz, P. (2004): Double Impact. The climate blockbuster 'the day after tomorrow' and its impact on the German cinema public, Potsdam Institute for Climate Impact Research (PIK), Report 92, Potsdam: PIK, retrieved from: www.pik-potsdam.de/research/publications/pikreports/.files/pr92.pdf (19th September 2008).

Richter, H. E. (1989): Die hohe Kunst der Korruption. Erkenntnisse eines Politik-Beraters, Hamburg: Hoffmann & Campe.

Richter, M.; Hurrelmann, K. (2006): Gesundheitliche Ungleichheit, Wiesbaden: VS-Verlag für Sozialwissenschaften.

Ries, G. (2004): Inhalt verpflichtet. Nachhaltigkeitsthemen der Medienbranche, Basel, Sarasani Sustainable Studie.

Rijs, K.; Meeuse, J.; Jurg, M.; Bouman, M.P.A. (2007): Formatief onderzoek uitgaanspubliek: Meningen van jongeren over uitgaan en harde muziek: Rapport van 94 chat-interviews onder uitgaande Nederlandse jongeren in de leeftijd van 16 tot 30 jaar, Deelrapport 1, Centrum Media & Gezondheid en GGD-Amsterdam.

Rimon II, J.G. (1989): Leveraging messages and corporations. The Philippine experience, *Integration*, 22, 33-44.

Rogers, E. M. (1976): New product adoption and diffusion, *Journal of Consumer Research*, 2, 290-301.

Rogers, E. M. (1995): Diffusion of innovations, New York: The Free Press.

Rogers, M. (2008): Arresting drama: the television police genre, *Studies in Learning, Evaluation Innovation and Development*, 5/2, 78-84.

Röll, F. J. (1999): Wie Filme Wirkung zeigen. Neue medienpädagogische Konzepte und Methoden am Beispiel ausgewählter Filme der Bundeszentrale für gesundheitliche Aufklärung. Ein Handbuch für den Einsatz von Filmen zur gesundheitlichen Aufklärung, Köln: Bundeszentrale für gesundheitliche Aufklärung.

Rorty, R. (1982): Consequences of pragmatism, Minneapolis: University of Missesota Press.

Rosengren, K. E.; Windahl, S. (1989): Media matter: TV use in childhood and adolescence, Norwood, NJ: Ablex.

Rubin, R. B.; McHugh, M. P. (1987): Development of parasocial interaction relationships, *Journal of Broadcasting & Electronic Media*, 31/3, 279-292.

Rubin, A. M.; Perse, E. M.; Powell, R. A. (1985): Loneliness, parasocial interaction and local television news viewing, *Human Communication Research*, 12, 155-180.

Ryerson, W. N. (2010): Programs and activities of Population Media Center, Shelburne, Vermont: Population Media Center (PMC).

Ryerson, W. N. (2008): Programs and activities of Population Media Center, Shelburne: Vermont, Population Media Center (PMC).

Ryerson, W. N. (2008): The effectiveness of entertainment mass media in changing behavior, Population Media Center, Series Edition, Shelburne, Vermont,

Sabido, M. (2004): The origins of Entertainment-Education. In: A. Singhal, M. Cody, E. M. Rogers and M. Sabido: *Entertainment-Education and social change. History, research and practice*, Mahwah, NJ: Lawrence Erlbaum Associates, 61-74.

Safranski, R. (2007): Romantik. Eine deutsche Affäre, München: Hanser.

Salmon, C. T. (1994): CDC conference summary report: using Entertainment-Education to reach a generation at risk, Atlanta, Georgia: Centers for disease Control and Prevention.

Salmon, C. T. (2000): CDC conference summary report: setting a research agenda for Entertainment-Education, Atlanta, Georgia: Centers for Disease Control and Prevention.

Samaniego, M.; Cortés Pascual, A. (2007): The teaching and learning of values through television, *International Review of Education*, 53, 5-21.

Sayre, S.; King, C. (2003): Entertainment & society: audiences, trends, and impacts, Thousand Oaks, CA, London, New Delhi: Sage.

Scales, M.; Hether, H. J.; Huang, G.; Freimuth, V.; Beck, V.; Berkowitz, M. S. (2006): Evaluating primetime TV show about public health investigations: content, impact and audience mix, paper presented to the annual meeting of american public health association, Boston, MA, 7th November 2006.

Schatzmann, L.; Strauss, A. (1973): Field research, Englewood Cliffs, NJ: Prentice-Hall.

Schmidt-Bleek, F. (2007): Nutzen wir die Erde richtig? Die Leistungen der Natur und die Arbeit der Menschen, München: S. Fischer Verlag.

Schrob, B.; Theunert, H. (2000): „Ein bisschen wählen dürfen..." Jugend - Politik - Fernsehen. Eine Untersuchung zur Rezeption von Fernsehinformationen durch 12 - 17Jährige, München: Kopaed.

Schuh, J. (2008): Involvement with celebrities: examining the relationships between similarity identification, wishful identification, and parasocial interaction, paper presented to the International Communication Association Conference 2008, Montréal, Canada, 22nd-26th May 2008.

Schulz, W. F.; Diffenhard, V.; Kreeb, M.; Motzer, M.; Rudel-Kreeb, A.; Russ, M. (2008): Recherchedatenbank B°CON für TV Journalisten und Nachhaltgikeitsakteure. In: C. Schwender, F. S. Schulz and M. Kreeb (Eds.): *Medialisierung von Nachhaltigkeit. Das Forschungsprojekt balance[ff]: Emotionen und Ecotainment in den Massenmedien*, Marburg: metropolis, 185-195.

Schütze, F. (1983): Biographieforschung und narratives Interview, *Neue Praxis*, 13/3, 283-293.

Schwan, H. (2008): Jürgen Emig. Angeklagter Gnadenlos, Frankfuter Allgemeine Zeitung (net), retrieved from http://www.faz.net/s/Rub9CD731D06F17450CB39BE001000D-D173/Doc~E1DD6B32064254D159D0149E3249F029D~ATpl~Ecommon~Scontent.html (28th March 2009).

Schwarz, U. (2004): Gesundheit in der Mediengesellschaft. Institutionelle Gesundheitsaufklärung und Fernsehunterhaltung, *Bundesgesundheitsblatt, Gesundheitsforschung, Gesundheitsschutz*, 47/10, 927-933.

Schwarzer, R. (1992): Self-efficacy in the adoption and maintenance of health behaviors: theoretical approaches and a new model. In: R. Schwarzer (Eds.): *Self-efficacy: thought control of action*, Washington DC: Hemisphere, 217-243.

Schwender, C.; Schulz, F. S.; Kreeb, M. (2008): Medialisierung von Nachhaltigkeit. Das Forschungsprojekt balance[f]: Emotionen und Ecotainment in den Massenmedien, Marburg: metropolis.

Servet, J. M. (1994): Paroles données, Le lien de confidance, La Revue du M.A.U.S.S., 4, 37-56.

Severin, W. J.; Tankard, J. W. (2001): Communciation theories: origins, methods, and uses in the mass media, New York: Longman.

Shattuc, J. M. (1997): The talking cure: TV talk shows and women, New York: Routledge.

Sherry, J. L. (2002): Media saturation and Entertainment-Education, *Communication Theory*, 12/2, 206-224.

Siegrist, J.; Marmot, M. (2006): Social inequalities in health: new evidence and policy implications, Oxford: Oxford University Press.

Silayan-Go, A. (1990): Entertainment for change and development: Will it work? In: P.L. Coleman and R. C. Meyer (Eds.): The enter-educate conference: entertainment for social change, Baltimore, MD: John Hopkins University, Center for Communication Programs.

Simon, J. (2004): Wirkung von Daily Soaps auf Jugendliche, Angewandte Medienforschung, *Schriftreihe des Medien Instituts Ludwigshaften*, 30, München: R. Fischer.

Singhal, A. (2008a): Where social change scholarship and practice went wrong? Might complexity science provide a way out of the mess? *Communication Development and Social Change*, 2/4, 1-6.

Singhal, A. (2010a): Communicating what works! Applying the positive deviance approach in health communication, *Health Communication*, 25/6, 605-606.

Singhal, A. (2010b): Personal communication with Avind Singhal about the positive deviance approach and its application to increase E-E activites in Germany, Berlin, 05th September 2010.

Singhal, A.; Rogers, E. M. (1989): Pro-social television for developent in India. In: R. E. Rice and C. Atkin: *Public communication campaigns*, 2nd edition, Newbury Park, CA: Sage, 331-350.

Singhal, A.; Rogers, E. M. (1999): Entertainment-Education. A communication strategy for social change, Mahwah, NY, London: Lawrence Erlbaum Associates.

Singhal, A.; Pant, S.; Rogers, E. M. (2000): Environmental activism through an Entertainment-Education Radio Soap Opera in India. In: M. Oepen and W. Hamacher (Eds.): *Communicating the environment: environmental communication for sustainable development*, Frankfurt: Peter Lang, 176-183.
Singhal, A.; Rogers, E. M. (2002): A theoretical agenda for Entertainment-Education, *Communication Theory*, 12/2, 117-135.
Singhal, A.; Cody, M. J.; Rogers, E. M.; Sabido, M. (2004): Entertainment-Education and social change. History, research and practice, Mahwah, NJ: Lawrence Erlbaum Associates.
Singhal, A.; Rogers, E. M. (2004): The status of Entertainment-Education worldwide. In: A. Singhal, M. J. Cody, E. M. Rogers and M. Sabido (Eds.): *Entertainment-Education and social change. History, research and practice*, Mahwah, NJ: Lawrence Erlbaum Associates, 3-20.
Singhal, A.; Sharma, D.; Papa, M. J.; Witte, K. (2004): Air cover and ground mobilization: integrating Entertainment-Education broadcasts with community listening and service delivery in India. In: A. Singhal, M. J. Cody, E. M. Rogers and M. Sabido (Eds.): *Entertainment-education and social change. History, research, and practice*, Mahwah, NJ: Lawrence Erlbaum, 351-375.
Singhal, A.; Chitnis, K.; Sengupta, A. (2005): Cross-border mass-mediated health narratives: Narrative transparency, "safe sex", and Indian viewers. In: L. M. Harter, P.M. Japp, M. and C. S. Beck (Eds.): *Co-constructing our health: the implications of narratives for enacting illness and wellness*, Mahwah, NJ: Lawrence Erlbaum Associates.
Singhal, A.; Rao, N.; Pant, S. (2006): Entertainmnt-Education and possibilities for second-order social change, *Journal of Creative Communication*, 1/3, 267-283.
Singhal, A.; Dura, L. (2008): Listening and healing in the Peruvian Amazon: an Assessment of Minga Peru's intercultural radio educative project to prevent and control domestic violence and HIV/AIDS, El Paso, Lima, Peru: Minga Peru/UN Trust Fund to Support Actions that Eliminate Violence Against Women.
Singhal, A.; Greiner, K. (2008): Performance activism and civic engagement through symbolic and playful actions, *Journal of Development Communication*, 19/2, 43-53.
Singhal, A.; Dura, L. (2009): Protecting children from exploitation and trafficking: using the positive deviance approach in Uganda and Indonesia, Washington, DC: Save the Children.
Singhal, A.; Buscell, P.; Lindberg, C. (2010): Inviting everyone: healing healthcare through positive deviance, Bordentown, NY: Plexus Press.
Singhal, A.; Greiner, K. (2010): Small solutions and big rewards: MRSA prevention at the Pittsburgh Veterans hospital. In: A. Singhal, P. Buscell and C. Lindberg (Eds.): *Inviting everyone: healing healthcare through positive deviance*, Bordentown, NY: Plexus Press, 47-67.
Singhal, A.; Wang, H.; Rogers, E. M. (2011): The rising of Entertainment-Education in communication campaigns. In: R. E. Rice and C. Atkin (Eds.): *Public communication campaigns*, 4th edition, Newbury Park, CA: Sage, forthcoming, 1-24 (manuscript pages).
Slater, M. D. (1997): Persuasion processes across receiver goals and message genres, *Communication Theory*, 7/2, 125-148.
Slater, M. D.; Rouner, D. (2002): Entertainment-education and elaboration likelihood: understanding the processing of narrative persuasion, *Communication Theory*, 12/2, 173-191.
Slater, M. D.; Rouner, D.; Long, M. (2006): Television dramas and support for controversial public policies: effects and mechanisms, *Journal of Communication*, 56, 235-252.
Sood, S. (2002): Audience involvement and Entertainment-Education, *Communication The-

ory, 153-172.
Sood, S.; Mernard, T.; Witte, K. (2004): The theory behind Entertainment-Education. In: A. Singhal, M. J. Cody, E. M. Rogers and M. Sabido (Eds.): *Entertainment-Education and social change. History, research and practice*, Mahwah, NJ: Lawrence Erlbaum Associates, 117-149.
Sood, S.; Rogers, E. M. (2000): Dimensions of parasocial interaction by letter writers to a popular Entertainment-Education soap opera in India, *Journal of Broadcasting and Electronic Media*, 44/3, 386-414.
Stark, S. (1997): Glued to the set, New York: Simon & Schuster.
Staudenmaier, P. (1996): Fascist ecology: the Green Wing of the Nazi party and its historical antecedents. In: J. Biehl, J. and P. Staudenmaier (Eds.): *Ecofascism: lessons from the German experience*, San Francisco: AK Press, 5-32.
Statistisches Bundesamt (2006): Datenreport 2006. Zahlen und Fakten über die Bundesrepublik Deutschland. Auszug aus Teil II, Berlin: Statistisches Bundesamt.
Spiegel Online (1996): Carl-Dieter Spranger, retrieved from http://www.spiegel.de/spiegel/print/d-9122365.html (02nd June 2009).
Spiegel Online (1997): Unser Mann in Thailand, retrieved from http://www.spiegel.de/spiegel/print/d-8693083.html (02nd June 2009).
Spiegel Online (2005): Entwarnung für den "Fahnder", retrieved from http://www.spiegel.de/kultur/gesellschaft/0,1518,366025,00.html (02nd June 2009).
Spoelstra, M.; Pienaar, W. (2008): Negotiation. Theories, strategies and skills, Cape Town: Juta and Co. Ltd.
Stack, S. (2000): Media impacts on suicide: a quantitative review of 293 findings, *Social Sience Quarterly*, 81/4, 957-971.
Stacks, D. W.; Salwen, M. B. (2009): An integrated approach to communciation theory and research, New York: Routledge.
Steele, L.; Dewa, C.; Lee, K. (2007): Socioeconomic status and self-reported barriers to mental health service use, *Canadian Journal of Psychiatry*, 52/3, 201-206.
Stegbauer, C. (2010): Reziprozität: Einführung in soziale Formen der Gegenseitigkeit, Wiesbaden: VS Verlag für Sozialwissenschaften.
Stivoro (2008): In iedere roker zit een stopper, Stivoro, Series Edition, Den Haag,
Stohl, C.; Cheney, G. (2001): Participatory practices/paradoxical practices: communication and dilemmas of organisational democracy, *Management Communication Quarterly*, 14, 90-128.
Strong, D. (2008): Audience involvement with "Khushiko Sansar", a children's TV show in Nepal: an Entertainment-Education initiative promoting positive attitudes and actions towards people with disabilities, thesis, Regent University.
Stolberg, S. G. (2001): CDC plays script doctor to spread its messages, New York Times, retrieved from http://www.nytimes.com/2001/06/26/science/cdc-plays-script-doctor-to-spread-its-message.html (15th July 2009).
Strauss, A. (1987): Qualitative analysis for social scientists, Cambridge: Cambridge University Press.
Strauss, A. (1991): Grundlagen qualitativer Sozialforschung. Datenanalyse und Theoriebildung in der empirischen soziologischen Forschung, München: Fink.
Strauss, A.; Corbin, J. (1990): Basics of qualitative research: Grounded Theory procedures and techniques, Newbury Park: Sage.
Strong, E. K. (1925): Theories of selling, *Journal of Applied Psychology*, 9, 75-86.
Summerfield, F. (2002): All you need is a good brainwashing, New Kensington, PA: Whitaker House.
Taylor, C. (1989): Sources of the self: the making of modern identity, Cambridge, MA: Har-

vard University Press.
Thompson, R. J. (1996): Television's second gold age: from Hill Street Blues to ER, Syracuse, NY: Syracuse University Press.
Tompkins, P. K.; Cheney, G. (1985): Communication and unobtrusive control in contemporary organizations. In: R. D. McPhee and P. K. Tompkins (Eds.): *Organizational communication: traditional themes and new directions*, Newbury Park, CA: Sage, 179-210.
Townsend, P.; Davidson, N. (1982): Inequalities in health: the black report, Middlesex: Penguin Books.
Treffer, U.; Baden, F. (2006): In aller Freundschaft. Schleichwerbung im öffentlich-rechtlichen Fernsehen: Was lief, ganz vertraulich, zur besten ARD-Sendezeit? Süddeutsche Zeitung (online), retrieved from www.sueddeutsche.de/wirtschaft/medien-in-aller-freundschaft-1.901595 (11th May 2009).
Trojan, A.; Legewie, H. (2001): Nachhaltige Gesundheit und Entwicklung. Leitbilder, Politik und Praxis der Gestaltung gesundheitsförderlicher Umwelt- und Lebensbedingungen, Frankfurt am Main: Verlag für Akademische Schriften.
Tufte, T. (2004): Entertainment-Education in HIV/AIDS communication: beyond marketing, towards empowerment. In: C. von Feilitzen and U. Carlsson (Eds.): *Promote or protect? Perspectives on media literacy and media regulations*, (Yearbook 2003), Göteborg: International clearinghouse on children, youth and media, 85-97.
Tufte, T. (2005): Entertainment-Education in development communication: between marketing behaviors and empowering people. In: O. Hemer and Tufte T. (Eds.): Media and glocal change: rethinking communication for development, Göteborg: Nordicom, 159-174.
Tuner, J. R. (1993): Interpersonal and psychological predictors of parasocial interaction with different television performers, *Communication Quarterly*, 41, 443-453.
United Nations (UN) (1987): Our Common Future. Oxford: Oxford University Press.
Usdin, S.; Singhal, A.; Shongwe, T.; Goldstein, S.; Shabalala, A. (2004): No short cuts in Entertainment-Education: designing Soul City step-by-step. In: A. Singhal, M. J. Cody, E. M. Rogers and M. Sabido (Eds.): *Entertainment-Education and social change. History, research, and practice* Mahwah, NJ: Lawrence Erlbaum Associates, 153-175.
Valente, T. W.; Poppe, P. R.; Merritt, A. P. (1996): Mass-media-generated interpersonal communciation as a source of information about family planning, *Journal for Health Communciation*, 1/3, 247-266.
Valente, T. W.; Murphy, S. T.; Huang, G.; Gusek, J.; Greene, J.; Beck, V. (2007): Evaluating a minor story-line on ER about teen obisty, hypertension and 5 A Day, *Journal of Health Communication*, 12/6, 551-566.
Valente, T. W.; Saba, W. P. (2001): Campaigns exposure and interpersonal communciation as factors in contraceptive use in Bolivia, *Journal of Health Communciation*, 6/4, 303-322.
Van Leeuwen, L.; Renes, R. J.; Leeuwis, C. (2012, accepted): Televised Entertainment-Education to prevent adolescent alcohol use: Perceived realism, enjoyment, and impact, *Health Education & Behavior*.
Vaughn, P. W.; Regis, A.; St. Catherine, E. (2000): Effects on an Entertainment-Education radio soap opera on family planning and HIV prevention in St. Lucia, *International Family Planning Perspectives*, 26/4, 148-157.
Volpers, H.; Bernhard, U.; Schnier, D. (2008): Public relations und werbliche Erscheinungsformen im Fernsehen. Eine Typologie persuasiver Kommunikationsangebote des Fernsehens, Berlin: Vistas.
Volpers, H.; Herkströter, D.; Schnier, D. (1998): Die Trennung von Werbung und Programm im Fernsehen. Programmliche und werbliche Entwicklungen im digitalen Zeitalter und ihre Rechtsfolgen, Opladen (Schriftreihe Medienforschung der Landesanstalt für Rund-

funk Nordrhein-Westfalen, Band 25).
Volpers, H.; Holznagel, B. (2009): Trennung von Werbung und Programm im Fernsehen. Zuschauerwahrnehmung und Regulierungsoptionen, Berlin: Vistas.
Vorderer, P. (2003): Entertainment theory. In: J. Bryant, D. Rosko-Ewoldsen and J. Cantor (Eds.): *Communication and emotion: essays in honor of Dolf Zillmann*, Mahwah, NY, London: Lawrence Erlbaum Associates, 131-153.
Vorderer, P.; Klimmt, C.; Ritterfeld, U. (2004): Enjoyment: at the hart of media entertainment, *Communication Theory*, 14/4, 388-408.
Waldrop, M. M. (1992): Complexity: the emerging science at the edge of order and chaos, New York, NY: Simon & Schuster.
Wallis, A.; Crocker, J. P.; Schlechter, B. (1998): Social capital and community building: part one, *National Civic Review*, 87/3, 253-271.
Waltz, M. (2006): Tauschsysteme als subjektivierene Ordnungen: Mauss, Lévi-Strauss, Lacan. In: S. Moebius and C. Papilloud: *Gift. Marcel Mauss' Kulturtheorie der Gabe*, Wiesbaden: VS Verlag für Sozialwissenschaften, 81-105.
Wang, H. (2008): Narrative engagement and persuasion of Entertainment-Education for social change: a critical integration of theories and constructs, Los Angeles: University of Southern California, unpublished paper.
Wang, H.; Singhal, A. (2009): Entertainment-Education through digital games. In U. Ritterfeld, M. J. Cody, & P. Vorderer (Eds.): Serious games: mechanisms and effects, New York Routledge, 271-292.
Watzlawick, P.; Beavin, J. H.; Jackson, D. D. (1969): Menschliche Kommunikation. Formen, Störungen, Paradoxien, Bern: Huber.
Weintraub Austin, E.; Pinkleton, B. E.; Fujioka, Y. (2000): The role of interpretation processes and parental discussion in the media's effects on adolescents' use of alcohol, *Pediatrics*, 105/2, 343-349.
Welzer, H. (2002): Das kommunikative Gedächtnis. Eine Theorie der Erinnerung, München: C. H. Beck.
White, W. L.; Popovits, R. M. (2001): Critical incidents: ethical issues in the prevention and treatment of addiction, Bloomington, IL: Lighthouse Institute.
Whitehead, M.; Dahlgren, G. (2006): Levelling up (part 1): a discussion paper on concepts and principles for tackling social inequities in health, Copenhagen: WHO Regional Office for Europe and WHO Collaborating Centre for Policy Research on Social Determinants of Health, University of Liverpool.
Whittier, D. K.; Kennedy, M. G.; St. Lawrence, J. S.; Seeley, S.; Beck, V. (2005): Embedding health messages into entertainment television: effect on gay men's response to a syphilis outbreak, *Journal of Health Communication*, 10, 251-259.
Wierlemann, S. (2002): Political correctness in den USA und in Deutschland, Dissertation, Berlin: Erich Schmidt Verlag.
Windeler, A.; Sydow, J. (2001): Project networks and changing industry practice - collaborative content production in the German television industry, *Organization Studies*, 22/6, 1035-1060.
Wilkin, H. A.; Valente, T. W.; Murphy, S.; Cody, M. C.; Huang, G.; Beck, V. (2007): Does Entertainment-Education work with Latinos in the United States? Identification and the effects of a telenovela breast cancer storyline, *Journal of Health Communication*, 12/5, 455-469.
Wilkinson, R.; Marmot, M. (2003): Social determinants of Health: the solid facts, World Health Organization (WHO).
Wilson, K. E. (2002): An evaluation of the CDC resource book for TV writers and producers, presentation to the American Public Health Association Annual Meeting, Phil-

adelphia, PA, November 2002.
Wimmer, R. D.; Dominick, J. R. (2000): Mass media research: an introduction, Belmont, CA: Wadsworth Publishing Company.
Winsten, J. A.; DeJong, W. (2001): The designated driver campaign. In: R. E. Rice and C. Atkin (Eds.): *Public communication campaigns*, 3rd edition, Thousand Oaks, CA: Sage, 290-294.
Wippermann, C.; Flaig, B. B.; Calmbach, M.; Kleinhückelkotten, S. (2009): Umweltbewusstsein und Umweltverhalten der sozialen Milieus in Deutschland, Berlin: Umweltbundesamt, retrieved from http://www.umweltdaten.de/publikationen/fpdf-l/3871.pdf (25th January 2010).
Witzel, K.; Kaminski, C.; Struve, G.; Koch, H. J. (2008): Einfluss des Fernsehkonsums auf die Angst vor einer Operation, *NeuroGeriatrie*, 5/2, 57-61, retvieved from http://www.witzel-chirurgie.de/PDFs/NG208_Koch.pdf (28th February 2011).
Witt, C. de (2007): Beiträge der Medientheorie(n) zu einer von Medien gestalteten Nachhaltigkeitskommunikation. In: G. Michelsen and J. Godemann (Eds.): *Handbuch Nachhaltigkeitskommunikation, Grundlagen und Praxis*, München: oekom, 175-183.
Wolf, M.J. (1999): The entertainment economy: the mega-media forces that are re-shaping our lives, London: Penguin Books.
Wollinka, O.; Keeley, E.; Burkhalter, B. R.; Bashir, N. (1997): Hearth nutrition model. Applications in Haiti, Vietnam, and Bangladesh, published for the US Agency for International Development and World Relief Corporation by the Basic Support for Institutionalizing Child Survival (BASICS), Project, Arlington, VA.
Würtenberger, T. (1987): Zeitgeist und Recht, Tübingen: Mohr.
Yoder, P. S.; Hornik, R.; Chirwa, B.C. (1996): Evaluating the program effects of a radio drama about AIDS in Zambia, *Studies in Family Planning*, 27/4, 188-203.
Zable, C. (2009): Wettbewerb im deutschen TV-Produktionssektor. Produktionsprozesse, Innovationsmanagement, Timing-Strategien, Wiesbaden: VS Verlag für Sozialwissenschaften.
Ziemann, A. (2007): Kommunikation der Nachhaltigkeit. Eine kommunikationstheoretische Fundierung. In: G. Michelsen and J. Godemann (Eds.): *Handbuch Nachhaltigkeitskommunikation, Grundlagen und Praxis*, München: oekom, 123-133.
Zillmann, D. (1988): Mood management: using entertainment to full advantage, Hillsdale, NJ: Lawrence Erlbaum Associates.
Zillmann, D. (1994): Mechanisms of emotional involvement with drama, *Poetics*, 23, 33-51.
Zillmann, D. (2000): The coming of the media entertainment. In: D. Zillmann and P. Vorderer (Eds.): *Media entertainment: a psychology of its appeal*, Mahwah, NJ: Lawrence Erlbaum Associates, 1-20.
Zillmann, D.; Cantor, J. R. (1977): Affective responses to the emotions of a protagonist, *Journal of Experimental Social Psychology*, 13, 155-165.
Zillmann, D.; Bryant, J. (1986): Exploring the entertainment experiences. In: J. Bryant and D. Zillmann (Eds.): *Perspectives on media effects*, Hillsdale, NJ: Lawrence Erlbaum Associates, 303-324.
Zillmann, D.; Bryant, J. (1994): Entertainment as media effect. In: J. Bryant and D. Zillmann (Eds.): *Media effects: advances in theory and research*, Hillsdale, NJ: Lawrence Erlbaum Associates, 437-461.
Zillmann, D.; Vorderer, P. (2000): Media Entertainment: the psychology of its appeal, Mahwah, NJ: Lawrence Erlbaum Associates.
Zimmerman, B.; Lindberg, C.; Plsek, P. (1998): Edgeware: lessons from complexity science for health care leaders, Dallas, TX: VHA Inc.
Zoller, H. M. (2000): A place you haven't visited before: creating the conditions for com-

munity dialogue, *Southern Communication Journal*, 65, 191-207.

Zoller, H. M. (2004): Dialogue as global issue management: legitimizing corporate influence in the transatlantic business dialogue, *Management Communication Quarterly*, 18, 204-240.

Zubayr, C.; Gerhard, H. (2010): Tendenzen im Zuschauerverhalten. Fernsehgewohnheiten und Fernsehreichweiten im Jahr 2009, *Media Perspektiven*, 03/2010, 106-118.

Weblinks

www.bildungsforschung.org
www.bundesverfassungsgericht.de
www.btg-bestellservice.de
www.casesjournal.org
www.faz.net
www.gooutplugin.nl
www.grasloewe.de
www.kjm-online.de
www.learcenter.org
www.miguelsabido.com
www.nytimes.com
www.pik-potsdam.de
www.scienceandentertainmentexchange.org
www.sound-soap.nl
www.spiegel.de
www.sueddeutsche.de
www.tipsvoorscripts.nl
www.umweltdaten.de
www.usatoday.com
www.wga.org

Appendix 1
US Entertainment-Education storylines and their audience effects (summative research results)

Source: The results are based on the data collection from the research stay (September - November 2008) at the USC / Annenberg School for Communication / Norman Lear Center, Hollywood, Health & Society program.

(1) ER (NBC) & Grey's Anatomy (ABC) – BRCA breast and ovarian cancer gene mutation
Hether, H. J.; Huang, G.; Beck, V.; Murphy, S. T.; Valente, T. W. (2008): Entertainment-Education in a media-saturated environment: examining the impacts of single and multiple exposure to breast cancer storylines on two popular medical dramas, *Journal of Health Communication*, 13/8, 808-823.

Findings:
- Viewers who saw both ER and Grey's Anatomy storylines were more likely to know that the BRCA gene mutation increases one's risk of breast cancer (AOR = 1.56, $p < .001$) and believe that mastectomy is a good option to prevent cancer (ß = .18, $p < .001$).
- The more episodes respondents watched across both shows, the more they intended to get tested for the BRCA gene (ß = .08, $p < .05$) and with each additional episode watched, were nearly 10 times more likely to schedule a breast cancer screening (AOR = 9.91, $p < .05$).

(2) 2004-2006 TV Monitoring cumulative analysis
Murphy, S. T.; Hether, H. J.; Rideout, V. (2008): How healthy is primetime? An analysis of health content in popular primetime television programs, A Kaiser Family Foundation report, September 2008.
Findings:
- During years 2004-2006, six out of every ten episodes of the top-rated scripted shows on TV had at least one health-related storyline.
- Episodes with health-related storylines increased from about half (51%) in 2004, to two-thirds (66%) in 2006.
- The frequency of health storylines was slightly lower for Hispanic viewers, and significantly lower for African American viewers.
- Unusual illness or disease storylines (26%) were featured significantly more frequently than the more prevalent health problems like heart disease (6%), cancer (5%) or diabetes (1%).
- Storylines focused more on the symptoms (65%), treatment (59%) and diagnosis (50%) of health conditions, when compared to prevention information (10%).

- Nearly two-thirds (61%) of all health storylines provided either a moderate (29%) or a strong (32%) level of educational content.

(3) ER (NBC) – youth heart disease, obesity, 5 A Day
Valente, T. W.; Murphy, S. T.; Huang, G.; Gusek, J.; Greene, J.; Beck, V. (2007): Evaluating a minor story-line on ER about teen obsity, hypertension and 5 A Day, *Journal of Health Communication*, 12/6, 551-566.
Findings:
- Viewers reported more healthy behaviors after seeing the storyline, i.e. exercising and eating healthy (AOR 1.65, p<.01).
- Viewers had more knowledge of 5 A Day compared with non-viewers (AOR 1.05, p<.05).
- Men had the greatest and most significant gains in knowledge (AOR 1.25, p<.01).

(4) Ladrón de Corazones (Telemundo) – breast cancer
Wilkin, H. A.; Valente, T. W.; Murphy, S.; Cody, M. C.; Huang, G.; Beck, V. (2007): Does Entertainment-Education work with Latinos in the United States? Identification and the effects of a telenovela breast cancer storyline, *Journal of Health Communication*, 12/5, 455-469.
Findings:
- Viewers had increased knowledge on 2 out of 3 items about cancer diagnosis and treatments after seeing the storyline (35% → 46%, p<.01; 8% → 21%, p<.01).
- Viewers who identified with characters in the storyline were more likely than other viewers to talk to others about the storyline/topic (64% vs. 44%, p<.001), and to call for more information, i.e. a clinic, health care place, or hotline number (21% vs. 12%, p<.001).
- Viewers were more likely to call for cancer information when an 800-number aired after a dramatic episode, compared to when it aired before an episode (45 vs. 20).

(5) The Bold and The Beautiful (CBS) – HIV stigma in Botswana
O'Leary, A.; Kennedy, M.; Pappas-DeLuca, K. A.; Nkete, M.; Beck, V.; Galavotti, C. (2007): Association between exposure to an HIV story line in The Bold and the Beautiful and HIV-related stigma in Botswana, *Aids Education and Prevention*, 19/3, 209-217.
Findings:
- Viewers held significantly less stigmatizing beliefs compared with non-viewers with TV access.

(6) ER (NBC) – Syphilis
Whittier, D. K.; Kennedy, M. G.; St. Lawrence, J. S.; Seeley, S.; Beck, V. (2005): Embedding health messages into entertainment television: effect on gay men's response to a syphilis outbreak, *Journal of Health Communication*, 10, 251-259.
Findings:

- Gay chat room visitors who saw the storyline were more likely than other visitors to say that they intended to get screened for syphilis (69% vs. 33%, p<.001) and to advise others to get tested for syphilis (56% vs. 31%, p<.05).

(7) The Bold and The Beautiful (CBS) – HIV hotline calls
Kennedy, M. G.; O'Leary, A.; Beck, V.; Pollard, W. E.; Simpson, P. (2004): Increase in calls to the CDC National STD and AIDS hotline following AIDS-related episodes in a soap opera, *Journal of Communication*, 54/2, 287-301.

Findings:
- Viewers who called for information when the CDC's 800-number for HIV-AIDS aired after a highly dramatic episode created the largest spike in callers to the number that year (5,313 call attempts). This was compared to callers to the 800-number when it aired on MTV, BET and 60 Minutes. The second highest number of calls (4,570 call attempts) was on National HIV Testing Day, when the hotline number was highly publicized in the media.

(8) Medical Investigation (NBC) – infectious disease and natural disaster investigations
Scales, M.; Hether, H. J.; Huang, G.; Freimuth, V.; Beck, V.; Berkowitz, M. S. (2006): Evaluating primetime TV show about public health investigations: content, impact and audience mix, paper presented to the annual meeting of american public health association, Boston, MA, 7th November 2006.

Findings:
- Respondents reported that after watching the program they were more likely to: follow recommendations of a medical or public health expert during a disease outbreak (61%), wash their hands regularly (57%), and be careful about foods/drinks that they consume (45%).
- Peak traffic to topic-specific CDC Medical Investigation Web pages coincided with airing of the program on Friday evenings.

(9) Grey's anatomy (ABC)
Kaiser Family Foundation (2008): Television as a health educator: a case study of Grey's Anatomy, Menlo Park, CA: Kaiser Family Foundation.

Findings:
- Regarding the question "Is it true or false, that if a woman who has HIV or AIDS becomes pregnant, there is nothing that can be done to prevent the virus from infecting her unborn baby" 53% of the audience say, it is false before watching the episode. One week after the episode, 76% said it is false and six weeks after the episode, 63% of the audience.
- Regarding the question "Is it irresponsible for a woman who knows she is HIV positive to have a baby?" 61% of the audience agreed before watching the episode. One week after watching the episode, only 34% agreed and six weeks after the episode 47%.
- Regarding the question "As far as you know, if a woman, who is HIV positive and

becomes pregnant and receives the proper treatment, what is the chance that she will give birth to a healthy baby – that is a baby, who is NOT infected with HIV?" Before watching the program, 15% of the audience was aware that with a proper treatment, an HIV mother's baby has a 98% chance of being born healthy. One week after the show, 61% were aware of the information. Six weeks later, 45% remembered the information correctly.

(10) Health Styles series (2000 and 2005)
- The US study series Health Styles confirms learning processes of health issues via entertainment TV. Half of the viewers consider the information shown on US entertainment television as accurate and trustworthy. When regular TV drama viewers were asked if they learned anything about a disease or how to prevent it from a TV storyline, two-third of the viewers responded positively. Additionally, one-third respond that they take action after the seeing the health messages on TV and for example decided to become organ donors.

Appendix 2
List of respondents, collaboration research
(1) USA – Hollywood, Health & Society

Name; Male (M) or Female (F) – Position, Organization

Hollywood, Health & Society Program (5):
- Sandra de Castro Buffington (F) - Director Hollywood, Health & Society Program
- Kathy Le Backes (F) - Former Project Manager, Hollywood, Health & Society Program
- Michelle Cantu (F) - Former Project Coordinator, Hollywood, Health & Society Program
- Vicky Beck (F) - Communication Consultant and Former Director of Hollywood, Health & Society Program
- Paula Patnoe Woodley (F) - Lecturer, Annenberg School for Communication and Journalism, University of Southern California, Former Consultant of Hollywood, Health & Society Program

Health Experts (4):
- Health expert (F) – respondent did not answer to the request for receiving final agreement to publish the personal details
- Deborah Glik (F) - Professor at the Department of Community Health Science, UCLA School of Public Health
- Elizabeth Bancroft (F) - MD, Medical Epidemiologist, LA County Department of Public Health
- William M. Lamers, Jr. (M) - M.D.

TV Professionals (4):
- Jeremy Kagan (M) - Tenured Professor at the School Of Cinematic Arts at USC and Founder of the Change Making Media Lab
- Elizabeth Klaviter (F) - Story Editor, Private Practice; Former Director of Medical Research, Grey's Anatomy and Private Practice
- TV professional (F) – respondent did not answer to the request for receiving final agreement to publish the personal details
- Producer (F) – respondent did not answer to the request for receiving final agreement to publish the personal details

(2) The Netherlands – Center for Media & Health

Centrum for Media & Health (3):
- Dr. Martine Bouman (F) - Director and Founder, Center for Media & Health
- Bo van Grinsen (F) - Former Project Worker, Center for Media & Health
- Hester Hollemanns (F) - Project Worker, Center for Media & Health

Health Experts (3):
- Marieke Wiebing (ma) (F) - Sr. Project Leader, STIVORO for a smokefree future
- Lonneke van Leeuwen (F) - Scientific Associate, Trimbos Institute
- Ninke Winkler-Prins (F) - in 2008 Lecturer Contemporary Visual Culture, Film & Television at the faculty Media & Entertainment Management, Stenden University Leeuwarden (2008); in 2011 Lecturer and researcher (marketing) communication & applied social media design at the faculty Art & Economics, Utrecht School of the Arts (HKU)

TV Professionals (3):
- Emiel Stubbe (M) - Project manager DNAMC, Albeda College
- Marc Linsen (M) - Managing director and scenariowriter, Broer producties
- Drs. Anne M.J. Huizinga (F) - Screenwriter and Tv-editor, currently at AVRO (formerly at Endemol NL)

International E-E Expert (1):
- Arvind Singhal, University of El Paso, Samuel Shirley and Edna Holt Marston Endowed Professor, and Associate Director, Sam Donaldson Center for Communication Studies, Department of Communication

(3) Germany – Study participants on E-E collaborations

No specifications can be given here (see chapter 5).

Appendix 3
Centrum for Media & Health: project overview (project selection):

Project	Time Frame	Form of E-E collaboration (if implemented)	E-E activity
Nederland in Beweging!-tv	1999-2010	Co-production	Consultancy
International E-E Conference	2000	-	Education (E-E event)
Costa!	2001	Inscript participation	Consultancy
Gezondheid in Beeld (Health on Screen)	2002-2005	-	Evaluation/Method (E-E research)
Radio Ruuanda Project	2003-2004	Co-production	Consultancy
Find out	2004-2006	Co-production	Evaluation/Method
E-E teaching modules	2004-today	-	Education (E-E curriculum)
Sound Effects campaign	2006-2009	Co-production	Evaluation/Method
Day of the Soap	Since 2006 (annual event)-today	-	Education (E-E event)
Talk, Show, Act method	2009-2010	-	Evaluation/Method
Tips for Scripts platform	2009-today	Service	Evaluation/Method
Internet Drama Series	2009-2011	Co-production / Independent production	Evaluation/Method
Reel to Real drama lines	2010-2012	Co-production / Independent production	Evaluation/Method
Positive Deviance method	2011-2013	-	Evaluation/Method

Appendix 4
Details on the methodology of the research study

Overview of Open Codings
Vorläufiges Kategoriensystem nach dem offenen Kodieren
MAXQDA 15.03.2010

Open Codings (preliminary category)	Open Codings (preliminary subcategory)	Example of narrative of Open Coding category	Frequency
Status quo TV Markt		„Also bei öffentlich-rechtlichen, also nicht bei allen, aber bei vielen gab es auf jeden Fall Themen- und Produktplacement. Und daraufhin ist eine Clearing-Stelle eingerichtet worden, die halt intern das alles klären und regulieren soll."	32
	Gesetz und seine Anwendung		47
	Wandel		4
	Trennung von Programm und Werbung		3
	Kritiker tragen selbst zu Entwicklungen bei		3
	Medienerfahrenheit des Zuschauers		7
	Detailliertes Gesetz bringt nichts		5
	„Raus kommen im Common Sense		8
	Produkt-/Themenbeistellung und Platzierung		21
	Verhältnis Produktionsfirma-Sender		4
	Rolle des Sender		17
	Produktionsbudgets zu gering		27
Empfehlungen		„Also es fehlt wirklich an Nachhaltigkeitsstories, ne. Das ist die Geschichte."	10
	Mehrere Medien-		3

Open Codings (preliminary category)	Open Codings (preliminary subcategory)	Example of narrative of Open Coding category	Frequency
	kanäle nutzen		
	Mehr Transparenz		13
Kooperation "oben aufhängen"		„Aber dadurch, dass die bereits auf Referatsebene hochkarätig besetzt waren und wir auch gleich mit unserem Produzenten da hingewackelt sind war klar, dass das relativ oder sehr hoch angesiedelt ist."	5
	„erfahrene TV Menschen"		2
	interstrukturell		3
	intrastrukturell		15
Einmaligkeit der Kooperation		„Ja, das ist wirklich sehr einzigartig und das ist auch ganz normal, dass es eben einzigartig ist (lacht)."	16
Verschleierungsstrategie		„Nee, ich weiß es nicht [mit Bezug auf konkrete Beispiele, die genannt werden sollen], aber was ich weiß dass ich ganz oft den Albert Maier dran hatte und der dann immer gesagt hat, nach, können wir nicht dies und das."	12
	Relativieren		18
	Zufälligkeiten		17
	Herunterspielen		17
Lizenzkooperationen		„Wir haben weder in das Drehbuch eingewirkt. Wir haben den TV Sender auch nicht mit irgendwelchen Geldern versorgt, sondern wir haben für einen ganz ganz geringen Beitrag die Rechte erworben das TV Format zu nutzen, um das in irgendeiner Form in den öffentlichen Verleih zu stellen."	18
	Lizenzrecht		3
	(kein) PR Motiv		3
	Keinen inhaltlichen Einfluss		4
	Bildungspaket		8
	Finanzen		3
	Trennung von TV-Produkt und Bildungspaket		6

Open Codings (preliminary category)	Open Codings (preliminary subcategory)	Example of narrative of Open Coding category	Frequency
	Kein Routinehandeln	„Es war, ja Neuland, wer sollte mir da etwas sagen."	9
	Offen sein	„Und man muss offen sein auch Dinge einfach mal auszuprobieren oder mitzumachen. Das ist vielleicht manchmal etwas schwer."	15
	Überlegtes intentionales Handeln	„Wir haben denen kommuniziert, wir wollen Kinder im Grundschulalter erreichen, wir wollen das Thema Nachhaltigkeit angehen und wir wollen spannende und Abwechslungsreiche neue Formate erproben."	15
	Einschaltquote	„Es gibt eben so eine ökonomische Sicht an die Dinge heran zu gehen. Und da wird man sagen, je weniger ich für je mehr Zuschauer bezahlen muss, desto besser."	11
	Angler/Wurm/Fischer Metapher	„Also, das ganz einfache Prinzip, dass der Wurm dem Fisch schmecken muss und nicht dem Angler. Das haben viele [Nachhaltigkeitsexperten] nicht so richtig begriffen."	16
	(Vor-)Erfahrung	„Ich habe überhaupt keine Erfahrungen damit. Wie gesagt, das war meine Einzige."	12
	Abschluss der Kooperation	„Die Kooperation hat eigentlich schon vorher geendet. Das war so 2006/2007."	3
	Vertrauen	„Also, da war Vertrauen gefragt, Vertrauensaufbau gefragt und das haben die [Kooperationspartner] mir auch abgenommen (lacht), Gott sei Dank."	11
	Begleitaktivitäten (zum TV Format)	„Wir haben um dieses Projekt herum, also um die Filmproduktionen herum eine ganze Reihe von Maßnahmen durchgeführt. Wir haben zum Beispiel mit dem TV Sender ein Spiel realisiert, das im Internet gezeigt wurde."	16
	Common Sense (CS)	„Wäre dies in der Öffentlichkeit herausgekommen, hätte es viel Ärger gegeben." „Wir haben immer betont von Anfang an... dass wir sozusagen Hilfestellungen geben, da wo es geht... und... die Serie weiterhin eigenständig ihr Ding trotzdem macht."	80

Open Codings (preliminary category)	Open Codings (preliminary subcategory)	Example of narrative of Open Coding category	Frequency
	Wertigkeit von Themen im CS		4
	Öffentlichkeit als kritische Instanz		18
Zeitgeist		„Ja da kann man auch schon sehen, dass wir auch ganz stark davon abhängig sind, was für ein Zeitgeist herrscht da draußen."	46
	Aktualität		14
„Gute Sache"		„Wenn es da eine Praxis gibt, dann deswegen, weil alle denken, dass sie doch eigentlich in gutem Glauben handeln und für eine gute Sache. Ich glaube das ist ein wichtiger Punkt. Und dass auch die kommerziell Beteiligten für sich in Anspruch nehmen, dass es doch für eine gute Sache ist."	4
Marktplatz		„Also, hat da jeder irgendwie etwas davon." „das ist halt so ein Geben und Nehmen."	62
	Tauschgaben (Geben, Nehmen, Erwidern)		138
Kooperationsrechtliche Grundlagen		„Auch da kann man etwas Sinnvolles machen, ohne in den Verdacht zu kommen Product Placement zu machen." „Das muss man halt in den richtigen Kontext einbringen. Aber das Ganze ist eine juristisch diffizile Geschichte und da braucht man sehr erfahrene Redakteure."	31
	(Un)Wissenheit/ (Un)Klarheit		10
	„willkürliche" Entscheidungen geknüpft an Einzelfall		30
Vermittler		„Es war ein Kommunikationsprojekt, dass man da wirklich so ein Medium dazwischen hat, dass eigentlich wirklich nur dazu da ist in beide Richtungen zu kommunizieren, und beide Richtungen zu kennen, dass man nicht aneinander vorbei redet."	13

Open Codings (preliminary category)	Open Codings (preliminary subcategory)	Example of narrative of Open Coding category	Frequency
Effekte/(Nachwirkungen) der Kooperation		„Ich sage mal, Sensibilisierungen gab es bei dem Ensemble. Weil dadurch, dass sich die Schauspieler eben damit [mit dem Umweltthema] auseinander setzen mussten."	5
Begleitforschung		„Wir haben einzelne Filme evaluiert, um zu gucken, wie wirken die, kommen die an, werden die Inhalte verstanden, die Botschaften verstanden, motivieren die sich mit dem Thema auseinander zu setzen."	32
	Finanzierung		3
	Einzigartig		2
	Formative Forschung		2
	Akquise von wissenschaftlichen Partnern		2
	Forschungsantrag		3
	unveröffentlicht		3
Vergleich mit anderen		„Es gab aber, wir haben es nicht direkt recherchiert, aber man kriegt ja auch so mit, was die Konkurrenz macht, was die anderen Formate machen."	1
Personenbezug versus Organisationsbezug		„Ich fand das schon ganz gelungen [die Kooperation]. Das Problem daran ist immer, das hängt so ein bisschen an Personen, ob die es wollen oder nicht." „Das war eine Art von Zusammenarbeit, die eine persönliche Freundschaft produziert hat."	35
Zeit		„Das brachte eine gewisse Zeitverzögerung zu Stande."	5
Celebrity Einbindung		„Ganz viele [Schauspieler] haben uns dann immer gefragt, was machen wir da jetzt eigentlich? Wir Schauspieler, Umwelttag? Muss ich da jetzt irgendwie sonst etwas erzählen? Dann haben wir gesagt, Leute ihr müsst jetzt nicht zu Umweltexperten mutieren, das glaubt euch auch kein Mensch. Ihr seid da, um das Thema Umwelt durch eure Präsenz nach vorne zu bringen."	11

Open Codings (preliminary category)	Open Codings (preliminary subcategory)	Example of narrative of Open Coding category	Frequency
Kooperationsvertrag		„Wir haben dann mit der öffentlichen Hand kooperiert. Da macht man auch immer einen Kooperationsvertrag, in dem dann aufgelistet wird, wer jetzt was übernimmt und wo die Verantwortungen liegen."	15
Pressearbeit		„Dann war nahe liegend, dass wir eine Auftaktpressekonferenz machen."	10
NE-Materialen		„Und was dann kam, na ja, können wir eben die Fachexpertise liefern. Wir haben sehr viel Materialien, Informationen, Links zu Informationsseiten."	5
Ständig absichern		„Ich will das jetzt auch nicht dramatisieren (lacht), aber es ist schon so, dass man darauf achtet. Und Sie haben es ja auch gemerkt bei dem Schreiben von Herrn Dillert, dass er immer noch aufpasst, bloß nicht gegen den Vertrag zu verstoßen. Ich bin da mittlerweile viel gelassener."	3
Inhaltlicher Einfluss/Finanzen		„Die Nachhaltigkeitsorganisation selber hat aber auch tatsächlich nie versucht, inhaltlich darauf Einfluss zu nehmen." „Dass das Ministerium oder wer auch immer das auch ist keine Gewalt über das Drehbuch hat oder ein Vetorecht ist mal eine unabdingbare Voraussetzung."	132
	Einstellen auf den anderen		2
	Grat wandern		11
	Normatives		7
	Unsicherheit/Angst/ Bedenken		19
	Auftraggeber-Auftragnehmer Verhältnis		2
	Konflikte		4
	Redaktionelle Freiheit/Programmhoheit		17
	Aug-in-Aug Partnerkonzept		74

Open Codings (preliminary category)	Open Codings (preliminary subcategory)	Example of narrative of Open Coding category	Frequency
	Finanzen und Handschlaggeschäft		55
	Drehbuch		23
	„Blut gerochen"		5
	Erwartungshaltung		5
Feldlogik		„Es war insofern interessant mal die andere Seite kennen zu lernen, auch zu sehen, wie diese Medienmacher denken, nach welchen Kriterien die überhaupt vorgehen."	11
	Zwei unterschiedliche Welten		7
	Entscheidungsstrukturen		12
	TV Seite		37
	Nachhaltigkeits (NE) Seite		30
Zustandekommen der Kooperation		„Die TV Serie und die Produzenten kamen auf unser Referat zu und haben gefragt, ob es ein Interesse gibt, dass wir ihnen, mit ihnen, in irgendeiner Form mit ihnen zusammen so eine Serie zum... zu produzieren, die sich dem Thema Klimaschutz widmet."	45
Erstes Treffen		„Da saßen dann drei ernste Männer und drei extremst lockere junge Frauen und haben sich erzählt, was man voneinander will."	17
	Gabentausch aushandeln und „beschnuppern"		9
	unvermittelt		4
Motive für die Kooperation		„Also, dass das auch authentisch dargestellt wird und in diesem Treffen wurde ausgelotet, was wäre realistisch, was wäre machbar und können wir machen."	3
	Inhalt und PR Motiv zusammen		16
	Wissensvermittlung		13
	Veränderung		14

Open Codings (preliminary category)	Open Codings (preliminary subcategory)	Example of narrative of Open Coding category	Frequency
	Ernst genommen werden/Anerkennung		3
	Aufklärung		33
	Inhalte vermitteln		32
	Zielgruppe (Mainstream) erreichen		41
	PR Motiv		65
	Motive TV Seite		164
	Motive NE Seite		19
Fiktion ist Realität für die Zielgruppe		„Ganz viele Leute [Zuschauer] unterscheiden da gar nicht großartig zwischen Realität, also zwischen den Schauspielern, die halt da einfach spielen und den Leuten, die die Schauspieler im realen Leben sind."	1
Mangelnde Planbarkeit		„Wir müssen fünf Jahre vorplanen, damit, sage ich mal eine Lösung entsteht. Das waren einfach so im Projekt die Schwierigkeiten, die konnten wir nicht richtig lösen. Das war nicht absehbar."	1
Eigenproduktionen		„Und also, dass ein Film produziert worden ist, ein großer langer Film auf Halde im Sinne von den bieten wir dann den Fernsehanstalten an, das habe ich nicht erlebt. Ich glaube, das wäre auch sehr unklug."	3

www.ingramcontent.com/pod-product-compliance
Lightning Source LLC
Chambersburg PA
CBHW051348290426
44108CB00015B/1928